Issues in Social Policy

Issues in Social Policy

Selections from *The CQ Researcher*

CQ Press

A Division of Congressional Quarterly Inc.
Washington, D.C.

CQ Press
A Division of Congressional Quarterly Inc.
1414 22nd Street, N.W.
Washington, D.C. 20037

(202) 822-1475; (800) 638-1710

www.cqpress.com

Printed and bound in the United States of America

04 03 02 01 00   5 4 3 2 1

A CQ Press College Division Publication

Director	Brenda Carter
Acquisitions editor	Charisse Kiino
Marketing manager	Julianne C. Rovesti
Managing editor	Ann Davies
Editorial assistant	Scott Kuzner
Cover designer	Dennis Anderson
Indexer	Joyce Teague
Composition	Jessica Forman
Print buyer	Liza Sanchez
Sales	James Headley

Photos: pp. 1 and 41: © AP; p. 61: © University of Wisconsin/Jeff Miller; p. 117: © Reuters; pp. 35 and 171: © AP.

"At Issue" pieces: p. 131: Reprinted with permission from David Gelertner.

Library of Congress Cataloging-in-Publication Data

Issues in social policy : selections from The CQ researcher.
p. cm.
Includes bibliographical references and index.
ISBN: 1-56802-619-6 (paper)
1. United States--Social policy--1993– 2. Social problems--United States. I. CQ researcher.

HN65.I86 2000
361.6'1'0973--dc21   00-060848

Contents

ANNOTATED TABLE OF CONTENTS

The ten *CQ Researcher* articles reprinted in this book have been reproduced essentially as they appeared when first published. In a few cases in which important new developments have occurred since an article came out, these developments are mentioned in the following overviews, which highlight the principal issues that are examined.

EDUCATION

School Vouchers

In April 2000 Florida adopted the nation's first statewide tuition voucher program. The Florida plan gives students at "failing" public schools state-funded "opportunity scholarships" that can be used to attend any school of their choice, including private religious schools. At least four other states are considering similar legislation. The constitutionality of using taxpayer money to send children to parochial schools was left unclear when the Supreme Court refused to hear a case challenging the voucher program in Milwaukee. Opponents say vouchers siphon money from struggling public schools. Furthermore, they argue, there is no definitive proof that student performance has improved in districts with voucher programs. But public support for vouchers and other school-choice plans appears to be growing, especially among minorities.

Zero Tolerance

A series of schoolyard mass killings in recent years has prompted school officials and lawmakers to impose mandatory punishments for a multitude of misbehaviors, many of them seemingly minor. Proponents credit tough disciplinary policies with driving school crime rates down. But critics question their effectiveness and worry about the impact the policies are having on individual rights. And civil rights advocates say the policies are being used to kick out minority, disabled and academically challenged students who might drag down standardized test scores. The latest school violence—for example, the shooting of a Michigan first-grader by another six-year-old—left little doubt that zero-tolerance policies will remain in force.

HEALTH CARE

Managing Managed Care

The managed-care industry succeeded in holding down health costs for most of the 1990s. But now it is under unprecedented attack from critics, who charge that HMOs and similar plans have seriously compromised the quality of care by excessively focusing on their bottom lines. With public frustration building, lawmakers in Congress are proposing a variety of regulatory remedies to rein in the power of health insurers to make critical care decisions. Reform advocates say the proposals would empower consumers and allow doctors to deliver patient care without interference. But managed-care advocates contend that the proposals would succeed only in driving up the cost of health coverage. The net result, they say, would be more uninsured people and bigger bills for working Americans.

Embryo Research

The use of embryos and aborted fetuses in scientific research is again under scrutiny, thanks to 1998's landmark isolation of primordial human embryonic stem cells. These "master cells" can evolve into virtually every kind of tissue in the body and could be the key to cures for conditions such as Parkinson's disease and diabetes. They also offer a never-before-seen glimpse into the earliest stages of human development. But anti-abortion groups and other critics contend that the privately funded work runs counter to a 1995 congressional ban on embryo research and want to bar taxpayer money from subsidizing the research, regardless of the potential benefits. Congress and the National Institutes of Health are trying to devise new guidelines and sidestep political minefields.

WELFARE AND SOCIAL SERVICES

Social Security

America's 76 million baby boomers pose a threat to the nation's social safety net. Simply put, the

Social Security system won't take in enough money to pay all of the boomers' guaranteed benefits as they retire over the next thirty years. To meet these obligations, the government will have to either raise workers' payroll taxes, cut benefits or take more drastic steps, such as raising the retirement age. A growing number of policy-makers are embracing calls to "privatize" the system and shift some payroll taxes to private retirement accounts. But a consensus is proving elusive.

Welfare Reform and Child Poverty

The child-poverty rate has declined slowly since 1993, and the rate of black child poverty is the lowest in history. But 13.5 million American children still live in poverty—the highest rate of any industrialized country. Conservatives attribute the decline to welfare reform, which forced millions of single welfare mothers to go to work. Child advocates like the Children's Defense Fund say that progress in reducing child poverty has slowed markedly and that cuts in social service programs have made the poorest families poorer. Meanwhile, child advocates question why states are amassing huge surpluses in federal welfare funds and why food banks and homeless shelters are seeing more and more children of the working poor, even as Congress dawdles in raising the minimum wage.

CRIMINAL JUSTICE

Death Penalty

A series of shocking murders in recent years has once again focused public attention on the death penalty. The deaths caused by the Oklahoma City bombers, the "Unabomber" and others have lent support to advocates of capital punishment. They continue to argue that capital punishment not only deters crime but also helps the families of murder victims find "closure." But opponents call for reform, if not abolition, of the death penalty. They point to disturbing evidence that non-white offenders are more likely to be executed for their crimes than white offenders and that poor inmates often don't receive adequate legal counsel. As proof they cite the cases of 75 people released from death row after courts reversed their convictions.

Prison-Building Boom

The number of Americans behind bars has grown to nearly 2 million, requiring federal and state governments to build an unprecedented number of prisons. Conservatives argue that although regrettable, the prison-building boom has helped to bring down the nation's high crime rate. But liberals and others say the United States is building prison cells when it should be combating crime by spending more money on education and drug treatment. In addition, they argue, other tough-on-crime measures, such as mandatory minimum sentences and truth-in-sentencing laws, are simply keeping minor felons in jail too long and at great expense to the taxpayers. Proponents of tough sentencing laws counter that they are needed as an antidote to lenient judges.

CIVIL RIGHTS

Racism and the Black Middle Class

Despite steady growth in the black middle class over the past thirty years, many African-Americans still believe they face race-based obstacles. As a result, they argue that affirmative action is still necessary to give even highly qualified blacks a fair chance at getting ahead. Others dispute the notion that discrimination is a serious problem and warn that the policy will hurt rather than help blacks by giving them a disincentive to work hard. At the same time, another debate rages over black flight to the suburbs. The American dream of a house in the suburbs only recently has become reality for many African-Americans. But some members of the black community say that successful blacks should move back to the cities to help disadvantaged African-Americans left behind.

Gay Rights

Vermont recently became the first state to grant marriagelike status to gay and lesbian couples. Elsewhere in the country, however, opposition to same-sex marriage remains strong. But other gay-rights measures are gaining support despite continuing opposition from conservatives. As of April 2000, 11 states and some 124 municipalities had anti-discrimination legislation, and many school districts had allowed high school students to form "gay-straight alliance" clubs. On the military front, the Defense Department is promising a crackdown on anti-gay harassment but is defending the "don't ask, don't tell" policy.

Preface

Do all children in the United States have access to good schools and are educational resources allocated equitably? Is their learning environment a safe one? Does managed care sacrifice the quality of medical services? How will social security provide for the nearly 80 million baby boomers who are set to retire in the next 30 years? Should same-sex marriages be legalized? These questions vex citizens and national leaders alike. There are no easy answers, and *Issues in Social Policy* does not present one-sided opinions or champion a particular perspective. Its balanced accounts of current issues in the realms of education, health, social services, criminal justice and civil rights allow instructors to explore these tough questions in a thorough manner, challenging their students to enter into the dialogue and form their own views.

This reader is a compilation of ten recent articles from *The CQ Researcher,* a weekly policy brief that brings into focus the often complicated and controversial issues on the public agenda. *The CQ Researcher* makes complex issues easy to understand. Difficult concepts are not oversimplified but are explained in plain English. Offering in-depth, objective and forward-looking reporting on a specific topic, each article chronicles and analyzes past legislative and judicial action as well as current and possible future political maneuvering. *Issues in Social Policy* is designed to encourage discussion, to help readers think critically and actively about these vital issues and to facilitate further research. It provides clear, real-world examples that add color and depth to the study of the policy process. Such examples give students a flavor of the substantive detail of a variety of policy areas while showing how policymaking at all levels of government—federal, state and local—affects their lives and futures.

The collection is organized into five subject areas that span a range of important social policy concerns. Indeed, the pieces were chosen purposely to expose students to a wide range of subjects, from civil rights to health care policy. We hope it will appeal to several audiences. It is an attractive supplement for social policy or welfare and poverty courses found in political science departments, policy programs and schools of social work. We also believe interested citizens, journalists and business and government leaders will turn to it to familiarize themselves with key issues, actors and policy positions.

The CQ Researcher

The CQ Researcher was founded in 1923 under a different moniker: *Editorial Research Reports.* ERR was sold primarily to newspapers, which used it as a research tool. The magazine was given its current name and a design overhaul in 1991. Today, *The CQ Researcher* is still sold to many newspapers, some of which reprint all or part of each issue. But the audience for the magazine has shifted significantly over the years, and today many more libraries subscribe. Students, not journalists, are now the primary audience for *The CQ Researcher.*

People who write for the *Researcher* often compare the experience to that of drafting a college term paper. Indeed, there are many similarities. Each article is as long as many term papers—running about 11,000 words—and is written by one person, without any significant outside help.

Like students, staff writers begin the creative process by choosing a topic. Working with the publication's editors, the writer comes up with a subject that has public policy implications and for which there is at least some controversy. After a topic is set, the writer embarks on a week or two of intense research. Articles are clipped, books ordered and information gathered from a variety of sources, including interest groups, universities and the government. Once a writer feels well informed about the subject, he or she begins a series of interviews with experts—academics, officials, lobbyists and people actually working in the field. Each piece usually requires a minimum of 10 to 15 interviews. Some especially complicated subjects call for more. After much reading and interviewing, the writer begins to put the article together.

Chapter Format

Each issue of the *Researcher,* and therefore, each selection in this book, is structured in the same way, beginning with an introductory overview of the topic. This first section briefly touches on the areas that will be explored in greater detail in the rest of the chapter.

Following the introduction is a section that chronicles

the important debates currently going on in the field. The section is structured around a number of questions known as "Issue Questions," such as "Should taxpayers help parents pay for private schools?" or "Did welfare reform help poor children?" This section is the core of each chapter: the questions raised are often highly controversial and usually the object of much argument among those who work in and think about the field. Hence, the answers provided by the writer are never conclusive. Instead, each answer details the range of opinion within the field.

Following these questions and answers is the "Background" section, which provides a history of the issue being examined. This look back includes important legislative and executive actions and court decisions from the past. Readers will be able to see how the current policy evolved.

An examination of existing policy (under the heading "Current Situation") follows the background section. Each "Current Situation" provides an overview of important developments that were occurring when the article was originally published.

Each selection ends with an "Outlook" section, which gives a sense of what might happen in the near future. This part looks at whether there might be new regulations afoot, anticipates court rulings and considers possible initiatives from the White House or Capitol Hill.

All selections contain other regular features to augment the main text. Each selection has two or three sidebars that examine issues related to the topic. An "At Issue" page provides opposing answers to a relevant question, from two outside experts. Also included are a chronology that cites important dates and events and an annotated bibliography, which details some of the sources used by the writer of the article.

Acknowledgments

We wish to thank many people for helping make this collection a reality. First is Tom Colin, editor of *The CQ Researcher,* who gave us his enthusiastic support and cooperation as we developed this collection. He and his talented staff of editors and writers have amassed a first-class library of *Researcher* articles, and we are privileged to have access to that rich cache. We also thankfully acknowledge the advice and feedback from the scholars who commented on our plans for the volume. In particular, we thank Richard Fording at the University of Kentucky, Lael Keiser at the University of Missouri, Elaine Sharp at the University of Kansas, Joe Soss at American University and John Tropman at the University of Michigan.

Some readers of this collection may be learning about *The CQ Researcher* for the first time. We expect that many readers will want regular access to this excellent weekly research tool. Anyone interested in subscription information or a no-obligation free trial of the *Researcher* can contact Congressional Quarterly at *www.cqpress.com,* or at (800) 638-1710.

We hope that you are as pleased with *Issues in Social Policy* as we are. We welcome your feedback and suggestions for future editions. Please direct comments to Charisse Kiino, in care of CQ Press, 1414 22nd Street, N.W., Washington, D.C. 20037, or by email at ckiino@cq.com.

—*The Editors of CQ Press*

1 School Vouchers

KATHY KOCH

It was one of the most anticipated Supreme Court decisions of recent years. The high court had been asked to review a pioneering program in Milwaukee, Wis., that allowed low-income children to transfer to private schools — including religious schools — at state expense. Opponents and supporters of school vouchers hoped the court would use the case to resolve a question that had long divided them: Can publicly funded voucher programs include religious schools without violating the constitutional separation of church and state?

In the end, neither side got the definitive ruling it wanted. The court announced Nov. 9 that it would not take up the case, letting stand a Wisconsin Supreme Court ruling the previous June that said Milwaukee's school-voucher plan did not violate the First Amendment's church-state separation clause.

Both opponents and supporters of school vouchers were disappointed by the court's action — or inaction, as some saw it — but each side put its own spin on the court's decision.

Voucher advocates claimed victory. If the Supreme Court justices had felt the Wisconsin program was clearly unconstitutional, they would have seized the opportunity to set the record straight, proponents said. "The Milwaukee decision was extremely strong and took a lot of wind out of opponents' sails," says Clint Bolick, litigation director for the libertarian-leaning Institute for Justice in Washington, D.C. "We're simply not hearing the constitutional argument as often as we were" prior to Nov. 9.

Meanwhile, admittedly disappointed opponents were quick to point out that the high court's refusal to hear the case did not mean the justices felt the law passed constitutional muster. "It is nothing more than a decision not to decide," says Elliot M. Mincberg, legal director of People for the American Way, a group that promotes First Amendment rights. "They may be waiting for a better case to come along before they rule on it."

Yet Mincberg and other voucher opponents concede that some state legislators will interpret the court's silence as a green light to push for similar programs elsewhere. Five states are considering voucher legislation this spring (*see p. 12*), and supporters are optimistic that at least one of those bills — a ground-breaking program in Florida — will become law before the Legislature adjourns later this month. If it withstands likely court challenges, the Florida law would for the first time provide vouchers for all children, regardless of family income level, who are attending poorly performing public schools.

Supporters of school vouchers claim that public opinion is shifting in their direction, and a recent Gallup Poll appears to back them up. While half of the respondents to the 1998 survey opposed "allowing students and parents to choose a private school to attend at public expense," opposition was down sharply from 1993, when 74 percent were against the idea. Over the same period, support for private-school choice rose from 24 to 44 percent.

Support for government-funded vouchers was actually higher when the question was worded slightly differently. Fifty-one percent of those polled in 1998 favored "allowing parents to send their school-age children to any public, private or church-related school of their choice with the government paying all or part of the tuition." Two years earlier, 43 percent of those polled favored the idea while 54 percent opposed it. Opinion was evenly divided in the 1997 poll, which is done annually for the Phi Delta Kappa educational fraternity. [1] (*See poll results, p. 4.*)

Tax-funded vouchers are often discussed under the rubric of "school choice," a broader category that encompasses privately financed tuition-reimbursement programs, tuition tax credits and expansion of public charter schools, which are exempted from many bureaucratic restrictions so that they are freer to innovate.

Choice supporters claim their cause has gained momentum in recent years, pointing to the following developments:

- More than 50,000 low-income students in 40 cities will receive vouchers from private philanthropists and foundations next year. [2]
- Last September, Wall Street investor Ted Forstmann and Wal-Mart heir John Walton announced they were launching a $100 million Children's Scholarship Fund to give four-year scholarships to 40,000 low-income children in grades K–12 via a nationwide lottery. The winners will be announced on April 21.
- The number of charter schools operating in the U.S. has nearly tripled in the past two years, rising from 441 in 1996–97 to 1,207 in 1998-99. [3] (*See sidebar, p. 10.*)

From *The CQ Researcher*, April 9, 1999.

Most U.S. Private Schools Are Religious

More than three-quarters of the nation's private schools are religious; half of all private-school students attend Roman Catholic schools.

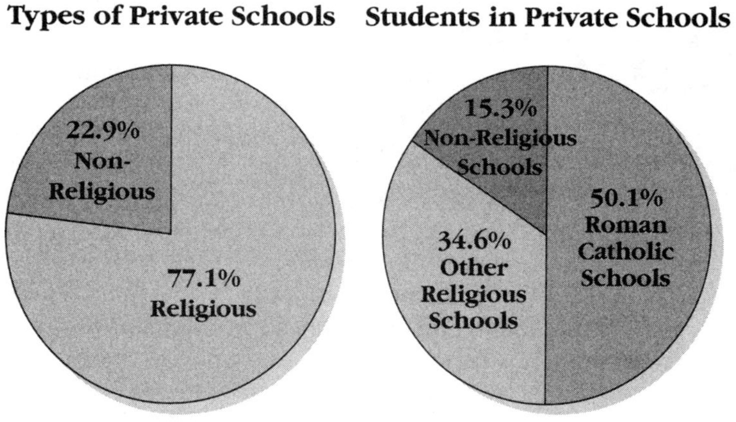

Source: "Private School Universe Survey, 1995-96," National Center for Education Statistics, U.S. Department of Education, March 1998.

• The Arizona Supreme Court on Jan. 26 upheld a state law allowing up to $500 a year in tax-free donations to scholarship funds at private schools, including religious schools. Voucher advocates hope the decision will boost efforts to get publicly funded vouchers approved by the Arizona Legislature later this year.

Supporters say vouchers and other school-choice options are getting more attention because they make sense, especially to lower-income parents in urban areas. Without some type of economic aid, these parents often have no choice but to send their children to local public schools that are often overcrowded, poorly equipped and understaffed.

"The clear tide of public opinion is moving in favor of choice, even among African-Americans," says Michael Guerra, executive director of the National Catholic Education Association. Randy Tate, executive director of the Christian Coalition, agrees. "As conservatives in Washington are grappling to find issues that resonate across ideological and political boundaries, school choice is one with broad-based appeal," he says.

Jim Carper, a specialist in the history of American education and an associate professor at the University of South Carolina at Columbia, detects a growing rift between the older black leadership of the 1960s, which he says "is committed to the public school system at any cost," and younger blacks who are open to discussing other educational options. "The desire for choice in education is very much alive and well in the African-American community," he says.

But while public support for school choice appears to be growing, it comes with strings attached. For instance, support for vouchers in the recent Gallup Poll was strongest if the government paid only part of the private school tuition tab. Only 48 percent favored subsidizing all the costs of private school tuition, while 52 percent favored partial compensation. And three-quarters of those polled believe any private school that accepts tax-funded vouchers should be held accountable to the state for how it spends the public's money, just as public schools are. And 70 percent say private schools that accept vouchers should be required to accept students from a broader range of ethnic and economic backgrounds and academic abilities than is now generally the case.

Many believe the question of accountability and concerns over admissions policies could well determine the outcome of the voucher debate. Private schools value their independence, and many vow not to accept voucher-supported students if the government interferes with their operations. Partly for that reason, opponents plan to fight state voucher legislation by trying to attach such requirements wherever voucher plans are proposed.

"If private schools are allowed to accept public money without being held accountable, the public is writing them a blank check," says Bob Chase, president of the National Education Association (NEA), the nation's largest teachers' union. "We would challenge any voucher program that does not have such requirements."

Chase disagrees with those who say the voucher movement is gaining momentum. Some supporters have become disenchanted with the concept, he says, because student academic performance has not improved as much as anticipated in districts with voucher programs. (*See story, p. 16.*) He also points out that voucher proposals were soundly defeated at the polls by voters in Oregon, California, Washington and Colorado over the last five years.

Sandra Feldman, president of the American Federation of Teachers, believes the momentum of the voucher movement will dissipate once the public understands the long-term impact. "It sounds terrific until you understand its Orwellian meaning: Give up on public education in America; stop investing in it, siphon off as much of its funding as you can to enable a few 'deserving poor' to go to private (mostly religious) schools and to hell with all the kids left behind," she wrote. [4]

The Clinton administration still staunchly opposes private school vouchers, although the president has indicated he would support charter schools and other programs offering greater choice within public schools. Private school vouchers "make my blood boil," Education Secretary Richard W. Riley told educators in Nashville last December. [5]

Gerald Tirozzi, then assistant secretary of Education for elementary and secondary education, said voucher programs are not the best solution to the problems facing public schools. For one thing, he pointed out, America's private schools can accommodate only about 6 million students. There are about 46 million children in public schools — a figure expected to reach 49 million by 2006.

A voucher system "can only accommodate a minimal number of public school students," Tirozzi wrote. "To think of vouchers as a credible solution to the problems of public education is to disregard most of America's students." [6]

Some opponents claim that school-choice advocates have a not-too-hidden agenda: While most of the focus to date has been on programs that would direct funds to low-income children and their parents, the critics say their ultimate goal is to make publicly funded vouchers available to all families, regardless of income.

Indeed, in Wisconsin some proponents want to do just that, threatening the fragile coalition of conservative Republicans and African-American leaders who crafted Milwaukee's original voucher program in the late 1980s. Currently those vouchers only go to families with incomes below 1.75 times the federal poverty level — about $28,000 for a family of four. Last August Milwaukee Mayor John Norquist shocked the black community when he said he favored eliminating the income cap and opening the program up to all students.

AP Photo/Mark Duncan

A teaching assistant brings a group of second-graders back from recess to Hope Tremont Academy, one of nearly 60 voucher schools in Cleveland, Ohio.

"I'll fight it," says Howard Fuller, the former superintendent of Milwaukee's schools and a staunch supporter of the current voucher program. Fuller, now director of the Institute for the Transformation of Learning at Marquette University, says "I don't support universal vouchers. I didn't get into this to get money for people who already have it."

"This is why most black groups like the NAACP are against vouchers," said Wisconsin state Rep. Annette Polly Williams, the author of the original voucher program. "Without the income cap, choice just becomes a free-market program that keeps richer families happy and Catholic and Lutheran schools solvent with state money without any commitment to improve public schools." [7]

"It's significant that there's any support" for vouchers among blacks, [8] says Fuller, "since all of the so-called top African-American leadership has relentlessly bombarded the community with how negative this program is. Yet I believe African-American parents want the same kind of choices that people with money have in America."

Bolick of the Institute for Justice does not deny that the school-choice movement may have a broader agenda than getting economically disadvantaged children out of failing urban schools. "It remains to be seen whether the movement will ever make the jump to middle-income kids," he says. "That really depends on how bad the public schools get."

As state legislatures craft voucher bills this spring, here are some of the issues they are debating:

Will vouchers force public schools to improve?

Giving parents money that allows them to pull their children out of failing public schools and send them to private schools will inject competition into the educational system, voucher advocates say. Public schools would then have to improve or risk losing billions of dollars in federal, state and local funds allocated based on school enrollment numbers, they argue.

"Education should not be a monopoly," says Tate of the Christian Coalition. "But right now you have

School Vouchers Are Gaining Support

The idea of giving government-funded vouchers to students who want to attend private schools is gaining support, according to a recent Gallup Poll, but support varies slightly depending on how the question is phrased.

1 *Should students be allowed to attend a private school at public expense?*

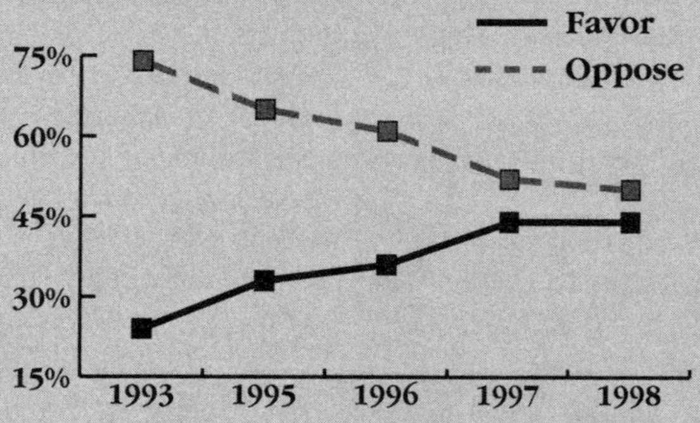

2 *Should parents be allowed to send their children to any public, private or church-related school of their choice with the government paying part or all of the tuition?*

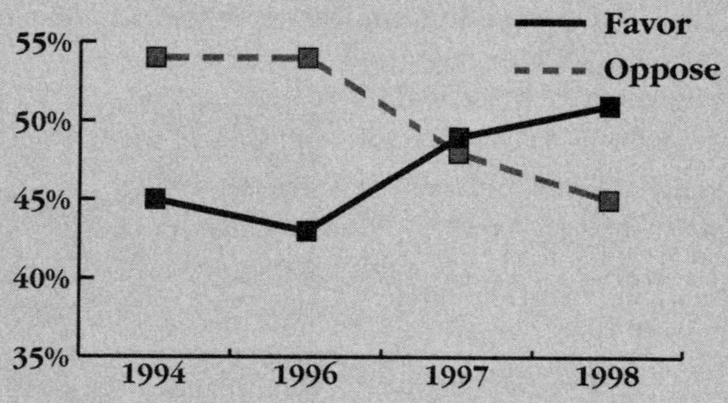

3 *Should government-issued vouchers cover all tuition costs, or just a portion of the costs?*

Voucher Covers All Tuition

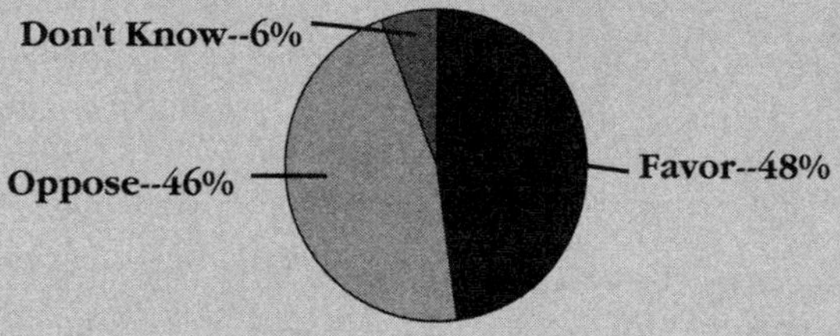

Voucher Covers Part of Tuition

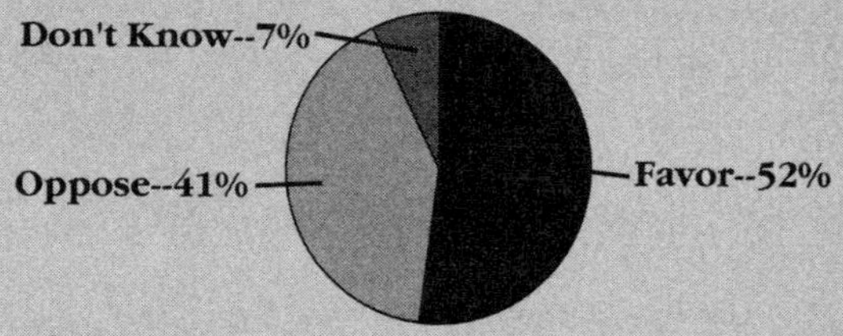

4 *Should private schools that accept government tuition payments be accountable to the state just like public schools are?*

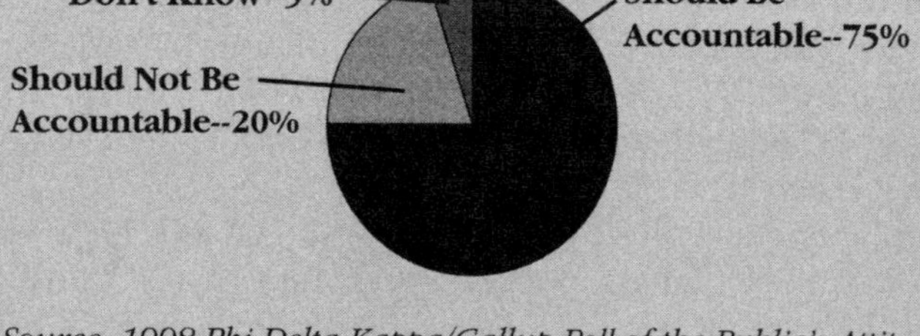

5 *Should private schools that receive public funding be required to accept students from a wider range of backgrounds and academic abilities than is now generally the case?*

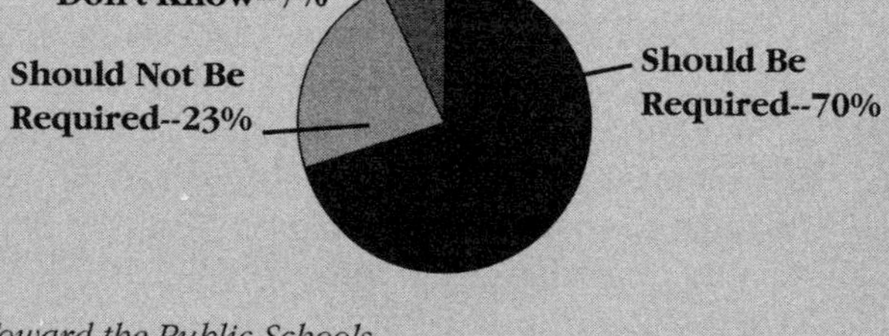

Source: 1998 Phi Delta Kappa/Gallup Poll of the Public's Attitudes Toward the Public Schools

Bill Clinton blocking the schoolhouse door, keeping children inside schools that don't work."

"I think the threat of vouchers has already helped to improve [public] education," says Joe McTigue, executive director of the Council for American Private Education. "And if the threat is enough to improve schools, imagine what the reality will do."

McTigue thinks the public's growing interest in vouchers is prompting the education establishment to support both education reform and public charter schools. Charter schools are small, tax-supported academies organized by parents, teachers or others in the community. They are freed from traditional regulations and red tape so they can focus on students educational needs. (*See story, p. 10.*) "Charter schools are kind of a 'safe' form of school choice," McTigue says. "They are designed to give parents more choice within the public-school setting."

Public school teachers and administrators also are becoming more parent-friendly, McTigue says. "There's an effort to provide parents with what they want, and to treat them more like consumers," he says. "This is partly in response to the overhanging cloud of vouchers on the horizon."

Bolick agrees. As parents are given more educational choice, he says, the only way public schools can compete is by improving their product. "And that's exactly what we've seen in Milwaukee, where public schools all of a sudden are personalizing their programs, issuing guarantees of success, etc."

Fuller is more cautious than Bolick in assessing the impact of Milwaukee's voucher program on the city's public schools. Until this year, he points out, Milwaukee's voucher program was relatively small, with only about 1,000 participants. Now that religious schools are eligible to participate, the program has expanded to 6,200 students.

Nevertheless, Fuller says, "We're beginning to see some signs of change. For the first time school administrators are running radio ads guaranteeing that they will teach your child how to read. For the first time in its 30-year history, the teachers' union and the administration reached a [contract] settlement six months before the old agreement expired. In that settlement, at least 12 schools began talking about seniority not being the basis for teacher staffing — something they said they would never do."

The NEA's Chase bristles at such talk. "I don't buy this education 'monopoly' language," he says. "Those are semi-inflammatory code words used by proponents of things other than vouchers."

Chase and other voucher opponents say there's no conclusive evidence that public schools improve because of private-school competition. Most of the improvements in student performance cited by voucher advocates can be attributed to the decades-old educational reform movement, Chase says. Voucher programs make those reforms more difficult to implement, he says. "How are public schools supposed to improve when they lose [financial] resources under voucher programs?" Chase asks.

"All this free-market talk really sounds good, but public schools are not widget factories," says NEA spokesman Stephen K. Wollmer. "They don't have control over their budgets the way a private company or a private school does. They can't borrow money and retool quickly if their product isn't selling."

The main flaw in the competition argument, Wollmer adds, is that private schools have much more latitude than public schools. "We don't have a level playing field," he says, noting that private schools do not have to accept students with behavior problems or special education needs, who are more expensive to educate.

Mincberg at People for the American Way criticizes voucher programs — including the one in Milwaukee — that allow vouchers to go to students who already were enrolled in private schools. Mincberg's group has sued one such program in the Southeast Delco school district in suburban Philadelphia, which he says was set up "explicitly to benefit kids already enrolled in private Catholic schools."

Mincberg also believes the voucher movement is diverting attention from programs proven effective at raising student achievement. He points to the Student Achievement Guarantee in Education (SAGE) program in Wisconsin. Students in the two-year-old program — which provides smaller class sizes and after-school programs — improved their test scores in reading, math and language arts more than students in either the regular public schools or voucher schools. (*See story, p. 16.*)

Are voucher programs that include religious schools constitutional?

Milwaukee's school voucher program has been operating for nearly a decade. Initially, the city only allowed vouchers to be used to send students to non-religious private schools. In 1995, however, the Wisconsin Legislature voted to include religious schools in the program. But the expansion was put on hold after it was challenged in court.

On June 10, 1998, the Wisconsin Supreme Court ruled that incorporating religious schools into the program did not violate either the state or the U.S. Constitution. The court said the program's expansion was driven largely by a "secular purpose" — to expand educational opportunities for poor children. Additionally, the court

Private Schools Set Their Limits

Most private schools would be willing to accept students from overcrowded urban schools in exchange for tuition reimbursement if they could maintain their current policies regarding curriculum, admissions, student assessment and other issues, according to a 1997 survey by the U.S. Department of Education. But most religious schools would not participate if they had to allow transfer students to opt out of religious instruction, and only 31 percent of the private schools show some degree of willingness to participate if they were required to accept students with special needs such as learning disabilities, limited English proficiency or low achievement.

Percentage Willing to Participate in Voucher Programs Under Various Conditions

Condition	Definitely Willing	Probably Willing	Possibly Willing	Probably Unwilling	Definitely Unwilling
Maintain current policies	60%	17%	15%	4%	4%
Random assignment of transfer students	19%	17%	18%	18%	28%
Accept special-needs students	7%	8%	16%	27%	41%
Participate in state assessments	18%	15%	24%	15%	27%
Permit exemptions from religious instruction or activities	19%	6%	8%	9%	57%

Source: "Barriers, Benefits and Costs of Using Private Schools to Alleviate Overcrowding in Public Schools," Final Report, 1998, U.S. Department of Education. The study was based on data collected from 22 large urban areas with overcrowded public schools. Percentages may not total 100 because of rounding.

noted, any child attending a parochial school under the program could be excused from religious instruction if his or her parents requested such an exemption.[9]

The American Civil Liberties Union, People for the American Way and affiliates of the state's largest teachers' unions appealed the decision to the U.S. Supreme Court. Both supporters and opponents hoped a Supreme Court ruling would clarify what many view as a host of confusing and contradictory decisions on state support of religious schools.

While the Supreme Court had never ruled on the constitutionality of vouchers, it had looked at other schemes to help parents with educational expenses. In 1973, for example, the court ruled in *Committee for Public Education and Religious Liberty v. Nyquist* that a New York state law granting parents reimbursements and tax credits for private school tuition was unconstitutional. The court said the law had the effect of subsidizing religious education because roughly three-quarters of parents receiving the reimbursements or credits sent their children to church-related schools.

But over the next two decades, the court handed down several apparently contradictory rulings, including *Mueller v. Allen* in 1983. In that case, the court held that an Ohio law offering a parental tax deduction for tuition was constitutional even though 93 percent of those claiming the deduction had children in religious schools.[10]

The Supreme Court's 8-1 decision not to review the Wisconsin case was widely interpreted as a victory for supporters of school choice. The Supreme Court has left intact "the most definitive court decision [on the subject] to date, which solidly supports the constitutionality of school choice," Bolick told a reporter.[11] "The court's action clears the way for states to embark on further experiments with educational choice," says Mike McConnell, a law professor and constitutional scholar at the University of Utah.

That's just not true, insists the NEA's Chase. "Except in Wisconsin, the issue is still not settled. The court decided not to tackle the issue. I think the question will eventually have to go before the Supreme Court."

"A definitive ruling by the U.S.

Supreme Court is absolutely necessary," Bolick agrees.

In the meantime, the Supreme Court left the Wisconsin high court's ruling on the law intact. That court said the program was constitutional because the state was not directly funding religious institutions. Instead, the court noted, the money was given to parents, who then decided where to spend it. The Milwaukee program "merely adds religious schools to a range of pre-existing educational choices available to [Milwaukee] children," the court said.

The question of whether religious schools should be allowed to accept publicly funded tuition vouchers is critical to the school-choice movement. More than three-quarters of all private schools in the U.S. — and most of those in low-income neighborhoods — are church-affiliated. (*See graphs, p. 2.*) Proximity is not the only consideration for low-income families.

"The only schools most poor parents can afford — even with a voucher — are overwhelmingly religious," Mincberg says. The fact that vouchers tend to "push" poor students toward religious institutions makes them unconstitutional, he maintains.

McConnell at the University of Utah says that while the constitutionality of school vouchers is not resolved, using public funds to attend church-related institutions is a well-established practice at the preschool and college levels. "It has been clear for quite some time that the old argument that it is unconstitutional for any governmental money to be used by religious institutions . . . just flies in the face of consistent and relatively uncontroversial practices," he says.

For instance, college students receiving federal education grants and loans are free to attend state universities as well as religious schools ranging from Catholic Notre Dame to Mormon Brigham Young, he points out. And families are free to use their federal child-care assistance to send their children to church-based day care, he says. "It just seems very peculiar to say that it's only between the first grade and 12th grade that the Constitution requires discrimination against religious institutions."

College and preschool education are "totally different animals than K-12," responds Chase, "because K-12 is compulsory. There's a big difference between someone being required to go to elementary and secondary school and someone choosing to go to college or to send their child to a day-care program."

Some proponents say voucher programs have a better chance of withstanding constitutional scrutiny if they include provisions allowing students to opt out of religious instruction — reasoning echoed by the Wisconsin Supreme Court ruling. But Mincberg disagrees. "It's not as if the only religion you get is in chapel every morning," he says. "Religion is embedded in the curriculums of church schools. That violates [Thomas] Jefferson's and [James] Madison's principle that not a farthing of compelled taxpayer dollars should go to support a religious point of view that [some] individuals disagree with."

Will vouchers hurt religious schools?

Some people fear that publicly funded tuition vouchers carry a hidden price tag: loss of independence.

"Government aid inevitably comes with strings attached," noted Howard P. Berkowitz, president of the Anti-Defamation League. [12]

"Private schools receiving vouchers ought to be held accountable for educating kids well, and should be subjected to the same performance and testing standards as public schools," says Mincberg. "They should also abide by [federal and state] civil rights laws and be fair in their selection of students."

Some voucher programs specifically prohibit private schools from discriminating based on race, religion, ethnicity or disability in their admissions policies. Those voucher laws usually require that students be selected randomly.

"We've found that some schools have random selection on paper and then, in practice, they don't," Mincberg says. "They were giving preference to Catholic students or students in the parish. Up to one-third of voucher schools in Milwaukee may be in violation of random-selection requirements."

Chase is particularly concerned about private schools that limit the enrollment of students with special-education needs, such as learning disabilities, limited English proficiency or low achievement. "About 75 percent of private schools right now do not offer any kind of special-education service," Chase says. "We would challenge any voucher program that does not have such requirements" for participating schools.

Such demands for accountability could slow the voucher movement. "If voucher programs expose [religious] classrooms to new layers of government oversight, the choice movement could be dead on arrival," writes Joe Loconte, William E. Simon Fellow in Religion and a Free Society at the conservative Heritage Foundation. [13]

Most private schools appear willing to participate if they can maintain their current policies regarding curriculum, admissions, student assessment and the like. But a recent Department of Education survey found that many private schools would resist accepting randomly assigned voucher students. And most religious schools would not join a voucher program if publicly supported students could refrain from participating in religious instruction or religious activities. [14] (*See chart, p. 6.*)

"No religious school — certainly no Catholic school — is going to participate in any plan that asks the school to cease functioning as a religious institution," says Guerra at the National Catholic Education Association. "It makes no sense for them to do that."

While most Catholic schools in Milwaukee are participating in the city's voucher program, most Lutheran schools are not. "We feel it would compromise our mission as a Christian school," said John Wesenberg, principal of Garden Homes Lutheran School. [15]

John Holmes, director of government affairs for the Association of Christian Schools International, says his members would balk at a provision allowing students to opt out of religious activities. "If you choose to go to a religious school, then that option should include the whole package of what that school is about," he says. "Otherwise you're going to cut the heart out of the mission of the institution."

McTigue at the Council for American Private Education says voucher programs should be designed to minimize government interference. "If you regulate schools to the point where the difference between school A and school B is Tweedledee and Tweedledum, you've eliminated pluralism and the right of parents to select a school that best matches their child's needs," he says. ■

BACKGROUND

Movement's Origins

There is little that is genuinely new about school-choice plans. Maine's "tuitioning" program has existed since the 18th century, Vermont's since 1869.

Tuitioning programs are New England's version of vouchers. Small towns with no public high school pay the tuition for residents who attend approved public or private high schools located outside the town. In Vermont, students were allowed to attend religious schools until 1961, when a state Supreme Court ruling outlawed using government funds to pay tuition in parochial schools.

In 1994 the same court reversed itself and allowed tuition reimbursement for parents sending their children to sectarian schools. But the state's education commissioner continued to refuse to allow tuitioned students to be reimbursed for parochial school tuition. So the school board of tiny Chittenden, Vt., sued the state, arguing that based on the 1994 decision it should be allowed to send 15 town residents to a local Roman Catholic high school. The case has been appealed to the Vermont Supreme Court, where a decision is expected in June.

Observers say some of the arguments being used in the Vermont case hark back to xenophobic prejudices that permeated debate in the 1800s, when the nation's public education system was being established. In state after state, taxes were being levied to finance public education, and truancy laws were being passed to ensure compulsory attendance. But as education historian Carper points out, the noble goal of free education for all was promoted with often ignoble motives. [16]

"The history of American education is based on pernicious anti-Catholicism," Carper says. "In the 1830s to 1850s, waves of Roman Catholic immigration pushed a lot of Protestant Americans into a common educational front in favor of compulsory public education."

In Maine, "tuitioning" students were allowed to attend religious schools until 1981, when the state disallowed the practice. But in 1997, the Institute for Justice sued Maine on behalf of parents from tuitioning towns who want to send their children to religious schools. The lawsuit argues that excluding religious schools violates constitutional guarantees of free exercise of religion and equal protection under the law.

After a lower court ruled against the parents, the case was appealed to the Maine Supreme Court, which heard oral arguments in November.

Voucher Proposals

While tuitioning programs have been around for centuries, most people trace the roots of the modern voucher movement to a seminal 1955 essay by free-market economist Milton Friedman. [17] He said vouchers would give parents greater flexibility in choosing their child's school, and would eventually improve public schools by injecting competition into the system. Vouchers would especially benefit the poor, he argued, because they often have no choice but to send their children to inferior local schools.

Eventually the federal government tested the voucher concept in a pilot program in elementary and junior high schools in the San Jose suburban school district of Alum Rock, Calif. The program ran from 1972 to 1976, but had lukewarm results, according to Denis P. Doyle, who ran the program. "It got a bad rap because it was not a startling success," said Doyle." [18]

In the early 1980s, the Reagan administration promoted a similar concept in the form of "tuition tax credits" for families with children at private and parochial schools. In 1990

Chronology

1950s-1970s

The perception that public schools are inadequate gives birth to the school-choice movement.

1955
Libertarian economist Milton Friedman publishes an essay proposing tuition vouchers as a way of expanding educational opportunities and improving public schools.

June 25, 1973
U.S. Supreme Court rules in *Committee for Public Education and Religious Liberty v. Nyquist* that a New York state law giving parents reimbursements and tax credits for the cost of private tuition in religious schools is unconstitutional.

1980s ***Concern about public education grows as student performance on the Scholastic Aptitude Test declines.***

June 29, 1983
Supreme Court upholds the constitutionality of a Minnesota law allowing parents to deduct part of their children's private or parochial school expenses from the family's taxable income in *Mueller v. Allen.*

1990s ***The first school voucher pilot programs and charter schools are created.***

1990
In April the Wisconsin Legislature establishes the first school voucher pilot program, helping 1,100 low-income students in Milwaukee to pay tuition at private non-parochial schools.

1991
The Minnesota Legislature creates the first charter-school program. Indianapolis businessman J. Patrick Rooney creates the nation's first privately funded voucher program in Indianapolis. His action spurs dozens of similar programs in other cities around the country.

1994
The Vermont Supreme Court allows tuition reimbursements for parents sending their children to sectarian schools. The school board of tiny Chittenden later sues the state, arguing that based on this decision it should be allowed to send 15 town residents to a local Roman Catholic high school.

1995
In June the Ohio Legislature creates a pilot voucher program in Cleveland. Under the program, vouchers can be used in religious or non-religious schools. In July the Wisconsin Legislature expands the Milwaukee program to cover 15,000 students and allows the vouchers to be used at religious schools.

1996
In May an Ohio appellate court declares Cleveland's voucher plan unconstitutional, on the ground that it violates the separation of church and state clauses of both the state and federal constitutions. The case is appealed to the Ohio Supreme Court.

1997
In January a Wisconsin trial court rules that the state's law expanding the Milwaukee voucher program to include religious schools is unconstitutional. The Institute for Justice sues Maine on behalf of parents who want to send their children to religious schools. The lawsuit argues that excluding religious schools violates constitutional guarantees of free exercise of religion and equal protection under the law.

1998
In June, the Wisconsin Supreme Court rules in *Jackson v. Benson* that the Milwaukee voucher program is constitutional under both the state and U.S. constitutions. Opponents appeal the decision to the U.S. Supreme Court. On Nov. 9 the court refuses to review it. Congress passes a $7 million program to provide 2,000 children in Washington, D.C., with vouchers of up to $3,200 apiece, but President Clinton vetoes the legislation in July.

1999
On Jan. 14 New York City's Republican Mayor Rudolph W. Giuliani proposes establishing a Milwaukee-style pilot voucher program in one of the city's school districts. On March 25 the Florida House of Representatives votes 71-49 to give "opportunity scholarships" to students who attend schools that receive a failing grade two years in a row on new statewide achievement tests.

Are Charter Schools the Answer?

Unhappy with the education their children are getting in public schools, some parents are taking matters into their own hands. For a few, the solution is home schooling. [1] Others are finding the financial resources to send their children to private schools. And a growing number are taking advantage of laws in their states that allow parents, teachers or others in the community to operate "charter" schools within the public school system.

These small, innovative academies are generally freed from many curriculum requirements and from such constraints as local teacher salary scales and collective-bargaining agreements. They are free to hire their own teachers and experiment with new teaching techniques. The idea is to relieve schools of bureaucratic burdens so that they can focus on students' educational needs.

"The [charter-school] movement was founded on the premise that when you eliminate red tape and give the principal decision-making power and encourage parents' input, that's an equation for success," says Joe McTigue, executive director of the Council for American Private Education.

Advocates believe competition from charter schools will stimulate public schools to be more innovative and more responsive to parents' concerns. "Competition from charter schools is the best way to motivate the ossified bureaucracies governing too many public schools," Sen. Joseph Lieberman, D.-Conn., wrote recently. [2]

Since the early 1990s, 33 states and the District of Columbia have passed legislation authorizing charter schools. More than 1,200 charter schools are in operation nationwide, and another 200 have been approved to open next year.

Many charter schools target students at-risk of falling through the cracks in traditional public schools. For instance, the Apple School in Lakeland, Fla., serves more than 100 children diagnosed with Attention Deficit Hyperactivity Disorder (ADHD). "Most charter schools target a specific population of kids," says Lakeland's administrator, Roy Williams.

Charter schools have drawn fire from some in the public school community. Bob Chase, president of the National Education Association, says he supports the charter-school concept but opposes "permissive" laws that "grant charter status not just to legitimate public schools but also to existing private schools, to home-schoolers and even to individuals and for-profit companies with no track record whatsoever in education." The charter-school movement is being used to get "backdoor funding for schools that remain effectively private by relabeling them 'charters,'" Chase says. [3]

The Center for Education Reform, which tracks and assesses charter-school laws in the states, insists the only way such schools can succeed is if the laws authorizing them contain few restrictions. This is the only way to guarantee that charter schools won't be regulated to death, the group says. "Yet today," the center notes in its latest report, "some charter-school laws are voluminous, reflecting the growing alarm felt by many in traditional public education venues toward this new form of public school." [4]

The center's report also criticizes communities for imposing new restrictions on charter schools. It points to Tucson, Ariz., as an example. "Having failed to ward off

Number of Charter Schools Rose Quickly

The number of charter schools operating in the United States has nearly tripled in the past two years.

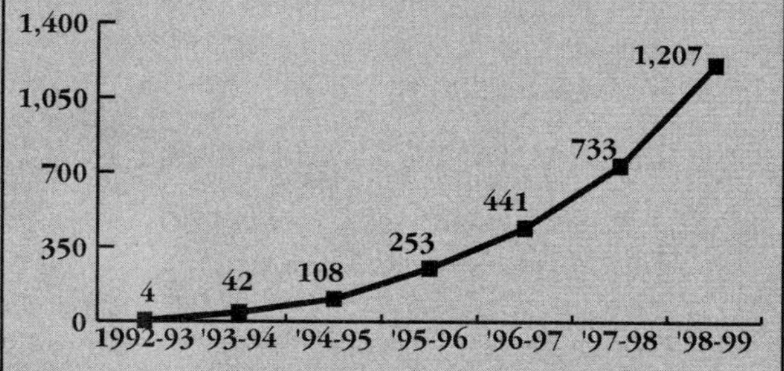

Source: The Center for Education Reform, "National Charter School Directory 1998-1999"

the Brookings Institution published a book by voucher advocates Terry M. Moe and John E. Chubb calling for a radical restructuring of American education. They recommended that public, private and religious schools compete for students in a free market. [19]

Then in the late 1980s, Polly Williams, an African-American state representative took up the school-choice banner in Wisconsin. Arguing that black parents were tired of having their children bused to outlying schools to achieve racial balance, she called for drastic action to improve neighborhood schools and proposed Milwaukee's voucher pilot program.

When it began in 1990, Milwaukee's program authorized $2,446 apiece for up to 1,100 low-income students to attend non-religious schools. The first year only 337 students participated because there were not enough private school spaces available. Enrollment jumped to 5,830 this academic year — from 1,501 last year — mainly because inner-city Catholic schools are now eligible to accept voucher students.

Proponents Worry That Regulations Will Limit Success

charters in their city, the [Tucson] City Council amended municipal zoning requirements to prohibit the opening of any new charter school not located on at least five acres or not having approved traffic patterns in place," the report says.

It's a common practice, notes Tracy Bailey, who oversees Florida's charter schools. "We call it regulatory reloading." [5]

There have been no nationwide studies to date that evaluate whether charter schools are more effective at educating students than traditional public schools. "It is still too early for a comprehensive report on the impact of charter schools, but so far results are encouraging," Lieberman wrote. He citied studies in Massachusetts and Minnesota showing students in charter schools surpassing state academic standards.

The Center for Education Reform's recent report also offers anecdotal evidence of charter schools' success, including test scores from students at two charter schools in California — Horizon Instructional Systems in Lincoln and the Vaughn Next Century Learning Center in San Fernando — that far exceeded district averages.

Arizona has 311 charter schools, more than any other state; 6 percent of Arizona's public school students are enrolled in charter schools this year. But a recent state evaluation found that students in charter schools "are not performing very differently from [students in] regular public schools." In math, students in traditional public schools showed gains equivalent to students in charter schools. By middle school, students attending charter schools for one or more years lagged behind students in regular schools, and the lag widened among high school students.

Lisa Graham Keegan, Arizona's superintendent of public instruction and an outspoken advocate of charter schools, puts a positive spin on the findings. The lags in achievement may be attributed to the fact that many charter schools focus on potential dropouts or other students who are failing in regular schools, she says.

Those students "tend to start at a lower point," said Rob Melnick, director of the Morrison Institute for Public Policy, which conducted the study. [6]

The study did offer clues about why charter schools are so popular: 79 percent of Arizona parents with children in charter schools felt their children were performing better academically, and 77 percent said their children had better attitudes about learning. Eighty-three percent of students in charter schools said they were doing better than at their previous school, while 77 percent liked their teachers better. [7]

NEA's Chase remains cautious. "I think there may be some merit in charter schools," he says. "My concern is that there is no silver bullet to improving schools. Yet there is this headlong rush into charter schools, especially in states like Arizona."

Chase says it is unfair for the states and federal government to pass legislation demanding increased accountability and improved test scores from the public schools — and basing teacher tenure and employment on those results — while exempting charter schools and private schools from those same requirements.

"People say the reason we need charter schools is that there is less regulation," he complains. "But you have legislatures that pass charter-school legislation today and then pass legislation increasing the amount of regulation of public schools."

"If public schools are overregulated, then why do they keep regulating them?" he asks.

---

[1] For background, see Charles S. Clark, "Home Schooling," *The CQ Researcher*, Sept. 9, 1994, pp. 769-792.

[2] Joseph Lieberman, "Schools Where Kids Succeed.," *Reader's Digest*, January 1999.

[3] Bob Chase, "Avoid Pitfalls in Charter School Law," *The [Memphis] Commercial Appeal*, March 28, 1999.

[4] "Charter School Laws: State by State Ranking and Profiles," The Center for Education Reform, November 1998.

[5] Quoted on "Charter Schools, Part I," *Morning Edition*, National Public Radio, Nov. 3, 1997.

[6] Quoted in Paul Davenport, "Study says charter students' gains similar to others," The Associated Press, March 15, 1999.

[7] *Ibid.*

But enrollment is still nowhere near the 15,000 students authorized by the state Legislature in 1995.

Since the program's inception the amount paid for each voucher has increased every year, reaching $4,894 in 1998-99. The total amount of educational funds shifted from Milwaukee public schools to private schools because of vouchers rose from $733,000 in 1990-91, the program's first year of operation, to $7 million in 1997-98. The amount of money lost by public schools rose sharply in 1998-99, to $28 million, after religious schools began participating in the program. [20]

Ohio was the first state to enact a law allowing religious schools to participate in a voucher program. Under Cleveland's 1995 pilot voucher program, 2,000 elementary school students were eligible to receive up to $2,500 to attend the private school of their choice. Although the law was the first to allow all students to receive vouchers, it stipulates that preference should be given to low-income students. The constitutionality of that law has been challenged, however, and is awaiting a ruling by the Ohio Supreme Court.

War in Milwaukee

In Milwaukee, the controversy over school vouchers remains as heated as ever. Teachers' unions, civil rights activists and anti-voucher groups are refusing to back down, despite the Supreme Court's refusal to review the law.

"It's like a war in Milwaukee," says former school Superintendent Fuller. "It's an issue that divides people politically, philosophically and ideologically. Now that the legal battle is over, [opponents] are going to try to regulate the program to death."

Judith Schaeffer, deputy legal director for People for the American Way, explains the group's position: "We believe strongly that if the program is to proceed, it must proceed lawfully. It's very clear that the regulations are being violated."

When the Wisconsin Legislature expanded the voucher program in 1995, it required participating schools to admit students by random selection and to allow students to opt out of religious instruction — two restrictions that in practice may discourage private schools from participating and give opponents additional ammunition to challenge such programs.

In fact, the People for the American Way Foundation (PFAWF) and the Milwaukee chapter of the NAACP filed a complaint with the state on Feb. 2 claiming that more than a third of the participating private schools may be violating the random-admissions requirement by giving preferential admissions to Catholics and siblings of current students.

"The voucher program was sold to Wisconsin legislators, and indeed defended before the Wisconsin Supreme Court, with the promise that all voucher students would get an equal chance to participate through random selection, not selection based on religious belief or other factors," says legal director Mincberg. "That promise has been broken."

"This new evidence that voucher schools are not obeying the law reinforces our strong belief that vouchers are the wrong choice for Milwaukee and throughout the United States," said PFAWF President Carole Shields. "We will continue to work with the NAACP and other concerned groups in Milwaukee to make sure that vouchers are not being used to open the door to new discrimination against schoolchildren there — and to oppose such programs around the country," she said. [21]

Milwaukee has clearly become ground zero in the public relations battle for hearts and minds in the voucher debate, Fuller says. "Anti-choice forces are doing everything they can to create the worst type of political and public relations environment imaginable." Vouchers have become a hot political issue in the city as well. "Money is pouring in for both sides in the current school board election in amounts I've never seen before," Fuller says.

Fuller's group recently held a symposium that brought together 200 African-Americans from around the country to study how to use school-choice options like vouchers, charter schools and tax credits. "We've got to figure out how to use these things to benefit our children," he says.

Carper at the University of South Carolina says African-Americans are more open to the idea of non-public education than they were in the 1960s. "Thirty years ago you wouldn't have found an African-American leader who would have even entertained the notion of vouchers or would have spoken of non-public education at all positively," he says, "and with good reason. A lot of non-public education frankly had racist baggage attached to it."

But private education is different now, he says. "I sit on a Christian school board here in Columbia, and we have one of the most racially and ethnically cosmopolitan schools in the state. It's a different world." ■

CURRENT SITUATION

Action in the States

After a decade of debate, there still are no statewide programs that permit parents to send their children to private schools at public expense. But proposals for pilot voucher programs and broader educational reforms are being debated across the country, particularly in states with Republican governors and conservative legislatures. "The states have become laboratories of school-choice experimentation," Bolick says.

Legislators in at least five states are considering voucher legislation this year: Florida, Texas, New Mexico, Pennsylvania and Arizona. New York City Mayor Rudolph W. Giuliani has proposed establishing a Milwaukee-style voucher system as a pilot program in one of the city's 32 community school districts.

In Florida, tuition vouchers are part of a broader education-reform package championed by newly elected Republican Gov. Jeb Bush, son of former President George Bush. Under the plan, Florida schools would be graded according to student performance on statewide achievement tests, which are already given to students in grades 4, 5, 8 and

10. Under the governor's plan, those tests would be given annually in grades 3-10. Students who attend schools that receive a "failing" grade two years in a row would become eligible for state-funded "opportunity scholarships" that could be used to attend the public or private schools of their choice. Schools receiving the highest grades would be eligible for additional state funds, which could be used as they see fit.

The vouchers would not be restricted to low-income families, but proponents argue that the principal beneficiaries are likely to be children from poorer neighborhoods. "If the schools are that bad, the middle- and upper-income kids will have fled," Bolick says.

The bill, which overwhelmingly passed the Florida House March 25 by a 71-49 vote, now goes before the state Senate, which is expected to take it up before the legislative session ends this month.

Critics of the Florida proposal say it does not include specific provisions holding private schools accountable for how they spend the public's money. Indeed, opponents tried to attach more than 80 amendments to the bill aimed at requiring private schools receiving state funds to be accountable. Among other things, the provisions would have required participating schools to administer the same statewide achievement tests that public school students must take, to undergo state financial audits and to abide by the same non-discrimination admission standards as public schools. All of the amendments were rejected by the Republican-controlled House.

"I am floored by the potential for waste, fraud and fiscal irresponsibility in this bill — and by the idea that we can fix our public schools by abandoning them," said Lisa Versaci, Florida director of People for the American Way. [22] Her group claims the proposed law would violate both the U.S. and Florida constitutions and has vowed to challenge it in court.

Nonetheless, supporters are confident the bill will pass. Vouchers were hotly debated during last year's governor's race and were strongly supported by then-candidate Bush. "Of all the states, I would put the odds very high for Florida to pass legislation this year," says Bolick.

In Texas, Gov. George W. Bush, a likely Republican presidential candidate, is supporting a bill that would extend school choice to low-income, low-performing youngsters in the state's six largest cities: Houston, Dallas, San Antonio, Ft. Worth, Austin and El Paso. Under the plan, which passed the Senate education committee March 24, students would receive vouchers worth 80 percent of the per-pupil funds allocated by the state and local school district; no more than 5 percent of a district's students could receive vouchers. Preference would be given to students at risk of dropping out of school.

It is unclear at this point whether the bill has the support of two-thirds of the Republican-controlled Senate, which it would need to be debated on the floor. It faces an even tougher challenge in the Democrat-controlled House, supporters say.

In Pennsylvania, Republican Gov. Tom Ridge unveiled a plan on March 11 to provide "supervouchers" worth $2,000-$4,000 a year to students attending schools classified as "academically distressed." The program would be limited to eight primarily urban school districts, which also would be granted broad powers to institute educational reform.

Earlier, Ridge proposed a groundbreaking pilot program that, if enacted, would allow families earning up to $75,000 a year to qualify for private-school vouchers. The money for the "middle-class" vouchers would not come from state education funds, however. Instead the state would appropriate $587.2 million in new money over five years. The proposed program was suggested by Catholic school officials in Pennsylvania as a means of reducing overcrowding in the public schools. Most of the 15 school districts selected for the program have a large number of Catholic schools. Bolick says the proposal emerged as a compromise between minority legislators, who pushed for the supervoucher plan, and Republicans, who lobbied for the statewide pilot program.

Arizona has more school choice than any other state in the country. There is complete open enrollment across district lines. The state also has the largest number of charter schools in the United States — 311, according to state Superintendent of Public Instruction Lisa Graham Keegan — and allows tax credits for private school scholarships, the plan recently legitimized by the Arizona Supreme Court.

Last July, Arizona enacted a pioneering school-financing plan called "student-centered education funding." Under the new law, which applies only to public schools, the state assigns each student the amount of per-pupil money spent by the state each year on non-capital expenses. When the student enrolls in the school of his choice — either a charter school or a regular public school — the state then releases the money to that institution.

"We used to finance education based on property taxes, like most of America," Keegan says. "Wealthier neighborhoods naturally got more money than lower-income neighborhoods, even though they were paying taxes at the same rate. It cannot be overstated enough how inherently unequal those systems are."

Now Keegan and Republican Gov. Jane Dee Hull are championing a statewide, Milwaukee-style voucher program that would provide about $4,800 a year for low-income students to use in any school of their choice, including religious schools. The measure passed the Arizona House March 15 and is now being considered in the state Senate.

In New Mexico, Republican Gov. Gary E. Johnson is committed to enacting some sort of school voucher program, but he faces a heavily Democratic legislature. Johnson recently proposed a precedent-setting voucher program, which would have phased in the first statewide, universal voucher program in the country. Beginning with low-income students the first year, the program would have eventually provided vouchers to all 330,000 students in the state, regardless of family income, by the end of the fourth year.

When the legislature refused to enact his proposal, Johnson threatened to veto the state budget, effectively shutting down the state government, unless the Legislature at least approved a pilot program for school vouchers. Because the legislative session ended without a budget, the governor is expected to convene a special legislative session before the fiscal year ends on June 30. [23] ■

OUTLOOK

Universal Vouchers?

Opponents say vouchers for low-income students are the nose of the camel peaking under the tent, paving the way for universal vouchers. They cite the voucher programs proposed this year in Florida, Pennsylvania and New Mexico, which do not specifically limit vouchers to low-income families.

"Without specific income caps, such programs could easily be expanded at a later date to become universal voucher programs," says Mincberg. Programs like the one being considered in Florida — which would give vouchers to any student in a low-achieving school — would be particularly easy to expand by simply using the laudable goal of raising state achievement standards, he argues.

"Ironically, as states increase the academic standards public schools must meet, the effect would be to make more and more students eligible for vouchers," Mincberg says, "without giving those schools the opportunity to improve before the kids start leaving. You wind up draining money and kids from those schools instead of focusing efforts on improving the schools."

Fuller says opponents are using the specter of universal vouchers as a scare tactic. "Clearly there are people who support universal vouchers, but I don't know of any nationwide effort to do that," he says.

Even in Milwaukee, where Mayor Norquist has come out in support of universal vouchers, the idea has never been officially proposed, Fuller points out. "Our coalition — which includes the mayor — has never united around universal vouchers, nor will we," he says. "There are too many people like myself who oppose them."

Tate of the Christian Coalition doesn't hide his support for universal vouchers. "I've said throughout the debate that if we want everyone to have an opportunity to achieve the American dream, every family should be able to send their children to a safe, secure and academically challenging school," he says. "But we need to start where the problem is most severe — in the inner cities where kids attend schools that most Americans don't want to drive past, let alone drop their children off at."

Bolick acknowledges that it could be difficult to stop the expansion of vouchers to other demographic groups. Once you have more school choice, he says, "it's not going to shrink. It's likely to grow, as more and more people demand the benefits. Whether it will make that jump to a universal choice plan, I just don't know."

Proponents predict that as more states embrace vouchers, more private schools will open up to fill the demand. "When the dollars are there, the market will open up and capacity will expand," says McTigue. "Black and Hispanic churches will establish schools in the inner cities. The private sector will respond, and educators fed up with the red tape in the public system will create new schools."

Many new private and charter schools have already opened up in Milwaukee. "The entire marketplace is in flux," says Bolick. "Who knows? Maybe one day we'll see movement back into improved Milwaukee public schools. That will be a sign that the program is succeeding."

Opponents remain skeptical. "Widespread use of vouchers will seriously undermine public education," Mincberg says. "The negative effect of vouchers will far outweigh any possible positive effects, due to the millions of dollars that will be drained away from the public school system."

And, Mincberg says, there is no guarantee that all this increased choice will actually result in better-educated children. "These voucher programs require no accountability," he says. "So you could be moving from a public school to a private school that is just as bad."

Others fear widespread use of vouchers could lead to a Balkanization of society and increased intolerance among future generations. "Public schools are the only institutions in our society where

At Issue:

Are voucher programs that include church-related schools constitutional?

yes

CLINT BOLICK
Litigation Director, Institute for Justice, Washington, D.C.

WRITTEN FOR *THE CQ RESEARCHER*, JULY 10, 1998

The Wisconsin Supreme Court answered the constitutionality question with a resounding "yes" last year. The question will linger until the U.S. Supreme Court delivers a definitive decision. But the First Amendment's plain meaning, buttressed by an unbroken line of recent U.S. Supreme Court precedents, suggests that well-crafted school-choice programs will survive constitutional scrutiny.

The actual First Amendment language reads: "Congress shall make no law respecting an establishment of religion." Clearly, the framers meant only to proscribe direct sponsorship of religion, a conclusion buttressed by constitutional history.

Moreover, the First Amendment guarantees citizens the right to "free exercise" of religion. When the two religion clauses are read together, it is clear that the First Amendment directs the state to chart a neutral course.

The strongest (and really only) precedent in the opponents' arsenal is the U.S. Supreme Court decision in *Committee for Public Education and Religious Liberty v. Nyquist*. The 1973 decision invalidated a New York "parochaid" program that provided tax benefits and direct subsidies for private education, most of which went to religious schools. The court reasoned that the aid had the impermissible "primary effect" of advancing religion. The court expressly left open the question of "a case involving some sort of public assistance (for example, scholarships) made available generally without regard to the sectarian-nonsectarian, or public-nonpublic nature of the institution benefited."

Two things have changed in the years since *Nyquist*. First, the nature of school choice: It is no longer designed to benefit particular schools but rather is a remedial effort to help expand the range of educational options. Second, the Supreme Court itself has changed: As the court observed only last year, First Amendment jurisprudence has "significantly changed" over the past decade, specifically "our understanding of the criteria used to assess whether aid to religion has an impermissible effect."

Allowing private- and religious-school options not only accords with First Amendment principles but also with the deeply entrenched constitutional principles of parental sovereignty and equal educational opportunities. Forty-five years ago in *Brown v. Board of Education*, the U.S. Supreme Court promised equal educational opportunities for all children. Upholding the constitutionality of school choice will be a major step toward fulfilling that promise.

no

ELLIOT M. MINCBERG
Legal Director, People for the American Way

WRITTEN FOR *THE CQ RESEARCHER*, MARCH 1999

Despite persistent assertions by the Religious Right to the effect that a Wisconsin law expanding vouchers to include religious schools was held constitutional by the U.S. Supreme Court, the court refused to hear the case — issuing no ruling on the merits one way or the other. Instead, it chose to let the Wisconsin law stand for the time being, subject to future rulings of the court.

The truth is that voucher programs that include sectarian schools grossly violate the constitutional separation of church and state. It is not simply that such schools might require students to engage in worship of other religious practices that violate their own or their parents' beliefs. It is that religion is in most sectarian schools entirely inseparable from academics.

According to the federal National Center for Education Statistics, more than half of all Christian schools describe "religious development," not academic excellence, as their top priority. Accordingly, faith is woven into the curriculum. In science class, for example, Christian schools are far more likely to ignore evolution in favor of Creationism. Sex-education classes are more likely to tailor instruction on birth control and disease prevention to their own religious doctrine or omit it altogether.

In short, voucher programs that fund religious instruction are unconstitutional because a primary effect is to advance religion. Quite simply, the majority of children participating in such voucher programs receive religious instruction paid for by taxpayers. That instruction will not just be in the form of worship services; it will be integrated into the curriculum from morning homeroom to biology, to literature to health, to after-school clubs and activities. Indeed, in Wisconsin, the law seems to permit schools to compel participation in religious worship over the objections of the student, or in the absence of written instructions from a parent.

Religious schools are created to advance a religious mission. That mission is perfectly reasonable and appropriate. But it may not be supported with tax dollars.

The Supreme Court ruled vouchers unconstitiutional in *Nyquist* in 1973, and will eventually break its silence on the current generation of voucher proposals. And when it does, it should stand by its previous rulings and strike down taxpayer financing of religious instruction, or it will ignore decades of settled constitutional law and key constitutional principles protecting religious liberty.

Do Students in Voucher Programs ...

For years, educators have been trying to determine whether students who use vouchers to attend private schools do better than those who remain in public school.

Not surprisingly, voucher opponents and proponents both say that their studies "prove" their position in the voucher debate. But no sooner has the ink dried on one study than the opposing side alleges bias and "bad social science."

"The right wing has conducted a profoundly deceptive public relations campaign seeking to persuade the media that these programs have been far more successful" than they have been, says People for the American Way, which opposes vouchers. In fact, "Some voucher students have done marginally better, some have done no better and some have fallen behind." [1]

"There are anecdotal instances that kids do better, and parents are more likely to be happy when they have chosen voucher programs," says Elliot M. Mincberg, the group's legal director. "But in terms of actual educational performance, I have not seen evidence that vouchers improve learning in any substantial way."

State-commissioned evaluations of the nation's two publicly funded voucher programs, in Milwaukee and Cleveland, showed no appreciable academic gains. Harvard University Professor Paul E. Peterson, a leading supporter of vouchers, has challenged both reports. In turn, the methodology and objectivity of Peterson and his colleagues have been widely challenged by researchers.

In a 1997 evaluation of Milwaukee's program, University of Wisconsin political science Professor John F. Witte found that voucher students did no better in reading compared with those who applied to the program but were rejected. But the voucher students performed better in math in the third and fourth years of the program. However, because half of the control-group students left the public school system and many of the least successful voucher students dropped out of the program, the findings were extremely "fragile," Witte said. [2]

After Witte reported his findings, voucher supporters lobbied successfully to eliminate the state requirement that participating schools gather achievement data necessary for a rigorous annual evaluation, Mincberg says.

Peterson says of the Witte report: "an acrid stench surrounds the manner in which the evaluator was selected." Peterson points out that Witte was chosen by Superintentendent of Public Instruction Herbert Grover, "no friend of school choice." "Instead of putting up the evaluation for competitive bid," Peterson writes, "he gave the assignment to John Witte," who "was known to have doubts about the advantages of private education." [3]

Peterson's study of the Milwaukee program found that math scores for third- and fourth-year participants were 5 and 11 percent higher, respectively, than the scores of voucher applicants who weren't chosen and remained in public schools. Reading scores for students who had been in the voucher program for three and four years averaged 3 and 6 percent higher, respectively, he found. Peterson claimed that if similar success could be achieved for all minority students nationwide, it could close the gap between white and minority test scores by more than one-half. [4]

But voucher opponents vehemently attacked Peterson's findings as methodologically flawed. Most concluded that he and his colleagues had compared a small, select group of voucher students with a tiny and disproportionately disadvantaged group of public school students, biasing results in favor of the voucher students. Because of high attrition rates among both sample groups, by the fourth year the two groups were "about as similar as apples and nails," said an American Federation of Teachers (AFT) analysis of the Peterson study. [5]

In a 1996 paper, Peterson and a colleague answered criticisms of their Milwaukee study. Among other things, they said that the claim that missing cases contaminate the results "is not supported by a detailed look at the available evidence." They also contended that the "assertion that the number of cases is too small to warrant the inferences [we] draw is unsupported." [6]

The AFT further complained that Peterson's study did not adequately compensate for the differing education levels of the students' parents. In a later analysis, when Peterson did control for parent education, he said he

people of all races and ethnic backgrounds learn to live together," says the NEA's Chase.

McTigue calls the Balkanization argument a "red herring." Private school graduates "are no less committed to democratic principles, pluralism and tolerance than graduates of other schools," he says, citing research by Jay P. Greene, an assistant professor at the University of Texas at Austin. Greene found that private schools are more racially integrated than public schools. [24]

The Balkanization argument "raises my blood pressure," Guerra says. Religious schools bring a vision to education entirely consistent with democratic ideals, he argues. Religious education promotes the common good of the community, "and not just individual advancement or corporate economic growth," he says.

. . . Outperform Students in Public Schools?

found no significant difference in achievement between voucher students and their public school peers.

A study by Princeton University Professor Cecilia Rouse found no improvement in reading but substantial improvement in math among voucher students in Milwaukee. Voucher proponents and opponents both claimed Rouse's findings buttressed their arguments.[7]

In another study, Rouse found that students in Milwaukee's experimental Student Achievement Guarantee in Education (SAGE) program, featuring public schools with small classes, keep pace with voucher schools in math and substantially outpace both private schools and city magnet schools in reading.[8]

Similarly, Professor Alex Molnar of the University of Wisconsin-Milwaukee also found that reducing class size is more effective than voucher policy in helping at-risk students. Molnar also studied SAGE students and found they outperform students who attend public or private schools with larger class sizes. Molnar found that African-American males particularly benefit from SAGE's smaller class sizes. Total reading, language arts and math scores for black males in the smaller classes rose 56 points in one year, compared with 39.4 points in non-SAGE schools.[9]

Nevertheless, Mincberg complains, Gov. Tommy G. Thompson, R-Wis., has proposed a budget for next year that would fund SAGE programs in only 40 percent of Milwaukee's schools, compared with 70 percent of eligible schools outside the city.

Peterson says he expects to get more conclusive results from his study of the School Choice Scholarship Foundation program in New York City. The privately funded program awarded 1,200 low-income students $1,400 a year to attend the religious or secular school of their choice. Because the recipients were selected via a lottery from among 20,000 applicants, Peterson says he is confident his comparison of the performance of voucher students and those not selected will be more credible than earlier studies, since they all came from the same pool of students.

Preliminary results after one year show that voucher students in the fourth and fifth grades scored 4 percentage points higher in reading and 6 points higher in math than their public school peers. However, in comparing all students in grades two through five, the voucher students scored 2 points higher in both subjects.

"The results from the first year of the New York City evaluation suggest that . . . there are clear benefits for low-income minority students that come from attendance in private schools," wrote Peterson.[10]

"There are dueling studies all over the place," concludes Clint Bolick, litigation director for the pro-voucher Institute for Justice in Washington, D.C. "But we should not give undue emphasis to the social scientists, who will undoubtedly continue to slug this out. The real experts are not the social scientists but the parents, who are voting with their feet."

---

[1] People for the American Way Foundation, "Myths and Facts about School Vouchers," undated Editorial Memorandum.

[2] John F. Witte, "Achievement Effects of the Milwaukee Voucher Program," Department of Political Science, Robert La Follette Institute, University of Wisconsin-Madison, Feb. 7, 1997.

[3] Paul E. Peterson and Chad Noyes, "Under Extreme Duress, School Choice Success," February 1996, chapter prepared for Diane Ravitch and Joseph Viteritti, eds, *New Schools for a New Century: The Redesign of Urban Education.*

[4] Jay P. Greene, Paul E. Peterson and Jiangtao Du, "Effectiveness of School Choice: The Milwaukee Experiment," March 1997.

[5] "A Critical Analysis of the Greene-Peterson-Du Paper," American Federation of Teachers Web site, September 1996, www.aft.org/research/reports/private/gdp/aftresp.htm.

[6] Jay P. Greene and Paul E. Peterson, "Methodological Issue in Evaluation Research: The Milwaukee School Choice Plan," Program on Education Policy and Governance, Harvard University, Aug. 29, 1996. Peterson is director of the program.

[7] Cecilia Rouse, "Private School Vouchers and Student Achievement: An Evaluation of the Milwaukee Parental Choice Program," *The Quarterly Journal of Economics*, Vol. 113, No. 2, 1998.

[8] Cecilia Rouse, "Schools and Student Achievement: More Evidence from the Milwaukee Public Choice Program," *Economic Policy Review*, 1998.

[9] Alex Molnar, "Smaller Classes, Not Vouchers, Increase Student Achievement," Keystone Research Center, 1998.

[10] Paul E. Peterson, "Vouchers and Test Scores," *Policy Review*, January-February 1999.

More Reforms

The public school system in the United States "can't possibly look the same in 10 years," say Arizona's Keegan. "It needs to be a better, more competitive mix of traditional public, charter and private schools."

Some think tuition tax credits and tax-free education accounts will become more popular than vouchers, because they are less likely to provoke government meddling. Congress last year passed a bill allowing parents to set aside as much as $2,000 a year per child into tax-free "education savings accounts" that could be used for private school tuition. President Clinton vetoed the bill last July, but it has been reintroduced this year. Idaho and Virginia are also considering tuition tax credit bills this spring, and citizens in Michigan and California are seeking referendums on tax credits in 2000.

The number of home-schooled students also is likely to grow, partly because of the growing variety of distance-learning programs available through technology.[25] "The traditional concept of school will change dramatically," McTigue predicts.

Mincberg foresees more standards-based, results-oriented public school reforms. "I think we will also see a greater push to reduce class size, particularly in the younger grades," he says. "And we'll see more teachers being hired and more school construction going on, as well as a greater commitment to resources dedicated to public schools, particularly in urban areas."

"We will no longer be throwing dollar bills at schools without structural change first," predicts Tate. "Schools not doing their job will be forced to do a better job. You will see a marked increase in test scores because more children will be in schools that challenge them."

Schools will be more responsive to the needs of children and families," says McTigue. "Monopolies are notoriously insensitive to the needs of their clients. But when you have the ability to take your business someplace else, the market becomes responsive to your needs.

"The key is to shift power from the bureaucrats to the families and parents," McTigue says. "Once the consumer gets control of this thing, everybody's boat is going to rise. It will be good for public education, private schools, home schools — the whole shebang." ■

FOR MORE INFORMATION

Council for American Private Education, PMB 457, 13017 Wisteria Dr., Germantown, Md. 20874; (301) 916-8460, www.capenet.org. This coalition of private-school associations seeks greater access to private schools for all Americans.

Institute for Justice, 1717 Pennsylvania Ave. N.W., #200, Washington, D.C. 20006; (202) 955-1300, www.instituteforjustice.org. This conservative public-interest law firm litigates cases involving parental school choice.

National Education Association, 1201 16th St. N.W., Washington, D.C. 20036; (202) 833-4000, www.nea.org. The NEA is the nation's largest teachers' union, with more than 2 million members. It works to defeat school-choice proposals through lobbying and litigation.

People for the American Way, 2000 M St., N.W., #400, Washington, D.C. 20036; (202) 467-4999; www.pfaw.org. This grass-roots organization promotes First Amendment rights through public-education programs.

Notes

[1] See Lowell C. Rose and Alec M. Gallup, "Public's Attitudes Toward the Public Schools," *Phi Delta Kappan*, September 1998.

[2] Figures from the Children's Educational Opportunity Foundation of America (CEO America).

[3] The Center for Education Reform, "National Charter School Directory 1998-99."

[4] Sandra Feldman, "Let's Tell the Truth," *The New Republic*, Nov. 24, 1997.

[5] Quoted in "School Vouchers," *USA Today*, December 18, 1998.

[6] Gerald Tirozzi, "Vouchers: A Questionable Answer to an Unasked Question," *Education Week*, April 23, 1997.

[7] Quoted in Derrick Z. Jackson, "The Corruption of School Choice," *The Boston Globe*, Oct. 28, 1998.

[8] A recent survey by an African-American think tank showed black support for vouchers is declining, contradicting the findings of the 1998 Gallup Poll. The 1998 telephone survey by the Joint Center for Political and Economic Studies found that between 1997 and 1998 African-American support for vouchers declined from 57 percent to 48 percent. Results are posted on the center's Web site, www.jointctr.org/selpaper/poll_edu.htm.

[9] See *Facts on File*, 1998, p. 409.

[10] For a summary of related Supreme Court rulings, see David Masci, "School Choice Debate," *The CQ Researcher*, July 18, 1997, pp. 625-648.

[11] Quoted in Mark Walsh, " 'Green Light' for School Vouchers?" *Education Week*, Nov. 18, 1998.

[12] Howard P. Berkowitz, "Think Twice About Vouchers," on the ADL's Web site at www.adl.org/frames/front_opinion.html. The ADL opposes tuition vouchers.

[13] Joe Loconte, "Will Vouchers Undermine the Mission of Religious Schools?" *Policy Review*, January-February 1999.

[14] "Barriers, Benefits and Cost of Using Private Schools to Alleviate Overcrowding in Public Schools," Final Report, U.S. Department of Education, Office of the Under Secretary, 1998.

[15] Quoted in Laconte, *op. cit.*

[16] For background, see Charles S. Clark, "Attack on Public Schools," *The CQ Researcher*, July 26, 1996, pp. 649-672.

[17] Milton Friedman, "The Role of Government in Education," in Robert A. Solo (ed.), *Economics and the Public Interest* (1955), pp. 127-134.

[18] Quoted in Clark, *op. cit.*, p. 662.

[19] John E. Chubb and Terry M. Moe, *Politics, Markets and America's Schools*, 1990.

[20] Figures are from the Wisconsin Department of Public Instruction.

[21] Press release, Feb. 2, 1999.

[22] Versaci's comments were made in a press statement the day of the House vote.

[23] See Mark Oswald, "Government shutdown looming if haggling persists," *The Santa Fe New Mexican*, March 23, 1999.

[24] Jay P. Greene and Nicole Mellow, "Integration Where it Counts," a paper prepared for delivery at the 1998 Annual Meeting of the American Political Science Association.

[25] For background, see Charles S. Clark, "Home Schooling," *The CQ Researcher*, Sept. 9, 1994, pp. 769-792.

Bibliography

Selected Sources Used

Books

Hanus, Jerome J. and Peter W. Cookson, Jr., *Choosing Schools: Vouchers and American Education*, American University Press, 1996.
Two university professors with opposing views on school vouchers debate the issues of whether vouchers will force public schools to improve, whether vouchers are constitutional and whether vouchers will improve student achievement.

McGroarty, Daniel, *Break These Chains: The Battle for School Choice*, Prima Publishing, 1996.
A fellow at the Institute for Contemporary Studies gives a blow-by-blow account of how low-income parents in Milwaukee fought to establish the nation's first voucher program and keep it alive despite opposition from the educational establishment and voucher opponents.

Articles

Feldman, Sandra, "Let's Tell the Truth," *The New Republic*, Nov. 24, 1997.
The president of the American Federation of Teachers argues that the momentum for vouchers will dissipate once the public understands the long-term impact. Vouchers will mean giving up on American public education, siphoning off as much of its funding as possible to enable a few "deserving poor" to go to private — mostly religious — schools, she argues.

Loconte, Joe, "Will Vouchers Undermine the Mission of Religious Schools?" *Policy Review*, January-February, 1999.
Voucher programs could end up being the Trojan Horse that exposed religious education to greater government control, argues Joe Loconte, William E. Simon Fellow in Religion and a Free Society at the conservative Heritage Foundation. As a result, many private schools will opt out of such programs and the choice movement could be dead on arrival, he contends.

Peterson, Paul E., "Vouchers and Test Scores," *Policy Review*, January-February 1999.
In preliminary results, this Harvard professor finds that students in the fourth and fifth grades in a private voucher program in New York City improved more in reading and math than their cohorts who were not chosen for the program. However, for students overall, in grades two through five, the difference was only 2 percent in both subjects.

Walsh, Mark, "'Green Light' for School Vouchers?" *Education Week*, Nov. 18, 1998.
The author discusses the impact of last November's U.S. Supreme Court decision not to review the Wisconsin ruling that school vouchers for parochial students are constitutional. Even though the court did not comment on the ruling, the court's inaction opened the way for voucher advocates to push for more state voucher programs.

Reports

"Barriers, Benefits and Cost of Using Private Schools to Alleviate Overcrowding in Public Schools," Final Report, U. S. Department of Education, Office of the Under Secretary, 1998.
A recent Department of Education study found that 66 percent of urban sectarian schools surveyed probably would not join a voucher program that exempted students from religious activities, and 46 percent would probably balk at requirements that they select students randomly.

"Charter School Laws: State by State Ranking and Profiles," The Center for Education Reform, November 1998.
This report by a pro-charter school organization evaluates state charter school laws according to whether they are weak or strong, and examines how they work in practice when implemented by local and state officials.

"Just Doing It: 1998 Annual Survey of the Private Voucher Movement in America," Children's Educational Opportunity Foundation of America.
This report summarizes how the private voucher movement grew from a single program in Indianapolis in 1991 to 34 programs serving 12,684 students in the 1997-98 school year.

Rees, Nina Shokraii and Sarah E. Youssef, "School Choice: What's Happening in the States," The Heritage Foundation, 1999.
The report gives an exhaustive state-by-state rundown of existing and proposed school-choice programs and related news.

Witte, John F., "Achievement Effects of the Milwaukee Voucher Program," Department of Political Science, Robert La Follette Institute, University of Wisconsin-Madison, Feb. 7, 1997.
A University of Wisconsin political science professor finds that voucher students showed only negligible test-score gains compared with non-voucher students even though they benefited from factors that usually increase educational achievement, such as parents' education, socioeconomic status and parents' academic expectations.

2 Zero Tolerance

Kathy Koch

On a school bus last fall in rural Mississippi, five high school students passed the time on the long ride home by tossing peanuts at each other.

But the fun ended when the driver got hit. She pulled over, called the police and had the boys arrested for assault, punishable by five years in prison. The criminal charges were soon dropped, but the teenagers were suspended and lost their bus privileges. Unable to make the 30-mile trip to school, all five dropped out.

The recent shooting death of a 6-year-old Michigan girl by another 6-year-old underscores the fear of violence that has invaded America's schools. But the strict, one-strike-and-you're-out policies being imposed to nip school violence and misbehavior in the bud sometimes go too far, critics say. Other examples from the public school crime blotter:

- A 6-year-old boy in York, Pa., was suspended for carrying a pair of nail clippers to school.
- A second-grader in Columbus, Ohio, was suspended for drawing a paper gun, cutting it out and pointing it at classmates.
- A 9-year-old Ohio boy was suspended after writing, "You will die an honorable death" as a fortune-cookie prediction for a class assignment.
- A 12-year-old Florida boy was handcuffed and jailed after he stomped in a puddle, splashing classmates.
- A 13-year-old boy in Manassas, Va., who accepted a Certs breath mint from a classmate was suspended and required to attend drug-awareness classes.
- Jewish youths in several schools were suspended for wearing the Star of David, sometimes used as a symbol of gang membership.

From *The CQ Researcher*, March 10, 2000.

Reuters/Rebecca Cook

A classmate shot and killed 6-year-old Kayla Rolland last month at school in Mount Morris Township, Mich.

Zero-tolerance policies punish all offenses severely, no matter how minor. School systems began adopting the tough codes after Congress passed the 1994 Gun-Free Schools Act, which required one-year expulsions for any child bringing a firearm or bomb to school.

But zero-tolerance rules in many states also cover fighting, drug or alcohol use and gang activity, as well as relatively minor offenses like possessing over-the-counter medications, disrespect of authority, sexual harassment, threats and vandalism. More than 90 percent of U.S. public schools had zero-tolerance policies for firearms or other weapons in 1997, and more than 85 percent had the policies for drugs and alcohol.

After the massacre last April at Columbine High School in Littleton, Colo., nervous legislators and school boards further tightened their zero-tolerance policies, creating what some critics call a national intolerance for childish behavior. In some jurisdictions, carrying cough drops, wearing black lipstick or dying your hair blue are expellable offenses. Even writing a paper about murder or suicide can land a student in trouble.

"Things got a lot worse post-Columbine," says John Whitehead, president of the conservative Rutherford Institute, a Charlottesville, Va., group dedicated to protecting civil liberties.

In the current atmosphere, merely displaying the image of a weapon is unacceptable, as Samantha Jones, of Nevis, Minn., learned. The 17-year-old Army recruit was forbidden from using her favorite photo of herself — sitting atop a howitzer at the local VFW post — for her yearbook picture.

"A real vortex has been created that sucks in otherwise good kids who make a single mistake," Whitehead says.

"Some call it zero-zero tolerance," says Paul Kingery, director of the Hamilton Fish Institute on School and Community Violence at The George Washington University.

He discovered that while the number of students expelled for firearms has decreased since 1994, expulsions and suspensions for non-gun offenses have skyrocketed.[1] In Chicago, for instance, expulsions jumped eightfold after zero-tolerance policies were adopted in 1995 for weapons, alcohol and drugs.

Meanwhile, because minor infractions are punished so severely, administrators are ratcheting up punishments for more serious offenses. Two-year and permanent expulsions are on the rise. In Pennsylvania, long-term expulsions jumped nearly 960 percent from 1996 to 1997, Kingery writes.[2]

To accommodate all the expulsions, the number of alternative schools in the United States jumped from 2,604 in 1994, when most zero-tolerance rules were enacted, to 3,380 in 1997, according to the U.S. Education Department.

Only nine states require expelled students to attend an alternative

Most Schools Adopt Zero Tolerance

School systems began adopting zero-tolerance policies after Congress passed the 1994 Gun-Free Schools Act, which required one-year expulsions for bringing a firearm or bomb to school. More than 90 percent of U.S. public schools had zero tolerance for firearms or other weapons in 1997.

U.S. public schools with zero-tolerance policies, 1996-97

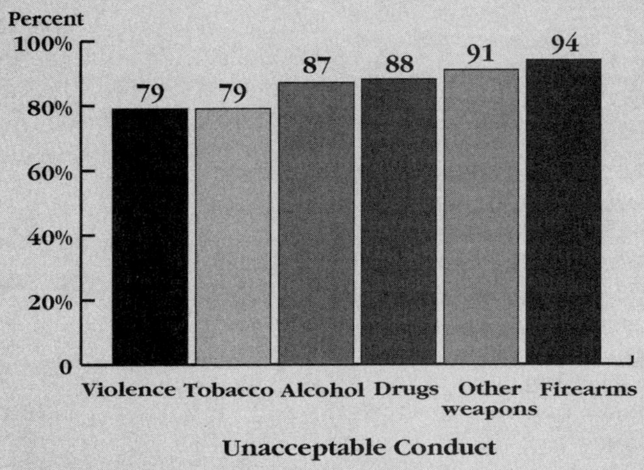

Source: U.S. Department of Education, "Principal-School Disciplinarian Survey on School Violence," 1997.

school. Research shows that expelled students who don't attend alternative classes are less likely to re-enter school and more likely to get mixed up in gang activity and drugs and otherwise run afoul of the law.

Critics say the biggest problem with zero-tolerance policies is their lack of flexibility, which prohibits officials from taking a child's age or past history into account.

"The absolute punishment applies whether you're carrying a nail clipper or a bazooka, Tylenol or illegal drugs," says Nadine Strossen, president of the American Civil Liberties Union (ACLU).

Strossen says school zero-tolerance policies grew out of drug-war laws that abolished discretion and curtailed civil liberties, such as mandatory minimum sentences, three-strikes-and-you're-out laws, civil-asset forfeiture and stop-and-frisk tactics.

"Judges were seen as too lenient," says Eugene Volokh, a professor of law at the University of California at Los Angeles, "and many people perceived that some school administrations tolerated things that shouldn't have been tolerated."

But critics say the zero-tolerance laws that resulted are either too vague or all-encompassing. One such law, an Alabama judge said recently, was unreasonable because it meant that "a sharpened pencil, chemistry supplies and a tennis racket could all be used as weapons." [3]

School administrators defend strict policies, arguing that they're needed because it's difficult to distinguish what is and isn't a weapon or gang-related paraphernalia. They say that students have been caught carrying hairbrushes with blades in the handles, or necklaces with large metal crosses made of knife blades. And gang symbols can range from a Star of David to a rolled up pants leg.

William Modzeleski, director of the Education Department's Safe and Drug-Free Schools Program, says local zero-tolerance policies go far beyond the federal gun-free schools legislation. "The federal law is very narrowly defined," he says. "It says a child should be expelled for bringing a firearm or bomb to school. Not drug-abusing behavior, not nail clippers, not nail files, not water pistols, not pellet guns."

The federal law also allows local administrators to waive or reduce the one-year expulsion if there are extenuating circumstances. In fact, about one-third of the students expelled for firearms serve less than a year's suspension, he says.

Modzeleski says some schools also may be misinterpreting an Education Department publication on recognizing troubled kids. It recommended that children exhibiting certain behaviors, like writing about death, be referred to a professional counselor. Yet some schools suspend such students.

"We have to send a message that we're serious about no guns and drugs," says Michael Resnick, associate executive director for advocacy and issues management at the National School Boards Association (NSBA). "We can't be fuzzy around the edges about that message."

Educators say they cannot relax their guard because life-threatening incidents continue to plague U.S. schools. Last fall, authorities shut down a Cleveland high school after uncovering a bomb plot. On Dec. 6, a 13-year-old honor student in Oklahoma took a semiautomatic handgun from his backpack and fired 15 rounds at classmates, injuring five. And on Feb. 29, there was the shooting in Michigan of first-grader Kayla Rolland.

While a handful of silly cases make headlines, most zero-tolerance cases involve real weapons, says Vincent Ferrandino, executive director of the National Association of Elementary School Principals (NAESP).

He rejects suggestions that the policies reflect administrators' fear of liability suits if violence should erupt in their schools. "These policies are meant to protect the kids," he says.

But Peter Blauvelt, president of the National Alliance for Safe Schools (NASS), says, "There are a lot of administrators who are comfortable having no discretion, especially when they have to discipline the mayor's child. It's much easier to say they must treat all kids the same because of zero-tolerance laws."

Allowing "flexibility" also allows more racial and ethnic discrimination, Ferrandino contends. But students' advocates say that zero tolerance disproportionately targets minorities, the poor and the disabled.

That was the charge made last fall by the Rev. Jesse Jackson, who led marches in Decatur, Ill., to protest the expulsions of six African-American teenagers for starting a brawl at a football game. White boys, Jackson said, never would have been expelled for two years for a fight that involved no weapons and no injuries.

Similarly, says Judith A. Browne, senior attorney for the Advancement Project, a civil rights group in Washington, D.C., the five Mississippi peanut throwers were treated harshly because they were black and the bus driver white.

Critics say zero-tolerance policies teach children to be intolerant and don't prepare them for making difficult judgments later in life. "School boards somehow expect children to value differences in each other when adults seem unable to differentiate between the behavior of 6-year-olds and 16-year-olds, between an aspirin and cocaine, and between a friendly, first-grade hug and a sexual attack," writes Bethany Baxter, an educational consultant.[4]

Expulsions Hit Black Students Hardest

In some large school districts, black students are three to five times more likely to be expelled than white students, according to a recent survey. Moreover, the percentage of blacks expelled far exceeds blacks' enrollment.

Public school expulsions, by race, 1998-99

School Location	Percentage Black	Percentage White
Austin, Texas		
Enrollment	18%	37%
Expulsion Rate	36%	18%
Boston		
Enrollment	55%	13%
Expulsion Rate	70%	9%
Columbia, S.C.		
Enrollment	78%	20%
Expulsion Rate	90%	9%
Los Angeles		
Enrollment	14%	11%
Expulsion Rate	30%	8%
Miami-Dade County, Fla.		
Enrollment	33%	12%
Expulsion Rate	48%	8%
Providence, R.I.		
Enrollment	23%	21%
Expulsion Rate	39%	13%
San Francisco		
Enrollment	18%	14%
Expulsion Rate	56%	11%

Source: The Applied Research Center, 1999

As parents, educators and policymakers debate the pros and cons of zero-tolerance policies, here are some of the questions they are asking:

Are zero-tolerance policies effective?

Proponents credit zero-tolerance policies with recent declines in crime and school weapons cases, even though they acknowledge there is little data to support that claim.

"All we have is anecdotal experience and the broad acceptance among administrators that zero-tolerance policies have been very helpful," says Ronald Stephens, executive director of the National School Safety Center, in Westlake, Calif.

"There is no good, quantitative research to show whether zero-tolerance policies are effective or ineffective," Modzeleski says. "But many educators and law enforcement officials will tell you that because of zero tolerance, we have less violence in schools than we had five years ago."

Federal statistics confirm that the number of crimes in schools per 1,000 students decreased from 155 in 1993 to 102 in 1997. There also were declines in the number of students carrying weapons to school and the number of student fights.

In Baltimore, school officials credit the aggressive zero-tolerance law adopted last spring with a 67 percent drop in arrests and a 31 percent decline in school crime in the first two months of the 1999-2000 school year. [5] And after Texas adopted zero tolerance for drugs and weapons, the percentage of teachers reporting that assaults on students was a "significant problem" dropped from 53 percent in 1993 to 31 percent in 1998. [6]

Moreover, says Stephens, the dramatic increase in the number of alternative schools around the country reflects the fact that zero-tolerance policies have "taken the troublemakers out of the schools and allowed the teachers to get back to the mission of teaching."

But critics argue that if zero tolerance were responsible for either falling street crime or the decline in school weapons-possession, proponents would have statistics showing that crime or weapons possession dropped faster in schools and communities with zero-tolerance policies than in those without them.

"They don't have those statistics," says Jason Zeidenberg, a policy analyst at the Justice Policy Institute. "It may just be that violent crime and drug use are down everywhere, so they are down in the schools as well," NASS' Blauvelt says.

Despite the lack of compelling statistics, 85 percent of principals, 79 percent of teachers and 82 percent of students credit zero-tolerance policies with keeping drugs out of schools, according to a 1998 Columbia University survey. [7]

However, a 1998 federal government survey of more than 1,000 school principals indicated that there were only minor improvements in school discipline and drug problems from 1990 to 1996. [8] The percentage of principals reporting "serious problems" with fighting, alcohol use and weapons possession dropped somewhat. But an increase was posted among principals who said tobacco and drug use, drug sales and verbal and physical abuse of teachers were "moderate or serious" problems.

"The bottom line is that the rate of school violence has remained fairly level since the early 1990s," wrote researchers Russell Skiba and Reece Peterson. [9]

School officials in Kansas suspended senior honors student Sarah Boman, 17, for displaying artwork at school that included a poem written from a madman's perspective. School officials considered it a threat and said Boman can return to school only if she had psychological testing.

The policies are highly effective at sending an unequivocal message to kids, says Gerald Tirozzi, executive director of the National Association of Secondary School Principals. "I can't prove that zero-tolerance policies alone were responsible [for the declines in violence], but with the violence going down, I'd like to think that message is sinking in."

But Skiba, an associate professor of counseling and educational psychology at Indiana University, says the right message may not be getting through, or may be reaching the wrong people. Several studies show that 35 to 45 percent of suspensions are for repeat offenders, he points out. "So we end up punishing honor students to send a message to bad kids. But the data indicate that the bad kids aren't getting the message."

While no studies show conclusively that get-tough tactics work, Skiba says there is good data showing the effectiveness of comprehensive violence-prevention programs focusing on conflict resolution, peer mediation, mentoring and bullying prevention.

Yet zero-tolerance policies are the quickest and cheapest way to put a program in place, Skiba says, "and it makes good rhetoric. We certainly need to set boundaries and limits. But let's not kid ourselves by thinking that we are going to solve school safety problems simply by drawing a line in the sand. Zero-tolerance policies by themselves will not ensure that our schools are safe."

But even proponents agree that the toughest policies won't totally eradicate violence, says John Mitchell, deputy director of education issues at the American Federation of Teachers (AFT). "If a kid is so driven that killing becomes the major thing in their lives, schools can't protect against that just with a zero-tolerance policy," he says. "Other things have to be put into place."

Modzeleski points out that zero-tolerance policies are only effective if they are developed with input from the parents and students and are relevant to the culture of the community and the age of the students. "What you do in Des Moines might be different from what you do in Dubuque," he says. "What is appropriate for a 17-year-old is not necessarily appropriate for a 7-year-old."

Effective programs also include early intervention, violence and gang prevention and programs to promote racial and ethnic tolerance. Efforts to get kids connected to their schools and communities through after-school opportunities, smaller schools, smaller classes and better-prepared teachers are also helpful, he says.

"If the policies are carefully worded, extremely narrowly focused and used in conjunction with a comprehensive violence-prevention program, they can be effective," says Gerald Newberry, executive director of the Health Information Network at the National Education Association (NEA). "And they must be communicated in a way that encourages co-operation, rather than rebellion."

But zero-tolerance measures that turn schools into military or penal institutions "foster anxiety, fear and insecurity — precisely the opposite of their intended effect," the ACLU's Strossen says.

Critics are particularly concerned about zero-tolerance programs run by 14 states that expel students without providing alternative educational opportunities.

"If a child is already ostracized and alienated, the most irrational response is suspension or expulsion," Strossen says. "You want to bring them back into the fold."

Are zero-tolerance policies constitutional?

Strossen maintains that students' rights to privacy, free speech and due process are being abridged by zero-tolerance rules. "Kids have been thrown out of school for completely innocuous things like wearing certain T-shirts, creating works of art or wearing the Star of David," she says.

The Supreme Court has ruled that children have a property interest in public education, and thus the government cannot deprive them of their education without due process, she says. The court ruled in the landmark *Tinker v. Des Moines* case in 1969 that neither students nor teachers shed their constitutional rights at the schoolhouse door, she adds.

"Yet, consistently, we see a whole host of actions being taken that violate civil liberties," Strossen says, "including everything from prosecuting parents when their children are truant, to throwing kids out of school for minor infractions, to censorial discipline for innocuous statements made on students' own Web sites."

Many lawsuits challenging zero-tolerance rules charge that students' rights to free speech were violated. In the wake of schoolyard murders by boys who first wrote about death or made verbal threats or dressed a certain way, teachers are quick to report — and schools prone to expel — a student for what he or she wore, drew or said.

Other challenges to zero-tolerance rules allege that schools failed to follow due-process procedures, Strossen says. Students must be given notice of the charge against them, she says, and allowed to respond to the charge before being penalized.

"But a lot of zero-tolerance policies are being automatically implemented without even giving the student an opportunity to respond," she says. Often the student doesn't even have the right to have a parent or lawyer present.

The Rutherford Institute's Whitehead says the constitutionality of a zero-tolerance code depends on the case and how the code is written. "Some of the policies I've looked at are vague and a bit overbroad, which I think goes to their constitutionality," he says.

Nonetheless, zero-tolerance policies have generally received favorable treatment from the current Supreme Court, which "almost always rules in favor of state laws, police actions and school actions," Whitehead says. "Starting with President [Ronald] Reagan's appointments, the court has shifted to the right," he says. "That has had a big impact on these cases."

For instance, in *Veronia School District v. Acton*, the court said in 1995 that student athletes have a reduced expectation of privacy and thus could be randomly tested for drugs without probable cause. "In another time, with a different court, you may get a different interpretation," Whitehead says. [10]

Charles B. Vergon, an attorney and professor of educational leadership at Youngstown State University, in Ohio, analyzed about 60 lawsuits brought on behalf of students expelled or suspended for weapons or firearms possession since 1990. In three-quarters of the cases, the schools' right to ensure safety on their premises was upheld, even though in some cases "a reasonable person could have taken a very different posture," Vergon says.

"School districts continue to enjoy substantial deference from the courts in governing the conduct of students at school and coming and going from school, particularly if it enhances the safety of students," he says.

NSBA staff attorney Julie Lewis

Expulsions in Chicago Rose Sharply

The number of students expelled in Chicago more than doubled in 1996-97, a year after the school board passed a strict zero-tolerance policy. Expulsions tripled in 1997-98 and are projected to keep rising.

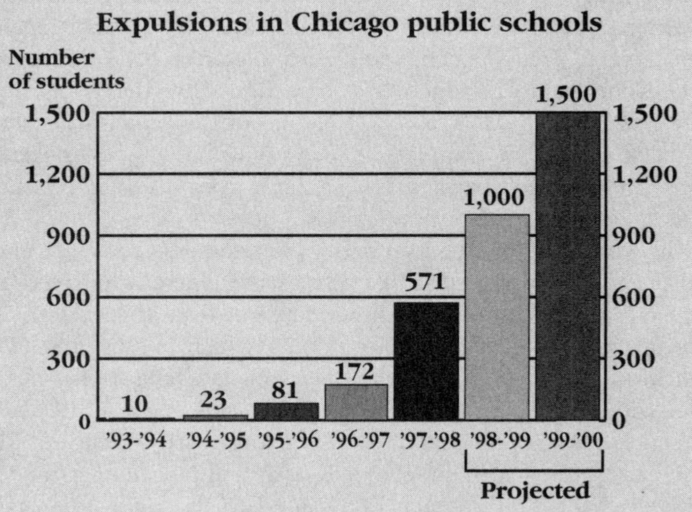

Source: Chicago Public Schools, "Measuring Progress Towards Goals," 1999

says zero-tolerance policies are usually upheld as constitutional unless they are too vague or overbroad, or the school district violates due-process rules, infringes upon students' free-speech rights or enforces the policies inconsistently.

"Most courts have been flexible in enforcing due process if they see that there was some procedure followed or notice provided," Lewis says. If a principal discusses the accusation with the student, many courts say the student received due process.

Ironically, Lewis says, some school districts are "broadening and broadening and broadening" their zero-tolerance policies, hoping to discourage civil-rights and equal-protection lawsuits. But instead, they now face more due-process and First Amendment suits, she says.

The University of California's Volokh says if zero-tolerance laws are properly written, and the school does not conduct an illegal search or otherwise violate the Constitution, they're perfectly constitutional. Even expulsions for artwork or writings dealing with death may not violate a student's right to free speech, he says.

In *Tinker v. Des Moines School District*, the Supreme Court held that schools can act if they have "reasonable anticipation" that a student's behavior will cause "material disruption" of school discipline, Volokh explains. For instance, if a student jokes about blowing up the school, the government could argue that it reasonably anticipated that such a joke would interfere with discipline because students would be frightened, rumors would get started or other kids might mimic the threat, he says.

"In the current atmosphere of heightened sensitivity, a school might punish something that in a particular context is disruptive, even though in another context it would be protected," Volokh says. For instance, a university recently removed a bulletin board photo of a military-history professor dressed in a mock Roman costume holding a sword. "The school said it creates a climate of violence," he says.

Schools' efforts to ban all images of guns are probably constitutional, he says. But they strike him as "a weird kind of fanatical, militant pacifism — an attempt to deny the fact that weapons exist and that sometimes they are useful, and that we pay people to operate them," he says. "Some schools are behaving in ways that are just plain silly," he says. "But silliness is not unconstitutional."

Are zero-tolerance policies fairly and consistently applied?

One of the rationales for zero-tolerance policies both in schools and law enforcement was to remove discretion from authorities and ensure that everyone would be treated equally.

"If you have a policy that clearly articulates what won't be tolerated, what the penalties are and it is consistently applied, that should minimize the extent to which you have discriminatory practices," says Tirozzi of the principals' association.

A discretionary policy allows authorities to consciously or subconsciously treat people from one group differently from those of another, Volokh says. "Zero-tolerance policies theoretically would diminish police discretion and the chance of racist enforcement," he says.

But critics argue that when zero-tolerance policies are actually applied in the real world, blacks, minorities, poor people and disabled students are expelled and suspended at higher rates than whites. Similarly, the critics say, racial stereotyping by police causes a disproportionate number of blacks and minorities to be stopped, frisked or arrested. For example, Strossen says, African-Americans make up 13 percent of the population and 13 percent of drug users. But blacks make up 74 percent of those incarcerated for drug use, she says.

The Decatur case brought this long-simmering controversy to the forefront. Lawyers for the six suspended youths produced statistics showing that 82 percent of Decatur students expelled in the past three years were African-American, although only 48 percent of the student population is black.

In addition, a recent survey of 12 large school districts showed that in some districts black students are three to five times more likely to be expelled than white students are. For instance, in Phoenix, blacks made up only 4 percent of the high school population but received 21 percent of the expulsions or suspensions. By comparison, only 18 percent of the whites — representing 74 percent of the enrollment — were suspended. Similarly, in San Francisco blacks account for 16 percent of the enrollment but 52 percent of the exclusions. [11]

Even the Department of Edu-cation's own figures show that in 1997 black students represented 17 percent of public school enrollment nationwide but 32 percent of those suspended — a disparity that has remained consistent since 1975.

"The recent school shootings were done primarily by white kids," Zeidenberg points out. "But African-American kids are the ones being disproportionately expelled and suspended. Is it really fair for them to bear the brunt of America's panic about school violence?"

However, "A numerical disparity does not by itself prove discrimination," Norma Cantu, assistant secretary of Education for civil rights, told the U.S. Commission on Civil Rights on Feb. 18. "It does not tell us the cause of the disparity."

The judge in the Decatur case agreed that disparate statistics alone don't prove discrimination. Judge Michael McCuskey upheld the students' suspensions on Jan. 11 after finding that the school district had not violated their civil rights. "Because the students failed to show that any similarly situated Caucasian students were treated less harshly," he wrote in his ruling, "they failed to establish that race played any role in the School Board's expulsion decision."

Reuters/Gary Caskey

Students attend a prayer vigil in Denver last April following a shooting spree by two Columbine High School students that left 15 people dead. The killings prompted many schools to strengthen their zero-tolerance policies.

Volokh agrees that raw, disparate numbers don't prove discrimination. "There may be a disproportionate amount of improper conduct in certain groups," he says. "For example, a disproportionate number of men are criminally prosecuted, but that doesn't necessarily mean there is an anti-male bias. It may be the case that men commit more crimes than women."

Although he admits that discrimination can occur, "Misbehavior is not evenly distributed among racial and ethnic groups," says Kent Scheidegger, legal director of the conservative Criminal Justice Legal Foundation in Sacramento, Calif. "It's possible they are being punished more because they are misbehaving more."

But researcher Skiba insists, "There's just no evidence of that whatsoever. There is pretty good evidence that this oversuspension is not the result of lower behavioral standards among black students," he says. "There seems to be more going on than that."

In a recent study, Skiba found no difference between the punishments meted out to black and white students once the students are referred to the office. But black students were twice as likely to be referred to the office as white students were. "The real disparity was in classroom referrals," he says.

Black students were referred more often for minor, more subjective behaviors like loitering, disrespect, threats, excessive noise and a catchall category called "conduct interference," he found. Whites were referred for less-subjective behaviors, such as smoking, vandalism, obscene language or using drugs or alcohol. "These things could be culturally bound," Skiba says. "A white female teacher might not be culturally sensitive to the difference in styles of African-American male students."

A study by the Civil Rights Project at Harvard University corroborated Skiba's findings. "African-American and Latino children are constantly being suspended for the more discretionary offenses, such as 'defiance of authority' and 'disrespect of authority,' " it said. "These categories of conduct clearly provide more latitude for racial bias to play a part." [12]

The ACLU's Strossen argues that such "invidious discrimination" is probably occurring in the classroom, when the teacher decides who to refer to the office, just as it does when a policeman decides who to stop and frisk or a prosecutor decides who to prosecute. "Studies have demonstrably shown that with minimum-sentencing guidelines discrimination apparently occurs at the police and prosecutor levels," she says. "I assume the same thing happens in the schools."

Even if the punishment meted out is the same once an offender appears before a principal or a judge, she says, "We'll never know all of the infractions committed by white kids that teachers decide not to treat as an infraction, partly because they know the punishment is going to be so harsh."

"Schools are more willing to recognize mitigating circumstances if they perceive the student as having 'a real future' that would be destroyed by expulsion," said Terry Keleher, program director at the Applied Research Center, in Oakland, Calif., which studies race and social-change issues. [13]

Disparate treatment of disabled students under zero-tolerance policies is more confusing, but no less controversial. Some observers complain that federal law creates a dual system of punishment in which disabled children who bring guns to school are treated less harshly than non-disabled students caught with a weapon at school.

But parents and advocates for the disabled cite statistics showing that, in fact, disabled students are twice as likely as non-disabled students to be expelled or suspended. They say schools use zero tolerance to get rid of disabled students that are difficult to handle or are not performing as well as others. ■

BACKGROUND

'We Need to Get Tough'

Presidential candidate Richard M. Nixon campaigned on "law and order" issues in the 1960s. Politicians in the '70s bragged of being "tough on crime." Then in the 1980s, as the government's "war on drugs" heated up, "zero tolerance" joined the lexicon.

The term probably first appeared in 1983, when the Navy cracked down on drug abusers. The Marines soon adopted a similar policy, and initiated random drug tests.

A year later, Congress passed the first mandatory-minimum sentencing law, specifying stiff, automatic penalties for drugs and firearms violations. Lawmakers also amended federal forfeiture laws, expanding the government's authority to seize private property suspected of being involved in commission of a crime.

By 1986, with the nation beset by crack cocaine and skyrocketing violence, President Ronald Reagan launched the "war on drugs," and Congress passed the Anti-Drug Abuse Act, which expanded the list of offenses covered by mandatory sentencing. [14]

The same year, Attorney General Edwin Meese III authorized Customs officials nationwide to seize the boats, automobiles, and passports of anyone crossing the border with even trace amounts of drugs.

Within months, angry citizens whose boats had been seized were testifying on Capitol Hill along with Customs and Coast Guard officials accused of trampling the rights and sometimes destroying the property of citizens, some later proved innocent.

But the administration continued on the attack. In May, Education Secretary William J. Bennett asked Congress to withhold federal education money from schools unless they adopted zero-tolerance expulsion policies for students using or dealing in drugs on school grounds.

"We need to get tough as hell and do it right now," Bennett told the House Select Committee on Narcotics Abuse and Control." [15]

Rep. E. Clay Shaw, R-Fla., supported Bennett's proposal, arguing, "We have to quit being bleeding hearts for every kid who's rotten to the core." [16]

But Bennett got little support from the rest of the Democratically controlled committee, which said it preferred drug-education programs to simple expulsion. "Are you suggesting that a junkie kicked out of school is no longer a junkie?" asked Chairman Charles B. Rangel, D-N.Y. [17]

Another section of the 1986 Anti-Drug Abuse Act contained the Drug-Free Schools and Communities Act, the precursor of today's Safe and Drug-Free Schools Act, the federal government's largest drug and violence-prevention activity. The act required schools to have policies prohibiting alcohol and drug use by youths.

"But it did not specify what was to happen once a kid was found possessing alcohol or drugs on school property," says the Education Department's Modzeleski, noting that the term "zero tolerance" does not appear in the act.

In 1990, the U.S. Customs Service discontinued its boat-impoundment program after a marijuana cigarette led to the seizure of a research vessel from the Woods Hole Oceanographic Institute.

Ironically, at about the same time that Customs was easing its policy, zero tolerance was catching on in the public schools. By late 1989, districts in California, New York and Kentucky had adopted zero-toler-

Chronology

1960s *Illegal drug trafficking skyrockets. Supreme Court recognizes free-speech rights for school students.*

1968
Mandatory drug testing begins for returning Vietnam War veterans.

1969
Supreme Court rules in *Tinker v. Des Moines Independent Community School District* that students' constitutional rights were violated when they were suspended for wearing black armbands to protest the Vietnam War.

1970s *Courts extend due-process protections to students and mandate equal education for the disabled.*

1971
President Richard M. Nixon declares the first "war on drugs."

1975
Supreme Court rules in *Goss v. Lopez* that students cannot be suspended without due process. Education for All Handicapped Children Act requires all children to be educated in the "least restrictive environment" possible.

1980s *Crack cocaine inundates inner cities, and homicide among juveniles, particularly young, black males, reaches epidemic proportions. First mass murders occur on school grounds.*

1982
An article in the *Atlantic* by researcher George Kelling espouses the "broken windows" theory of policing, providing the basis for later zero-tolerance tactics in cities and schools.

1983
Navy and Marines adopt zero-tolerance drug policy.

1984
Congress passes Comprehensive Crime Control Act, requiring a federal commission to develop mandatory-sentencing guidelines for federal judges. Congress mandates stiff penalties for drug and firearm offenses.

1986
President Ronald Reagan launches a second "war on drugs." Congress passes Anti-Drug Abuse Act, doubling the number of federal mandatory minimums in effect. Federal and state governments begin seizing boats, automobiles and homes of drug suspects.

Jan. 13, 1988
Supreme Court rules in *Hazelwood School District v. Kuhlmeier* that school officials can censor student expression for "legitimate pedagogical concerns."

Sept. 26, 1988
A 19-year-old gunman opens fire on a Greenwood, S.C., schoolyard, killing two and wounding nine.

1989
On Jan. 17, a man with an assault rifle kills six children and wounds 30 on a Stockton, Calif., playground.

1990s *Congress bans guns from school grounds; mass murders committed by students erupt at decade's end.*

1990
President George Bush signs Gun-Free School Zones Act.

1992-93
Fifty-five violent deaths occur at schools and school functions.

1993
Washington state mandates life imprisonment for repeat felons.

1994
California and 12 other states pass "three-strikes-and-you're-out" legislation. Congress passes Omnibus Crime Bill, which includes mandatory drug sentences, and the Gun-Free Schools Act.

1995
Supreme Court strikes down 1995 Gun-Free School Zones Act and upholds random drug testing of school athletes. Crime reverses its upward trend, except for homicides by teenage boys, which skyrockets.

1997-98
Students commit mass murder five times within eight months in rural schools; 13 students and faculty die and 47 are wounded.

April 20, 1999
Two teenage boys shoot and kill 13 people at Columbine High School in Littleton, Colo., and then commit suicide.

Feb. 29, 2000
Six-year-old Kayla Rolland is shot and killed by a classmate at an elementary school in Michigan.

Are Students Losing Legal Rights . . .

In Texas recently, a high school student was sent to juvenile jail for five days without a hearing after writing a Halloween horror story in which a teacher and some classmates were shot.

Constitutional scholar Jamin Raskin cites the "unbelievable and shocking" case as an example of due process being denied to a student because of a zero-tolerance policy.

In the 1970s and '80s, the war on drugs accustomed American students to such anti-drug tactics as warrantless drug testing, locker searches and drug-sniffing dogs nosing around their cars and bookbags.

But student rights eroded even faster in the '90s as schools embraced zero-tolerance discipline policies to address school violence, say legal scholars like Raskin, a professor at American University. Following a recent spate of mass murders at schools, lawmakers and school officials adopted zero tolerance for behavior that even implies violence. Now, students are being suspended for writing about death, suicide or murder or for drawing pictures of guns.

"Discipline codes should discourage some of the negative writing that goes on," says John Mitchell, deputy director of education issues for the American Federation of Teachers. "Schools shouldn't be compelled to display work that isn't uplifting."

Students have always had fewer First Amendment rights than other citizens, says Eugene Volokh, a law professor at the University of California at Los Angeles. "When you're talking about K-12 education, the government has much more authority than it does over private citizens," he says. But in the 1960s, the Supreme Court expanded those rights, a trend that some say has been dramatically reversed in the past two decades.

"From the Warren Court era to the Rehnquist Court era, there has been a progressive decline in constitutional protection for students' rights," says Raskin, author of *We the Students*, a new textbook on students' rights.

Others disagree. "I don't think students' rights have declined," says Edwin Darden, senior staff attorney for the National School Boards Association (NSBA). "There's been an evolution to try to balance the needs of school districts and the needs and rights of the students."

The courts have been "very thoughtful" about how to achieve that balance, Darden says. But constitutional rights don't exist in a vacuum, he says, and the courts have had to weigh schools' need to ensure the safety of all students against the rights of the individual. "The courts have often ruled in favor of the schools."

Raskin says the Supreme Court "aggressively defended" students' First Amendment rights its 1969 *Tinker v. Des Moines Independent Community School District* ruling. The court said students should not be prevented from wearing black armbands to protest the Vietnam War unless it would cause "material and substantial disruption of school activities or invasion of the rights of other students."

As Justice Abe Fortas wrote in the case: "Neither students nor teachers shed their constitutional rights to freedom of speech or expression at the schoolhouse gate."

But by the late 1980s, Raskin says, the reconstituted court's *Hazelwood School District v. Kuhlmeier* ruling upheld the authority of schools to censor student publications "for almost any reasonable purpose."

Raskin says another constitutional right being "violated all over the country by zero-tolerance policies" is the right to due process. In the years before zero tolerance, students had a right to hear and respond to the charges against them before being expelled or suspended. But now, Raskin says, "Students are automatically suspended without a hearing."

The tough, new policies reflect longstanding complaints by politicians that liberal court rulings allowed chaos to reign in classrooms because educators had to jump through procedural hoops to expel disruptive students. Many observers say the current crackdown is a backlash to those procedural excesses.

"The only due process right that the Supreme Court has given students is that they must be given some notice of the charge against them and some opportunity to respond," says Nadine Strossen, president of the American Civil Liberties Union (ACLU). "It can be completely informal, it can be verbal and it can be after the punishment has been meted out, and students have no right to a lawyer. To even call it 'due process' is an exaggeration.

"It's nothing compared with what you would get if you were accused of even a misdemeanor outside of the school," she says. "Yet the life-destroying consequences can be at least as great if you're talking about someone being thrown out of school."

However, students' rights have expanded in two areas, Raskin says. High school students may now sue their

ance expulsion policies for drugs or gang-related activity. By 1993, schools across the country had cracked down on tobacco, alcohol and disruptive activities, as well as drugs and weapons.

After an American Association of University Women survey showed that 81 percent of students in grades eight-11 said they had been sexually harassed at least once in school, many schools also instituted zero tolerance for sexual harassment.

Zero tolerance was also becoming more popular with local lawmakers and soon was being applied to everything from pollution and trespassing to skateboarding, racial intoler-

. . . Or Getting More 'Care' From Schools?

school for student-on-student sexual harassment if the school knew about it and did nothing to stop it. And many state courts have ruled in recent years that corporal punishment is unlawful, he points out.

Legal experts predict that the next two frontiers for students'-rights litigation will involve what Raskin calls school "cyber-censors," and efforts by schools to extend their disciplinary authority to off-campus student behavior.

In the aftermath of the shootings at Columbine High School in Littleton, Colo., some schools are cracking down on students who put material on their home Web pages that criticizes or threatens school personnel.

Except for those posting bomb threats, students have generally won their court challenges to such policies, especially if it merely involved the right to criticize the school administration and caused no disruption in classes, Raskin says.

Darden says the courts will also be seeing more challenges of schools trying to discipline students for what they do during non-school hours. "It's the next big wave of school litigation over the next two years."

For instance the Texas legislature recently passed a law requiring the expulsion of any student who commits a felony or an assault, or distributes drugs or alcohol near school property. Many states are requiring that schools be notified when a student runs afoul of the law, even though it was not on school property or during school hours. Some of those students are summarily expelled or suspended.

Darden says these new laws are efforts by the school districts to tell students, "We care about the whole person. When you do things that are dangerous to yourself, like using drugs or alcohol, the school district cares about that and will not look the other way."

But others find them a disturbing trend. "It would be ridiculous for the school to get involved, unless perhaps the student was arrested for rape," says Kent Scheidegger, legal director of the conservative Criminal Justice Legal Foundation in Sacramento, Calif. "You wouldn't want a suspected rapist in the school. But arrested for marijuana possession? That doesn't make any sense. That should be a matter for parents and the juvenile courts. That's what they're there for."

Darden says it is often the parents who are "asking, begging and cajoling" the school districts to impose tough behavior standards off-campus. If the school is randomly testing kids for drugs, it's easier for a student to resist peer pressure, parents argue.

"Except for the most extreme circumstances, schools really have no rightful authority to discipline students for activity off-campus," says Peter Blauvelt, president of the National Alliance for Safe Schools (NASS). "I think you have to make a case that the child's presence in school causes an undue risk of violence to others at school if a student got caught smoking marijuana or drinking on Saturday night and the school wants to expel him, I think that's ridiculous," Blauvelt says.

"It's much easier for politicians to demand a crackdown on the most silly and imagined transgressions," Raskin says. "So we have some kid spending five days in juvenile detention for writing a ghost story."

John Whitehead, president of the Charlottesville, Va.-based Rutherford Institute, a conservative group dedicated to protecting civil liberties, worries about the long-term impact of zero-tolerance tactics. "You're teaching kids that they live in a totalitarian society," he says. "This generation has been raised being searched without a warrant, being strip-searched and having their urine tested without probable cause. You'll have a whole set of people who will be conditioned to promote order over rights.

"You also have a whole segment of society that is being repressed," Whitehead says. "They operate on a subterranean level, because they really don't have free speech. They have secret signals, eye movements and code words."

Further, he says, "Many kids are smoking as a way to rebel. And younger and younger kids are drinking. I think it's a way of shoving it into the faces of the adults."

He says much of the violence erupting among kids already is the result of repressed anger. "Sooner or later they will blow," he predicts.

Whitehead says adults are sending kids the wrong message with zero-tolerance policies. "The message kids are getting is that some crazy adult game is being played here, and that the rules are really stupid," he says. "The adults say they're teaching kids about 'justice' when they say they must treat every infraction the same. But how is it justice to treat someone with a pair of nail clippers the same as you treat someone with an Uzi?"

ance, homelessness and boom boxes.

'Broken-Windows' Approach

In 1990, President George Bush signed the Gun-Free School Zones Act into law, prohibiting the possession or discharge of a firearm near a public school. The act claimed Congress had the right to act under its power to regulate interstate commerce. But the Supreme Court disagreed, ruling in 1995 that Congress had exceeded its constitutional powers. By then, lawmakers had gone back to the drawing board and enacted the 1994 Gun-Free Schools Act, which tied enforcement to the federal government's spending power.

'Get Tough,' Younger Students Say

Middle-schoolers in Tustin, Calif., advocated tougher policies on alcohol and marijuana than local high school students.

1. When should students be suspended for marijuana or alcohol violations?

MS	HS	All	
72	41	55	A. Always.
24	50	38	B. In repeat or severe cases.
5	9	7	C. Never.

2. When should police be notified about marijuana or alcohol violations?

MS	HS	All	
63	34	49	A. Always.
32	53	42	B. In repeat or severe cases.
5	13	9	C. Never.

3. When should counseling be required for students with a marijuana or alcohol violation?

MS	HS	All	
57	38	47	A. Always.
36	48	42	B. In repeat or severe cases.
7	15	11	C. Never.

4. Should students be allowed to avoid transfer if they agree to random drug testing?

MS	HS	All	
33	44	39	A. Yes.
47	42	44	B. Sometimes, depending on the circumstances.
20	14	17	C. No.

Note: All totals do not add to 100 due to rounding.
Source: Tustin Unified School District, Orange County, Calif., February 2000

That prompted state legislatures to begin requiring local school districts to implement zero-tolerance policies for firearms and bombs. Many of the new laws also included anything that could be used as a weapon.

"There is no universal definition of a weapon," Modzeleski says. "A belt buckle is a weapon, a rat-tail comb is a weapon. So are box cutters and baseball bats."

Meanwhile, zero tolerance got a boost from *Fixing Broken Windows*, a 1996 book by George L. Kelling and Catherine M. Coles. They argue that ignoring minor problems in cities, like broken windows or graffiti, eventually leads to an increase in serious crime.

Republican Mayor Rudolph W. Giuliani based his anti-crime program in New York City on the theory, adding panhandlers, graffiti and street peddlers to the proscribed list. His "broken-windows" policy was first outlined in a 1982 *Atlantic* article by Kelling.

After crime in New York declined dramatically, the policy was widely adopted. "Mayor after mayor has rediscovered that disorderly behavior creates fear and leads to serious crime," Kelling said. [18]

Is Violence Declining?

The string of recent school shootings has added to the perception that violence is increasing in schools. Nine mass homicides on school grounds in less than two years have left 29 dead. [19]

But education and juvenile-justice officials continue to insist that children are safer in schools than in their own homes. Except for the recent shootings, overall school violence has been fairly steady for the past 20 years. And according to the NCES survey, the behaviors that school principals list as "serious or moderate" discipline problems were not violent activities but tardiness (40 percent) and absenteeism (25 percent). Twenty-one percent of the principals listed fighting as a serious problem, but only 5 percent considered gangs serious, and 2 percent listed weapons possession or physical abuse of teachers. [20]

"Despite public perceptions to the contrary, the current data do not support the claim that there has been a dramatic, overall increase in school-based violence in recent years," said researcher Irwin Hyman. [21]

But Stephens of the school safety center says that just looking at official statistics on school violence is misleading. "We have redefined deviancy over the last couple of decades," he says. "In some schools, a fight is not reported unless there is blood on the floor.

"There is a disincentive for administrators to report crime in their schools," he says, because principals are afraid they will be blamed for doing an inappropriate job. To get a true picture of school violence, you must look at reported incidents, unreported incidents and underreported incidents."

"We've seen a tremendous growth in the number of alternative schools at the elementary level, because so many younger children are acting out violent behavior," Stephens says. "Some of the aggression that before was being experienced at the middle school and high school levels is being manifested in the elementary grades."

But Kathy Christie, a policy analyst at the Education Commission of the States, says she has not seen a huge jump in the number of alternative schools being built for elementary-grade students. ■

CURRENT SITUATION

Alternative Schools

The Clinton administration wants Congress to require all school districts to provide alternative education for any student expelled or suspended for disciplinary reasons. Under current federal law, that's required only if a child is disabled, and the Senate voted last May to rescind that requirement.

"It ought to be a basic American principle that no student should be punished by being denied an education," said Education Secretary Richard W. Riley after a Dec. 9 meeting with Jesse Jackson. Excluded students should receive "appropriate supervision, counseling and educational services so they can meet state [academic] standards."

But, according to the Education Commission of the States, only nine states require schools to provide alternative schooling, and it's optional in 25 states. In 14 states, no laws govern alternative services.

As a result, only 43 percent of the students expelled for carrying a firearm to school in 1997 were sent to alternative schools. Law-enforcement groups complain that by not providing alternative services, schools are dumping their discipline problems onto the streets.

But even when suspended students get alternative education, the quality of the education they receive is sometimes questionable. "Usually they are warehouses — dumping grounds for the worst teachers, administrators and students," says George Washington University's Kingery. "There have been no evaluations of their quality."

An alternative school is defined as any school that addresses the needs of students that cannot be met in a traditional school. Other than that, there is no standard definition of what constitutes an alternative school. The Education Department is preparing a survey of the nation's more than 3,400 alternative schools — which serve 1 percent of the nation's youngsters — to determine their characteristics.

The quality of education in alternative schools "clearly is a civil rights issue if the kids who are there are disproportionately kids of color, and the schools are demonstrably of poor quality," says Mary Frances Berry, chairman of the Commission on Civil Rights.

Witnesses told the civil rights panel in February that some teachers and administrators — pressured by school boards to raise overall test scores or face pay cuts or dismissal — are using zero-tolerance policies to push out low achievers and learning-disabled students who perform poorly.

"The growing popularity of zero-tolerance school-discipline policies during a period of rapidly raised academic standards and high-stakes testing is not accidental," said Joan M. First, executive director of the National Coalition of Advocates for Students. "There are two ways to change standardized test scores. Either children learn more, or the composition of the test pool changes. Zero tolerance effectively accomplishes the latter."

"With the new standardized tests, there's an awfully strong urge on the part of teachers and principals to get rid of students," agreed Cruz Reynoso, a law professor at the University of California at Los Angeles and vice chairman of the civil rights panel. "I've heard that from many sources in California."

NASSP General Counsel Steven Yurek admitted, "It is a very big issue for schools."

Others complained that by escalating the sheer number of minority students excluded from public education, zero-tolerance policies are reversing gains made since the Supreme Court's 1954 *Brown v. Board of Education* decision promised equal educational opportunities for all children.

"Zero-tolerance laws are challenging the whole concept of universal public education," says Ruth Zweifler, executive director of the Student Advocacy Center of Michigan. "Instead, we've moved to an, 'If they deserve it, then we'll give it to them' attitude."

Harsh zero-tolerance policies are "sweeping uncounted numbers of our most vulnerable and needy children into the streets," where they remain "uneducated, unserved and unsupervised," she said.

"If we find that what we have heard is verifiable across the board," Berry says, "the Education Department's Office of Civil Rights should investigate the situation in alternative schools. It ought to be taken up as a very serious issue."

The commission will discuss the issue further on April 14. "We don't want chaos and disorder to reign in the schools," Berry says, "but quite clearly there is something going on here regarding how kids of color and

Prohibited in Providence

Brass knuckles. Hand grenades. Mace. Toy guns. Students who bring those or other banned items to school face automatic expulsion in Providence, R.I., which passed a much more restrictive zero-tolerance policy than the federal Gun-Free Schools Act.

Federal law

- Guns
- Explosive devices
- Silencers and mufflers
- Bombs, grenades, rockets, missiles and mines

Providence policy

- Guns
- Explosive devices
- Silencers and mufflers
- Bombs, grenades, rockets, missiles and mines
- Realistic replicas of firearms
- Knives
- Razors
- Gas repellent, mace
- Martial-arts devices
- Objects that could inflict bodily harm: blackjacks, chains, clubs, brass knuckles, nightsticks, pipes, studded bracelets, etc.
- Any object that gives the appearance of any of the above.

Source: Applied Research Center, Feb. 18, 2000

disabled kids are dealt with under these discipline policies."

Amending IDEA

If Congress required all expelled or suspended students to be sent to alternative schools, it would resolve the controversy over the disparate treatment of disabled students under zero-tolerance policies.

Under the 1997 amendments to the Individuals with Disabilities Education Act (IDEA), special-education students — whose disabilities can range from stuttering to serious emotional disturbance — have extra protections from zero-tolerance policies. If a disabled child brings a weapon to school, he may be immediately removed from school and suspended for 10 days, during which time the school must determine whether the offense was a manifestation of his disability. If not, the student may be expelled for a year, the same as a non-disabled child. Unlike a non-disabled student, however, he must be given free alternative education.

The protections were designed to prevent schools from expelling disabled students just because they might be more difficult or expensive to educate.

If bringing the weapon to school was a manifestation of the child's disability, the school may let the child back into school after a 10-day suspension, or, if the school determines that the child is a danger to himself or the other students, the school may send him to an alternative school for 45 days. Then, the school can ask an independent hearing officer to determine whether the child is ready to return to school, a procedure that can be repeated indefinitely.

The 45-day reviews were put into the law so schools could not "just kick the student out and forget about him," says Lilliam Rangel-Diaz, a member of the National Council on Disabilities board. But the policy has generated a lot of resentment, especially among parents of regular-curriculum kids expelled without getting alternative education or review hearings every 45 days.

"IDEA overrides state and federal zero-tolerance-for-firearms laws," Lewis says. "They contradict one another. This policy ties the hands of school administrators, and it's creating a lot of problems."

School administrators complain that if a disabled student threatens a student or a teacher, they cannot expel him as they could a non-disabled student. And parents of general-education students are starting to realize that their kids have less protection than a disabled student does. "Now after a kid gets expelled, some parents are asking for retroactive coverage under IDEA," Lewis says.

Educators and parents are also upset about the cost of providing alternative services for expelled disabled students. "When you run alternative schools with an 8-to-1 student-to-teacher ratio, that comes at a cost to the other students who are sitting in bigger classes," said Edward Kelly, superintendent of schools in Prince

At Issue:

Should disabled students be disciplined differently under zero-tolerance policies?

yes

KEVIN P. DWYER
President, National Association of School Psychologists

WRITTEN FOR *THE CQ RESEARCHER*

Misguided efforts by some Congress members to amend the Individuals with Disabilities Education Act (IDEA) perpetuate the public's erroneous impression that the law creates a dual-discipline system that prevents schools from removing a child with a gun from school. Nothing could be further from the truth.

The law was amended in 1997 so that any gun-carrying child can be removed. Schools can expel a student with disabilities who brings a gun to school for one year — just as they do other students — if the behavior was not the result of the child's disability.

After removal, students also receive continued education in an alternative program. If it is determined that the behavior resulted from a student's disability, the law allows the child to be suspended for 10 days while determining if the student poses a danger. If so, the school can expel the student indefinitely, but the case must be reviewed every 45 days.

Congress included these rights to protect students with disabilities from discrimination. Students with disabilities often present challenges. Without due process, these students would be removed disproportionately by schools that decided providing services was too costly, time consuming or inconvenient. But Congress acknowledged that children with disabilities, like all children, have the right to a free, appropriate, public education.

Now some in Congress contend the alternative-education requirement should be dropped because other students don't receive such services. But withdrawing educational services from any student does not make our schools and streets safer.

Leaving any student free to roam the streets without supervision is a prescription for increasing crime. Research affirms that expelling troubled children without educational and mental-health services increases dropout rates, drug use and overall juvenile crime.

To get this message to Congress, we have developed a Safe Streets, Safe Schools effort — involving 50 education, mental-health, student-services and child-advocacy groups — to support providing alternative education and crisis-intervention for all students.

But that effort cannot fall upon the education community or the justice system alone. States and local jurisdictions must work together to fund and implement services for all students with challenging behavior.

To balance the movement toward zero tolerance for guns, drugs and violence in schools, we must also have zero tolerance for academic failure for all students.

no

SEN. JOHN ASHCROFT, R-MO.

WRITTEN FOR *THE CQ RESEARCHER*

In light of the tragic school shootings, we must ask ourselves if federal education laws do all they can to promote school safety. America's classrooms must be safe and secure for students to get a world-class education.

Our general policy is commendable: Zero tolerance for weapons. Under the federal Gun-Free Schools Act, states receiving federal education funds were required to pass laws mandating an immediate, one-year expulsion for students who bring weapons to school.

Unfortunately, this policy does not apply to one out of every eight students subject to another federal law, the Individuals with Disabilities Education Act. Under IDEA, a student with a weapon typically is returned to the classroom in as few as 45 days. This category includes individuals who have serious emotional disturbances and behavior disorders. Schools have no power to expel these students if their disability caused them to bring a gun to school. If it didn't, schools can expel the student, but still must continue to provide full educational services.

Hence, schools are subject to a dangerous dual-discipline system that handcuffs them from removing violent students. It is deeply distressing that federal law requires that some who bring guns to schools be returned to a classroom filled with kids who want and deserve a safe and secure setting in which to learn.

Missouri teachers, parents, principals and superintendents have told me that we must do something in Washington to end this dual-discipline system that threatens the safety of children and invites a mass tragedy.

In response, I have authored the School Safety Act, which gives schools authority to remove any student who has a weapon at school. Congress voted overwhelmingly to include this provision in juvenile-justice legislation that now awaits conference committee action.

My legislation abolishes the dangerous double standard for weapons and returns control to where it belongs — local schools. Teachers, principals and superintendents care deeply about students with special needs. I trust these individuals to make the right decisions, including making special exceptions on a case-by-case basis. Dangerous and disruptive students are a small minority and pose a threat to all students.

A safe and orderly learning environment is critical to our children's success in school. Local schools must have the authority and flexibility to keep classrooms safe by being able to remove any student with a weapon from the classroom.

William County, Virginia. "The good student is shortchanged." [22]

Administrators say their greater responsibility is to the 2,500 other students that attend a typical high school, rather than the one kid who is expelled.

Under the provision approved by the Senate last May, introduced by Sens. John Ashcroft, R-Mo., and Bill Frist, R-Tenn., disabled students who bring firearms to school would be treated the same as non-disabled students, regardless of whether or not the action resulted from their disability. Thus, if the state where the student lives is not required to provide educational services during the expulsion period, neither child would receive services.

"If you bring a gun or firearm to school, you should be treated the same, if you have a disability or no disability," Frist told fellow senators on May 20.

The amendment was attached to the juvenile-justice bill, which is not expected to go anywhere this year. However, Sens. Edward M. Kennedy, D-Mass., and Patrick J. Leahy, D-Vt., are expected to introduce an amendment to the education reauthorization bill this month requiring all expelled students to receive alternative education.

Dozens of advocacy groups support the amendment, including the two major teachers' unions and the National Parent-Teachers Association, as well as the Clinton administration. The bill would require the Education, Justice and Health and Human Services departments to share the cost of the alternative services.

The amendment is also supported by sheriffs, district attorneys and police and law enforcement groups like Fight Crime, Invest in Kids, which represents victims of violence.

"Giving a gun-toting kid an extended vacation from school and from all responsibility is soft on offenders and dangerous for everyone else," said the victims' group in opposing Ashcroft-Frist.

Supporters of mandatory alternative education often point to the tragic case of Kip Kinkel, the 14-year-old Oregon boy who was suspended for bringing a gun to school. He was not required to attend alternative classes. He went home and killed his parents, then returned to school later to shoot and kill two students and wound 25.

Reuters/Scott Olson

After several black high school students from Decatur, Ill., were suspended for two years for fighting at a football game, the Rev. Jesse Jackson and others said zero-tolerance policies unfairly target minorities.

Zero-Zero Tolerance

The administration also has proposed that Congress require any school receiving federal education funds to have "sound and equitable" discipline policies. Although neither the House nor the Senate has acted on the proposal, school districts across the country are revisiting their zero-tolerance policies anyway, partly after pressure from parents.

"After all of the bad press, people are saying, 'Let's calm our jets a bit and think through this a little more,' " Newberry says.

But while some lawmakers are trying to make their laws less harsh, most are trying to broaden the definition of what is covered. "There has been a tremendous amount of activity in the state legislatures on this subject," says Christie of the Education Commission of the States.

Often legislators try to impose zero tolerance for drug and alcohol sales or consumption on school grounds. But the proposals usually don't make it through the legislature once lawmakers realize how damaging the consequences of long expulsions would be, she says.

"Zero-tolerance policies were initially put into place to ban lethal weapons from school grounds," she says. "Having a beer in your locker probably doesn't rate up there with carrying a weapon that could threaten the life of another student."

Some school districts are extending zero tolerance to cover off-campus behavior, punishing kids who get into trouble with the law on weekends, even for non-violent behavior like alcohol or marijuana use.

More and more schools are moving to ban images of guns on school grounds. Several school districts have taken rifles out of the hands of color guards, and one would not allow students re-enacting a Civil War battle to carry fake wooden muskets.

"Schools are reluctant to glorify

guns in any way right now," Tirozzi says. "You're seeing a knee-jerk Pavlovian response when people ban images of guns or weapons."

If a policy oversteps good sense, communities generally let their elected school board know about it, Resnick says. "Ninety-six percent of school board members in this country are elected. So there's a real opportunity for self-correction."

Tirozzi would like to see school boards limit their zero-tolerance policies to weapons, drugs and serious altercations, and return discretion to local superintendents. "Even the federal law mandates that for firearms superintendents should have discretion," he says.

The national associations representing elementary and secondary principals issued a joint statement in January asking school districts to consider three critical areas when reviewing zero-tolerance policies: the age of the child; fitting the punishment to the "crime" and ensuring that educational services are continued.

Blauvelt suggests that school boards should adopt the language in federal and state laws governing illegal drugs and weapons. "An aspirin is not a 'controlled and dangerous substance,' " he says. "Midol is not a 'controlled and dangerous substance.' "

Ferrandino of the elementary school principals association advises school boards to make sure policies are developed with community input and have reasonable penalties and allow for discretion. "There needs to be some sort of rationality and balance brought to the discussion," he says.

The National School Boards Association's Resnick agrees. "Hopefully, when you have a policy that can have as great an impact — positive and negative — on individual children as zero-tolerance policies can have, they are being developed with substantial community input," he says.

Mitchell of the AFT says school boards should be careful not to confuse zero-tolerance policies with discipline codes. Zero tolerance should be reserved for very serious offenses, he says. Less serious infractions should be covered under a discipline code, which allows for graduated consequences proportionate to the offense and punishes repeat offenses more severely than first-time offenses, he says. For instance, "A 'true weapon' should be covered by zero-tolerance policies," Mitchell says. "But a look-alike weapon should be covered by a school discipline policy."

The Rutherford Institute's Whitehead suggests that by relying on student courts for minor infractions, "You can get the decision out of the hands of one guy who's afraid of losing his job."

But most important, he says, zero-tolerance policies should only apply to "real offenses, like carrying real guns, real knives and real drugs — like cocaine — and not Alka-Seltzer."

Schools also should provide adequate due process and alternative educational services for expelled students, others say. "I don't know of any other situation in which an individual can be arrested, or put in jail or punished without some form of due process," Stephens, of the school safety center, says. "After all, we even have an appeal process for traffic tickets." ■

OUTLOOK

Ebb and Flow

Educators predict that for the immediate future, the zero-tolerance pendulum will continue to swing back and forth. "It's cyclical," researcher Skiba says. "Every time there's another school shooting, you see a new round of ever-tougher zero-tolerance policies, followed in a few weeks by new community and parental outcries about violations of basic rights and common sense."

"Like any other reform issue, these things tend to ebb and flow," the Education Department's Modzeleski says. "Some places are already backing off from zero tolerance. We recommend that policies be reviewed on a regular basis."

George Washington's Kingery hopes that there will be "a little more reason" applied to zero-tolerance policies, and that the quality of alternative education will come under more scrutiny.

If zero tolerance is a backlash to judges and school administrators having broad discretion, says the University of California's Volokh. "Maybe there will be a backlash to the backlash. Maybe we will decide that we can't have a one-size-fits-all rule, and we should return discretion to the individual principals."

"Zero tolerance is now in the court of public opinion," Whitehead says. "All the major magazines have criticized it lately, and now even the teacher groups are saying, 'Let's have some reason.' "

But most agree that schools will not entirely abandon strict discipline, and that the public will continue to support zero tolerance for extreme acts involving guns, violence and drugs.

The NEA has launched a public-education campaign to get school districts to think in terms of a comprehensive, community-generated school-safety program that addresses the entire education system, including physical plant, teacher training, early elementary intervention, effective mental-health programs, crisis intervention and conflict resolution.

"We must move from a knee-jerk reaction to one in which we are willing to invest a lot of dollars over the long term," the NEA's Newberry says. "Until school boards come up with money and creative plans to address these larger issues in a comprehensive way, we're not really going to solve the problem."

Ferrandino of the elementary school principals' group says many school districts are trying to make schools smaller and gentler places. "Since these school shootings began, we have learned that there's much that both the schools and communities can do to create an environment where students can feel they belong and are valued as individuals," he says. Among other things, principals are trying to reduce class size and student anonymity. Other schools have developed community relationships with social-service agencies and are getting parents more involved in the schools.

"I think it is quickly being recognized that smaller might be better," Ferrandino says.

Others advocate more after-school and youth-development programs, both of which are more expensive and require long-term commitments — and time — from adults.

Sadly, two weeks before Kayla Rolland was shot in Michigan, several experts tied the future of zero tolerance to what the nation decides to do about guns. "Handgun availability is part of what is driving this ridiculous response on the part of the schools," Newberry says.

"I would love to say that within 10 years we won't need policies like zero tolerance," Tirozzi says. "By then, I would hope we will have gotten weapons out of the hands of youngsters, parents will be doing a better job in the household and we will have changed the kind of things that are projected onto movie screens. But unless and until this society comes to grips with its love affair with violence, and as long as children can easily obtain weapons, these problems will continue to come into the schoolhouse.

"When society zeroes out violence, we'll be happy to zero out zero tolerance," he says. ■

FOR MORE INFORMATION

National Association of Elementary School Principals, 1615 Duke St., Alexandria, Va. 22314-3483; (703) 684-3345; www.naesp.org. This association of elementary and middle school principals conducts workshops for members on federal and state policies and programs.

National Association of Secondary School Principals, 1904 Association Dr., Reston, Va. 20191-1537; (703) 860-0200; www.nassp.org. This group, which includes college-level teachers of secondary education, conducts training for members and serves as an information clearinghouse.

National School Boards Association, 1680 Duke St., Alexandria, Va. 22314; (703) 838-6722; www.nsba.org. This federation of school board associations monitors legislation and regulations affecting public-education funding, local governance and education quality.

National School Safety Center, 4165 Thousand Oaks Blvd., Suite 290, Westlake Village, Calif. 91362; (805) 373-9977; www.nssc1.org. The center was created by presidential directive in 1984 to meet the growing need for additional training and preparation in the area of school crime and violence prevention.

Notes

[1] Of the 100,000 students expelled nationwide during the 1997-98 school year, 3,930 were expelled for bringing a firearm to school under the Gun-Free Schools Act. That was a 31 percent drop from the previous year's total, according to Department of Education statistics.

[2] The statistics are from an unpublished study by Kingery, "Suspension and Expulsion: New Directions."

[3] See *Dothan City Board of Education v. V.M.H.*

[4] Quoted in "The Intolerance of Zero Tolerance," Intellectual Capital.com, Aug. 19, 1999.

[5] Robert C. Johnson, "Decatur Furor Sparks Wider Policy Debate," *Education Week*, Nov. 24, 1999.

[6] "The Fight's Not Over, *The New Republic*, Dec. 6, 1999.

[7] "National Survey of Teens, Teachers and Principals," National Center on Addiction and Substance Abuse, Columbia University, 1998.

[8] "Violence and Discipline Problems in U.S. Public Schools: 1996-1997," National Center for Education Statistics, 1998.

[9] Russ Skiba and Reece Peterson, "The Dark Side of Zero Tolerance: Can Punishment Lead to Safe Schools?" *The Kappan*, January 1999.

[10] For details, see Kathy Koch, "Drug Testing, *The CQ Researcher*, Nov. 20, 1998, p. 1014.

[11] The unpublished study was conducted by the Applied Research Center, in Oakland, Calif.

[12] "Education Denied: The Negative Impact of Zero Tolerance Policies," The Civil Rights Project at Harvard, February 2000.

[13] Keleher testified before the U.S. Civil Rights Commission on Feb. 18, 1999.

[14] For background, see Margaret Edwards, "Mandatory Sentencing," *The CQ Researcher*, May 26, 1995, pp. 465-488.

[15] "Zero tolerance on drugs urged," *Houston Chronicle*, May 21, 1986.

[16] James J. Kilpatrick, "Get tough with kids who use, sell drugs," *Houston Chronicle*, June 17, 1986.

[17] *Houston Chronicle*, *op. cit.*, May 21.

[18] Harry Bruinius, "In Giulianiville, it's a case of law vs. order," *The Christian Science Monitor*, Nov. 9, 1999.

[19] For background, see Kathy Koch, "School Violence," *The CQ Researcher*, Oct. 9, 1998, pp. 881-904.

[20] Violence and Discipline Problems in U.S. Public Schools, 1996-1997, The National Center for Education Statistics, February, 1998.

[21] Quoted in Skiba and Peterson, *op. cit.*

[22] Dennis Cauchon, "Zero-tolerance policies lack flexibility," *USA Today*, April 13, 1999.

Bibliography

Selected Sources Used

Books

Kelling, George L., and Catherine Coles, *Fixing Broken Windows: Restoring Order and Reducing Crime in Our Communities*, Martin Kessler Books, 1996.
The Rutgers University professor and his co-author argue that ignoring minor problems in cities, like broken windows or graffiti, eventually leads to an increase in serious crime. Kelling first outlined the approach in a 1982 *Atlantic* magazine article.

Raskin, Jamin B., *We the Students: The High School in the High Court*, Congressional Quarterly, 2000.
An American University constitutional law professor outlines precedent-setting Supreme Court cases involving drug testing, locker searches, school newspaper censorship, sexual harassment and free speech.

Articles

"Zero tolerance on drugs urged," *Houston Chronicle*, May 21, 1986.
Education Secretary William Bennett becomes the first official to ask Congress to withhold federal education funds unless schools adopt "zero-tolerance" expulsion policies for drug dealing on school grounds.

Baxter, Bethany, "The Intolerance of Zero Tolerance," Intellectual Capital.com, Aug. 19, 1999.
A consultant to colleges argues that school officials do not model good judgment by setting up zero-tolerance policies that treat all offenses equally harshly.

Cloud, John, "The Columbine Effect," *Time*, Dec. 6, 1999.
Zero tolerance sounds like a good way to treat violence in schools, but experts say it may have gone too far.

Grier, Peter, and Gail Russell Chaddock, "Schools get tough as threats continue," *The Christian Science Monitor*, Nov. 5, 1999.
Educators are struggling with how to implement get-tough safety rules meant to stop student shootings.

Johnson, Dirk, "Schools' New Watchword: Zero Tolerance," *The New York Times*, Dec. 1, 1999.
This overview looks at how zero-tolerance school discipline has replaced more traditional punishment.

Skiba, Russ, and Reece Peterson, "The Dark Side of Zero Tolerance: Can Punishment Lead to Safe Schools?" *The Kappan*, January 1999.
The authors argue that increasingly broad interpretations of zero tolerance have resulted in a near epidemic of suspensions for seemingly trivial events, increasing the likelihood that excluded students will get involved in drugs and gangs.

Wing, Bob, and Terry Keleher, "Zero Tolerance: An Interview with Jesse Jackson on Race and School Discipline," *Colorlines*, spring 2000.
Jackson contends that zero-tolerance polices disproportionately target minority students.

Reports and Studies

Keleher, Terry, Applied Research Center, March 1999.
In a survey of 12 large school districts across the country, the public-policy institute found that black students are three to five times more likely to be expelled than white students in some districts.

Kingery, Paul, "Suspension and Expulsion: New Directions," Hamilton Fish Institute, unpublished 1999 study.
Kingery found that expulsions and suspensions are rising nationwide and that longer and permanent expulsions are at an all-time high.

National Center on Addiction and Substance Abuse, "National Survey of Teens, Teachers and Principals," 1998.
The Columbia University research center found that 85 percent of principals believe zero-tolerance policies keep drugs out of schools.

National Center for Education Statistics, "Violence and Discipline Problems in U.S. Public Schools: 1996-1997," 1998.
This survey of more than 1,000 school principals found mixed and minor improvements in school discipline and drug problems.

The Civil Rights Project at Harvard, "Education Denied: The Negative Impact of Zero Tolerance Policies," February 2000.
A briefing paper prepared for the U.S. Civil Rights Commission argues that zero-tolerance policies are having a disproportionate impact on African-American and Latino children.

U.S. Department of Education, "Report on State Implementation of the Gun-Free Schools Act," August 1999.
This annual report shows that in the 1997-98 school year, 3,930 students were expelled for bringing a firearm to school, a 31 percent drop from the previous year.

3 Managing Managed Care

Adriel Bettelheim

Backlash against managed care usually takes the form of fiery speeches from reform-minded politicians or the telling of horror stories by patients denied access to critical care.

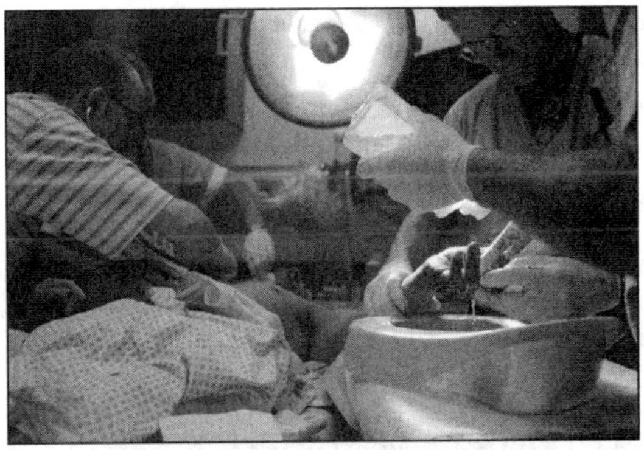

But things took a turn toward the unusual in March, when 15,000 frustrated doctors — average income $166,000 a year — joined a labor union. They pledged to fight managed care companies that they say delay reimbursements, make them work longer hours and excessively meddle in patient care.

"Our major agenda is to organize every employed doctor in this country," said Barry Liebowitz, leader of the dissident physicians.

The odd alliance of affluent professionals and a traditionally blue-collar union reflects the depth of the debate over America's medical system. Managed care companies, which now serve approximately 160 million Americans, are under unprecedented attack by a variety of critics, who say they have sacrificed the quality of medical services by excessively focusing on financial results.

A survey last September by the Kaiser Family Foundation and Harvard University found Americans are increasingly worried about managed care. Sixty-five percent of the respondents favored some government involvement to protect consumers in managed care plans compared with 52 percent the year before. And 73 percent favored giving consumers the right to sue their health plans, compared with 64 percent in 1997.

The debate in the last Congress over managed care regulation and President Clinton's proposed "Patients' Bill of Rights" got sidetracked by partisan bickering and the Monica Lewinsky scandal. But with the 2000 elections less than 19 months away and consumer frustration building, lawmakers are again trying to address public concerns. At least a half-dozen members of Congress have proposed competing versions of patients'-rights legislation that would impose new regulations on health insurers and strip away their decision-making power. Several of the measures would amend the Employee Retirement Income Security Act of 1974 (ERISA), which exempts many health plans from state laws and prevents millions of patients from suing managed care firms. [1]

The proposed regulations also deal with more fundamental issues, such as whether managed care "gatekeepers" should continue to decide what procedures are "medically necessary." But Republicans and Democrats remain sharply divided over how far regulations should go, making it unclear whether the two sides will compromise and pass legislation or turn health-care reform into a campaign issue in next year's elections.

"The $64,000 question is what kind of debate does Congress want, and are the problems real, perceived or just designed to protect health-care providers?" says Karen Ignagni, president of the American Association of Health Plans (AAHP). Ignagni argues that new regulations will only drive up health costs by imposing new layers of red tape, making it more difficult for working people to afford coverage.

Health-provider groups like the American Medical Association (AMA) counter that the time is ripe for reform, citing numerous examples in which, they say, health plans trampled on patients' rights. Many physicians, long bitter over plan administrators' ability to overrule their decisions, want to revert back to something resembling a traditional fee-for-service system, in which insurers agreed to pay for whatever care the doctor ordered.

"There are some good managed care plans out there, but as the opportunity to make a buck increases, a number are cutting here and there and coming up woefully short of what acceptable standards for care should be," says Texas family physician Nancy Dickey, president of the AMA.

The health-care debate comes as more and more Americans are being funneled into managed care plans through their employers. Approximately 60 percent of the population — and 85 percent of Americans with employer-based health insurance — receive their care through managed care. Some 71 million are enrolled in the most prevalent type of managed care program, a health maintenance organization (HMO). Many managed care companies also are angling for retirees covered by Medicare, who have the option of switching from the traditional coverage the government program offers to an HMO.

Polls suggest a majority of plan enrollees are satisfied with the quality of care they receive. But many people complain that they have had problems getting permission from managed care plans to see medical specialists or pay emergency room

From *The CQ Researcher*, April 16, 1999.

Concern About Managed Care Rose

Americans have become increasingly concerned about the quality of managed care and more supportive of consumer-protection proposals, according to a recent survey by the Kaiser Family Foundation.

Does government need to protect consumers from not getting the care they need from managed care firms?

Are managed care plans doing a bad job serving consumers?

Should consumers have the right to sue their health plans?

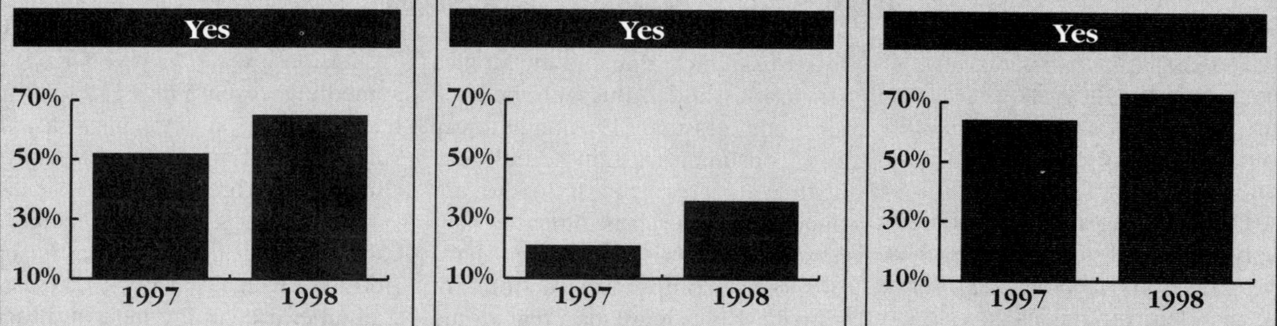

Source: Kaiser Family Foundation, "Kaiser-Harvard Survey on Americans' Views on the Consumer Protection Debate," Sept. 17, 1998

bills — and they say they have no place to turn when a claim is denied. They also aren't sure whether they want to pay more for added protections. A recent Employee Benefit Research Institute (EBRI) survey found that 46 percent of respondents favor increasing government regulation of health insurance in theory, but only 20 percent favor drafting more rules if they would increase health insurance costs by $50 per month or more.

Health-care economist Paul Fronstin, who conducted the survey, says Americans are reluctant to pay more for added protection because they treat health insurance differently from other essentials. While they may be willing to spend more to go to a better college or buy a fancier car, they are not willing to pay out-of-pocket for extra services or protection, and thus will accept whatever coverage their employer provides.

The anti-managed care sentiment is ironic to some because most experts give the industry credit for holding down health costs for most of the 1990s. By using their purchasing power to extract price concessions from doctors, hospitals and other health-care providers, plans were able to reverse a trend of double-digit premium increases. The federal Health Care Financing Administration (HCFA) reports that health-care spending growth was 4.8 percent in 1997, the last year for which complete figures are available, compared with a high of 12.2 percent in 1990. [2]

Some economists estimate that, by next year, managed care companies will be saving Americans as much as $300 billion a year on health care. Much of the cost controls came at a time when new diagnostic tests and technologies and a host of novel drugs were exerting upward price pressure. Indeed, many HMOs kept premiums deliberately low to attract new employer groups, suffering crushing financial losses. Many are expected to raise premiums 6-9 percent this year to firm up their balance sheets.

Despite the cost controls, managed care companies managed to anger many different groups. Uwe Reinhardt, a professor of health-care economics at Princeton University, says health plans unwisely focused on shortening patients' hospital stays, leading to highly publicized incidents, such as mothers being kicked out just one day after delivering their babies.

Plan administrators also were reluctant to provide basic customer information, such as the background of plan physicians and how satisfied current enrollees were with services. Moreover, Reinhardt says industry leaders were slow to spend on information systems that could track key variables — such as the outcomes of treatments — and gauge the quality of care. Some state and federal lawmakers now are demanding the information as part of patient-protection legislation.

The result has been growing consumer dissatisfaction and the perception that health plans are compromising quality for cost. The Foundation for Taxpayer and Consumer Rights recently sued one of the nation's largest HMOs — Kaiser Permanente — alleging its advertising fraudulently portrayed plan doctors as not subject to financial constraints on patient care.[3]

Medical caregivers have also jumped into the managed care fray, accusing HMO gatekeepers of restricting patient access to their services. The 15,000 doctors who recently became members of the AFL-CIO-affiliated Service Employees International Union joined some 600,000 registered nurses, medical technicians and home health aides who had already joined the union in the hope of gaining leverage in negotiating contracts with HMOs and other managed care providers. Some large employers, responding to their workers' complaints, have even begun bypassing managed care companies altogether and contracting directly with doctors and hospitals.

Faced with the public outcry, managed care providers are trying to mollify critics by advocating more external reviews of their decisions. By allowing enrollees to appeal coverage decisions to outside professionals, the plans hope to clean up their image and obtain some legal protection from liability suits. The pace quickened in January after a Superior Court jury in San Bernardino, Calif., ordered Aetna US Healthcare of California to pay the widow of a cancer patient $120.5 million for rejecting a doctor's request to try experimental bone marrow treatment for a rare form of stomach cancer.[4] Plans also are agreeing to help pay the costs of members participating in clinical trials of experimental drugs.

Higher Health-Care Costs Predicted

Major U.S. employers predict that their health-care costs will increase by up to 11 percent in 1999, compared with last year's 3.7 percent increase.

Type of Plan	Anticipated Increase	Average Cost Per Employee
Health-maintenance organizations	6–9%	$3,532
Point-of-service plans	6–9%	$4,012
Preferred provider organizations	5–8%	$4,312
Traditional indemnity plans	9–11%	$4,910

Source: Survey by Hewitt Associates of 2,000 health plans and 200 employers.

It's unclear whether the changes will affect the calls for federal reforms. Democrats, who have been closely linked to health-care reform since the Clinton administration's failed 1993 health plan and generally score well with the issue in elections, are under pressure to produce some legislation during the current Congress. This time around they may have an easier time exerting influence on Republicans, who hold slim majorities in both the House and Senate and need Democratic support to pass practically any measures.

Many GOP lawmakers believe some reforms are necessary but find excessive regulations don't square with their anti-regulatory leanings. They also are feeling pressure from big business, which believes new regulations will lead to steep premium increases that they will have to pay. To avoid being labeled do-nothings, lawmakers may pass a series of limited measures dealing with specific proposals — say, expanded emergency-room care or better access to specialists. Another proposal under consideration, sponsored by Rep. Tom Campbell, R-Calif., would give physicians and other health-care providers immunity from antitrust laws so they can negotiate as groups with health plans over fees and services. Campbell says it would give health professionals the same leeway labor organizations now enjoy; critics contend it could immunize anti-competitive activities by the doctors.

"They say it takes seven years to produce legislation that is complex," Rep. Charlie Norwood, R-Ga., a dentist who has proposed bills similar to Democratic plans, mused recently. "This is complex, and we're only in our fifth year."

Interest groups on both sides of the debate are trying to influence the outcome. Managed care reform advocates sponsored a "Patients' Bill of Rights Day" on April 9, featuring rallies around the country pressing for more federal protection for patients. The managed care industry is trying to persuade presidential and congressional candidates in the 2000 elections that managed care reform isn't high on voters' agendas. The AAHP in January polled 300 likely Republican primary voters in New Hampshire, finding 85 percent in managed care plans were satisfied with their coverage. The poll also showed that a candidate's stance on reform ranked low among factors likely to influence voters.[5]

As lawmakers and policy experts debate how to manage managed care, here are some of the questions they are asking:

Should managed care legislation strip away decision-making power from insurers?

For many Americans, the question of who decides what is medically necessary was brought home last June by a declaration from Kaiser Permanente. The powerful HMO told its 9 million members it wouldn't cover the $10 cost of the popular anti-impotence pill Viagra. Barely a month later, HCFA, which administers the Medicare and Medicaid programs, announced that Medicaid, a federal-state program for the poor, must cover Viagra in cases where a doctor believes it's medically necessary to treat erectile dysfunction.[6] The conflicting decisions unleashed a heated debate over which stance was correct and whether Kaiser and other HMOs were letting cost considerations interfere with the quality of care.

Doctors and insurers have long been in conflict over who should decide when health care is medically necessary. Physician groups led by the AMA contend that performance reviews, practice guidelines and other managed care cost controls undermine physicians' autonomy, preventing them from choosing what is right for the patient. The added paperwork justifying decisions to insurers also eats into doctors' incomes.

Seizing on the current anti-HMO sentiment, the doctors are mounting an intense lobbying effort to include medical-necessity provisions in any patient-protection laws that are considered by the current Congress. Such provisions would effectively take away insurers' ability to determine what patient care is necessary.

"Patients are extraordinarily frustrated by the current system of care," says AMA President Dickey. "We should have some guidelines that let health plans demonstrate a [decision by a] physician is out-of-date, or not cost-effective. But to just have a box [on a form indicating coverage is denied without providing a rationale for the decision] really leaves patients hung out to dry."

Doctors complain that a growing number of managed care firms are arbitrarily denying coverage for a wide range of accepted treatments that don't fall within the insurers' guidelines, such as physical therapy for a child with cerebral palsy. Doctors also complain that managed care firms use contracts with carefully worded language that says, in essence, certain good practices are nonetheless not necessary practices. This makes it harder for patients to appeal decisions, the physicians contend.

Sara Rosenbaum, a professor of public health and health services at George Washington University, coauthored a study documenting HMO decision-making practices in the Jan. 21 issue of *The New England Journal of Medicine*. The study describes how medical directors at large HMOs often ignore published medical studies, national experts and guidelines of the Food and Drug Administration and National Institutes of Health when they make coverage decisions. For example, Rosenbaum cites insurers' unwillingness to cover growth-hormone therapy for children with an endocrine disorder even though 96 percent of pediatric specialists approved the treatment.[7]

With public sentiment increasingly tilted against managed care, lawmakers are embracing the doctors' pitch. "Too often, HMOs and other insurance companies deny services that ought to be covered by saying that the services are not medically necessary," Sen. Edward M. Kennedy of Massachusetts, ranking Democrat on the Senate Health, Education, Labor and Pensions Committee, said during a March hearing.

Pending proposals in the Senate and House would prohibit group health plans from "arbitrarily interfering with" covered health services when a physician determines they are medically necessary. The physician may be the patient's primary-care doctor or a specialist to whom the patient was referred. The language was included in legislation proposed by Kennedy and Senate Minority Leader Tom Daschle, D-S.D. It also is part of measures sponsored by Rep. John D. Dingell, D-Mich., Rep. Greg Ganske, R-Iowa, and Sen. John H. Chafee, R-R.I.

Insurers counter that doctors are trying to go back to the unconstrained fee-for-service system that threw health-care costs out of kilter in the 1970s and '80s. With providers interpreting the scope of coverage under a contract, the insurers say they can't assure that health dollars will be spent fairly or equitably on safe and proven medical treatments. Health-plan administrators add that physicians' complaints about autonomy are a red herring, pointing to insurance industry studies that show as many as 97 percent of doctors' recommended courses of treatment are approved by managed care firms.[8]

"These proposals would give virtual carte blanche to treatments that are unnecessary, and sometimes even dangerous," says Chip Kahn, president of the Health Insurance Association of America (HIAA). "The result would be consumers pay higher premiums and receive lower-quality health care."

Kahn says the pending proposals would saddle health plans with legal barriers to challenging coverage, making it easier to file fraudulent claims or undertake risky medical procedures. HCFA estimates that fraud accounts for more than $100 billion of the nation's health-care spending.

And just as managed care foes roll out horror stories about denied coverage, insurers offer examples of doctors who abuse the system — a Pennsylvania physician who was convicted on 59 counts of illegally distributing narcotics to drug abusers and dealers, saying the drugs were "medically necessary," or the New York community center director who stole nearly $1 million by fraudulently billing the state for more than 25,000 psychiatric sessions that never took place. [9]

Ultimately, the dispute over medical necessity could be decided by outside reviews by independent experts. Groups such as the Healthcare Leadership Council — a Washington-based coalition of hospital, pharmaceutical and other health-care industry executives — say they would support legislation that allowed patients to make binding, independent appeals if doctors and insurers have a dispute.

Many health plans already are implementing such appeals procedures, but the industry is opposed to government regulations mandating them. Kahn says consumers can patronize those plans that offer appeal rights. But he adds that health insurers still have a fiduciary responsibility to all customers not to pay for unnecessary care.

Will tougher regulations lead to a rationing of health care?

The fundamental question underlying the managed care flap is the same question that fueled past battles over regulating airlines, telecommunications and electric utilities: Should the government impose reforms or allow the free market to sort things out and give consumers all of the necessary protections?

The question packs added punch in the case of health care because many Americans believe access to emergency care, experimental treatments and medical specialists already is restricted and will get worse in the future. What's unclear is whether proposed patient-protection regulations will improve access to the health system or intensify the pressure to cut costs and ration care.

In essence, the whole point of managed care is rationing. Insurers promote the health services and providers they believe are the most cost-effective and limit access to those that aren't. The managed care industry says passing laws that would guarantee clients a choice of doctors, more power in selecting treatments and expand the right to sue their plans would drive up costs and raise premiums, ultimately leaving more Americans uninsured. [10]

"In the end, real working people are going to pay either directly or indirectly for whatever Congress mandates," AAHP President Ignagni says. "The fundamental question is whether patient-protection legislative proposals are really in the patients' interests."

Ignagni and others point to the experience of the late 1980s and early '90s, when the increased use of diagnostic tests, new drugs and technologies and more physician visits combined to sharply drive up the nation's health-care costs. Insurers raised the cost of coverage, and employers passed on the increases to workers. Many young and low-income workers opted out of their health plans entirely rather than ante up. Some businesses made the decision for them by dropping coverage altogether.

The number of uninsured Americans has been a growing concern for policy-makers. EBRI estimates that

"There are some good managed care plans out there, but as the opportunity to make a buck increases, a number are cutting here and there and coming up woefully short of acceptable standards for care."

—Dr. Nancy Dickey, president, American Medical Association

Industry Warns About New Regulation

The managed care industry says increased government regulation will drive up employers' premiums or reduce the value of benefits that plans offer members. Some believe this will ultimately lead to more health-care rationing.

Possible Effects If Employers' Premiums Rise 10 Percent

• Increased employer contributions (1999-2003):	$116.7 billion
• Increased employer contributions per covered worker (1999-2003):	$1,593
• Decrease in number of insured individuals in 1999:	3.2 million
• Total potential wage loss (1999-2003):	$122.8 billion
• Wages lost per covered household (1999-2003):	$1,869

Source: Barents Group, April 21, 1998

about 43 million people currently have no health coverage. [11] Federal law allows workers to purchase insurance if they leave a group plan without having another plan to join. But policy experts say insurers commonly screen applicants for "pre-existing conditions" and charge them many times the normal price if something is found. As a result, affordable insurance is only available to a handful with a clean bill of health.

Reform-minded lawmakers say regulation is needed now precisely so market power will be shifted back in consumers' direction. With consumer complaints on the rise, the politicians argue that new patients'-rights laws would help tens of millions of managed care participants who currently don't have any legal protections because of the nation's patchwork system of regulating health care. These lawmakers say patients should be active participants in their care and treatment, and have access to a fair process to resolve differences with their insurers and doctors.

Under the current regulatory scheme, states are the primary regulators of employer-based health insurance. Some 15 states have enacted health-care consumer protections. According to a recent U.S. General Accounting Office survey, they range from improved access to emergency services and specialists to prohibitions on "gag rules" that some contend prevent doctors from discussing treatments that won't be covered by insurance. [12]

But the federal Employee Retirement Income Security Act of 1974 pre-empts state laws for the approximately 48 million people enrolled in self-insured group health plans (plans typically sponsored by large companies in which the employer, rather than an outside insurance company, assumes the financial risk). The ERISA exemption protects these plans from member lawsuits and requirements that they open their networks to a broader selection of health-care providers.

"Even where states have acted to deal with particular problems, too often the action fails to provide the full protection patients need," Sen. Kennedy says.

While lawmakers appear to agree on broad principles for overhauling managed care, they remain divided along partisan lines on specifics. Republicans, favoring an approach that keeps regulation to a minimum, have offered a proposal in the Senate that would extend protections to the 48 million Americans in self-insured plans. The GOP plan is spearheaded by Sen. James M. Jeffords, R-Vt., chairman of the Senate Health, Education, Labor and Pensions Committee.

Democrats, though, say there are at least 113 million Americans in managed care who need federal protection because of the hit-or-miss nature of state regulations. They include state employees and workers who buy health insurance independently. [13]

"Enormous differences exist today in the protections that are afforded to people based on the accidental happenstance of a consumer's state of residence, and the payer and form of that consumer's health plan," says Ronald Pollack, executive director of the liberal-leaning advocacy group Families USA.

Regardless of whether regulations are passed, few experts predict health-care rationing will go away. Instead, they say, decisions about painful cuts will gradually shift from insurers to health-care professionals, employers and the workers themselves. Some corporations confronted with premium increases may elect to forgo buying health coverage for workers and instead give their employees vouchers or lump-sum payments. The workers will then have to decide what is the most appropriate coverage they can buy for that amount. Similarly, insurers who face higher costs may increase deductibles and copayments, forcing plan members to decide if they want to pay more for certain procedures.

"You can't avoid the reality of rationing, it just will shift from sector to sector," says Mark Hall, professor of law and public health at Wake Forest University and author of the 1997 book *Making Medical Spending Decisions.*

Health-care economist Fronstin predicts current labor conditions may prevent consumers from shouldering too much of the burden. With skilled labor in demand, he thinks companies will go out of their way to avoid passing along premium increases, cutting administrative costs and taking other steps to keep workers happy.

"As long as there's a tight labor market, employers will be very reluctant to do anything to create more job openings," Fronstin says. "But if there's a recession, costs will be shifted, and you could end up with many more people uninsured."

Should physicians and hospitals be subject to performance ratings or guidelines?

Cleveland Health Quality Choice was one of the first communitywide efforts in the nation to measure the quality of local health care. But come July, the nonprofit health program will shut its doors permanently, a victim of the topsy-turvy health-care market.

Launched in 1989 by a group of businesses alarmed by spiraling medical costs, the program issued semiannual report cards on how 27 northern Ohio hospitals cared for patients suffering from serious conditions like heart attacks and strokes. The businesses anticipated using the results as guides to buying health coverage for their workers. Plan administrators even took the unusual step of releasing the report cards to the public,

AP Photo/Kaiser Permanente

Industrialist Henry J. Kaiser, second from left, visits the Kaiser shipyard in Portland, Ore., in 1942, with President Franklin D. Roosevelt. In 1945, Kaiser opened enrollment in his company's prepaid health-care system to the public.

hoping the evaluations would show that simply choosing the cheapest health-care providers was, in fact, not always cost-effective in the long run.

But problems soon developed. Hospitals complained that the plan didn't always allow for differences in the severity of patients' illnesses and even accused each other of falsifying results. A spate of hospital mergers changed the nature of health-care contracting, forcing purchasers to decide whether to contract with all or none of the hospitals in a group and reducing the need for individual hospital performance ratings.

In January, the Cleveland Clinic and the eight hospitals in its system — which reluctantly participated in the program in the first place, largely to avoid losing insurance contracts — decided the approximately $2 million annual cost of compiling the data wasn't worth the effort and dropped out of the program, effectively dooming it.

"We focused on the quality of health care when everybody else was focused on cost," says Dr. Dwain Harper, the program's director. "When something like this fails, it's the community that loses."

The Cleveland Health Quality Choice plan's experience illustrates the dilemmas surrounding health-care quality standards. While advocates say such measures are needed to protect and inform consumers in an increasingly complicated marketplace, it's difficult to agree on precisely what to measure, how the measurements should be compared and whether the results should be used internally or released to the public.

Many believe some type of agreed-upon standards are necessary because health care in the United States varies widely from region to region, rendering traditional medical guidelines for specific procedures inadequate. Dartmouth Medical School researchers have documented how fewer than three out of every 200 breast cancer patients in Rapid City, S.D., received breast-conserving surgery instead of mastectomies, while in suburban Elyria, Ohio, 96 out of 200 did. The two procedures are deemed about equally effective. In gerontological care, spending for hospital treatments during the last six months of life is nearly twice as much in retiree-rich Greater Miami ($14,212 per person) as in Minneapolis ($7,246), the Dartmouth researchers found. [14]

Another argument for standards is that not everyone agrees on what is generally accepted care. A recent study in the AMA's *Archives of Internal Medicine* found more than 47 percent of 1,710 patients who had recurrent heart attacks between 1986 and 1995 had not received aspirin, beta-blockers and lipid-lowering drugs to control cholesterol after the first attack. Doctors in recent years have increasingly turned to the medications to reduce the risk of cardiovascular death. [15]

Doctors and hospitals are traditionally reluctant to endorse a single treatment as the most effective, arguing that medical cases are almost always too complicated to merit such a black-and-white approach. However, managed care companies and big employers increasingly have used their market power to impose statistical guidelines, which they say accurately point caregivers in the right direction.

In the early 1990s, a group of employers and HMOs developed the Health Plan Employer Data and Information Set (HEDIS), a now widely accepted standard that measures how frequently people in health plans receive more than 40 basic tests and services. While groundbreaking, the quality reports have been criticized as being heavily weighted toward primary-care — such as cancer screening and cholesterol tests — and inadequate for measuring how seriously ill people are treated.

More recently, the health-care community has embraced "outcomes research," a more complicated type of assessment that systematically tracks a patient's clinical treatment and responses to the treatment. This involves the use of still-evolving statistical measurements to account for differences between patients. An effective grading system could, for instance, track the success rate of coronary bypass surgeries while recognizing that certain teaching or research hospitals in a community see more complex heart cases.

To date, there is no single accepted standard for measuring quality of care. The AMA recently launched an accreditation program aimed at evaluating physicians' clinical performance and patient-care results. The program, which would release results to the public, is viewed skeptically by some as an attempt by doctors to set standards for each other instead of leaving the task to regulators or insurers. [16]

"Our opponents like to portray us as arbitrary, having little regard for outcomes research," says AMA President Dickey, defending the effort. "It's really a question of determining the best medical practices and digging beneath the political rhetoric."

Managed care also is incorporating new quality reviews as part of the industry's accreditation process. The National Committee for Quality Assurance (NCQA), a watchdog agency set up by the managed care industry to police health plans, announced in March that, starting in July 2000, it will begin requiring accredited plans to submit to outside reviews by specialists if they deny patients access to certain care or procedures. The move is designed to fight perceptions that managed care makes decisions based on cost considerations instead of what's best for the patient. It also could blunt proposed congressional legislation that would make it easier for patients to sue their health plans if certain coverage is denied. [17]

"A health plan that does well under Accreditation 2000 [the new review process] puts its members first," says NCQA President Margaret O'Kane.

Meanwhile, large employers in several cities are teaming up to launch independent programs similar to Cleveland Health Quality Choice. In Dayton, Ohio, a coalition of businesses that assumes financial risk for insuring 70,000 employees plans to issue a community report card on area hospitals within two years. In Texas, doctors and hospitals in Dallas and Fort Worth are working with large employers in the area to develop a report card for health-care consumers based on benchmarks such as recovery times and complication rates from procedures.

"This information is not available today in our marketplace," Sue Nelson, manager of health promotions and benefits for Dallas-based Texas Instruments Inc., recently told the *Dallas Morning News*. "If you were to go out and seek medical care, we believe you should know answers to the key questions." ■

BACKGROUND

Cost Concerns

After resoundingly rejecting President Clinton's 1993 plan for government-run health care, Americans appeared content to let for-profit managed care companies figure out how to balance medical costs with quality of care. The industry's failure to do so has created turmoil throughout the health-care system and new fears about the availability of care to millions of patients and employers.

Managed care companies absorbed more than $800 million in losses over the past two years, prompting a wave of mergers and consolidations. In December, Aetna Inc. purchased Prudential Health

Chronology

1880s-1920s

The concept of modern health care evolves with the advent of group practices, health insurance and community rating.

1883
William Mayo and his son, William James, open the Mayo Clinic in Rochester, Minn., becoming the first medical group practice.

1911
The Equitable Life Assurance Society of America writes the first group coverage employee life insurance policy. Interest from big employers leads to expansion of employee benefits, including '"medical catastrophe coverage," the first fee-for-service indemnity plans.

1929
Baylor University contracts with its hospital to provide care for the university's faculty for a flat rate per person. This "community rating" system becomes the predecessor of Blue Cross health plans.

1940s-1950s

Large-scale major medical plans evolve out of wartime industry.

1941-1945
A shortage of skilled workers and a wartime freeze on wages and corporate profits lead companies to expand employee health benefits. Collective bargaining and favorable court decisions help unions win generous health benefits that are standardized into fee-for-service medical plans.

1945
Industrialist Henry J. Kaiser provides health-care coverage and services on a prepaid basis for his shipyard workers in Oakland, Calif., and Vancouver, Wash., then opens the plan to the public. The plan evolves into Kaiser Permanente, the first managed care organization, now serving about 9 million clients.

1950
More than 100 rural health plans exist, and about 20 HMOs are in operation. The St. Louis branch of the Teamsters, the Appalachian United Mine Workers and the Detroit United Auto Workers have prepaid group coverage.

1959
The Federal Employee Health Benefit Program is formed.

1960s-1980s

The advent of government-financed health systems leads to greater demand for medical services, driving up health-care spending.

1965
Medicare is enacted. The tax-payer-financed system provides the elderly and disabled with access to short-term medical services. At enactment, slightly half of those age 65 and older have hospital insurance.

1988
Allied-Signal Corp. cancels the health-care arrangements of 80,000 employees and dependents and transfers them into the HMO plans of Cigna Corp. Cigna agrees to cap Allied-Signal's health-care costs for three years. The trend of employers channeling workers into managed care accelerates.

1990s

Managed care organizations hold down health-care inflation but encounter public backlash.

1991-1997
Increases in HMO premiums among firms with more than 200 employees slow from 12.1 percent to 2 percent.

1993
The Clinton administration proposes the National Health Security Act, designed to provide all Americans with health insurance. Spearheaded by first lady Hillary Rodham Clinton, the plan is defeated by a coalition of business interests, the medical lobby and Republicans.

1996
Fifty million Americans now receive health care through employer-sponsored HMOs, up from 15 million in 1985. Another 50 million are in preferred-provider organizations (PPOs).

1997
A proposed "Patients' Bill of Rights" is issued by Clinton's Advisory Commission on Consumer Protection and Quality in the Health Care Industry.

1999
Enrollment in managed care plans continues to surge despite complaints about service. Congressional Democrats and Republicans offer differing versions of health-care consumer bills.

Care — the latest in a series of acquisitions that has essentially concentrated power around six big insurers: Aetna, Cigna, United Healthcare, Foundation Health Systems, Pacificare and Wellpoint Health Networks. [18]

These combined companies wield enormous power in some cities, giving them the ability to dictate prices and lock dissenting doctors and hospitals out of their networks. In some areas, insurers have used so-called "all-or-nothing" contracts to pressure doctors to participate in their lowest-paying health plans. The practice has sparked several nasty disputes; 400 Texas doctors in Arlington and Fort Worth left Aetna last year and refused to see the insurer's patients. [19]

Despite the intense pressure to cut costs, a growing number of observers question how much more efficiency the industry can squeeze out of the health-care market. Health plans recently have experienced problems keeping control of rising drug costs and the demand for expensive medical technologies. One industry survey last year found the number of drug prescriptions filled per 1,000 HMO members rose 7 percent over 1997 figures. And with the majority of workers now in some form of managed care, insurers can't rely as much on the one-time savings from switching people over from traditional indemnity plans. [20]

Princeton University economist Reinhardt blames managed care's woes on timing and economic conditions. Reinhardt says it was easier to cut costs and force health-care rationing on employers and workers during the recession of the late 1980s and early '90s, when employees were worried about losing their jobs. Now, the economy is strong, labor markets are tight and employers must offer generous fringe benefits to attract skilled workers. As a result, health plans are under pressure to be more flexible. Increasingly, HMOs and their gatekeeper systems are giving way to less restrictive point-of-service contracts and "preferred provider" networks, which allow patients to obtain care from outside the managed care network.

"Boom times in the economy have eroded the power of selective contracting and, thereby, clipped the wings of managed care," Reinhardt wrote in a 1998 essay, "The Managed Care Industry in Perspective." He says the industry increasingly is powerless to impose market discipline and is "slouching once again to something resembling . . . warmed-over, fee-for-service indemnity insurance." [21]

That hasn't stopped health-care consumers from worrying about the future — and harboring suspicions about their plans. The spate of HMO "horror stories" over the past two years has fueled the perception that many people are receiving substandard care, even though managed care executives contend they sometimes are being blamed for medical accidents that could happen in any health-care system. Doctors also are reminding patients about the freedom they have lost in procuring health care and raising their anxiety over further rationing. Public opinion is so brittle that Helen Hunt's tirade against her HMO in the 1998 movie "As Good As It Gets" drew standing ovations in some theaters.

Meanwhile, employers are concerned about managed care mergers limiting the choice of available health plans and raising premiums. In Philadelphia, the Aetna-Prudential merger has given the combined company a projected 39 percent share of the health-care market. Aetna and a large Blue Cross company, Keystone Health Plan East, together control more than four out of every five members of Philadelphia-area managed care networks.

"A marketplace this large should not be subject to a near monopoly," Alan Hillman, director of the University of Pennsylvania Health Policy Center, told *The New York Times* in January, soon after the merger was announced. Hillman says the financial demise of either big provider would leave one health plan in charge of care for a large percentage of the working population.

Search for Solutions

Big business, consumers and health professionals are all appealing to Congress for legislative remedies. But lawmakers remain divided over how to respond to the various concerns.

Republicans, in keeping with their generally anti-regulatory leanings, prefer market-based solutions. One option broached by Rep. Bill Thomas, R-Calif., influential chairman of the House Ways and Means Subcommittee on Health, House Majority Leader Dick Armey, R-Texas, and others, would shift health care away from the current employer-based system to one based on tax credits. [22] Most of the proposals would offer a refundable tax credit to individuals who buy health insurance. In theory, this would give consumers more control over how much coverage they want to buy and spur managed care companies to compete on price and service, not on how they can limit benefits in ways hidden to most consumers.

It wouldn't be the first time the federal tax code is used to shape social policy — proposals already abound to use tax credits for education and long-term care. But critics say the approach ignores the fact that high-risk individuals with pre-existing conditions probably won't be able to find affordable, comprehensive policies unless the government forces

Employers Now Make Many Choice Decisions

The Clinton administration's 1993 health-care reform proposal foundered in large part because many Americans didn't want the government to decide what medical care they receive. Instead, the task is falling to the nation's large employers, who increasingly are channeling employees and their dependents into managed care and, in the process, defining the health-care marketplace.

The practice dates to 1988, when Allied-Signal Corp. canceled the health-care plans of 80,000 employees and their dependents and transferred them into Cigna Corp.'s HMO plans.[1] In return, Cigna gave the company a discounted price and agreed to cap Allied-Signal's health-care costs for three years. The move saved the company millions of dollars and soon had corporate executives across the country chanting the managed care mantra.

Yet studies show that employees often have little choice in selecting what managed care coverage they receive. A 1998 survey of 21,000 employers conducted by the RAND Corp. and the Research Triangle Institute found that only 17 percent of workers employed by private companies were offered a choice among plans. Only one-third of the businesses with 100 or more employees allowed workers to select from a variety of plans. The survey also found that only one-quarter of the large businesses gave employees anything beyond basic plan descriptions.

Paul Ginsburg, president of the Center for Studying Health System Change, says despite the fact that most workers weren't given a choice of health plans, they did have more choice of physicians than in the past. That's because employers, responding to worker concerns, expanded hospital and physician networks within the managed care framework.

"It's important to recognize that employers have responded to consumer demands for choice," Ginsburg says.

The situation is less optimistic for smaller businesses, who have less clout negotiating health coverage and are more sensitive to premium increases. Some — particularly in retail trade, agriculture and resources — have stopped offering health coverage at all, or only give their employees limited choice.

Choice is important because experts say workers are sensitive to small changes in the cost of premiums. One 1997 study in the *Journal of Health Economics* documented how 26 percent of health-plan members switched to a cheaper plan when the monthly premium for their own plan rose by $10. The sensitivity primarily benefits HMOs, whose premiums usually are slightly lower than indemnity insurers and preferred provider organizations that offer more choice.

Some lawmakers and public-policy experts have suggested reforming health insurance so it is no longer employer-based. They note that by switching from one managed care company to another, a big company can force thousands of workers and their families to leave their personal physicians. Reform advocates also contend that most big employers aren't concerned with the quality of care, just the cost, and lack the means to measure how well their workers are being cared for. A number have suggested using tax credits to allow workers to buy their own health coverage.

Employers say they want to continue to sponsor health plans, noting they now provide coverage for 150 million workers and their families and finance one-third of all health-care spending in the United States. But they fear new federal mandates on managed care will drive up the cost of insurance at a time when tight labor markets dictate they must offer generous benefits to retain workers.

"The marketplace is responding to the needs and desires of consumers," Marcia Comstock, a health-care policy fellow at the U.S. Chamber of Commerce, testified at a U.S. Senate hearing in March. "Mandating today's favored practices or services runs counter to . . . quality improvements and drives up costs unnecessarily."[2]

[1] For background, see Thomas Bodenheimer and Kip Sullivan, "How Large Employers Are Shaping the Health-Care Marketplace," *The New England Journal of Medicine*, Vol. 338, No. 14 (April 2, 1998), pp. 1003-1007.

[2] Comstock testimony before Senate Committee on Health, Education, Labor and Pensions, March 11, 1999.

insurers to cover them. The size of subsidies for low-income families and the working poor also would have to be substantial to cover the full cost of coverage.

Some critics, such as Rep. Pete Stark, D-Calif., ranking Democrat on the Ways and Means Health panel, believe employers will use the availability of the credits as an excuse to stop providing health coverage that would be preferable to anything that could be bought with the credits. Others believe Congress should instead address underlying problems in the insurance industry, like the lack of standards for what health procedures should be covered.

"None of the tax-credit proposals adequately addresses the need for reform in the [insurance] market. In the absence of such reform, tax-credit proposals could seriously erode health coverage for individuals and families with substantial pre-existing conditions," the advocacy group Consumers Union recently declared.

With the 2000 campaign season looming and odds stacked against substantial reforms, GOP leaders are

How States Are Regulating Managed Care

Here are some of the most common types of patient-protection legislation and the states where they are in force:

Prevent health plans from penalizing doctors who discuss options not covered by the plan or inform patients about grievance or appeal rights:

California, Colorado, Connecticut, Florida, Kentucky, Maryland, Massachusetts, Minnesota, New Jersey, New York, Ohio, Oregon, Pennsylvania, Texas, Vermont.

Protect enrollees if a health insurer denies coverage for emergency services because enrollee didn't seek prior approval:

California, Colorado, Connecticut, Florida, Kentucky, Maryland, Minnesota, New Jersey, New York, Ohio, Oregon, Pennsylvania, Texas, Vermont.

Allow women in health plans to designate obstetricians and gynecologists as their primary-care physicians:

California, Connecticut, Kentucky, Maryland, Minnesota, New Jersey, New York, Oregon, Pennsylvania, Texas, Vermont.

Force managed care firms to provide easier access to medical specialists:

California, Colorado, Connecticut, Florida, Minnesota, New Jersey, New York, Ohio, Oregon, Pennsylvania, Texas, Vermont.

Require managed care firms to list prescription drugs they normally cover, and/or disclose providers for obtaining drugs not on the list:

California, Connecticut, Florida, Kentucky, Minnesota, New York, Oregon, Pennsylvania, Texas, Vermont.

Source: "Managed Care: State Approaches on Selected Patient Protections," March 11, 1999, U.S. General Accounting Office

likely to offer more modest, piecemeal proposals. But they are expected to clash with the goals of President Clinton and congressional Democrats, who believe Republicans won't go far enough in giving patients the protection they need. The differences were evident at last month's 13-hour markup of the Senate Republicans' patients'-protection bill, when Democrats on the Senate Health, Education, Labor and Pensions Committee offered 18 amendments that were all defeated by party-line votes. The bill — which relies on market-based solutions but has been criticized for covering just the 48 million Americans in self-insured health plans — was finally approved by a 10-8 vote, with all Republicans voting for it and all Democrats opposing it.

Democrats want any reforms to apply to all Americans with private insurance, and they continue to press for provisions that would make it easier for patients to sue managed care providers for denial of treatments. Republicans oppose such measures, saying they would drive up health-care costs, increase the number of frivolous lawsuits and prompt employers to scale back the health benefits they now offer.

Despite such tensions, some observers believe it's still possible for lawmakers to arrive at a bipartisan solution. Republican congressional leaders this year are allowing committees with jurisdiction over health care to draft and approve managed care legislation — a process that will give Democrats more input and could result in a degree of bipartisanship. Last year, the Republican managed care bill was written outside the committee process by a GOP health-care task force that didn't solicit Democratic input. The task force produced a bill that narrowly passed the House by a vote of 216-210, mostly along party lines, and drew a veto threat from Clinton, who said it didn't provide enough patient protections.

"I'm encouraged by the consensus that has emerged on the core elements of a Patients' Bill of Rights," Sen. Jeffords says. "I believe we have an obligation to act responsibly, without unduly raising the cost of health coverage or upsetting the existing balance between state and federal regulation of health coverage." ■

CURRENT SITUATION

'Managed Competition'

For most of the 1990s, employers embraced managed care as a way

Uninsured Americans Now at 43 Million

Managed care gets credit for controlling medical costs and offering a private-sector solution to the nation's health-care woes. But a number of studies suggest Americans who are unable to get into its health plans are finding it increasingly difficult to obtain essential medical services.

The number of uninsured Americans has risen from 37 million in 1992 to approximately 43 million today. Health-care economists blame increasingly expensive premiums, cutbacks in employer coverage and other cost pressures stemming from the changing medical environment. And experts caution the traditional safety net of charity care is eroding as doctors and hospitals struggle with shifting reimbursement policies and limits on federal aid.

"Many people don't focus on the uninsured because they're busy gauging the opinions of people who are already in health plans, who, for the most part, are satisfied because they're healthy," says Paul Fronstin, health-care economist for the Employee Benefit Research Institute. "The fact is the problems with the uninsured are getting worse, and something needs to be done."

The uninsured are usually defined as those people who don't have health coverage through employer-based plans, Medicare or Medicaid. An estimated 30 million are members of low-income working families who can't afford to buy coverage but also aren't poor enough to qualify for Medicaid, the federal-state health program for the indigent. Most people in this group are less likely to receive basic care and tend to delay seeking treatment until they get seriously ill, sometimes requiring emergency-room visits.

Many health-care providers provide charity care to these people knowing they won't get compensated — an American Medical Association study estimates that doctors provide about $11 billion worth of free or discounted care annually. Some have tried to shift the cost to their insured patients. But with managed care tightening payments to doctors, hospitals and clinics, recouping the losses is more difficult, leading some practitioners to abandon the practice altogether.[1]

A recent study sponsored by the Washington-based Center for Studying Health System Change illustrates the problem. The study of 12,000 physicians, published in March in the *Journal of the American Medical Association,* found that doctors whose income depends the most on HMOs and other managed care organizations devote, on average, 40 percent less time to charity care as doctors with little involvement in managed care.[2]

In addition, doctors who practice in regions with a large number of managed care plans spent less time providing charity care, regardless of how many managed care patients they saw in their own practice. The survey found more than 77 percent of respondents said they still provide at least 10 hours of care to uninsured patients each week.

An earlier study by the center found that, in states where Medicaid programs rely heavily on managed care, uninsured people were less likely to have a primary-care physician or have visited a doctor or clinic for regular care in the past year.

Managed care companies respond that employers and state governments, not health insurers, are to blame for the added pressure on health care's bottom line. Both the American Association of Health Plans and the Health Insurance Association of America contend the managed care industry has improved the quality of care by keeping medical inflation down, thus making health insurance more affordable. AAHP President Karen Ignagni cites industry studies showing that even a 1 percent increase in premiums can result in 300,000 more people losing health coverage.

Federal officials and health-plan administrators are taking some efforts to widen access to care. Congress in 1997 approved a $24 billion, five-year program to provide coverage for the nation's approximately 11 million uninsured, non-Medicaid-eligible children. Similarly, HMO giant Kaiser Permanente has earmarked money to treat uninsured children and asked doctors to work in clinics that cater to at-risk, uninsured patients.[3]

Peter Cunningham, author of the two Center for Studying Health System Change studies, says lawmakers should get more involved. He suggests providing direct funding to care for the uninsured or compensating health-care providers for the charity care they deliver by creating a pool of money financed by federal and private sources.

"The research suggests that the holes in the safety net may be widening," Cunningham says.

[1] See Amy Goldstein, "Physicians Cutting Back Charity Work," *The Washington Post,* April 5, 1999, p. A1.

[2] See Peter Cunningham et al., "Managed Care and Physicians' Provision of Charity Care," *Journal of the American Medical Association,* Vol. 281 (March 24/31, 1999), pp. 1087-1092.

[3] Goldstein, *op. cit.*

of keeping costs in line. But many privately believed they could do an even better job containing health-care inflation if they banded together to collectively purchase health insurance. With premiums on the rise, more and more are.

Last year, nine Chicago-area businesses — including Ford Motor Co., Bank of America and Navistar International Transportation — negotiated 1999 premiums with local HMOs at rates that were just 4 percent above last year's level. That's less than half of what most employers are expecting to pay this year. After five years of little or no premium growth, three-quarters of American businesses expect health insurance rates to rise an average of 9 percent this year, according to the benefits consulting firm William Mercer.

"We saw the HMO market in Chicago merging, and costs were going up, so we felt by coming together we could expand our leverage," Larry Boress, executive director of the alliance — the Chicago Business Group on Health — told the *Chicago Tribune*.[23]

Group purchasing is built around what health-care experts call the concept of "managed competition." The companies jointly solicit proposals for health coverage and evaluate the resulting bids to obtain competitive rates and certain performance guarantees. In the process, they bypass insurance companies who traditionally act as middlemen and impose their own restrictions on care. The added clout allowed the Chicago-area companies to require the HMOs to provide employees with preventive medical services, such as mammograms, or participate in wellness programs.

But joint purchasing isn't always easy. Thomas Bodenheimer, a family and community medicine specialist at the University of California at San Francisco School of Medicine, says it can be difficult to get participating companies to agree on a standard set of benefits so that all involved are essentially buying the same insurance product. The companies also have to abide by the joint negotiating process and agree not to bargain on the side for even cheaper insurance from managed care providers.[24]

Purchasing groups have been used in a number of different ways across the country with varying success. One of the oldest is the Cleveland-based Council of Smaller Enterprises, which began as a joint-purchasing program for small businesses in the late 1970s and today offers insurance to 13,000 companies with 200,000 employees and dependents. Organization officials say the group's leverage in negotiating rates has pushed insurance costs in northern Ohio down 20 percent below the national average.

A more recent example is the Pacific Business Group on Health, formed in the early 1990s by Wells Fargo, Bank of America and other large San Francisco-area employers. The coalition, which now includes 33 companies and more than 3 million members, negotiates premiums with managed care companies and ties 2 percent of the premium to performance. If the organizations don't provide appropriate preventive care, as defined by the coalition, they must pay back the amount. This summer, the coalition will try to expand its system to include smaller businesses, which tend to experience higher rate increases because they have less negotiating power.

An arguably more dramatic variation on the theme is found in Minneapolis and St. Paul, Minn., where a 29-company coalition, the Buyers Health Care Action Group, for the past two years has contracted directly with groups of hospitals and physicians, essentially designing its own care systems. Bodenheimer says the coalition — which includes corporate giants 3M, General Mills and Honey-well — succeeded in creating a price war among health-care providers, driving down premiums 8.5 percent below what they would have been had the companies contracted through HMOs. But, he adds, the alliance adopted a complicated system for reimbursing the health professionals, preventing some of the savings from being translated immediately into expanded medical services.[25]

The Clinton administration and many local governments believe joint purchasing could be the way of the future, particularly for small businesses that currently are experiencing premium increases of 10-13 percent this year. Clinton has proposed a tax credit for small businesses with fewer than 25 workers that establish purchasing alliances, also known as "health marts." Clinton proposed a similar incentive for purchasing pools in his 1993 health plan. Several localities, among them New York City, also have launched their own pilot programs with business groups to form new purchasing alliances.[26]

Drop in Care Denials

Health insurers say they aren't concerned about direct contracting and other collaborative efforts driving them out of business. Managed care executives contend only the largest corporations have the financial means to independently process claims, deal with customer complaints and offer workers a choice of several health-care options. "It's going to be difficult for all but the largest groups of employers to do it," says HIAA's Kahn, predicting some alliances may eventually contract with health plans for claims processing and other administrative functions.

If managed care companies are not fazed about the potential shift in power, new data suggest they appear to be making a concerted effort to be more accommodating to patients. Health-care statistics collected by several states over the past two years indicate health plans actually are not denying much care, despite the well-publicized horror stories about HMOs cutting off access to medical treatments.

New York, New Jersey and Connecticut, among others, have began to require managed care plans to

At Issue:

Should legislators shift responsibility for interpreting "medical necessity" from insurers to health-care providers?

yes

RICHARD F. CORLIN, M.D.
Speaker, American Medical Association House of Delegates

FROM A STATEMENT TO THE SENATE COMMITTEE ON HEALTH, EDUCATION, LABOR AND PENSIONS, MARCH 2, 1999.

There is currently no issue more pressing than the question of who determines the "medical necessity" of patient care. . . . Consider, for instance, how integral the determination of medical necessity is for sound internal and, especially, external appeals programs. . . . [R]egardless of how sound and effective the actual appeals procedures may be, if the "medical necessity" standard that is being applied in both the internal and external appeals is arbitrarily dictated by the plan administrator or plan documents, the patient will never be guaranteed a fair, objective evaluation of the appropriate level of covered treatment. . . .

Information-disclosure requirements can also be adversely influenced by how "medical necessity" is determined and by whom. For instance, many plans in their information-disclosure statements indicate that the plan will provide coverage for all "medically necessary" treatment. As a result, patients and prospective enrollees believe that they are covered for all medical treatment which is clinically appropriate. . . . When the patient suffers an illness, however, plans that have arbitrarily defined the term "medical necessity" can deny coverage for a wide range of accepted treatments that do not fall within their own arbitrary definition of medically necessary treatment. . . .

Frequently, a patient's right to have access to specialty care hinges on whether the plan decides that it is not medically necessary based on an arbitrary definition of "medical necessity" crafted by the plan. . . . In such a case, upon appeal, if further constrained to use only the plan's "medical necessity" definition, the final outcome would deny needed patient care. Under appeals regulations currently in effect, a patient can be "slow walked" through an appeals process, while awaiting referral to an appropriate specialist. . . .

Reviews of managed care contracts last year revealed that language imposing "lowest cost" criteria had been included in many contracts' definitions of medical necessity. Health plans' concern about their profits remains the driving force behind these definitions, which emphasize cost and resource utilization over quality and clinical effectiveness. To say the least, this is alarming both to patients and to physicians. . . . The AMA believes that "medical necessity" or "medical appropriateness" decisions are ultimately medical decisions and must continue to be treated as such. Permitting health plans to decide "medical necessity" according to financial or cost considerations creates a dangerous precedent.

no

HEALTH INSURANCE ASSOCIATION OF AMERICA

FROM "MEDICAL NECESSITY AND HEALTH PLAN CONTRACTS," MARCH 1999.

The question is provoked by legislation that has been proposed on Capitol Hill and in many states. At first blush, such legislation, which would place determinations of "medical necessity" solely into the hands of treating physicians, seems innocuous, even reasonable: Why shouldn't treating physicians define what is medically necessary? But, in fact, this proposed change — which would have a detrimental effect on health care in America — reflects the widespread public confusion about "medical necessity" as a boundary of health coverage and "medical necessity" as a clinical determination by a treating physician.

The "medical necessity" provisions in currently proposed federal legislation represent a radical rewriting by public officials of the contract between insurers and health plans and their customers. When the provider, rather than the health plan or insurer, interprets the scope of coverage under the contract, health plans and fiduciaries cannot guarantee to the insured that health-care dollars are being spent fairly and equitably on medical treatments that are safe, proven and effective. Indeed, such legislation could give some providers incentives to overtreat patients to enhance their incomes. Under such a regime, who can doubt that insurers' denials of payment or determinations of non-coverage would be regularly challenged?

In effect, the proposed "medical necessity" provisions represent an attempt to turn back the clock. Such proposals would do more than simply return the health-care system to the unconstrained fee-for-service system of payment that was responsible for the double-digit inflation in health-care costs of the 1970s and 1980s. It would undermine efforts by all types of health-plan delivery models, from HMOs through PPOs and fee-for-service coverage. Even in the earlier era of fee-for-service medical coverage, insurers reviewed claims to ensure that the services already delivered had in fact been medically necessary.

Far from protecting patients, passage of such legislation would be deeply inimical to the interests of health-care consumers, driving up the cost of medical care and possibly even placing patients in harm's way. The legislation would needlessly raise costs for plans, thereby promoting premium increases and reducing the affordability of health insurance. In the long run, such legislation threatens to diminish the availability of coverage and increase the number of the uninsured.

Glossary for a New Millennium

The advent of managed care has created a new lexicon. Here are some of the more commonly used health-care terms:

Managed Care — A catchall term that refers to a wide variety of health-care organizations, including health maintenance organizations (HMOs) and preferred provider organizations (PPOs), which control costs by monitoring how member doctors and hospitals treat patients, and by limiting access to specialists and certain expensive procedures.

Fee-for-Service — The traditional system of paying doctors for services rendered, as opposed to by salary or a fixed amount.

Third-Party Payer — The insurer, employer, government or other party that mediates between doctors and patients and negotiates fees for medical services. This is the opposite of when patients make payments out-of-pocket directly to a doctor or other health-care provider.

Utilization Review — A system used by many health insurers and health-care providers to monitor doctors' diagnoses, treatment and billing practices. The reviews are designed to lower costs by discouraging unnecessary treatment but have been criticized for interfering with physicians' decisions.

Medicare — The government-financed health-care system that provides the elderly and disabled with access to short-term medical services. Funded by payroll deductions and general revenues, the plan covers acute illnesses but doesn't cover prescription drugs or routine hearing, vision and dental care.

Health Maintenance Organization (HMO) — A health-care plan that provides health services for members who prepay a premium that generally covers a range of health services with limited co-payments.

Preferred Provider Organization (PPO) — A health-care provider who furnishes services on a negotiated fee schedule. Enrollees are offered a financial incentive to use doctors on the preferred list and must pay a deductible and co-payment to use out-of-network physicians.

Point-of-Service Plan — A managed care plan that combines features of prepaid and fee-for-service insurance. Enrollees decides whether to use network or non-network providers when care is needed, and are usually charged large co-payments for choosing the latter.

Managed Competition — One approach to health-care reform in which health plans compete to serve the needs of enrollees. Typically, enrollees are offered a choice of plans during an open season.

Community Rating — The practice of setting premium rates based on the cost experience of a managed care plan's entire membership, instead of a particular employer group.

Capitation — A health insurance payment mechanism in which health-care providers are paid a fixed amount of money each month per insured person to cover services over a period of time.

Cost Shifting — A situation in which a health-care provider compensates for decreased revenue from one payer, say an uninsured person, by increasing charges to another.

Source: George Halvorson, *Strong Medicine*, 1993.

report incidents of care denials and how they were resolved. While the information is still incomplete, it suggests health plan administrators now appear reluctant to second-guess physicians, possibly fearing lawsuits or political backlash. [27]

The records show HMOs primarily denied access to medical specialists who weren't part of their network, or refused to pay for treatments the plans decided weren't essential for a patient's recovery. Also denied were experimental procedures, such as bone-marrow transplants. But the relative numbers were low: the six largest managed-care firms in New York have averaged about 2.5 appeals per 1,000 patients. In New Jersey, the state last year recorded just 69 appeals from some 2.5 million enrollees in managed care plans.

The figures bear out managed care executives' contention that the amount of denials and the appeals they generate is overstated. But the low numbers concern some health-care experts, who say plan administrators are abdicating their responsibility to control health costs, likely in response to the political pressures. There is "an urgent need for managed care to second-guess decisions by physicians [that] subject patients to needlessly risky surgery and needlessly costly tests," Alain Enthoven, a health economist and one of the academicians who coined the concept of managed care in the 1980s, proclaimed recently in *The New York Times*. [28] ■

OUTLOOK

Rx for Medicare?

While Congress and the Clinton administration ponder ways to rein in managed care, lawmakers simultaneously are looking at ways the industry can help solve the financial squeeze surrounding the federal Medicare program.

Medicare provides subsidized health insurance to 39 million elderly or disabled Americans. But with costs rising faster than revenues, the $207 billion-a-year system is projected to go broke in about 2008, when the first of 77 million "baby boomers" born between 1946 and 1964 begin retiring. One solution would be to introduce some form of managed competition by having the government offer incentives for private managed care plans to compete against traditional health insurers, which pay fixed rates for specific medical services. This could be accomplished by giving the elderly health-care vouchers with which they could shop for the most appropriate coverage. Because recipients are presumably more sensitive to price and quality than government bureaucrats, this system — called "premium support" — would, in theory, deliver more benefits and better care at a lower price. [29]

But the recent experience of a federal commission charged with finding a solution to Medicare's woes shows how politically difficult it is to introduce such reforms — and more broadly raises questions about whether it's at all possible to overhaul the American health system. The 17-member commission, after a year of study, in March came up one vote short of the 11 needed to endorse formal recommendations to Congress or President Clinton. Members were divided over a plan offered by panel co-chairman Sen. John B. Breaux, D-La., that would have given seniors a fixed amount of money to buy private health insurance. Opponents, particularly more liberal Democrats appointed by President Clinton, said it wouldn't necessarily save money and questioned whether it would undermine a 1960s Great Society pact to protect the nation's sick and needy.

Breaux has indicated he may take another stab by introducing legislation in the Senate. Clinton, meanwhile, has offered his own solution, proposing to divert nearly $700 billion of government surpluses over the next 15 years to shore up Medicare.

Managed care reform and Medicare reform are separate but closely related issues. Len Nichols, a health-care economist at the Urban Institute in Washington, estimates federal and local governments buy health care for approximately 27 percent of Americans through Medicare and Medicaid. Annual spending for these beneficiaries amounts to nearly 40 percent of all health services delivered — worth more than $500 billion. With a flood of current workers set to retire early in the next century and health-care costs on the rise, policy-makers know they have to control the program's costs. They can't without changing the fundamental way health care is delivered and paid for — likely through some kind of managed care legislation. But the system is so complex — and the current pace of medical breakthroughs so fast — that government regulators can't keep up.

The federal government already has tried to link managed care to Medicare. In 1997, lawmakers created Medicare+Choice, a program that created more health insurance options for seniors by making it easier for private managed care plans to enter the Medicare market. About 17 percent of all Medicare beneficiaries have since switched to HMOs, and many like their willingness to pay for preventive services and prescription drugs that currently aren't covered under traditional Medicare coverage.

The federal government has set up pilot programs in several cities to see whether Medicare costs could be reduced if HMOs had to bid for senior-citizen patients. But patient and health-care professionals' concerns that benefits would also be cut led to the scuttling of the programs in Baltimore and Denver. Implementation of a program in Phoenix, where 40 percent of area seniors are enrolled in Medicare HMOs, has been delayed.

Plan administrators also complain the government's reimbursement policies haven't adequately kept up with rising costs. In response, many managed care plans unexpectedly dropped out of Medicare or scaled back their service areas over the past two years, leaving approximately 500,000 seniors stranded. Most had to go back to conventional Medicare coverage.

"It is absolutely impossible to micromanage health care in the 21st century," Breaux said, after his panel deadlocked on the latest Medicare debate.

That assessment is shared by many experts, who caution there is no "magic bullet" to answering the larger question of how to improve health-care quality and keep costs down. Indeed, most say any practical solution will require politically unpalatable sacrifices from beneficiaries, health-care providers and insurers.

"We can no longer start our public debate with the false but comforting assumption that our social abundance can support social safety nets and minimum entitlements to everyone in society," University of Chicago legal scholar Richard A. Epstein writes in his 1997 book *Mortal Peril: Our*

Inalienable Right to Health Care?

AAHP's Ignagni puts it equally bluntly: "Republicans and Democrats both want to do something. The question is what is it, and can each side get beneath the political debate and truly assess the costs and benefits?" ■

FOR MORE INFORMATION

American Medical Association, 515 N. State St., Chicago, Ill. 60610; (312) 464-5000; www.ama-assn.org. National trade group for physicians, residents and medical students. Actively lobbying for managed care reforms that would strip away certain decision-making powers away from health insurers.

American Association of Health Plans, 1129 20th St., N.W., Suite 600, Washington, D.C. 20036; (202) 778-3200; www.aahp.org. Large national trade association for managed health-care plans and organizations. Is fighting managed care reform efforts and lobbying for changes to current Medicare-reimbursement formulas.

Health Insurance Association of America, 555 13th St., N.W., Washington, D.C. 20004; (202) 824-1600; www.hiaa.org. National group for health insurance companies that write and sell health insurance policies. Lobbying against managed care reforms that would allow patients to sue their plans and give enhanced decision-making powers to doctors.

Employee Benefit Research Institute, 2121 K St., N.W., Suite 600, Washington, D.C. 20037; (202) 659-0670; www.ebri.org. Nonprofit organization that conducts research on health insurance coverage, health-care utilization and health-care cost containment and studies the health-delivery system.

Consumers Union of the United States, 1666 Connecticut Ave., N.W., Suite 310, Washington, D.C. 20009; (202) 462-6262; www.consumersunion.org. Advocacy group that publishes *Consumers Report* and lobbies on health-care issues nationally and on the state level.

Notes

[1] For background, see Kenneth Jost, "Patients' Rights," *The CQ Researcher*, Feb. 6, 1998, pp. 97-120, and Sarah Glazer, "Managed Care," *The CQ Researcher*, April 12, 1996, pp. 313-336.

[2] See Katherine Levit et al., "National Health Expenditures in 1997: More Slow Growth," *Health Affairs*, November/December 1998, pp. 99-110.

[3] See Milt Freudenheim, "Group Sues to Halt Kaiser Permanente Ads," *The New York Times*, March 18, 1999, p. C7.

[4] See Julie Marquis, "HMO Case Renews Debate on Patients' Rights," *Los Angeles Times*, Jan. 22, 1999, p. A3.

[5] See Karen Foerstel, "Health Care Forces Fight To Frame the Debate," *CQ Weekly*, April 3, 1999, pp. 799-801.

[6] See Michael Conlan, "It's Up, Down: Medicaid Covers Viagra, But Insurers Cite Safety Concerns," *Drug Topics*, July 20, 1998, p. 18.

[7] See S. Rosenbaum, et al., "Who Should Determine When Health Care Is Medically Necessary?" *The New England Journal of Medicine*, Vol. 340, No. 3 (Jan. 21, 1999), pp. 229-232.

[8] See Dahlia Remler et al., "What Do Managed Care Firms Do to Affect Care?" *Inquiry*, Vol. 34 (fall 1997), pp. 196-204

[9] See "Fraud: The Hidden Cost of Health Care," Health Insurance Association of America, 1996.

[10] See Ellyn Spragins, "Making HMOs Play Fair," *Newsweek*, May 4, 1998, p. 88.

[11] For background, see "Sources of Health Insurance and Characteristics of the Uninsured," Employee Benefit Research Institute Issue Brief No. 204, December 1998.

[12] See U.S. General Accounting Office, "Managed Care: State Approaches on Selected Patient Protections," March 1999.

[13] See Karen Foerstel, "Debate on Managed Care Legislation Diverges Along Familiar Lines," *CQ Weekly*, March 20, 1999, pp. 701-702.

[14] See "The Dartmouth Atlas of Health Care 1998," *American Hospital Publishing*, 1998.

[15] See Danny McCormick et al., "Use of Aspirin, Beta-Blockers and Lipid-Lowering Medications Before Recurrent Acute Myocardial Infarction: Missed Opportunities for Prevention?" *Archives of Internal Medicine*, 159:561-567 (March 22, 1999).

[16] See Judith Graham, "Physician Performance Initiatives Gain Ground," *1999 Comparative Performance Data Sourcebook*, Faulkner & Gray Inc.

[17] See "NCQA To Require Independent Appeals," A.M. Best Co./BestWire, March 16, 1999.

[18] See Milt Freudenheim, "Concern Rising About Mergers in Health Plans," *The New York Times*, Jan. 13, 1999, p. A1.

[19] See Peter Kilborn, "400 Doctors in Dallas Break Contracts with Aetna's HMO," *The New York Times*, Oct. 20, 1998.

[20] See Michael Casey, "HMOs Tally Up Costs and Raise Their Rates," *Medical Industry Today*, Feb. 2, 1999.

[21] For background, see Stuart Altman and Uwe Reinhardt, "Strategic Choices for a Changing Health System," *Health Administration Press*, 1996.

[22] See Mary Agnes Carey, "Managed Care Overhaul Shows New Signs of Life," *CQ Weekly*, Jan. 16, 1999, pp. 129-134.

[23] See Bruce Japsen, "Employers Pool Muscle," *Chicago Tribune*, Dec. 24, 1998, p. B1.

[24] For background, see Thomas Bodenheimer and Kip Sullivan, "How Large Employers Are Shaping the Health Care Marketplace," *The New England Journal of Medicine*, Vol. 338, No. 14 (April 2, 1998), pp. 1003-1007.

[25] *Ibid.*

[26] See Jennifer Steinhauer, "Health Insurance Costs Rise, Hitting Small Business Hard," *The New York Times*, Jan. 19, 1999, p. A1.

[27] See Michael Weinstein, "Managed Care's Other Problem: It's Not What You Think," *The New York Times*, Feb. 28, 1999, p. C1.

[28] Quoted in *Ibid.*

[29] See Robert Pear, "Politically and Technically Complex, Medicare Defies a Sweeping Redesign," *The New York Times*, March 18, 1999, p. A23 and "Medicare Reform: Promises, Promises," *The Economist*, March 27, 1999, pp. 29-30.

Bibliography

Selected Sources Used

Books

Altman, Stuart, and Uwe Reinhardt, eds., *Strategic Choices for a Changing Health-Care System*, Association for Health Services Research, 1996.
Two prominent health-care scholars outline policy and management issues, including health-care spending, rationing and reorganization of the delivery system.

Anders, George, *Health Against Wealth*, Houghton Mifflin, 1996.
A *Wall Street Journal* reporter documents how the HMO system can turn against patients confronting medical emergencies and serious diseases.

Epstein, Richard, *Mortal Peril: Our Inalienable Right to Health Care?* Addison-Wesley, 1997.
A University of Chicago legal scholar argues that a hands-off approach to regulating health care will guarantee greater access to quality medical care for more people.

Halvorson, George, *Strong Medicine*, Random House, 1993.
America's health system focuses on procedures, not outcomes, creating massive waste, a managed care executive contends.

Articles

Cunningham, Peter, et. al., "Managed Care and Physicians' Provision of Charity Care," *Journal of the American Medical Association*, Vol. 281 (March 24/31, 1999), pp. 1087-1092.
Health-system changes may be affecting the ability of doctors to provide care with little or no compensation from patients who are uninsured and underinsured and may result in decreased access to physicians for uninsured patients, researchers say.

Lewis, Diane, "Doctors Join Union to Fight Ills from HMOs," *The Boston Globe*, March 2, 1999, p. A1.
In an attempt to regain clout lost to HMOs, 15,000 doctors have joined a new alliance formed by the AFL-CIO and promised to fight managed care by spending $1 million over the next year to bring discontented physicians into their fold.

McLaughlin, Catherine, and Paul Ginsburg, "Competition, Quality of Care and the Role of the Consumer," *The Milbank Quarterly*, No. 4, Vol. 76 (December 1998), p. 737.
Two health-policy experts argue there is little evidence of any relationship between competition and the quality of medical care.

Millenson, Michael, "What Doctors Don't Know: Problems With the Health-Care System," *The Washington Monthly*, December 1998, No. 12, Vol. 30, p. 8.
A journalist-turned consultant argues that physician autonomy in making health-care decisions isn't always a good thing.

Rosenbaum, Sara, et al., "Who Should Determine When Health-Care is Medically Necessary," *The New England Journal of Medicine*, Vol. 340, pp. 229-232 (Jan. 21, 1999).
The authors argue that physicians, not insurers, should be responsible for deciding what care patients receive.

Samuelson, Robert, "Myth of the Managed Care Monster," *The Washington Post*, July 29, 1998, p. A21.
The economics columnist argues that, if Americans can get whatever health care they — or their doctors —want, then society will ultimately be worse off.

Reports

"Medical Necessity and Health-Plan Contracts," Health Insurance Association of America, March 1999.
A health-insurance industry analysis of proposed congressional patients'-rights legislation outlines how new regulations would mean higher costs and lower-quality care.

"Sources of Health Insurance and Characteristics of the Uninsured," Employee Benefit Research Institute, Issue Brief No. 204, December 1998.
A nonpartisan group provides comprehensive summary data on the insured and uninsured populations in the nation and in each state and discusses the characteristics most closely related to individuals' health-insurance status.

Nichols, Len, "Health-Care Quality: At What Cost?" No. 13 of the series "The Future of the Public Sector," The Urban Institute, May 1998.
As Medicare and Medicaid adopt cost-control techniques used in managed care, the author argues that the uninsured will find it even more difficult to afford medical treatment.

4 Embryo Research

ADRIEL BETTELHEIM

Last fall, teams of scientists working separately at the University of Wisconsin and Johns Hopkins University made a groundbreaking discovery — and kicked up a tempest.

The researchers isolated from human embryos and fetuses a primitive variety of cells that are capable of developing into virtually every kind of tissue in the body. The so-called stem cells could provide valuable tools for curing ailments such as Parkinson's disease and diabetes, if scientists can learn how to train them to grow into a desired healthy body part.

"These findings . . . bring medical research to the edge of a new frontier that is extraordinarily promising," National Institutes of Health (NIH) Director Harold Varmus said, echoing the optimism that swept the scientific community. "It is not too unrealistic to say that this research has the potential to revolutionize the practice of medicine and improve the quality and length of life."

But while the findings generated headlines and drew comparisons to landmark moments in 20th-century science, they also reignited a simmering legal and ethical debate over embryo research. Scientists, theologians, politicians and government officials have sparred in recent months over whether a 1995 federal ban on funding research on embryos should apply to stem cells. Congress and the NIH are attempting to devise new guidelines in light of the developments. But officials first must arrive at a consensus on such thorny philosophical questions as when life begins, and whether an embryo has the same moral status as a person.

"It's a watershed issue that cuts

From *The CQ Researcher*, December 17, 2000.

deeply into the future of the biomedical community," says Ronald M. Green, chairman of the Ethics Institute at Dartmouth College. "Science is forcing us to rethink our ethical, moral and religious considerations, but all the recent developments make it difficult to draw lines in the sand."

Human stem cells are hardly the first scientific discovery in recent years to challenge people's beliefs in this way. The advent of recombinant DNA technology in the 1970s led to developments allowing scientists to clone sheep and other mammals, raising the very real but unsettling prospect that human beings also could be replicated. [1]

Around the same time, scientists developed a deeper understanding of how DNA carries chemical messages, allowing them to identify specific human genes linked to diseases, and, possibly, certain types of behavior. That has raised questions about how much of our existence is predetermined, and whether science should be allowed to intervene via techniques such as gene therapy. [2]

The stem cell discovery could potentially have even more profound meaning, because it offers a glimpse at human life in its simplest form. The microscopic clumps of cells are found in the interior of days-old embryos before they develop rudimentary nervous systems and are capable of achieving something resembling awareness.

When isolated in culture dishes, the cells — through a still-unknown mechanism — can grow into specific body parts, such as brain cells or heart muscle. They also can replicate indefinitely in the laboratory, providing a potentially endless source of replacement tissue. Scientists have watched with amazement as some of the cells spontaneously evolve into tiny bundles of beating heart muscle, clumps of nerves or even hair and teeth. [3]

However, scientists don't yet know how to make a stem cell "committed" to becoming a particular body part. And they still aren't sure whether the spare body parts they create won't be rejected by the patient's immune system — a problem that frequently arises in organ transplants.

Some of the stem cells were extracted from spare embryos created in fertility clinics that were deemed unsuitable for implantation in the womb. Others came from the gonads of aborted fetuses. Because of uncertainties over whether the existing funding ban applies to stem cells, the University of Wisconsin and Johns Hopkins scientists relied on private funding for their work, including financing from Geron Corp., a Menlo Park, Calif., biotechnology firm with a strong interest in anti-aging products.

Most scientists believe the stem cells are biologically closer to other types of cells — say, blood cells — than to a complete embryo. They argue the government should fund research into how the cells can be coaxed into becoming a specific type of tissue, pointing to the wide-ranging health benefits that could follow. With this knowledge, researchers say they could perform tasks like creating new bone and cartilage cells for patients suffering from osteoporosis or arthritis, or nerve cells for stroke victims or people with spinal cord injuries.

"The world would be better off if public funding were available, because it would allow the best biomedical scientists in academia to enter the field," says James A. Thomson, the University of Wisconsin biologist who first isolated the human stem cells and used them to grow heart tissues. "Although a great deal of basic research needs to be done before these cells can lead to human therapies, I believe in the long run they will revolutionize many aspects of transplantation medicine."

However, anti-abortion groups and many Catholic theologians oppose using taxpayer money to fund the work, arguing the scientists are destroying life to advance their research. The critics, who believe that life begins at conception, contend the stem cells, however primitive, are distinct entities that have the same moral status as humans. They criticize the researchers for playing up the biological qualities of the stem cells while paying less attention to the methods that extract them from embryos. And they worry that advances in cloning will soon lead scientists to create embryos specifically so they can extract their stem cells.

"These embryos are far beyond conception; fertilization has taken place and we have a genetically unique individual," says C. Ben Mitchell, senior fellow at the Center for Bioethics and Human Dignity, a nonprofit group in Bannockburn, Ill., that is leading the fight against federal funding. "Giving an embryo a different moral status based on the time of gestation is simply an act of arbitrariness. There's no scientific evidence to point to a specific time when the moral status moves higher."

Public figures and advocacy groups are already joining the debate. Groups advocating for victims of various diseases have mounted a major lobbying push in favor of federal funding, even going as far as recruiting the help of conservative Sen. Strom Thurmond, R-S.C., an abortion foe whose daughter suffers from juvenile diabetes, and 33 U.S. Nobel Prize winners.

Opponents, including the National Conference of Catholic Bishops, have issued strongly worded position papers supporting the ban, saying any researcher who understands the origin of the stem cells is "morally complicit" in their destruction. Those coming out against federal funding include no less than 70 members of Congress and former Surgeon General C. Everett Koop.

Lawmakers considering what to do must first consider the 1995 ban, authored by Rep. Jay Dickey, R-Ark. that prohibits spending federal money on any biomedical research involving human embryos outside the womb. [4] The ban, which didn't contemplate the extraction of stem cells, has been attached for the past four years as a rider to the annual bills that fund NIH.

Congress could elect to expand the ban so it explicitly mentions stem cell research. Lawmakers also could take the more dramatic step of extending the ban to privately funded research — a move that experts say would almost certainly would trigger legal challenges because it could infringe on individuals' reproductive rights. Congress also could elect to simply let the ban stand and defer to NIH on the issue of stem cell research — a move that appears increasingly likely given the sharp philosophical divide over the issue.

NIH in December released draft guidelines recommending the funding of stem cell research based on a legal opinion by Harriet Rabb, general counsel of the U.S. Department of Health and Human Services (HHS). [5] The opinion states that stem cells "do not have the capacity to develop into a human being, even if transferred to the uterus." As a result, Rabb wrote, destruction of the cells during the course of research wouldn't constitute the destruction of an embryo. President Clinton's National Bioethics Advisory Commission and the American Association for the Advancement of Science (AAAS) have similarly endorsed federally funded stem cell research.

To get around the issue of the current funding ban, NIH said it would not use federal funds to create embryos for research but would support studies that use embryos developed by private sources. Moving with caution, the agency is seeking public comment on the draft guidelines and has assembled an oversight panel to review grant proposals.

"The ethical and social issues associated with stem cell research are complex and controversial and require thoughtful discourse in public fora to reach resolution," Varmus says.

But critics say the NIH's preliminary decision reflects a concerted effort to defy the funding ban and present a new definition of an embryo. "The researcher's temptation is to think that if something technically can be done it ethically should be done," Richard Doerflinger, associate director for policy development for the National Conference of Catholic Bishops, told a Senate Appropriations subcommittee hearing on stem cell research last December. "A civilized society will appreciate the possibilities opened up by research, but will insist that scientific progress must not come at the expense of human dignity." [6]

Geron is watching the debate closely. It wants to learn how to convert a patient's ordinary cells into stem cells that then can be used for transplantation and self-repair. The company announced in May that it

At the Beginnings of Life

The isolation of human embryonic stem cells, shown below, represents a landmark in biomedical research and offers the highest-resolution view yet into early human development. Controversy arises because stem cells are isolated from aborted fetuses or early-stage embryos.

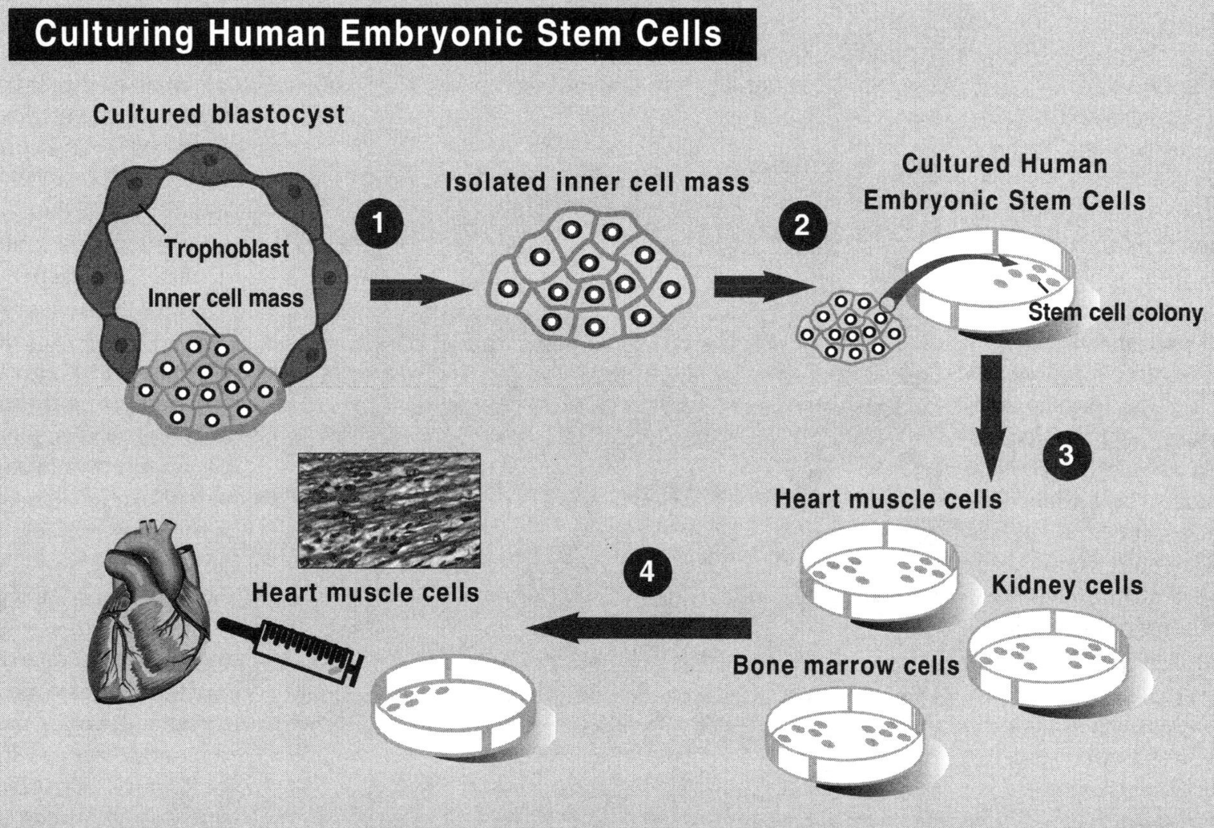

1 Scientists isolate the inner cell mass from a microscopic five-day-old embryo, or blastocyst.

2 The cells are placed in a tissue culture dish and mixed with growth factors that allow them to mature into stem cells.

3 When the growth factor is removed, the stem cells differentiate into specific cell types. University of Wisconsin researchers used stem cells to grow heart tissues while scientists at Johns Hopkins University coaxed them into becoming nerve cells.

4 Other body parts could be grown in this way and used to treat assorted ailments, such as heart disease.

Source: University of Wisconsin–Madison

formed a $20 million research alliance with the Roslin Institute of Scotland, which first focused worldwide attention on cloning in 1997 by creating Dolly, a cloned sheep. But Geron has denied it is interested in creating cloned human embryos.

Geron's involvement has made some observers uneasy because it operates entirely outside the scope of the funding ban and, by extension, without any federal oversight. Dartmouth ethics expert Green, among others, believes federal funding of stem cell research would ensure that other companies entered the field, and that NIH or some other federal authority would oversee the scope of the work.

"You would have a serious ethical issue if some company, not necessarily Geron, were deliberately creating embryos only to dismember them, and reaping huge financial benefits," Green says.

Geron says it convened its own ethics panel for advice on how to proceed, adding it understands the moral questions and general unease swirling around stem cell research.

"We are sensitive to the ethical issues surrounding our respective technologies," Geron President and Chief Executive Officer Thomas Okarma said in announcing the alliance with the Roslin Institute. "Both our organizations have been and remain committed to pursuing these technologies in an open and responsible manner."

As scientists, ethics experts, religious leaders and government officials continue to debate stem cell research and what it means for broader experiments involving human embryos, here are some questions they are asking:

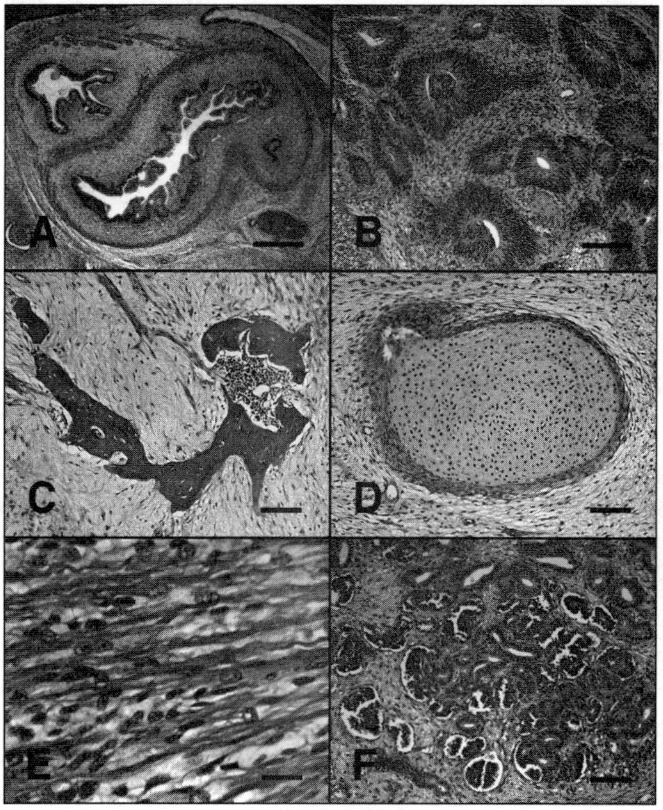

University of Wisconsin–Madison/*Science* magazine

The human embryonic stem cells isolated at the University of Wisconsin–Madison randomly differentiated into a variety of cell types: (A) gut, (B) neural, (C) bone marrow, (D) cartilage, (E) muscle and (F) kidney.

Is the use of stem cells from embryos morally or ethically wrong?

The isolation of human stem cells created tensions between two of the modern world's most important ethical commitments: curing disease and protecting human life. For many, resolving the issue hinges on drawing a series of careful distinctions about the source and nature of the stem cells.

The Johns Hopkins researchers' technique of extracting stem cells from aborted fetuses has stirred up slightly less controversy because the research didn't affect the ultimate fate of the embryos. Notwithstanding the separate and incendiary national debate over abortion, using stem cells from already-dead fetuses has been likened to the well-established medical practice of obtaining donor tissue from cadavers. Many experts additionally believe this research would currently qualify for federal funding because of the wording of the congressional ban on embryo research.[7]

The University of Wisconsin team's use of spare embryos from fertility clinics is much more controversial. About 16,000 embryos are created in clinics each year, the majority of which are deemed unsuitable for transplantation in the mothers' wombs. They typically are stored in liquid nitrogen and eventually discarded. However, using them to obtain stem cells involves the direct destruction of the embryos — an act that is expressly singled out in the congressional funding ban.

President Clinton's 17-member National Bioethics Advisory Commission believes the federal government should fund researchers using these two extraction techniques because a ban would conflict with the ethical goals of medicine — namely healing, prevention of disease and research. But the panel draws a distinction between the use of existing embryonic tissue and the hypothetical creation of a "research embryo" strictly so it can be used as a source of stem cells. The ethics panel says "there is no compelling reason" to generate an embryo for purposes other than creating a child, and recommends against using taxpayer funding for research using embryos produced for research purposes.[8]

Harold Shapiro, president of Princeton University and chairman of the ethics panel, says coming to some moral agreement on issues of birth and death is difficult because science is constantly evolving and testing individuals' beliefs. The result, he says, is anxiety about the future direction of technology and, in some cases, a temptation to "stop" science.

"We need new sources of reflection to enrich the ongoing ethical debates," Shapiro said. The "nervousness, ethical malaise, anxiety or even foreboding reflect, I believe, a shared understanding that humankind's destiny will not be decided in full in the laboratory or at the genetic level, where we have a lot more confidence in our ability to find solutions." [9]

Some theologians parse the ethical question differently, drawing distinctions not between the source of the embryos but between whether they exist inside or outside of the womb. Four leading theologians took this tack in October, when they wrote to Congress contending that human stem cell research can be conducted ethically and in harmony with religious principles.

"According to our religious beliefs, all human life must be protected," the theologians wrote. "However, they also indicate that there is a significant difference between an embryo suspended in liquid nitrogen that will never be implanted inside a womb, and an unborn child who is already in the womb." The group added that religious teachings stressing compassion for the sick further justify federal funding of the research.*

Theologians also are re-evaluating the question of precisely when life begins, postulating that such a thing as a "pre-embryo" may exist. Following this line of thinking, it may be permissible to extract stem cells before the embryo reaches some critical developmental milestone in which it becomes a distinct entity — for instance, the point at which it is capable of dividing in two to form twins.

However, opponents of stem cell research contend such distinctions are designed to achieve political compromises and don't address the broader ethical issues surrounding experiments on human subjects. The critics say society must rigorously apply those principles or face the prospect of treating people as things.

"Members of the human species who cannot give informed consent should not be the subjects of an experiment unless they personally may benefit from it, or the experiment carries no significant risk to harming them," says the National Conference of Catholic Bishops' Doerflinger. He notes that U.S. law already allows for such considerations, permitting states to pass statutes prohibiting harmful experiments on human embryos, despite prohibitions on restricting access to abortions.

The Center for Bioethics and Human Dignity rejects using compassion for the sick as justification for conducting stem cell research, saying the Bible teaches that people are not free to pursue good ends through immoral or unethical means.

"We must not sacrifice one class of human beings to benefit another," says the center's Mitchell, citing as an example the use of data from Nazi medical experiments on concentration camp inmates to gain insights into human physiology.

Both groups believe the correct ethical approach would be to find alternate sources for stem cells. Indeed, lab techniques have been identified that could stimulate growth and specialization of stem cells extracted from adult tissues, bone marrow or umbilical-cord blood. However, scientists say those stem cells aren't biologically equivalent to the ones found in embryos and are less capable of evolving into the desired tissue.

Experts believe the debate over ethics will continue but that new scientific discoveries will gradually make the potential applications of stem cell research overshadow the moral reservations. Arthur Caplan, director of the Center for Bioethics at the University of Pennsylvania, predicts patient-advocacy and disease-related interest groups will besiege undecided lawmakers with evidence that stem cell research can create such medical miracles as virus-free blood or help repair spinal-cord damage until the politicians give in. "That lobby, I think, will overwhelm moral reservations," Caplan said. [10]

Should stem cell research be eligible for federal funding?

To patient-advocacy groups, Michelle Puczynski is a living argument for federal funding of stem cell research. The 15-year-old from Toledo, Ohio, was 13 months old when she was diagnosed with juvenile diabetes. Since then, she has taken 16,500 injections of insulin simply to survive. The advocates, who invited Puczynski to a Washington news conference in May, say the government should bankroll research into how stem cells can be grown into insulin-producing pancreatic cells. Such cells could then be injected into Michelle's body to begin reversing the debilitating condition.

"Events in the lab are overcoming the fear of the unknown," says Daniel Perry, executive director of the Alliance for Aging Research and head of Patients' Cure, a Washington-based coalition of 35 patient organizations advocating federal funding. "This debate needs to include the voices of people who face tragic and catastrophic illnesses — conditions that potentially could be relieved."

But Congress has been leery about giving its blessing to new varieties of developmental biology. The 105th Congress took up a measure to ban a process known as somatic cell nuclear transfer that could be used to

* The letter was signed by Margaret Farley, a Roman Catholic nun and professor of Christian ethics at Yale University Divinity School; Nancy Duff, a Presbyterian theologian and associate professor at the Princeton Theological Seminary; Rabbi Elliott Dorff, professor of philosophy at the University of Judaism in Los Angeles; and Abdulaziz Sachedina, an Islamic scholar at the University of Virginia.

Stem Cells' Unlimited Potential

Researchers believe that human embryonic stem cells can be grown into a variety of body parts, enabling them to fight many common afflictions.

Cells Derivable From Stem Cells	Target Diseases
Insulin-producing cells	**Diabetes**
Nerve cells 	**Stroke, Parkinson's disease, Alzheimer's disease, Spinal cord injury**
Heart muscle cells 	**Heart attacks, Congestive heart failure**
Liver cells	**Hepatitis, Cirrhosis**
Blood cells	**Cancer, Immunodeficiencies**
Bone cells 	**Osteoporosis**
Cartilage cells 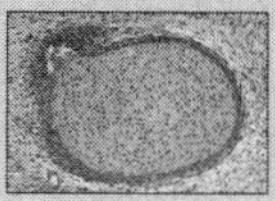	**Osteoarthritis**
Eye cells	**Macular degeneration**
Skin cells	**Burns, Wound healing**
Skeletal muscle cells	**Muscular dystrophy**

Source: Geron Corp.

create a human embryo. The process involves replacing the nucleus of an egg cell with another cell that wouldn't multiply if left in its original state. The remaining part of the egg cell can "program" the new nucleus to multiply. Scientists believe the process could help them clone cells that could treat cancer, heart disease and other conditions, but lawmakers expressed serious concerns about creating carbon copies of living or dead people. The Senate finally voted against taking up the bill because it was too broadly written. [11]

Defenders of stem cell research this year tried to insert a measure in a Senate spending bill that would have permitted government-supported research on spare stem cells donated by couples who went through in-vitro fertilization. But the provision was stripped out by Sen. Arlen Specter, R-Pa., chairman of the Senate Appropriations subcommittee that controls NIH's budget, who said the issue should be decided outside the budget process. Specter and Senate Majority Leader Trent Lott, R-Miss., indicated they will introduce legislation in February to define the conditions for federally supported stem cell research. [12]

The 1995 congressional funding bars the use of federal money for research in which embryos are "destroyed, discarded or knowingly subjected to risk, injury or death" but doesn't specifically mention stem cells. One key question surrounding the ban and its effect on the current research is whether stem cells can develop into embryos on their own and, thus, should fall under the funding ban. The answer appears to be "maybe."

Scientists at the University of Toronto in 1993 grew entire mice out of stem cells. But the scientists first wrapped the stem cells in an envelope of genetically modified cells that couldn't grow into part of the fetus but helped the stem cells attach to the wall of the female mouse's uterus. Without this kind of artificial protection, many scientists believe the stem cells alone aren't capable of evolving into a person. [13]

"Embryonic stem cells on their own can't make certain embryonic tissues, they can't form an embryo and we aren't cloning here," says John Gearhardt, director of the division of developmental genetics at the Johns Hopkins School of Medicine. He is the scientist who coaxed stem cells isolated from the gonads of aborted fetuses into becoming nerve cells.

But Gearhardt points out there are

different kinds of stem cells. He believes the ones he and the University of Wisconsin's Thomson isolated are "pluripotent" stem cells, meaning they are capable of becoming a wide array of human tissues but cannot become cells of the placenta or other tissues needed for implantation in the womb.

However, the scientists can't be sure. That is because very early in development, an embryo is also believed to possess "totipotent" stem cells that can form every kind of cell in the body. The researchers can't test whether the cells they isolated are totipotent because it would involve injecting the stem cells into another embryo to create a test environment to determine whether the cells retain all of their developmental powers. That would conflict with virtually all accepted ethical guidelines.

Rep. Dickey, the author of the congressional funding ban, says that such uncertainties are precisely why the ban should be applied to stem cells. He says scientists should study stem cells in animals and in less controversial adult cells without getting involved in politically volatile embryo research. He adds NIH's preliminary indications that it will fund stem cell research are a deliberate attempt to flout the law.

"Any NIH action to initiate funding of such research would violate both the letter and spirit of the federal law banning federal support for research in which human embryos are harmed or destroyed," Dickey wrote Secretary of Health and Human Services Donna E. Shalala in May.

Dickey has numerous allies. Sen. Sam Brownback, R-Kan., calls the research "immoral, illegal and unnecessary," adding, "there are better, more promising avenues to follow in order to continue our fight against some of the diseases with which we are battling." Brownback issued a highly critical position paper on stem cell research this summer that was endorsed by Catholic and Protestant anti-abortion leaders.

Despite the passionate feelings, political realities are thwarting the critics from enacting legislation. Dickey in September indicated he would draft an amendment to NIH's fiscal 2000 spending bill that would have extended the ban to stem cells. But he was talked out of the move by House Majority Whip Tom DeLay, R-Texas, who was seeking to eliminate controversial amendments in an effort to speed up the budget process. The fight will likely continue during the next Congress.

"Congress is crossing a moral Rubicon, and the people fighting the abortion wars see [stem cell research] as a kind of proxy for the fight over when does life begin," says the Alliance for Aging Research's Perry. "We're taking a middle-of-the-road approach and hoping NIH will release its guidelines soon so we can develop a funding policy through an honest, thorough and open process."

Reuters/Brendan McDermid

The use of human embryonic stem cells in medical research is rekindling the debate over whether fetuses should be considered human beings. Above, abortion foes from Operation Rescue protest at an abortion clinic in Niagara Falls, N.Y., last April.

Are the potential benefits of stem cell research being oversold?

A hiker suffers a serious heart attack in a remote part of a national park. By the time he reaches a hospital, only one-third of his heart is still working. Eager to return to active life, he provides doctors with a sample of his skin cells, which are then injected into specially prepared, donated human eggs. The eggs are grown in a lab for a week, developing into early-stage embryos that yield stem cells that are a perfect genetic match for the patient. Doctors grow the stem cells into heart-muscle cells, inject them into the patient and watch as the new cells begin to replace old damaged ones. Before long, the patient is restored to health.

This hypothetical scenario — outlined recently in *Scientific American* magazine by Roger Pedersen, a stem cell researcher at the University of California at San Francisco — illustrates the tremendous potential for therapeutic cures arising from stem cell research. If it were possible to control how stem cells differentiate into body parts, Pederson writes, the resulting cells could potentially help repair damage from Parkinson's disease, diabetes and other debilitating conditions that result from the death or damage of one or several cell types.[14]

But observers caution there are huge scientific hurdles ahead, and that significant health benefits from the current research may not be seen for decades, if ever. In particular, some worry that researchers — under pressure to produce and deliver results for politicians, potential investors and the public — may be hyping the field's potential before they even know whether stem cell-based transplantation works in humans.

"I hate to be the skunk at the garden party, but the probability of success simply isn't guaranteed," says Charles Jennings, editor of *Nature Neuroscience*, a scientific journal. "The brain, for example, has a hundred-billion neurons in an incredibly complicated array, firing 10 to 100 actions every second. You just can't expect to go patch up the holes in it with cellular putty-filler."

Jennings and others question whether stem cell researchers are moving too quickly toward human clinical trials without fully understanding the underlying science and possible risks. Without knowing precisely what kind of brain cells govern certain neurological functions, for example, the skeptics say it will be difficult to pinpoint a cure for Parkinson's disease — a progressive disorder characterized by the loss of dopamine-producing neurons in the brain. It also will be hard to recruit patients for trials on potential therapies. To test the efficacy, scientists will need one group that receives transplanted cells and another control group that receives a placebo. But skeptics question how many people will be willing to volunteer to have holes drilled into their heads or needles injected into their brains, on the chance they may receive an unproven treatment.

"Neural transplantation is quite risky," Jennings says. "And once the new cells are implanted, it's difficult to monitor physiological changes because you can't just decide to biopsy that part of the brain. It raises major concerns."

Some patient advocates have elected to remain silent on stem cell research until the outcome of experiments and the political debate become clearer. The American Cancer Society last summer pulled out of the Patients' Cure coalition, reportedly over internal policy disagreements. The organization also had received a letter from Cardinal William Keeler of Baltimore asking the cancer society to reconsider its membership. Officials denied that pressure from the Roman Catholic Church influenced their decision, saying they were conducting their own analysis of the issue and at some point in the future would issue a policy statement. [15]

Even some lawmakers generally sympathetic to scientific causes are openly expressing reservations about endorsing a major government role in stem cell work. Specter describes the issue as "fuzzy" — intriguing because of the medical potential but also fraught with troubling legal and moral implications. "I don't think you can rush to judgment on it," he says. "This is obviously on the cutting edge."

Most scientists acknowledge there are concerns but defend pushing forward, saying stem cell research is doing more than just promising future cures. It also is offering insights into events that can't be studied directly in the human embryo. The University of Wisconsin team, for example, has observed how stem cells differentiate into the three primary "germ lines" in the body, and subsequently into arrays of tissue cells, including cartilage, bone, muscle and neural and gut cells. Understanding these steps will yield new insights into birth defects, infertility and miscarriage, according to Thomson. And testing how specific, differentiated cells respond to certain drugs will allow researchers to sort out which medications are helpful or harmful. [16]

"We're not just a bunch of cowboys looking to stick strange cells into the heads of people," says Ronald McKay, a leading stem cell researcher and chief of the laboratory of molecular biology at the National Institute of Neurological Disorders and Stroke in Bethesda, Md. "This work has appeal to many different segments of the scientific community because stem cells give us a tool to look at very complex cellular functions."

Many researchers in the field are now focusing on chemicals that can act as growth factors and stimulate stem cells to produce specific kinds of cells. Researchers at Washington University School of Medicine in St. Louis, for example, found that the vitamin A derivative retinoic acid seems to stimulate a set of genes in stem cells to make them produce neurons while inhibiting genes that trigger other types of cell formation. [17]

Gearhardt of Johns Hopkins and other prominent researchers take pains to note that stem cell work is not a new, hype-driven branch of science but builds on more than a half-century of pioneering work in developmental biology. Viewed in this context, he says it is reasonable to expect careful, steady progress, but no breathtaking applications overnight.

"Our work is simply an extension of work that's gone on for decades," Gearhardt says. "We're taking discoveries that go back to the 1930s and '40s and just applying them to humans." ■

BACKGROUND

Early Breakthroughs

Scientific breakthroughs like the discovery of penicillin and the

Chronology

1960s *Biologists studying mice begin to postulate how "master cells" existing in embryos can create different kinds of tissue. However, they can't isolate the cells. Meanwhile, other types of fetal research yield a vaccine against measles and improved treatment of blood diseases.*

1970s *Embryo research accelerates and becomes a public issue.*

1973
The U.S. Supreme Court recognizes the constitutional right to abortion in *Roe v. Wade.*

1975
The U.S. Department of Health and Human Services (HHS) bars research on live fetuses but allows studies on dead fetuses or their tissues if permitted by state law.

1980s *Scientists continue their studies and begin transplanting fetal tissue. Anti-abortion groups oppose the use of biological materials from aborted fetuses.*

1981
Researchers in England and the United States derive stem cells from mouse embryos at an early stage. This allows them to begin developing cultures in laboratories to prompt the stem cells to form certain tissues.

1988
Scientists at the University of Colorado perform the first fetal tissue transplant on a patient with Parkinson's disease. HHS imposes a moratorium on federal funding of fetal tissue transplant research.

1990s *New discoveries offer a detailed view of early human development — and fan controversies.*

1993
Scientists at the University of Toronto announce they grew an entire mouse from individual stem cells extracted from mouse embryos. The experiment proves stem cells can grow into an entire healthy organism. President Clinton, in one of his first acts as president, removes prohibitions on fetal tissue research.

1994
A panel of experts convened by the National Institutes of Health (NIH) concludes that public funds should be spent on embryo research, as long as the embryos in question were not created strictly for research purposes. President Clinton soon after announces that his administration will forbid taxpayer funding for research with human embryos, regardless of their source.

1995
Congress incorporates language in the spending bill that funds NIH forbidding taxpayer funding for research with human embryos, regardless of their source. The ban is included in subsequent annual spending bills. University of Wisconsin researchers isolate the stem cells of a monkey and discover unique properties inherent to primates.

November 1998
Scientists at the University of Wisconsin and Johns Hopkins University announce that they isolated human embryonic stem cells for the first time.

Jan. 19, 1999
NIH Director Harold Varmus announces the federal government can pay for some stem cell research, as long as publicly funded researchers don't grow the cells themselves.

May 4, 1999
Geron Corp., in Menlo Park, Calif., forms an alliance with the Roslin Institute of Scotland to blend stem cell research with the cloning technology that produced Dolly the sheep in 1997.

June 28, 1999
The National Bioethics Advisory Commission recommends that federally funded scientists be allowed to extract stem cells from human embryos, as well as conduct research on embryos derived by others.

Aug. 18, 1999
The American Association for the Advancement of Science endorses private and public research on stem cells, citing the potential medical benefits to individuals.

polio vaccine have long given Americans hope that other still common afflictions such as cancer, heart disease and mental illness could be stopped, too. In fact, progress has come painfully slow. Consider that when President Richard M. Nixon signed the National Cancer Act in 1971, marking the official declaration of war on the disease, many scientists believed they were within a decade of curing or controlling the disease. Nearly 30 years later, scientists are still learning the basic underpinnings of the disease and how to prevent specific cancers. [18]

It is precisely because of this incremental nature of scientific research that the isolation of human embryonic stem cells is both a watershed event and only the latest development in nearly a half-century of research into human tissue growth and transplantation. It may take many more decades — if ever — before the knowledge is harnessed into practical therapies that allow the body to replicate parts of itself.

The idea of a "master cell" that could prompt many kinds of tissue growth began to gain currency in the 1960s, when scientists noticed that cancerous cells in mice could form several different types of tissue. The discovery had limited research applications, however, and scientists for nearly two decades were unable to create non-cancerous, self-renewing stem cells from mouse embryos.

In 1981, researchers at the University of Cambridge in England and the University of California at San Francisco were able to derive stem cells from mouse embryos at an early, 100-cell stage. This allowed scientists to begin tinkering with cultures that could allow the cells to multiply. They also were able to combine mouse stem cells with separate embryos, giving rise to a genetically hybrid mouse. But the researchers soon learned there were major differences in developmental biology between mice and humans, leading to research on higher mammals.

In 1995, the University of Wisconsin's Thomson isolated the stem cells of a monkey. The work was notable because Thomson soon noticed unusual characteristics as he closely examined the behavior of stem cells. For instance, he found that primate stem cells quickly differentiated into various tissues unless they were grown in tissue culture dishes along with a special type of mouse cell called a "feeder cell" that prevents them from specializing. Scientists don't yet understand how the feeder cells work — a hurdle that will have to be overcome if they are ever to generate enough tissue for commercial purposes. [19]

Thomson subsequently applied his primate stem cell extraction technology to spare embryos from fertility clinics, which enabled him to perform the first successful extraction of human stem cells in February 1998. Around the same time, Johns Hopkins' Gearhardt also isolated and cultured human stem cells. Gearhardt's work arose out of two decades of research on how genetic errors give rise to Down's syndrome, a condition that occurs when one of an embryo's chromosomes copies itself once too often.

"It feels great [to be first], but it's just the beginning," Thomson says. "Up until this point, we've had no way to study questions about human development during the early weeks so we can see all of the critical decisions being made in the body plan. This gives us a nice source of material to study."

The University of Wisconsin and Johns Hopkins each patented the respective extraction techniques the scientists used and then licensed them to Geron. The biotech company believes it could be on the cusp of a financial bonanza if the stem cells can be harnessed to provide anti-aging products. But company President Okarma acknowledges this will involve much more research, including developing a much better understanding of human development. [20]

Unanswered Questions

One big question is why are stem cells so active in embryos but hardly in evidence after birth? Each of the body's cells carry the organism's unique genetic code imprinted in DNA and, theoretically, could use it to create replacement tissue during adulthood. But other than regenerating skin cells and occasionally mending some bone fractures, the human body outside of the womb typically does not take advantage of this option. In contrast, salamanders and certain other animals can regrow tails and limbs. [21]

Another focus is the cellular mechanism that shuts off stem cell division, which centers on the portion of a chromosome called a telomere. Cells are born with a length of telomere that gets shorter each time a cell divides. Conventional human cells divide about 50 times, then die of old age — a driving factor in the broader phenomenon of human aging. However, Geron scientists have perfected a way of building telomeres back up with an enzyme called telomerase. Scientists using the enzyme have been able to make stem cells divide 200 times or more, creating healthy cells that could increase the life span. But it's still unclear whether they can make enough cells to save a patient suffering from the late stages of conditions such as Alzheimer's disease or cirrhosis of the liver.

Longer term, stem cell research could be used to replace a human

Religious Views Vary on Stem Cell Research

Stem cell research, and the broader issue of using fetal tissue for biomedical purposes, has prompted a broad spectrum of religious views. The following sampling is culled from a one-day workshop organized by the National Bioethics Advisory Commission last May at Georgetown University.[1]

■ **Catholicism** — Roman Catholics view human life as a continuous progression from single-cell embryos to death, according to Edmund D. Pellegrino, director of the Center for Clinical Bioethics at Georgetown University Medical Center. Catholics therefore object to extracting stem cells from aborted fetuses or spare embryos from fertility clinics, believing that those who do are destroying the equivalent of a human being. They also are highly skeptical about designating just those embryos that are past a certain stage of development as human beings, viewing the practice as arbitrary.

A differing view is offered by Margaret Farley, a Catholic nun and professor of Christian ethics at Yale University Divinity School. Farley believes a case can be made for stem cell research and raises the possibility that embryos in their earliest stages of development may not constitute an individual human entity. She believes the break point may be when the embryo develops the first signs of a nervous system and can begin to respond to its surroundings, usually around 14 days after conception.

■ **Judaism** — Jewish law doesn't bestow legal status on embryos outside the womb. Moreover, it doesn't recognize fetuses as a human beings until they emerge from the uterus, regarding them during the first 40 days of gestation "as if they were simply water," according to Rabbi Elliot Dorff, professor of philosophy at the University of Judaism in Los Angeles. Therefore, current stem cell research is permissible, and even in keeping with the Jewish tradition of accepting both natural and artificial means to overcome illness. Judaism still prohibits abortions except when absolutely necessary, but it wouldn't frown on using stem cells extracted from a fetus to save other people's lives if the abortion were performed for sufficient reason.

■ **Islam** — Islamic law doesn't provide a universally accepted definition of "embryo" or define specifically when the fetus becomes a moral-legal being, according to Abdulaziz Sachedina, professor of Islam in the department of religious studies at the University of Virginia. A majority of Shiite and Sunni scholars divide pregnancies into two stages by the end of the fourth month, when they believe ensoulment takes place. Therefore, Sachedina says, research using stem cells from early-stage embryos is an act of faith in God, so long as the purpose is to improve human health.

■ **Eastern Orthodox** — This faith has a long tradition of encouraging medical healing but believes it should be done according to God's will, not our own, according to Demetrios Demopulos, pastor at Holy Trinity Greek Orthodox Church in Fitchburg, Mass. Therefore, embryos shouldn't be sacrificed in experiments, no matter how worthy the goal is. Demopulos says the prohibition on research using human embryos should be upheld in the public sector and even extended to the private sector.

■ **Protestantism** — Protestant faiths are split on stem cell research. Gilbert C. Meilaender Jr., a Christian ethicist at Valparaiso University in Indiana, says using stem cells from aborted fetuses or spare embryos is an example of the strong using the weak. Society is trying to benefit some members at the expense of others who have already been condemned to die, in this view.

However, Ronald Cole-Turner, a professor of theology at the Pittsburgh Theological Seminary and chair of the United Church of Christ committee on genetics, believes stem cell research should continue because it promises great benefit. His major concern is that the medical benefits will be distributed only by means of the market and won't be available to underprivileged members of society.

[1] See "A Look At . . . Science and Religion," *The Washington Post*, June 13, 1999, p. B3.

body's faulty genes with healthy DNA. Biologists currently perform gene therapy by loading the healthy DNA onto viruses that provide a means of transport. However, the body's immune system often rejects these treatments. This has frustrated medical efforts to weed out recessive genes that cause conditions like sickle-cell anemia. However, stem cell-based gene treatments have the potential to be far more efficient because they could carry the patient's own DNA with only the undesired, recessive gene altered. With stem cells' capacity to multiply, some genetic diseases that are now incurable could be defeated. However, such techniques would likely prompt a new debate over medical ethics because they would essentially alter human heredity.[22]

Oversight System

The prospect of stem cell researchers tinkering with human genetics has prompted differing views of how far the government should go in regulating the field. If federal funding for stem cell research is approved, the AAAS believes existing government agencies can oversee potential applications of the technology. The Food and Drug Administration would have the authority to regulate the development and use of human stem cells used as biological products to diagnose, treat or cure a disease. Similarly, the National Bioethics Advisory Commission and the separate Recombinant DNA Advisory Committee could work with physicians, patient disease groups, religious leaders, Congress and funding agencies like NIH to assure that appropriate safeguards are in place, the AAAS says.

The bioethics commission believes there should be a system of national oversight supplemented by local independent review boards to ensure that research can proceed under specific conditions. The ethics panel believes supervision of scientists who derive stem cell lines should begin at the local level so the university or other sponsoring institution and other interested parties take responsibility for ensuring the researchers' ethical conduct. The local boards also could review consent documents and oversee the sharing of research materials with foreign institutions.

On a national level, the ethics panel is urging HHS to establish a national oversight panel of scientists and representatives from other fields to ensure that research is conducted in an ethically acceptable manner. "In an ethically sensitive area of emerging biomedical research, it is important that all members of the research community, whether in the public or private sectors, conduct the research in a manner that is open to appropriate public scrutiny," the ethics panel says in its report endorsing federal funding of stem cell research.

Echoing some of the panel's conclusions, Dartmouth ethics expert Green says, "We need to have federal funding of this research, but the best researchers have to remain under open scrutiny as they continue to develop the field. Scientists have to be aware of the need to draw ethical lines, and that people [opposed to their work] aren't just a bunch of medieval anti-Copernicans." ■

CURRENT SITUATION

Startling Discovery

Until recently, most scientists dismissed the notion that transplanting brain cells could cure serious head injuries or neurological disorders such as Alzheimer's and Parkinson's diseases. Now they are reconsidering the possibilities in light of some startling new evidence.

Researchers in Sweden and the United States over the past year have uncovered pathways in which the brain produces a small but consistent number of new nerve cells, contradicting the long-held belief that the adult brains of humans and other primates can only lose cells, not gain them. [23] At the center of the activity are neural stem cells that can grow into a wide variety of brain cells.

The news was startling because scientists previously thought that the complexity of the human brain prevented the constant production of new cells; essentially, the addition of extra cells would only disrupt the organ's orderly flow of electrical signals. But researchers working with adult macaque monkeys found that stem cells appear to stimulate creation of new nerve cells in the fluid-filled ventricles deep in the brain. The new cells then migrate over a week or more to the cortexes, where they subsequently send out connections to other nerve cells. The researchers now are trying to interrupt production of the new cells to see if the animals' behavior changes.

"Doctors might . . . be able to stimulate stem cells to migrate into areas where they usually do not go and to mature into the specific kinds of nerve cells required by a given patient," neuroscientists Gerd Kempermann and Fred H. Gage of the Salk Institute for Biological Studies in La Jolla, Calif., wrote recently in *Scientific American*. "Although the new cells would not regrow whole brain parts or restore lost memory, they could, for example, manufacture valuable amounts of dopamine [the neurotransmitter whose depletion is responsible for the symptoms of Parkinson's disease] or other substances."

The findings have inspired a new burst of research into the brain's functions, long one of the biggest mysteries in biology. But while the discoveries ignited popular interest and inspired news headlines such as "Can I Grow a New Brain?" researchers caution that the brains of Alzheimer's victims and stroke patients don't appear to try to repair themselves, indicating the regenerative efforts may not be enough to overcome the most serious brain injuries. And they dismiss the futuristic scenario of whole-brain transplants as virtually impossible due to the sheer number of cells and the complex ways they are arrayed. [24]

If the latest research continues to appear promising, scientists expect to give animals various tests and learning tasks to see whether they can influence the stem cells to channel brain cells to various parts of the organ. One study performed on rats showed that if the rodents were trained in tasks involving a brain part called the hippocampus, which influences learning, memory and emotion, more new cells migrated to the part.

Key Questions About Stem Cells and Embryos

Following are some of the questions being raised by ethicists and other concerned Americans about current embryo research:

Why is so much attention being focused on stem cells? Scientists for decades knew that the cells existed, but only recently have been able to isolate them in laboratories. Watching how the cells differentiate into body parts gives researchers the best glimpse yet into the mysteries of early human development. Furthermore, learning how to "train" the cells to evolve into desired tissue could bring a host of promising new medical treatments. But some religious leaders and anti-abortion groups oppose the practice of extracting the cells from embryos and aborted fetuses, which they believe have the same moral status as a human being. Moreover, they worry that scientific advances may prompt researchers to clone embryos strictly so they can be tapped for their stem cells.

Can't scientists obtain stem cells from another source? Yes. Stem cells can also be extracted from adult tissue or from biological materials like umbilical cord blood. However, biologists say these stem cells are different from the ones that are extracted in the embryonic stage and display less of a tendency to differentiate. Thus, their usefulness in research is limited. Opponents of embryonic research say federal money should be directed toward finding new uses for this variety of stem cells.

Isn't there already a ban on using embryos in federally funded research? Yes. President Clinton and Congress have both forbidden taxpayer funding for research with human embryos, regardless of their source. However, lawmakers have also enthusiastically supported research on fetal tissue, as long as investigators don't have a connection with the abortion that provides the tissue source. This has created a curious dichotomy and made it more difficult for lawmakers to sort out whether stem cells actually fall under a funding ban, and whether Congress even has the legal authority to weigh in on the research.

Will stem cell research eventually allow people to clone themselves? It's not inconceivable. However, most experts believe stem cell technology will be primarily used to generate an endless supply of spare parts, such as heart muscle tissue, bone or cartilage. It also could be used in tandem with gene therapy to eliminate undesirable genetic traits in a person that give rise to diseases. That poses a new set of ethical questions, such as are we creating a new bioengineered subspecies of man.

Why are Geron Corp. and other biotechnology companies so interested in the field? Some of the companies want to turn people's ordinary cells into stem cells, then treat them so they can replicate indefinitely. This could provide a source of replacement tissue for deteriorating and diseased tissue and help reverse the aging phenomenon. Other companies want to study how stem cells differentiate to prevent miscarriages and birth defects or help infertile people conceive children.

While stem cells are showing new promise for brain research, they simultaneously are being shown to have less-than-anticipated utility in other areas of medicine. New research is showing that a cancer treatment consisting of high doses of chemotherapy accompanied by stem cell transplants may be no better than ordinary chemotherapy for women with advanced stages of breast cancer. [25]

The regimen was thought to be effective for patients whose breast cancer had spread to other parts of the body. Aggressive chemotherapy would kill the tumor, along with the undesired side effect of killing healthy bone marrow. Afterward, rapidly dividing stem cells previously filtered from the patient's blood would be transplanted back into the body to take up the bone marrow's function and grow new blood cells. Breast cancer is the primary reason such "autotransplants" are now performed. However, a recent study of 1,188 women with metastatic breast cancer treated in North America, Brazil and Russia found the treatment could not reverse the disease in the most serious cases.

"Everyone expected this to be the miracle," says Mary Horowitz, scientific director of the Autologous Blood and Marrow Transplant Registry of North America at the Medical College of Wisconsin and one of the study's authors. [26] She said the results would help breast cancer patients make more informed decisions, perhaps discouraging those with slim odds of survival from trying it as a last resort. ■

OUTLOOK

Future of Cloning

As science continues to challenge people's definitions about what it means to be human, it is likely that more controversial public policy decisions will be made surrounding issues of birth and death. Embryo research provides an important crucible, in the opinion of many experts, because it challenges society to find ethically acceptable applications of its rapidly expanding knowledge about the human condition.

The scientific discoveries surrounding stem cells actually are less of a concern to many people than the potential applications of the work — and what limits should be placed on the technology. Such worries were raised last fall when a Worcester, Mass., company, Advanced Cell Technology, created stem cells by cloning the nucleus of a human cell into a cow egg. The cow eggs are much easier to obtain than human eggs and could provide a more practical way of transplanting a person's own stem cells to replace damaged tissue.

However, critics worried that the company had created a strange cow-human hybrid and called for new controls on cloning technology. Company officials responded that the cells in question could not possibly grow into a viable creature and that they were strictly interested in biomedical applications.[27]

Cloning is the likely "next step" in the stem cell saga.

Science journalist Gregg Easterbrook, a senior editor at *The New Republic*, writes that, while stem cell research is in itself scientifically promising, it really serves as a means of accumulating the technical know-how to eventually clone human beings. This may not be something to necessarily fear, in Easterbrook's view, because cloned individuals could not be created as anything but babies and would still be subject to the character-shaping effects of their generation's particular upbringing. Dictators would not be able to make carbon copies of themselves, as has been suggested in popular fiction and Hollywood movies. Instead, there would be beneficial effects, such as providing the means for infertile people to conceive and raise children.

"We should not be squeamish about cloning just because it mixes reproduction, technology and the new," Easterbrook writes. "Owing to the stem cell breakthrough, there now stands the prospect that our children will not only live healthier lives but that their children will be the final generation of Homo sapiens, supplanted by Homo geneticus or whatever comes next. . . . If all goes well, the advent of control over our own cells might offer our grandchildren many things we would wish for them."[28]

AFP Photo/Luke Frazza

Harold Varmus, director of the National Institutes of Health, discusses the possible uses of stem cells during hearings before the Senate Appropriations Subcommittee on Labor, Health and Human Services and Education on Dec. 2, 1999.

Bioethicist Dorothy C. Wertz of the Shriver Center in Waltham, Mass., predicts human cloning will become a treatment primarily used in fertility clinics, similar to egg donation or in-vitro fertilization. She notes both of those techniques were initially criticized as ethically unacceptable but gradually became commonplace.

"The most likely use of cloning would be by people who cannot have children in the usual way and who want to have a child who is like themselves, rather than inviting an unknown stranger's genes into the family," Wertz wrote in the *Gene Letter*, a scientific journal. "Eventually, cloning on a limited basis will become an accepted reproductive technology."[29]

But such acceptance won't begin without more clear-cut rules governing reproductive medical research. President Clinton in 1994 prohibited federal funding from being used to clone human beings, saying, "each human life is unique, born of a miracle that reaches beyond laboratory science."[30] Federally funded scientists could extract DNA from fetal tissue until late last year, when NIH temporarily banned work that used fetuses to create stem cells. Meanwhile, it isn't clear whether Congress or any federal agency can regulate embryo research done in private — or the donation of embryos from thousands of fertility clinics.

Dartmouth ethics expert Green says a widespread ban on cloning and similar technologies won't work because no one will get all countries to agree on what is ethical science. People who want to seek out cloning procedures will travel to countries where the technology is tolerated, while research in countries with cloning bans will be stifled. He believes it's better to permit such research but subject it to strict ethical guidelines.

"There's a deep ethical need to draw lines, defend human life but not just be ignorant and resistant to

At Issue:

Should the federal government fund research involving stem cells derived from embryos remaining after infertility treatments?

yes

National Bioethics Advisory Commission

FROM "ETHICAL ISSUES IN HUMAN STEM CELL RESEARCH," EXECUTIVE SUMMARY, SEPTEMBER 1999.

Research involving the derivation and use of human ES [embryonic stem] cells . . . remaining after infertility treatments should be eligible for federal funding. An exception should be made to the present statutory ban on federal funding of embryo research to permit federal agencies to fund research involving the derivation of human ES cells from this source under appropriate regulations that include public oversight and review. . . .

The current ban on embryo research is in form of a rider to the appropriations bill for the Department of Health and Human Services (DHHS), of which the National Institutes of Health (NIH) is a part. The rider prohibits use of the appropriated funds to support any research "in which a human embryo [is] destroyed, discarded or knowingly subjected to risk of injury greater than that allowed for research on fetuses in utero." . . .

The ban, which concerns only federally sponsored research, reflects a moral point of view either that embryos deserve the full protection of society because of their moral status as persons or that there is sufficient public controversy to preclude the use of federal funds for this type of research. . . . In our view, the ban conflicts with several of the ethical goals of medicine and related health disciplines, especially healing, prevention and research. These goals are rightly characterized by the principles of beneficence and non-maleficence, which jointly encourage pursuing social benefits and avoiding or ameliorating potential harm.

Although some may view the derivation and use of ES cells as ethically distinct activities, we do not believe that these differences are significant from the point of view of eligibility for federal funding. That is, we believe that it is ethically acceptable for the federal government to finance research that both derives cell lines from embryos remaining after infertility treatments and that uses those cell lines.

Although one might argue that some important research could proceed in the absence of federal funding for research that derives stem cells from embryos remaining after infertility treatments (i.e., federally funded scientists merely using cells derived with private funds), we believe that it is important that federal funding be made available for protocols that also derive such cells.

Relying on cell lines that might be derived exclusively by a subset of privately funded researchers who are interested in this area could severely limit scientific and clinical progress.

no

Richard M. Doerflinger

Associate director for policy development, Secretariat for Pro-Life Activities, National Conference of Catholic Bishops

FROM TESTIMONY BEFORE THE SENATE APPROPRIATIONS SUBCOMMITTEE ON LABOR, HEALTH AND HUMAN SERVICES AND EDUCATION, DEC. 2, 1998.

In discussions of human experimentation, the researcher's temptation is to think that if something technically can be done it ethically should be done — particularly if it may lead to medical benefits or advances in scientific knowledge. A civilized society will appreciate the possibilities opened up by research but will insist that scientific progress must not come at the expense of human dignity. When this important balance is not maintained, abuses such as the Tuskegee syphilis study or the Cold War radiation experiments become a reality.

In deciding whether to subsidize various forms of human experimentation, legislators are not merely making an economic decision to allocate limited funds. On behalf of all citizens who pay taxes, they are making a moral decision. They are declaring that certain kinds of research are sufficiently valuable and ethically upright to be conducted in the name of all Americans — and that other kinds are not.

By such funding decisions, government can make an important moral statement, set an example for private research and help direct research toward avenues which fully respect human life and dignity as they seek to help humanity. . . .

A remaining question involves the other avenues for advancing stem cell research, or for advancing the medical goals to which this research is directed, without exploiting developing human beings. Last year, for example, we proposed to Congress that there may be nine promising alternatives to the use of cloning to provide stem cells — and eight of these seem to involve no use of embryonic stem cells at all.

In the same few weeks that these embryo experiments garnered such national attention, significant advances were reported in two of these areas: the use of growth factors to help hearts grow new replacement blood vessels and the use of stem cells from placental blood to treat leukemia and other illnesses.

It would be sad, indeed, if Congress' attention were to focus chiefly on those avenues of research which garner front-page news precisely because they are ethically problematic. Instead, Congress has an opportunity to use its funding power to channel medical research in ways which fully respect human life while advancing human progress.

change," Green says. "If we can't develop a basic understanding of things like stem cells, it will be an impediment to our progress as a society." ■

FOR MORE INFORMATION

Center for Bioethics and Human Dignity, 2065 Half Day Road, Bannockburn, Ill. 60015; (847); 317-8180, www.bioethix.org. This non-profit group is spearheading opposition to federally funded stem cell research on material derived from embryos, arguing the work entails destroying human beings.

Geron Corp., 230 Constitution Dr., Menlo Park, Calif. 94025; (650) 473-7700; www.geron.com. This biotechnology company funded the recent research into stem cells and licensed patents from the academic institutions where the work took place. It hopes to combine stem cell technology with cloning to create new anti-aging products.

National Institutes of Health, 1 Center Dr., Building 1, Suite 126, Bethesda, Md. 20892; (301) 496-2433; www.nih.gov. This branch of the Department of Health and Human Services supports and conducts biomedical research into causes and prevention of disease and would oversee federally supported research on stem cells and embryos. It now is devising guidelines on stem cell research.

Patients' Coalition for Urgent Research, 2021 K St., N.W., Suite 305, Washington, D.C. 20006; (202) 293-2856. This coalition of more than 30 patient advocacy and disease groups actively lobbies for federal funding for embryo and stem cell research, citing myriad potential health benefits.

Notes

[1] See David Masci, "The Cloning Controversy," *The CQ Researcher*, May 9, 1997, pp. 409-432.

[2] See Adriel Bettelheim, "Biology and Behavior," *The CQ Researcher*, April 3, 1998, pp. 289-312.

[3] For background, see Roger A. Pedersen, "Embryonic Stem Cells for Medicine," *Scientific American*, April 1999, pp. 68-73.

[4] See *CQ Almanac 1995*, pp. 11-55-11-60.

[5] See Charles Marwick, "Funding Stem Cell Research," *Journal of the American Medical Association*, Vol. 281, No. 8, p. 224 (Feb. 24, 1998).

[6] Testimony before the Senate Appropriations Subcommittee on Labor, Health and Human Services and Education, Dec. 2, 1998.

[7] For background, see Sarah Glazer, "*Roe v. Wade* at 25," *The CQ Researcher*, Nov. 28, 1997, pp. 1033-1056.

[8] See National Bioethics Advisory Commission, "Ethical Issues in Human Stem Cell Research," September 1999.

[9] From the Andre Hellegers Lecture, Kennedy Institute of Ethics, Georgetown University, December 1998.

[10] Quoted in Paul Smaglik, "Stem Cell Scientists Caution Clinical Applications Remain Years Away," *The Scientist*, Vol. 12, No. 23, Nov. 23, 1998, p. 1.

[11] See *CQ Almanac 1998*, p. 19-3.

[12] See Paulette Walker Campbell, "Fight Over Stem Cell Research Is Unlikely to Tie Up Spending Bill," *The Chronicle of Higher Education*, Oct. 15, 1999, p. A36.

[13] See Gina Kolata, "When a Cell Does an Embryo's Work, a Debate Is Born," *The New York Times*, Feb. 9, 1999.

[14] Pedersen, *op. cit.*

[15] See "Two Republicans Endorse Stem Cell Research Funding," Reuters, July 30, 1999.

[16] See Nicholas Wade, "Scientists Cultivate Cells at Root of Human Life," *The New York Times*, Nov. 6, 1998, p. A1.

[17] Pedersen, *op. cit.*

[18] See Adriel Bettelheim, "Cancer Treatments," *The CQ Researcher*, Sept. 11, 1998, pp. 785-808

[19] See Rick Weiss, "Stem Cell Discovery Grows Into A Debate," *The Washington Post*, Oct. 9, 1999, p. A1.

[20] See testimony before the Senate Appropriations Subcommittee on Labor, Health and Human Services and Education, Dec. 2, 1998.

[21] See Gregg Easterbrook, "Medical Evolution," *The New Republic*, March 1, 1999, pp. 20-25.

[22] Easterbrook, *op. cit.*

[23] See Gerd Kempermann and Fred H. Gage, "New Nerve Cells for the Adult Brain," *Scientific American*, May 1999, pp. 48-53.

[24] See David Brown, "Brain Regenerates Cells, Study Says," *The Washington Post*, Oct. 15, 1999, p. A2.

[25] See Philip A. Rowlings et al., "Factors Correlated With Progression-Free Survival After High-Dose Chemotherapy and Hematopoietic Stem Cell Transplantation for Metastatic Breast Cancer," *Journal of the American Medical Association*, Vol. 282, No. 14, (Oct. 13, 1999), pp. 1335-1343.

[26] Quoted in Marilynn Marchione, "Study Shows When Treatments for Breast Cancer Are Most Effective," *Milwaukee Journal Sentinel*, Oct. 13, 1999, p. 1.

[27] See Faye Flam, "Despite Objections, Hopes Rise for Material That Could Repair Human Ailments," *The Philadelphia Inquirer*, June 27, 1999.

[28] Esterbrook, *op. cit.*

[29] See "Conclusion: The Future of Cloning," *Gene Letter*, Vol. 3, Issue 1, August 1998

[30] See "Human Cloning Discouraged," The Associated Press, March 4, 1997.

Bibliography

Selected Sources Used

Books

Cook-Deegan, Robert, *The Gene Wars: Science, Politics and the Human Genome*, W.W. Norton, 1996.
The former director of the Biomedical Ethics Advisory Committee gives a firsthand account of efforts to launch the Human Genome Project and the politics surrounding the biomedical research community.

Lyon, Jeff, and Peter Gorner, *Altered Fates: Gene Therapy and the Retooling of Human Life*, W.W. Norton, 1996.
Two reporters explore the possibility of curing thousands of genetic conditions by transplanting properly coded genes for defective ones. They also explore the genetic roots of aging, psychology and intellect and discuss the biomedical possibilities from cloning human embryos.

McGee, Glenn, (ed.)., *The Human Cloning Debate*, Berkeley Hills Books, 1998.
Numerous perspectives on the promise and challenges from cloning in the wake of the 1997 creation of Dolly, the sheep. Special emphasis on the philosophical implications of human cloning.

Quesenberry, Peter J. (ed.), *Stem Cell Biology and Gene Therapy*, Wiley-Liss, 1998.
A somewhat technical look at stem cell research and gene therapy. Topics covered include preparations of stem cells, possible therapies and new clinical applications.

Articles

"Comment: Stem Cell Research," Mary Woodard Lasker Charitable Trust, 1998.
A comprehensive review of key scientific, policy and ethical issues surrounding stem cell research and how it may relate to the 1995 congressional ban on embryo research. Included are perspectives from politicians, religious leaders, government officials and prominent scientists.

Hoffman, Paul, "Can I Grow A New Brain?" *Time*, Nov. 8, 1999, p. 94.
This portion of *Time*'s Visions 21 series focuses on the use of neural stem cells to repair damage and even recreate parts of the brain.

Marwick, Charles, "Funding Stem Cell Research," *Journal of the American Medical Association*, Vol. 281, No. 8, p. 224 (Feb. 24, 1999).
Account of how the National Institutes of Health decided it can fund research on stem cells from human embryonic tissue, despite the statutory ban on research involving human embryos.

Pedersen, Roger A., "Embryonic Stem Cells for Medicine," *Scientific American*, April 1999, pp. 68-73.
A stem cells researcher at the University of California at San Francisco details the far-reaching potential of stem cell-derived therapies if scientists are able to coax the cells into making perfectly matched tissues for transplantation.

Smaglik, Paul, "Stem Cell Scientists Caution Clinical Applications Remain Years Away," *The Scientist*, Nov. 23, 1998, p. 1.
Biologists still have years of work before patients will receive either stem cell-derived tissue transplants or stem cell-based gene therapy, scientists agree.

Wade, Nicholas, "Scientists Cultivate Cells at Root of Human Life," *The New York Times*, Nov. 6, 1998, p. A1.
The first report of the isolation of human embryonic stem cells and an early analysis of the thicket of ethical and legal questions that the discovery prompted.

Weiss, Rick, "Stem Cell Discovery Grows Into A Debate," *The Washington Post*, Oct. 9, 1999, p. A1.
The new field of stem cell research faces major tests in the laboratory and in Congress as the fiscal 2000 federal budget cycle draws to a close.

Reports

American Association for the Advancement of Science, "Stem Cell Research & Applications," Aug. 18, 1999.
After hearing from scientists, religious leaders and government officials, the association endorses federally funded stem cell research, saying it holds enormous potential for contributing to mankind's understanding of basic human biology.

National Bioethics Advisory Commission, "Ethical Issues in Human Stem Cell Research," September 1999.
A White House ethics panel examines pressing issues surrounding stem cell research and concludes the federal government should have a funding and oversight role.

5 Social Security

ADRIEL BETTELHEIM

Like many people of her generation, Claire McGrath is a loyal defender of Social Security. The 73-year-old retired state employee from Syracuse, N.Y., relies on her $916 monthly benefit check to pay her bills and views the program as a vital safety net for the elderly. But she worries it may not be around for her grandson after politicians get through tinkering with it.

"I think we need to leave it the way it is because Social Security at least guarantees you'll receive something," McGrath says. "I know there are a lot of strains on the system, and I don't blame younger people for griping about how much they have to pay into it. But I'd hate to see them monkey with it and put us at more risk."

For decades, lawmakers who considered changing the Social Security system risked incurring the wrath of seniors like McGrath and being accused of dismantling one of America's great domestic-policy programs. So few tried that the program became known as the "third rail" of American politics; touching it meant instant death.

Lately, however, Social Security could more accurately be described as a lightning rod for far-reaching reform proposals.

Since President Clinton proposed a national dialogue on Social Security in his State of the Union address in January, Congress and Washington think tanks have been abuzz with proposals to overhaul the 63-year-old retirement system. Many plans envision "privatizing" the system by redirecting some payroll taxes from retiree benefits to individual savings plans tied to stocks and bonds. Others call for gradually raising the retirement age or even allowing the government to invest the Social Security trust fund in the stock market.

Updated by Adriel Bettelheim, June 1, 2000.
Originally published October 2, 1998, as "Saving Social Security."

The shift in thinking is vindication for conservative and libertarian think tanks and politicians, who have long argued the present system operates like a Ponzi scheme because it relies on current workers to pay retirees more than they paid into the system. With an unprecedented 76 million baby boomers born from 1946-1964 expected to retire over the next 30 years, even some liberal Democrats concede the so-called pay-as-you-go system can't survive in its present form.

"The energy in social policy right now is to privatize," says Sen. Daniel Patrick Moynihan, D-N.Y., one of Social Security's staunchest defenders, who stunned many in March by proposing a reform plan that featured personal retirement accounts. "Any effort to keep Social Security will have to acknowledge the people who want to get rid of it, the people who are saying that government is taking your money and cheating you." [1]

Clinton and Republicans and Democrats in Congress discussed the future of the program at various town hall meetings and in other settings but could not agree on a package of comprehensive reforms. The concept of privatization resurfaced as a theme in the 2000 presidential race between George W. Bush, who favored the idea, and Al Gore, who defended the existing system.

However, recent volatility in the stock market is dampening enthusiasm for quick legislative solutions. Stock market gyrations tied to financial turmoil in Russia and Asia led former Labor Secretary Robert B. Reich, among others, to predict the privatization movement will stall. "Social Security was supposed to be an insurance system," he says. "The stock market is anything but an insurance system. It's more like a casino."

The calls for change are largely driven by predictions that the Social Security trust fund will face a severe financial squeeze early in the next century. According to actuarial projections, the trust fund will go broke by 2037, when benefits paid to retirees exceed revenues the system collects. The incoming money — from payroll taxes paid by current workers and their employers and the self-employed plus the interest Social Security earns on the government bonds it buys — will only be enough to pay 75 percent of all old-age, disability and survivors' benefits due. To pay the remainder, the government will have to increase taxes, cut benefits, restrict Social Security eligibility or make more drastic changes. [2]

But the reform movement is driven by more than just accounting projections. Changing public attitudes about pensions and investments have made many baby boomers and younger workers receptive to the idea of a retirement system based on accumulated wealth. The popularity of employer-sponsored 401(k) retirement plans, fueled by the bull market of the 1990s, has already tied thousands of current workers' retirement sav-

The Graying of America

In 1900 only one in 25 Americans was 65 or older, but by 2040 the number will be one in four, putting a severe strain on the Social Security system.

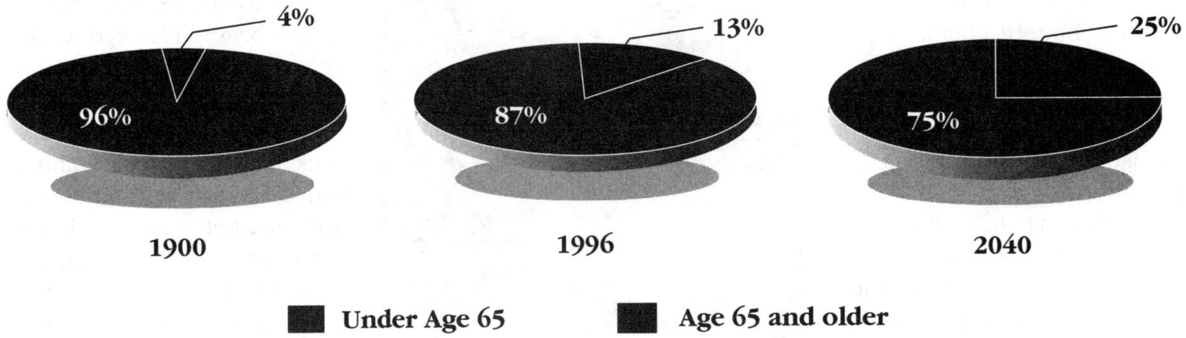

Source: National Commission on Retirement Policy, "Can America Afford to Retire: The Retirement Security Challenge Facing You and The Nation," January 1998

ings with personal investments. Surveys also suggest younger workers are so disillusioned with government that many don't expect Social Security to even exist by the time they retire. A 1994 poll by the youth advocacy group Third Millennium found more respondents ages 18-34 believe UFOs exist than believe they will ever receive Social Security.

"To maintain anything approximating today's opportunities for seniors in the future — and to do so without doing a massive injustice to younger people — we must make major changes in a system of public entitlements that now passes out huge windfalls regardless of need," says Peter Peterson, a former secretary of Commerce under President Richard M. Nixon and a member of the Clinton administration's Bipartisan Commission on Entitlement and Tax Reform.

Privatization advocates like Peterson argue that setting up personal retirement accounts would raise money to finance Social Security without raising taxes. The Concord Coalition, a Washington interest group that advocates policies to eliminate the federal budget deficit, estimates workers could earn 7 percent returns by investing the money they now pay into Social Security taxes in stocks instead. Currently, the Social Security taxes that aren't immediately applied to paying retirees' benefits are invested in safe but low-yielding U.S. Treasury bonds that only pay 1 or 2 percentage points above inflation. The Concord Coalition analysis assumes stocks will perform at their 75-year historical averages. [3]

However, skeptics respond there's no guarantee the stock market will continue to perform at record highs and note workers' retirement savings could be threatened by market downturns lasting several years. Additionally, placing a portion of payroll taxes into private accounts reduces the amount of money available for traditional, guaranteed monthly Social Security benefits. Privatization foes such as John Sweeney, president of the AFL-CIO, say cutting guaranteed payments would be especially harmful to low-wage workers, who have less to invest and now count on a Social Security benefit formula that is weighted in favor of people with low career earnings.

Several other proposals would attempt to reduce the strain on Social Security by raising the retirement age, which is already scheduled to increase to 67 from 65 by 2022. Raising the age further to 70, as has been proposed in several plans, means Social Security wouldn't have to start paying recipients as soon and, presumably, won't have to pay them for as long. Supporters of the idea say a higher retirement age additionally corresponds to Americans' increased longevity. In 1935, when Social Security was created, the average 65-year-old was expected to live about 12.6 more years. Today, that person is expected to live 17 additional years; by 2040 he will be expected to live at least 19 more years. [4]

Yet another reform plan would allow the Social Security system to invest its trust fund in common stocks, instead of the low-yielding government bonds. Advocates say the plan could boost the system's investment returns while preserving the core elements of the government's social safety net. However, polls show many current workers and senior citizens are skeptical about the government's ability to make the right investment decisions and worry about whether the proposal would leave Washington with too much influence on pri-

Understanding Social Security

• Social Security, created in 1935, is the most costly item in the federal budget. The program provides old age, survivors' and disability insurance to approximately 45 million Americans. Workers and their employers fund the system by each paying payroll taxes equivalent to 6.2 percent of covered wages. Self-employed individuals pay 12.4 percent of taxable self-employment income. The Internal Revenue Service collects the taxes and deposits the money in government-administered accounts known as the Old Age and Survivors and Disability Insurance Trust Funds (OASDI).

• The payroll tax revenues are used to pay benefits to those people currently collecting Social Security pensions, a system known as pay-as-you-go. Any excess of taxes over benefit payments is invested in U.S. Treasury bonds, which earn the average rate of return on publicly traded government debt. Social Security taxes also pay for Medicare, the national health program for the elderly. The services that are funded come under Medicare Part A and include inpatient hospital care and skilled nursing care.

• Workers who accumulate enough earnings credits become eligible to receive a Social Security pension when they reach the early retirement age of 62 or become too disabled to continue working, regardless of age. A workers' dependent spouse and non-adult children can draw monthly survivors' pensions when the worker dies.

Social Security is a defined-benefit pension program, meaning each pension is based on the worker's average career earnings and on the age when the worker or worker's dependents first obtain the pension. The exact amount of the payout is determined by a formula that is codified in law and updated annually to reflect changes in wages and consumer prices.

The Social Security benefit formula is deliberately tilted in favor of workers with low career earnings, those who face an unusually high risk of becoming totally disabled and married couples with only one wage earner. It's possible to make generous payments to these groups because high-wage workers, unmarried and childless workers and dual-income married couples receive less favorable treatment under the system.

• In 1999 the Social Security system took in $526.6 billion from payroll taxes and bond interest and paid out $385.8 billion in benefits to retired and disabled workers and their families. Administrative costs totaled $3.3 billion. The system's assets increased $133.7 billion, to $896.1 billion, and the trust funds earned $55.5 billion on bond interest.

• The trust funds are expected to be able to cover benefits until 2037. However, the 2000 Social Security trustees' report states that benefit payments will begin to exceed income in 2015, and that interest income on the Treasury bonds will be able to keep total income ahead of benefit payments only until 2025. After that, the trust funds will begin to decline until they are exhausted by 2037. At that point, tax revenue will be able to pay only three-quarters of benefit obligations.

Sources: Social Security Administration, Brookings Institution

vate capital markets.

It is difficult to predict whether or when any substantial reforms will be passed. Recrafting a landmark social policy program is a difficult and politically risky task for any new president to lead with. It is more likely that Congress and the White House will continue to seek incremental reforms. One such change took place in the spring of 2000, when the Republican-controlled Congress and the Clinton administration agreed to scrap the program's earnings limit. The Depression-era provision was designed to keep older workers out of the workforce at a time of high unemployment by reducing their Social Security benefits for every dollar they earned above a designated threshold. At the time of the debate, more than 800,000 seniors between the ages of 65 and 69 were losing $1 in Social Security benefits for every $3 they earned beyond $17,000. Lawmakers argued an unusually tight labor market and the federal budget surplus created ideal conditions for lifting the limit without appearing fiscally irresponsible.

And with financial markets around the world subject to turbulence, Republicans and Democrats alike may have second thoughts about replacing the present system with individual accounts that rely on the compounded earnings power of stocks and bonds.

"Clearly there are a lot of risks to achieving reforms," says Social Security Commissioner Kenneth Apfel. "But the best thing for the American people is the long-term security of the Social Security system, and continuing to talk about the need for reform . . . is centrally important."

"Nobody really knows what will happen until the president weighs in," says Henry Aaron, senior fellow in economic studies at the Brookings Institution. "Everyone is putting [reform proposals] on the table. But it's up to the administration to really start the debate by coming up with its own plan. And making large-scale changes to social programs is often fraught with peril."

Elderly Are Fastest-Growing Group

Due to the large number of aging baby boomers, Americans 65 and older are the fastest-growing segment of the population.

Population Growth by Age Group (1995-2040)

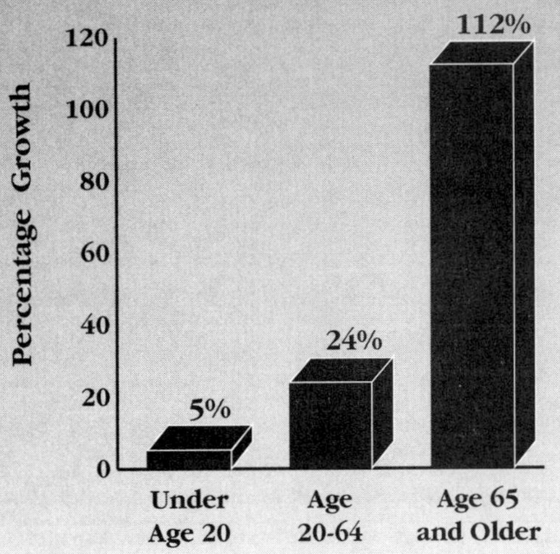

Source: National Commission on Retirement Policy, "Can America Afford to Retire: The Retirement Security Challenge Facing You and The Nation," January 1998

As policy-makers mull further changes to the system and debate its long-term viability, here are some questions they are asking:

Can the existing system survive without major reforms?

The early architects of Social Security and many liberal Democrats shake their heads at all of the recent proposals to change the system. Most believe Social Security can continue to provide a safety net for retirees and their survivors if Congress simply makes minor adjustments, occasionally raising payroll taxes or recalculating the way benefits are paid. Doing so would address concerns about the system's solvency while still guaranteeing that benefits will stay about where they are.*

"The key point is that we do not need to panic," says Rep. Jerrold Nadler, D-N.Y., who disputes the view that the system is in a financial crisis. "Social Security's status as a risk-free, guaranteed benefit program is, for millions of Americans, the sole protection against economic misfortune. That rock-solid dependability must be preserved."

Liberals like Nadler accuse reform advocates of manufacturing a crisis that pits generation against generation. They note Social Security has worked well for more than 60 years by providing a steady stream of monthly payments that beneficiaries can rely on. It also has helped lift millions of seniors out of poverty.

Robert Myers, who served as chief actuary of the Social Security Administration from 1947–1970 and deputy commissioner in 1981 and 1982, says the existing system was never intended to be an unchangeable or contractual program. Rather, its founders envisioned Congress stepping in to make gradual adjustments when demographic or accounting factors necessitated change.

"Fixing the system is easy, but finding the fix that fits both politically and socially is trickier," Myers says. "Some 80 million retirees and survivors will be drawing benefits from Social Security the year it is supposed to go broke. Having them go from a check one month to nothing the next is unthinkable. The country wouldn't stand for it."

Defenders of the system say the projected financial squeeze isn't as severe as it's being depicted. They note Social Security actuaries project the program's deficit will amount to only 1.89 percent of taxable payroll over the next 75 years. While that's a cause for some concern, program advocates argue a small tax increase could solve the problem without having to take more dramatic steps like raising the retirement age or making steep reductions in benefits.

One remedy being discussed among liberal House Democrats would increase the wage base for Social Security taxes by lifting the cap on income subject to the payroll tax. The current payroll tax is 12.4 percent (with 6.2 percent each paid by workers and employers) on salaries up to $68,400 a year. About 6 percent of all workers make more than that ceiling. Other options include extending the program to many federal government workers who are now excluded from participating in it, or means-testing the program to avoid paying benefits to rich retirees.

Another proposal to save the present system comes from Robert Ball, who served as commissioner of Social Security from 1962-1973. Ball believes the government can leave benefits roughly at current levels without significant new taxes as long

* The average monthly benefit for a retired worker in 1999 was $780.

Would Women Lose Under Privatization?

The image of an elderly widow living off her monthly Social Security check is frequently evoked in debates over the retirement program. However, the push to overhaul the program is raising questions over whether older women would gain or lose under a privatized system.

Some backers of the current system contend privatization could unfairly penalize professional women and dependent spouses for a variety of reasons. First, working women typically earn less than men (71 cents for every $1, on average), and therefore have fewer funds to invest in individual savings accounts. Dependent spouses, who now are automatically entitled to 50 percent of their husband's benefits, would lose the subsidy in a system based on private accounts. Some private savings plans may also be set up to expire at death, leaving the survivor without benefits.

Women also tend to be more averse to risk when making investment decisions. A recent U.S. General Accounting Office study of women in their prime earning and saving years shows they are less likely than men to invest in potentially higher yielding but risky assets like stocks, meaning they would be at risk of having accumulated less in their private accounts at retirement. [1]

"Difficult as Social Security reform will be, our most serious challenge may be ensuring fair treatment for women," says Rep. Barbara B. Kennelly, D-Conn., ranking Democrat on the House Ways and Means Subcommittee on Social Security.

However, privatization proponents say the current system needs to be changed precisely because it cheats working women by using an outdated "model family" with a stay-at-home mom. When the program was designed, few married women worked outside the home. If benefits were to be calculated based on one's own work history, millions of widows would be left with nothing when their husbands died.

In 1939, lawmakers introduced spousal benefits that automatically entitled a woman to half of her husband's benefits, regardless of whether she had paid payroll taxes. Thus a woman who worked all of her life and paid a significant amount of taxes into the system could receive a smaller retirement benefit than a woman who never worked, even if their household incomes are identical.

The American Society of Actuaries estimates that for a family making $68,400 in pre-retirement income, a stay-at-home spouse would be entitled to a Social Security widow's benefit of $1,354 per month, compared with $1,082 for a widow who brought home half of the household income.

The disparity becomes even larger for couples who make a combined $34,200 in annual pay. The actuaries project the stay-at-home spouse would receive a monthly check of $1,082 on being widowed, while a wife who brought home half of the income draws a monthly benefit of only $674.

Cato Institute analyst Darcy Ann Olsen adds that working women typically qualify for smaller payouts under the present system because they frequently leave the work force for extended periods of time during their peak earning years to raise children. [2]

The Cato Institute endorses a system that consists entirely of individual investment accounts, in which a husband and wife split contributions and ownership of the accounts 50-50. If both spouses contributed 10 percent of earnings to the accounts, the think tank calculates all categories of women would be better off than under Social Security or hybrid plans that provide guaranteed minimum benefits and individual accounts.

Gender equity will continue to receive attention as the privatization debate pushes forward, particularly because two-thirds of working women have no other pension plan. "Too many women, minority women in particular, will find themselves about to enter a financial prison when they retire," says Jeffery Lewis, executive director of the Teresa & H. John Heinz III Foundation, a Washington public policy think tank.

[1] See U.S. General Accounting Office, "Social Security Reform: Implications for Women's Retirement," Dec. 31, 1997. For background, see Sue Kirchhoff, "Proposed Fixes Could Widen Social Security Gender Gap," *CQ Weekly*, April 25, 1998, pp. 1038-1044.

[2] See Darcy Ann Olsen, "Greater Financial Security for Women with Personal Retirement Accounts," Cato Institute Briefing Paper No. 38, July 20, 1998.

as it finds a way to earn higher returns on its reserves. His solution would allow Social Security to invest about 40 percent of its trust funds in stocks, 30 percent in corporate bonds and the rest, as now, in government debt.

"There is no financial crisis in Social Security. But it does need adjustment," Ball says. He notes other federal retirement systems such as the Federal Employees Thrift Plan place their reserves in stocks without placing participants at significant risk. [5]

However, critics say such proposals ignore the fact that the program's fiscal situation is only expected to get worse as more baby boomers begin to collect benefits. Adding to the concerns are worrisome demographic trends. Medical advances are making people live longer, meaning they will collect benefits longer. People also are retiring earlier. And the tendency toward smaller families is moving the nation closer to zero population growth, meaning there will be fewer workers in coming generations to pay taxes into the system. [6]

Daniel Mitchell, a senior fellow

Low-Income Retirees Depend on Social Security

Social Security accounted for nearly 90 percent of the retirement income received by low-income Americans in 1995.

Sources of Income for Americans, 1995

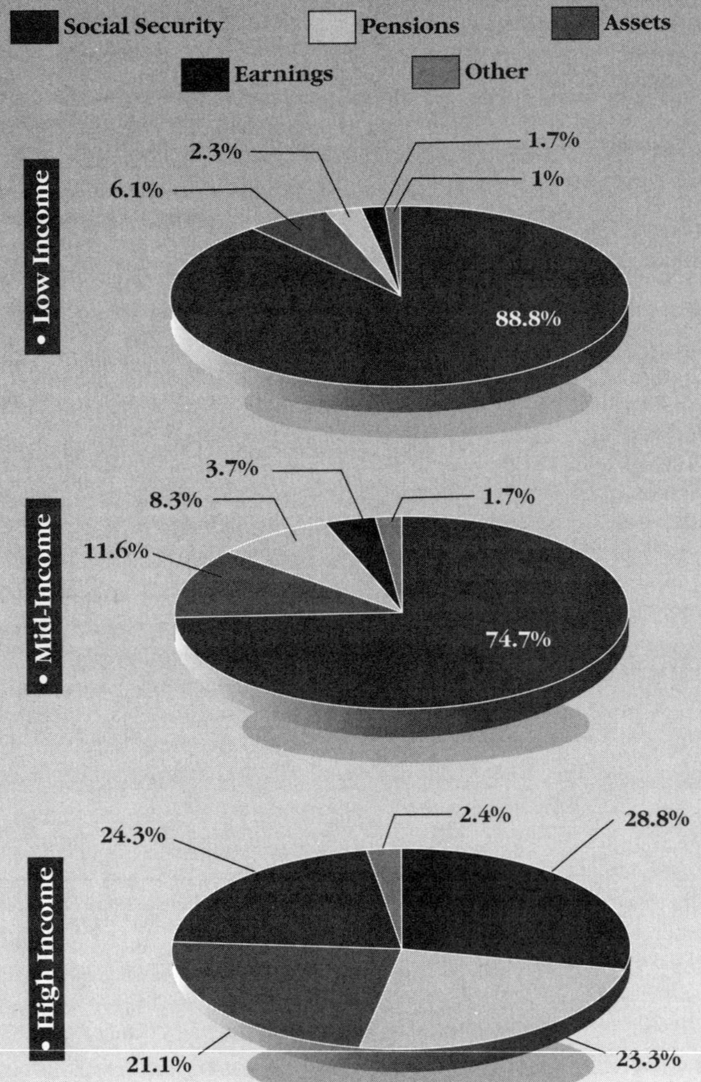

Percentages do not add to 100% due to rounding

Source: National Commission on Retirement Policy, "Can America Afford to Retire: The Retirement Security Challenge Facing You and The Nation," January 1998

at the conservative Heritage Foundation, says the combined effect will be staggering liabilities for the Social Security trust funds. By 2075, the last year for which the Social Security Administration projects numbers, Mitchell calculates the trust funds will have a total shortfall of $20 trillion, adjusted for inflation. Eliminating the future deficit would require a 54 percent increase in payroll taxes, a 33 percent reduction in benefits or a combination of those approaches. Mitchell argues it would be far easier to scrap the current system of promised benefits in favor of a privatized system based on accumulated wealth.

"The important question to ask is whether the price tag for moving to a private system is smaller or larger than the amount of money lawmakers would have to find to fulfill the promises of the current system," Mitchell says.

Another important question is whether young workers are willing to pay higher payroll taxes to maintain the government's promise to retirees. Supporters of higher taxes say even a 2 percent hike will leave American workers paying less for social insurance than many Western Europeans.

However, Third Millennium Executive Director Richard Thau is alarmed by the prospect of ad infinitum payroll tax increases to keep the Social Security trust fund in balance. "The idea of raising taxes further just to fund the existing system isn't going to fly," he says. "The majority of young people believe the real challenge is to pre-fund the system and avoid the demographic tsunami that will come when the baby boomers retire."

Clinton, without endorsing a plan, has voiced concerns about raising payroll taxes. And Moynihan says long-time supporters should face up to reality and enact more forward-thinking reforms now, while the government has a balanced budget and before Social Security's woes become overwhelming. "If we continue to treat this program as the untouchable 'third rail' of American politics, we could find one day in the not very distant future that the system has vanished," he says.[7]

Impact of Shrinking Work Force

There were 3.7 workers per beneficiary in the Social Security system in 1970, but by 2075 the number of workers is expected to have dropped to 1.8, providing less income for the system.

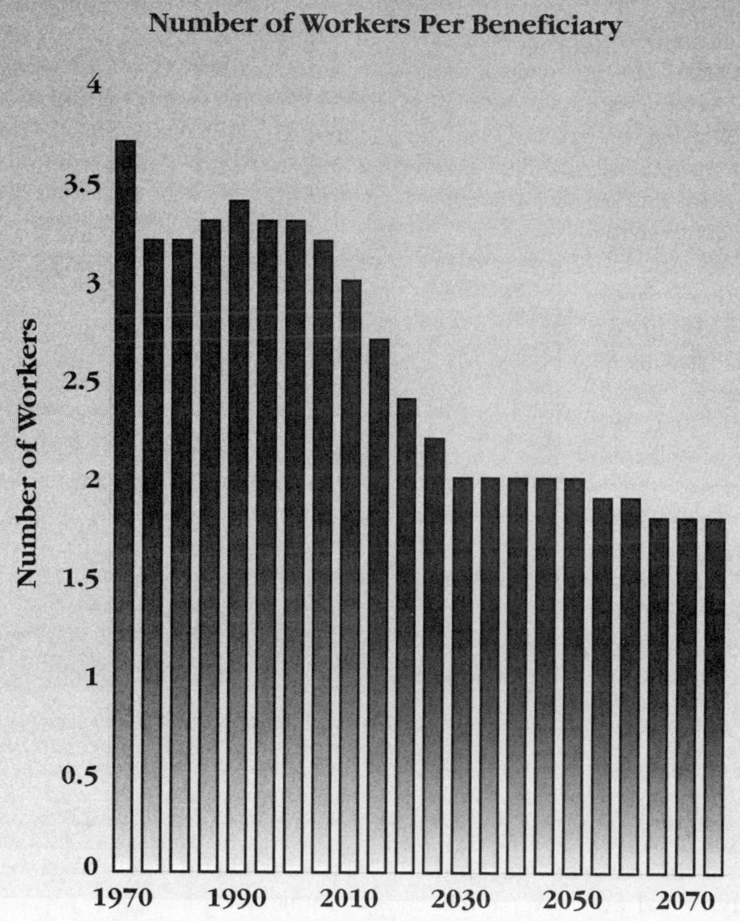

Source: National Commission on Retirement Policy, "Can America Afford to Retire: The Retirement Security Challenge Facing You and The Nation," January 1998

Should individual savings accounts be included in any reforms?

In 1981, the government of Chile decided to replace its financially strapped pay-as-you-go national pension system with a program based on individually owned, privately invested accounts. The results dramatically exceeded expectations.

By requiring all covered or dependent workers who entered the work force after 1981 to place 10 percent of their monthly earnings in a savings account, government leaders boosted the national savings rate nearly threefold and solidified the developing nation's capital and labor markets. Old-age, disability and survivors' pensions in the privatized system paid 50-100 percent more than under the old system.

The bigger payouts, combined with other free-market reforms, have more than doubled economic growth in the developing nation from its historical 3 percent annual pace to an average of 7 percent per year over the past 12 years, according to Jose Pinera, the former minister of labor and now an international consultant on pension reform.[8] Argentina, Australia, Bolivia, Colombia, Mexico, Peru, the United Kingdom and Uruguay, among others, have since shifted to pension systems that rely on private accounts. *(See story, p. 91.)*

Privatization advocates say a similar move by the United States would be economically advantageous, delivering bigger pensions to workers and helping the economy grow faster. Some believe the emphasis on personal savings would have the added feature of encouraging more individual responsibility at a time when the nation prepares for a surge in its elderly population.

"Individual Americans should have a stake in the economy and more control over their own retirement benefits and the timing of when they retire," says Rep. Jim Kolbe, R-Ariz. "When you talk about security of the current system, it's illusory in the sense that you either have the political insecurity that exists today, or you have some kind of an economic risk that exists [in future years]."

Privatization would differ from Social Security in two important ways. First, the amount a worker receives at retirement depends entirely on how much one contributes to the savings plan and how well the investments perform. Put another way, those who set aside more and invest wisely enjoy more comfortable retirements. Secondly, pensions are paid out of an individual's accumulated savings instead of financed by taxes on active workers.

With some 45 million Americans currently collecting Social Security, it would be impossible to immediately switch to a private system. At least a half-dozen pending proposals envision a gradual transformation that would offer young workers the chance to voluntarily invest a portion of their wages into a private system while ensuring that retirees and people planning to retire soon would continue to receive the traditional benefits.

One of the most detailed plans offered so far comes from the National Commission on Retirement Policy, a bipartisan group of lawmakers, economists, actuaries and business executives assembled by the Washington-based Center for Strategic and International Studies. The plan would divert 2 percent of the current 12.4 percent payroll tax into individual savings accounts. Workers could choose among several investment options, including mutual funds tied to stocks. The plan also would increase the retirement age to 70 by 2029. The early retirement age, when people can stop working and receive reduced benefits, would increase to 65 from 62 by 2017.[9]

AARP

President Clinton discusses the Social Security system at a recent forum sponsored by the American Association of Retired Persons (AARP) and the Concord Coalition.

The presumed higher rate of return from private accounts would be offset in reduced guaranteed monthly Social Security payments. But the plan would design the cutbacks to hit the wealthy more than people with lower incomes. It also calls for a minimum benefit — 60 percent of the poverty line for people who have worked at least 20 years, rising to 100 percent for people who have worked at least 40 years — and would allow Social Security recipients to continue working without losing their benefits.

The bipartisan plan is expected to carry weight on Capitol Hill and is cosponsored by Sens. Judd Gregg, R-N.H., John B. Breaux, D-La., and Reps. Kolbe and Charles W. Stenholm, D-Texas. Another well-received centrist proposal is the plan offered by Moynihan and Sen. Bob Kerrey, D-Neb., that leaves the traditional Social Security system more or less intact but would allow workers to set up voluntary personal savings accounts funded by a 2 percent cut in the payroll tax. Workers would be given a number of investment options, all tax-deferred. While details remain to be worked out, employers would likely collect the money and send it to the Social Security Administration, which would oversee the investments.[10]

A 2 percent tax cut isn't enough for some lawmakers and public-policy experts. One far-reaching reform proposal suggests that two-thirds of payroll taxes be diverted to personal investment accounts. The plan is backed by the Cato Institute, a libertarian think tank that has been one of the prime movers behind Social Security reform.

Most budget experts agree that the economic arguments for privatization are valid but say the plans still raise troubling practical questions. One concerns "transition costs." Because money has to be found for existing pension payments at the same time workers will be asked to contribute to new private accounts, Congress would probably have to raise taxes or borrow money to keep both systems financially sound for several decades. The higher taxes would effectively replace the lost payroll taxes that were shifted into the private accounts, according to Brookings Institution senior fellows Gary Burtless and Barry Bosworth.[11]

Privatization critics add that the new system's reliance on market performance creates winners and losers — a radical departure from Social Security's New Deal pledge to guarantee the elderly well-defined benefits. Moreover, it could subject workers' savings to stock market volatility and high fees charged by administrators who run the investment plans.

"With all the turmoil in Asia and Russia right now, we might want to think twice about betting on go-go financial markets," says Sen. Paul Wellstone, D-Minn. "There will always be millions and millions of Americans who depend solely on Social Security for their retirement security." *(See graph, p. 84.)*

Warren B. Rudman, the former Republican U.S. senator from New Hampshire who now chairs the Concord Coalition, acknowledges the debate could be affected by recent stock market volatility. But he says steps could be taken to minimize risks to older workers, perhaps by closing any privatization plan to workers 50 years old and over.

Oddly silent in the current debate are Wall Street investment firms, which stand to gain billions of dollars in management fees if private investment accounts are adopted. Some investment firms that provide both administrative services and investment advice quietly support diverting payroll taxes into personal investments but don't want to visibly lobby and risk being accused of acting out of self-interest. [12]

Other financial service firms are equally worried about the cost of administering thousands of small new retirement accounts, fearing lawmakers will draft new regulations to lessen recipients' investment risk. The concerns have intensified as August's stock market tumble wiped out many investors' recent gains and threatened to give the high-flying mutual fund industry a black eye.

Matthew Fink, president of the Investment Company Institute, the trade group for the mutual fund industry, says investors aren't well-served by extreme proposals on either side of the Social Security debate. Investment firms support a "targeted, moderate approach" that would allow, but not require, workers to invest some portion of their Social Security tax in individual accounts, he says.

Should the retirement age be raised?

It took a generous buyout offer to convince Carrie Cusano to retire before age 70 from her job as a purchasing agent at Southern Connecticut State University in New Haven.

"A lot of us are just old enough to retire but young enough to work, and are quite capable of staying on," says Cusano, now 74. "Raising the retirement age is a good idea because more and more people are working longer."

Many of the plans to overhaul Social Security propose allowing workers like Cusano to remain on the job longer in order to strengthen Social Security's financial solvency. The plans assume that delaying the time when workers collect benefits means the government won't have to pay retirees for as long and can invest some of the money to build up Social Security's reserves. Brookings economist Burtless estimates even a

"The best thing for the American people is the long-term security of the Social Security system, and continuing to talk about the need for reform . . . is centrally important."

— Kenneth Apfel, commissioner, Social Security Administration

one-year increase in the retirement age will result in approximately a 7 percent reduction in an average worker's total lifetime benefits.

Raising the retirement age is nothing new. In 1983, the National Commission on Social Security Reform, headed by current Federal Reserve Board Chairman Alan Greenspan, raised the retirement age as part of a package of reforms designed to save the system. The retirement age will increase in stages from 65 to 67 by 2022, while the early retirement age remains at 62. However, workers who opt out early will get only 70 percent of the full Social Security benefit.

The new bipartisan plan from the National Commission on Retirement Policy proposes taking the Greenspan commission's concept further by raising the early retirement age to 65 by 2017 and increasing the normal retirement age to 70 by 2029. The Moynihan-Kerrey plan would make similar adjustment to the normal retirement age, but not until 2073.

Such plans would reverse an early 1990s trend in which older workers like Cusano were targeted in downsizings and early retirement programs. Indeed, some companies now facing labor shortages are hiring back on a part-time basis the same workers who left several years ago. In 1998, the labor force participation rate for men ages 55 to 64 was 67.5 percent, up from 65.5 percent in 1994. The participation rate for women in the same age bracket has risen steadily since the 1970s and was 50.5 percent last year. [13]

However, allowing workers to stay on the job longer could still pose problems. The U.S. General Accounting Office in July released an analysis saying millions of Americans, primarily in lower-paying blue-collar jobs, are more likely to suffer health problems well into their 60s than contemporaries in white-collar jobs. A delayed retirement age could force them to work in pain or with debilitating conditions, such as arthritis, lung disease or emotional disorders. Some might have to apply for disability benefits, increasing the cost of that program to the government. [14]

Raising the retirement age could also weigh heavily against certain ethnic groups. African-American males, for example, live nearly eight fewer years on average than white males. Raising the retirement age to 70 could prevent large numbers from drawing a pension.

There also is ample evidence that many Americans simply count on retiring early. A majority of workers, 53 percent, now start drawing Social Security benefits at 62. According to one recent analysis, America's post-World War II affluence, more generous Social Security benefits and private pension accumulations have led most workers to expect to spend, on average, one-third of their adult lives in retirement. [15]

University of Minnesota political scientist Lawrence Jacobs has analyzed public opinion polls dating to the 1970s and finds consistent opposition to raising the retirement age, sometimes exceeding 60 percent. Jacobs finds greater support for raising payroll taxes, though few are enthusiastic about that prospect. [16]

"When Americans have been asked to set spending priorities in the federal budget, they have expressed overwhelming support for maintaining or expanding the [Social Security] program," Jacobs says.

Yet Americans, perhaps paradoxically, seem receptive to working at least part of the time they are retired. Eighty percent of 2,001 baby boomers polled in June for the American Association of Retired Persons plan to work at least part time after they formally retire. Thirty-five percent said they would do it mainly for the interest or the enjoyment work provides, 23 percent wanted the money and 22 percent envisioned starting their own business or working full time at a new job or career.

Politicians began to acknowledge these desires in the spring of 2000, as Congress passed, and President Clinton signed, legislation to scrap the limit on how much outside income retirees age 65 to 69 may earn and still collect their Social Security benfits. The so-called "earnings test" was a relic of the Depression, when it was used to discourage older workers from entering the workforce and make room for younger, unemployed workers. Under the rule, individuals ages 65 to 69 lost $1 in benefits for every $3 they earned above an annual limit—$17,000 at the time of repeal. The individuals who lost benefits were compensated with "delayed retirement credits" after age 70. There are no earnings limits for individuals age 70 and above.

A robust economy, federal budget surpluses and a shortage of skilled workers convinced lawmakers they could lift the limit without appearing to be fiscally irresponsible. Some advocates said it would encourage more retirees to re-enter the workforce and remain active without suffering financial consequences. It also would allow U.S. companies to better tap the experience and input of its older workers.

"Given the increased longevity and generally improved health of many retirees, the prospect of an aging society and a slower-growing workforce, it is critical that we find ways to better tap the valuable and underutilized skills of older workers," Jane Baumgarten, a board member of AARP, said at the time.

BACKGROUND

Belated Action

Germany's "Iron Chancellor," Otto von Bismarck, established the first social security system in 1889 to ease the financial pain of unemployment in his increasingly industrialized nation. Many historians suggest the move was less out of compassion for displaced workers than an effort to blunt Social Democratic critics of his military buildup.

Britain, Russia, France, Uruguay, Chile and Japan soon had similar versions of government-run old-age pension programs. Each provided elderly citizens with defined benefits based on strict eligibility rules. The programs were financed by current workers, their employers, or both.

However, retirement plans remained relatively rare in the United States during the first decades of the 20th century. Many in the country viewed social security as a socialistic European import that was out of sync with the Jeffersonian philosophy of self-reliance and minimal government. There were other more practical reasons: Most of the economy was still agricultural, and people could live off the riches of the land. In 1930, only about 15 percent of all workers were covered by any type of retirement plan. [18]

The Great Depression changed the equation. The financial crash wiped out industrial and trade union plans, leaving workers without pensions. Most seniors' savings disappeared in bank collapses. With few other means of support and a dearth of available jobs, many elderly people flocked to New York, Massachusetts and other states with old-age pension programs. Some hard-pressed state governments were forced to cut benefits or refused to accept new pensioners.

Facing mounting political pressure, Congress in 1935 passed the Social Security Act proposed by President Franklin D. Roosevelt, putting millions of retirees under a retirement plan for the first time. Originally, the program only aided retired workers age 65 and above — not their dependents — and was financed by a 2 percent payroll tax that was shared equally by employer and employee on the first $3,000 of wages.

Opposition to the payroll tax at first was intense, leading Roosevelt to shrewdly depict the system as a kind of

Chronology

1930s-1940s
As part of the New Deal, President Franklin D. Roosevelt launches the Social Security system.

1935
Roosevelt signs the Social Security Act, putting millions of workers under a retirement plan.

1937
The Federal Insurance Contribution Act (FICA) requires workers to pay taxes to support the Social Security system.

1939
Congress adds benefits for dependents of retired workers and surviving dependents of deceased workers.

1940
The first monthly benefit check is paid to Ida Mae Fuller, a retired law clerk in Ludlow, Vt.

1950s-1960s
Congress increases Social Security benefits and expands the number of workers covered.

1954
Coverage is extended to farm operators and most farm and domestic workers.

1956
Congress adds disabled workers over age 50 to the program. Women become eligible for benefits at age 62, rather than 65.

1961
Men become eligible to receive early retirement benefits at 62.

1965
Concern about the elderly leads to enactment of Medicare.

1970s ***Congress passes Social Security increases immediately before the U.S. economy falters.***

1975
Annual cost-of-living adjustments passed by Congress take effect, indexing benefits to inflation. The formula overstates the inflation rate by 25 percent, forcing the program to make larger payouts than necessary.

1977
Congress corrects the mistake and increases the payroll tax rate. Social Security is now thought to be actuarially sound.

1980s ***Social Security enters another financial crisis.***

1982
Inflation grows faster than wages, contrary to government projections. For the five years ending in 1982, inflation is more than 50 percent while real wages decline 7 percent. This forces the program to pay out far more than it takes in.

1983
Acting on the recommendations of the Greenspan commission appointed by President Ronald Reagan, Congress cuts benefits, delaying annual cost-of-living increases and gradually increasing the retirement age.

1985
Social Security trust funds are moved "off budget" so that the funds earmarked for the Social Security system can be tracked separately from the rest of the federal budget.

1990s ***Government actuaries predict current taxes are insufficient to cover Social Security benefits when baby boomers retire.***

1994
Social Security trustees predict the trust funds will run out of money by about 2030, seven years earlier than they projected in 1993.

1996
The trustees report the system will begin to run deficits in 2012. All members of a trustees' advisory panel recommend investing some or all of Social Security funds in the private sector.

1998
Congress and the White House continue to grapple with ways to shore up Social Security.

2000s ***Social Security runs out of money.***

2011
The first baby boomers collect benefits.

2037
Social Security system will no longer be able to pay all the benefits promised to retirees.

insurance program that was financed out of "premiums" workers paid for coverage in their old age. In fact, there were no individual accounts where workers' contributions were stashed for their own retirements. Instead, the existing work force was taxed to subsidize the benefits to current retirees. Asked about this discrepancy by an aide, Roosevelt responded, "That account is there so that those sons of bitches up on the Hill [Congress] can't ever abandon this system after I'm gone." [19]

At the time of Social Security's passage, American society was very different from today. There were many more workers than retired people, and the average American was only expected to live to 61, meaning many would never receive a single Social Security check. The result was a windfall for the very first retirees. Ida Mae Fuller, a retired law clerk from Ludlow, Vt., received the first Social Security check — for $22.54 — on Jan. 31, 1940. She had contributed only $22 to the system. At the time of her death 35 years later, her benefits totaled $22,000.

Bettmann/UPI

President Franklin D. Roosevelt signs the Social Security Act in 1935.

Signs of Trouble

Between 1935-1980, Congress gradually expanded the scope of Social Security, covering more people and paying out progressively larger benefits. In 1939, Congress added benefits for dependents and survivors of a deceased worker. In 1950, the program was extended to agricultural workers, the self-employed, members of the armed forces and disabled people age 50 and above. In 1961, President John F. Kennedy pushed through Congress a 20 percent increase in benefits and an early retirement provision that offered payouts and survivor benefits to men at age 62.

The 1970s brought the first signs of trouble, as it became apparent Social Security couldn't finance all the benefits it promised. After decades of robust economic growth and low inflation, growth slowed and prices rose. Demographics also shifted; there had been 16 workers for every retiree in 1950, but by 1970 the figure had fallen to about 3.7. Adding to the problem were automatic cost-of-living increases, introduced in 1972, which indexed Social Security benefits to inflation.

By 1977, Social Security was facing a crisis. President Jimmy Carter and Congress responded by nearly doubling taxes — passing a then-record $227 billion tax increase — and slowing down the growth of future benefits. The changes were billed as long-term solutions. But when the U.S. economy took another downturn in the early 1980s, workers' wages fell and the system faced a second financial squeeze.

In 1982, President Ronald Reagan convened a bipartisan commission to discuss Social Security reforms chaired by economist Greenspan. The commission recommended delaying cost-of-living increases, taxing the benefits of higher-income retirees and gradually increasing the retirement age from 65 to 67 by 2027 — changes that were adopted by Congress in 1983.

Greenspan predicted the reforms would keep Social Security solvent until at least 2068. However, Social Security's trustees now think the trust fund surplus will run out some 30 years sooner — by 2032. The trustees assume wages will grow more slowly than the Greenspan-led commission believed in 1983. Additionally, there are fewer workers and more retirees than when the commission did its work in the early 1980s.

The Greenspan commission also didn't fully recognize that surpluses would temporarily build up in the years before the first baby boomers retire, according to the Congressional Research Service. As a consequence, the opportunity to capture and invest Social Security surpluses to anticipate later deficits didn't even come up for discussion in 1983. [20]

In the late 1980s, it became evident that surpluses were indeed occurring and being used to finance the government's

Many Nations Trying Pension Reform

At least a dozen countries have attempted to overhaul their social security systems in recent years. Here are some of the approaches that have been taken:

• **CHILE** — Gen. Augusto Pinochet installed the world's first privatized national pension system in 1981. It requires those who enter the work force after 1981 to automatically invest 10 percent or more of their wages in an individual retirement account, which isn't taxed until withdrawal. Older workers have the option of remaining in the traditional social security system.

The retirement funds had accumulated $30 billion by last year and were widely credited with solidifying the emerging nation's capital markets. However, in the past year Chile's stock market has lost more than 25 percent in dollar terms due to declining exports to Asia and falling copper prices tied to Japan's economic slowdown. The average retirement fund has declined about 5 percent over the past 12 months, and some economists fear a recession could end years of steady growth.

• **BRAZIL** — In an attempt to streamline the economy and reduce debt, President Fernando Henrique Cardoso tried to reform social security this year by offering a constitutional amendment to raise the retirement age. The Brazilian Congress rejected the proposal in May as labor unions and rivals charged the changes would have penalized manual and unskilled laborers, who tend to enter the work force at younger ages and would therefore be required to work more years.

Officials are pledging to revisit minimum-age requirements for social security after the October elections. Under Cardoso's plan, men had to work until they turned 60 and had been employed for 35 years to qualify for pensions. Women had to be at least 55 and to have worked for 30 years.

• **POLAND** — Legislation is being considered that allows creation of private pension funds with tax-deductible contributions. The criteria for granting disability allowances have also been tightened. The reform plan, similar to Chile's, is making its way through the Polish parliament.

• **GREAT BRITAIN** — A privatization plan begun by Prime Minister Margaret Thatcher in 1988 features two tiers. All workers pay into the basic government pension plan, which provides a defined benefit. But higher-income workers can leave a supplementary government plan or their employers' pension plan and invest their contributions elsewhere, presumably for higher returns.

The restructuring has allowed the British to amass more than $1 trillion in retirement savings while controlling entitlement spending. The system is credited with helping Britain remain more vibrant and economically competitive than many other European countries by providing plentiful capital for British companies through the financial markets. However, individuals have lost billions of dollars by succumbing to high-pressure sales tactics from some financial firms. Some companies are compensating them for losses, but the actions of others have sparked criminal investigations.

• **AUSTRALIA** — The Labor government in 1986 began implementing a retirement system based on mandatory private savings. By 2002, when the system is fully in place, workers will have to set aside 9 percent of their income in designated investment funds. Contributions are now taxed before they are invested in the funds. The coalition government is reviewing its tax code and studying whether it should convert to a tax-deferred system.

Sources: Heritage Foundation, The New York Times, *news reports.*

annual operating budget. Sen. Moynihan tried to correct this by proposing to temporarily roll back payroll taxes, then raise them again after 2015 to meet rising costs, reaching a combined employer-employee Social Security tax of 16.2 percent by 2050. However, Congress never adopted the proposal.

More recently, Social Security actuaries have predicted the payroll tax would have to be even higher than Moynihan suggested to meet costs by the middle of the next century — perhaps in the range of 18-19 percent, according to American Enterprise Institute economist Carolyn Weaver.[21] ■

CURRENT SITUATION

Political Football

In his 1998 State of the Union address, President Clinton urged Congress to deal with Social Security's problems before spending any projected federal budget surpluses. But most observers say the issue is far more complicated than the White House depicts.

Social Security now takes in about $100 billion a year more from payroll taxes and interest income than it pays out in retiree benefits. The big surplus is factored into federal budget forecasts and tends to obscure the deficit that actually is incurred running government programs. The Congressional Budget Office (CBO), for instance, projects an overall federal surplus of $80 billion in fiscal 1999, rising to $251 billion in fiscal 2008.

Congressional Republicans, mainly in the House of Representatives, question the wisdom of keeping such a large reserve and think a portion of the surplus ought to be used to finance tax cuts for working couples, investors and heirs to large estates. But House Democrats and a bipartisan majority in the more cautious Senate believe cutting taxes would ignore the challenge of fixing Social Security before the first baby boomers retire and the program begins to operate in the red. [22]

In reality, the surplus is part of a larger game of accounting sleight-of-hand surrounding the Social Security program. The money from payroll taxes and interest income technically is invested in Social Security's trust funds. But the government really borrows it to cover year-to-year operations. In exchange, it issues the retirement system special Treasury IOU's. When it comes time for Social Security to redeem the claims plus interest, the U.S. Treasury will have to borrow from the public or levy taxes.

As a result, some economists say there is virtually no difference between applying budget surpluses to pay down the overall national debt or using it specifically for Social Security. Many suspect Clinton was really using the Social Security message in the State of the Union to appear fiscally prudent and pressure Republicans not to pass election-year tax cuts.

White House officials disagree with the assessment, saying it is possible to strengthen Social Security's financial position by applying the surplus to it. Gene Sperling, assistant to the president for economic policy and Clinton's point man on Social Security, says the president wasn't seeking a commitment that the surplus be spent in a particular way, just that it be reserved until lawmakers have a better idea of how much is needed to save the system. [23]

"If the surpluses are drained away in the short term [via tax cuts], we're just digging ourselves in a deeper hole," adds Social Security Commissioner Apfel.

Heading into the 2000 presidential elections, Democrats expected to hammer Republicans over their plans to overhaul the system, arguing the GOP is endangering Social Security so that it can pass tax cuts and extend other breaks for the rich. But perhaps the greater risk for Republicans is relying on long-term economic forecasts to make decisions about Social Security reform and tax policy. Even a slightly incorrect assumption about economic growth could mean the real surplus is off by billions of dollars. And global economic uncertainty could lead to more undesirable side effects. The CBO has warned that financial turmoil in regions such as Asia and Russia could hurt export markets and significantly slow U.S. economic growth.

"The energy in social policy right now is to privatize. Any effort to keep Social Security will have to acknowledge the people who want to get rid of it, the people who are saying that government is taking your money and cheating you."

— Sen. Daniel Patrick Moynihan, D-N.Y.

OUTLOOK

Impact on Saving

Many experts say the most enduring legacy of the Social Security debate may be a shift in the way Americans view personal savings. For decades, retirement income was likened to a three-legged stool — a leg for pension, a leg for savings and a leg for Social Security. But with the Social Security system under stress and employer-guaranteed pensions being replaced with 401(k) plans whose size depends on individuals' investment skills, more emphasis is beginning to be placed on personal savings habits.

"There seems to be a certain irrationality at work," says Stanford University economist John Shoven. "If you ask younger Americans, 'Do you think you're going to get anything from Social Security?' they answer, 'I don't think I'm going to get very much.' And if you ask them, 'Are you saving enough?' they answer, 'No. I should be saving 10 percent. I'm only saving 2 percent.' But then if you ask them, 'How well off do you think you'll be when you retire?' The answer is, 'I'll be fine.' " [25]

Indeed, studies show many Generation Xers save very little be-

At Issue:

Will privately invested retirement accounts relieve the financial squeeze facing the Social Security system?

EDWARD H. CRANE
President and CEO, Cato Institute, Washington, D.C.

FROM AN ADDRESS DELIVERED IN PARIS, DEC. 10, 1997, REPRINTED IN* VITAL SPEECHES OF THE DAY, *APRIL 15, 1998.

yes

I believe there is no economic issue facing the world today that is more important than converting public pension programs from pay-as-you-go government-run systems into individually capitalized, privately owned retirement systems. . . .

One of the reasons for the growing popularity of replacing a pay-as-you-go plan with an individually capped, fully funded plan is that Americans seem to intuitively know what is demonstratively true. Namely, that the returns from a privately invested retirement account will be significantly greater than the return one receives on one's alleged "investment" in Social Security. To repeat, in the United States the payroll tax is not invested, just as it's not invested in most social security systems around the world. It goes directly into payouts to current retirees, with whatever excess there may be going to help finance the federal government's deficit spending. The government leaves "Special Treasury Notes" in a so-called trust fund when it purloins these excess funds, but to see that the trust fund is a fraud, one need only consider the options facing the government whether these "bonds" are in the trust fund or not.

In the year 2010 or sooner, by our estimates, the cash flow from payroll taxes will be insufficient to meet the benefits due current retirees. Assuming the government will live up to its obligations (there is good reason to believe it will not, but for the sake of argument we will give it the benefit of the doubt), once the system's cash flow turns negative and the Social Security Administration turns to the national government for help, the government can come up with the necessary funds by: 1) increasing taxes 2) increasing borrowing 3) reducing benefits or 4) reducing other government spending. Now suppose the Special Treasury Notes are presented to the national government by the Social Security Administration for redemption to make up for the shortfall. The government, in order to raise the funds to redeem the bonds is faced with precisely the same four options as if there were no trust fund at all.

Thus, when the American government officials smugly point to the approximately $2 trillion in accumulated special Treasury Bonds that are expected to be in the trust fund by 2010 and tell us that this will help finance the system until 2029 and that therefore there is no crisis, they are being disingenuous, to put it kindly. There is no trust fund in the United States and the crisis is at hand, particularly for younger workers who face the prospect of negative rates of return on their payroll taxes over their entire working lives.

HENRY AARON
Senior Fellow, The Brookings Institution

FROM TESTIMONY BEFORE THE SENATE BUDGET COMMITTEE, JULY 23, 1998.

no

Advocates of private accounts have claimed that the returns to pensioners will be higher under a privatized system than under Social Security. This claim is the exact opposite of the truth for reasons that have been developed cogently in scholarly research and can be expressed simply in non-academic terms. Furthermore, private accounts would expose individual workers to risks that are now broadly shared among workers and across generations.

The logic is straightforward. Payments to support Social Security (or Social Security and private accounts) go for two purposes: to pay Social Security benefits for current or future beneficiaries that exceed reserves (the so-called unfunded liability); and to build reserves [for] future retirees.

Whether to curtail Social Security benefits for the current elderly and those soon to retire is an important issue, but it is entirely independent of the issue of privatization. Whatever decision Congress makes on this divisive issue, current workers will have to pay the same amount for those benefits, whether we retain Social Security in its current form or gradually shift to some alternative. Current workers who support benefits for the current beneficiaries derive no personal financial gain whatsoever from paying those taxes. This situation is the inescapable consequence of decisions made over the past half-century to pay larger benefits to retirees than the payroll taxes paid on their behalf could justify. Paying out those taxes as current benefits rather than retaining them as reserves produced what policy analysts call the "unfunded liability," the obligation to pay benefits to current retirees and to currently active workers in excess of accumulated reserves. We can debate whether or not it was wise to pay those benefits and build up this unfunded liability, but we cannot avoid paying it except by reneging on commitments to current beneficiaries and older workers. On this score, there is no difference at all between the return to workers under a gradual transition to privatized accounts of any kind and retention of Social Security.

Any difference between the returns workers receive under a privatized system and under Social Security must come from the taxes paid above those necessary to support current benefits and go to accumulate reserves. The average returns from similarly invested assets would be lower under private accounts than they would be under Social Security because private accounts would be more costly to administer, and these extra costs would reduce the amounts available to support pensions

FOR MORE INFORMATION

If you would like to have this CQ Researcher updated, or need more information about this topic, please call CQ Custom Research. Special rates for CQ subscribers. (202) 887-8600 or (800) 432-2250, ext. 600, or E-mail Custom.Research@cq.com

American Association of Retired Persons, 601 E St., N.W., Washington, D.C. 20049; (202) 434-2277; www. aarp.org. This national membership organization for persons age 50 and over monitors legislation and issues affecting older Americans and provides members with training, employment information and volunteer programs.

Brookings Institution, 1775 Massachusetts Ave., N.W., Washington, D.C. 20036; (202) 797-6000; www.brookings.org. This centrist-to-left-of-center think tank assesses the effectiveness of public-policy programs and is generally skeptical of sweeping plans to overhaul Social Security.

Cato Institute, 1000 Massachusetts Ave., N.W., Washington, D.C. 20001; (202) 842-0200; www.cato.org. This libertarian think tank advocates private-sector solutions to public-policy issues and is sponsoring a $3 million program to study privatization of Social Security.

Heritage Foundation, 214 Massachusetts Ave., N.E., Washington, D.C. 20002; (202) 546-4400; www.heritage.org. This conservative think tank studies Social Security privatization around the world and advocates a similar strategy for the United States.

National Commission on Retirement Policy, 1800 K St., N.W., Washington, D.C. 20006; (202) 775-3242; www.csis.org. This arm of the Center for Strategic and International Studies tries to foster bipartisan solutions to problems with federal entitlement programs and has crafted a centrist proposal to reform Social Security.

Social Security Administration, 6401 Security Blvd., Baltimore, Md. 21235; (410) 965-3120; www.ssa.gov. This federal agency administers the national Social Security and Supplemental Security Income programs.

cause they are busy paying off student loans and starting families. But the problem extends to other generational groups. The U.S. Department of Labor estimates that more than 50 million workers lack any kind of pension. Various academic studies show the current Social Security system actually may reduce private saving by as much as 50 percent because it promises retirement income. The studies note retirement typically is one of the main reasons people save.

Privatization advocates say the various plans to set up IRAs will change saving habits because workers will be setting aside a percentage of their wages in private accounts, instead of sending in contributions that are immediately spent on paying benefits.

But some doubt that privatization would automatically increase savings. Brookings economists Burtless and Bosworth believe setting up new accounts will probably result in workers cutting their contributions to IRAs, 401(k)s and their other existing voluntary retirement plans. Also, they note Social Security is caught in an accounting Catch 22: lowering payroll taxes to divert money to the new accounts will force the government to borrow more money from individual investors to meet its current obligations. Thus, money that would have been saved by the investors is being used to pay benefits.

"In order to boost national saving, a privatization plan must reduce someone's consumption," Burtless and Bosworth argue. They say this could only be accomplished by a privatization plan that cuts benefits to existing and soon-to-be retirees.

Clinton and other lawmakers have urged workers to save more by making a conscious decision to join 401(k) plans and other savings programs while the Social Security dilemma is worked out. Experts say that kind of forward thinking could effectively sidestep what promises to be a drawn-out debate over a volatile political issue.

Joining the plans on one's own to boost savings "is really important," says Alicia Munnell, a management professor at Boston College and former member of the president's Council of Economic Advisers. "Life is complicated, and people have children and other immediate demands, and thinking about sitting down and saving for retirement at 30 is hard." [26] ■

Notes

[1] See James Glassman, "Moynihan's Social Security Plan," *The Washington Post*, March 24, 1998, p. A19. For background, see Sarah Glazer, "Overhauling Social Security," *The CQ Researcher*, May 12, 1995, pp. 417-440 and Richard L. Worsnop, "Age Discrimination," *The CQ Researcher*, Aug. 1, 1997, pp. 682-705.

[2] For background, see "1998 Annual Report of the Board of Trustees of the Federal Old-Age and Survivors Insurance and Disability Insurance Trust Funds," Office of the Chief Actuary, Social Security Administration, April 28, 1998.

[3] On average, large-company stocks registered returns of 10.5 percent while smaller companies' stocks returned 12.5 percent annually.

[4] See Peter Peterson, *Will American Grow Up Before It Grows Old* (1996), pp. 21-27.

[5] For background, see Robert Ball, "A Secure System," *The American Prospect*, No. 29, November-December 1996, pp. 34-35.

[6] See Martynas Ycas, "The Challenge of the 21st Century," *Social Security Bulletin*, winter 1994, pp. 3-9.

[7] From Sen. Daniel Patrick Moynihan, "How to Preserve the Safety Net," *U.S. News & World Report*, April 20, 1998, p. 25.

[8] See testimony before the House Ways and Means Subcommittee on Social Security, Sept. 18, 1997.

[9] See Richard Stevenson, "Bipartisan Group Urged Big Changes in Social Security," *The New York Times*, May 19, 1998, p. A1.

[10] See Ronald Powers, "Moynihan Backs Social Security Privatization," The Associated Press, April 6, 1998.

[11] See Gary Burtless and Barry Bosworth, "Privatizing Social Security: The Troubling Trade-Offs," *Brookings Institution Policy Brief*, No. 14, March 1997.

[12] For background, see Brett Fromson, "A Safety Net Whets Wall St. Appetites; Social Security Proposals Could Mean Billions in Fees," *The Washington Post*, Jan. 7, 1997, p. C1.

[13] See Robert Samuelson, "Older Workers, New Patterns," *The Washington Post*, Nov. 12, 1997.

[14] For background, see U.S. General Accounting Office, "Social Security Reform: Raising Retirement Ages Improves Program Solvency but May Cause Hardship for Some," July 15, 1998.

[15] C. Eugene Steuerle, Edward Gramlich, Hugh Heclo and Demetra Smith Nightingale, *The Government We Deserve: Responsive Democracy and Changing Expectations* (1998).

[16] See Lawrence Jacobs and Robert Shapiro, "Myths and Misunderstandings About Public Opinion Toward Social Security: Knowledge, Support and Reformism," a paper prepared for the 10th Annual Conference of the National Academy of Social Insurance, Jan. 29-30, 1998, Washington, D.C.

[17] See Pete DuPont, "Punish Productive Seniors?" *The Washington Times*, Aug. 14, 1998.

[18] For background, see Peter Ferrara and Michael Tanner, "A New Deal for Social Security," Cato Institute, 1998, pp. 13-32.

[19] See Dorcas Hardy and C. Colburn Hardy, *Social Insecurity* (1991), pp. 7-12.

[20] See Congressional Research Service, "The Social Security Surplus," Nov. 21, 1988, pp. 28-31.

[21] See Carolyn Weaver, "Social Security Reform after the 1983 Amendments," paper delivered at the annual meeting of the Eastern Economic Association, Boston, Mass., March 18-20, 1994.

[22] For background, see Andrew Taylor, "Social Security Surplus Shaping Up As an Election Year Battleground," *CQ Weekly*, July 25, 1998, pp. 1999-2000.

[23] Interview in *Roll Call*, June 22, 1998, p. 3.

[24] See Robert Pear, "Wait 'Til Next Year, Gingrich Admits on Big Tax Cuts," *The New York Times*, Aug. 7, 1998.

[25] For background, see "Geezer Boom," *Hoover Digest Selections*, summer 1997, No. 3, pp. 20-23.

[26] See Jerry Morgan, "Americans Retiring Without a Stool or a Nest Egg to Sit On," *Newsday*, June 14, 1998, p. F6.

Bibliography

Selected Sources Used

Books

Steuerle, C. Eugene, Edward Gramlich, Hugh Heclo and Demetra Smith Nightingale, *The Government We Deserve: Responsive Democracy and Changing Expectations*, Urban Institute Press, 1998.
Four respected academics illustrate how federal spending commitments made years ago are conditioning the United States' economic future. Explores how many Americans now expect to spend a significant share of adulthood in retirement.

Peterson, Peter, *Will America Grow Up Before It Grows Old?*, Random House, 1996.
The former Commerce secretary under President Richard M. Nixon and chief executive officer of Lehman Brothers argues that economic disaster lies ahead if the United States continues to ignore its low savings rate and unsustainable commitments to retirees.

Carter, Marshall, and William Shipman, *Promises To Keep: Saving Social Security's Dream*, Regnery, 1996.
Two executives at State Street Bank and Trust Co. outline a privatization plan they say will guarantee full benefits to retirees, reduce workers' taxes and cut the Social Security system's unfunded liability by 60 percent.

Ferrara, Peter, and Michael Tanner, *A New Deal for Social Security*, Cato Institute, 1998.
An economist and a public-policy expert trace Social Security from its inception, contending the program's problems are the result of a fundamental flaw: Social Security taxes aren't saved or invested in any way.

Articles

Miller, Matthew, "Rebuilding Retirement: A Dramatic Shift in Generational Politics Sets the Stage for Major Social Security Changes," *U.S. News & World Report*, April 20, 1998, pp. 20-26.
A well-written analysis of how politicians who previously tiptoed around Social Security's problems are now offering sweeping plans to overhaul the system.

Rankin, Robert, "Privatizing Social Security has Pitfalls, Promise," Knight-Ridder News Service, July 27, 1998.
A good overview of rival plans to privatize Social Security and how the debate is being shaped in three White House-sponsored forums around the country.

Wildavsky, Ben, "Working Solutions," *National Journal*, July 4, 1998, pp. 1560-1564.
Explores how the concept of raising the retirement age has gained currency in the Social Security debate.

Krauss, Clifford, "Social Security, Chilean Style," *The New York Times*, Aug. 16, 1998.
Chile kicked off the push to privatize Social Security with a set of sweeping reforms in 1981. But the author says it has proven no panacea for the insecurities people feel when thinking about retirement.

Reports

Burtless, Gary, and Barry Bosworth, "Privatizing Social Security: The Troubling Trade-Offs," *Brookings Institution Policy Brief*, March 1997, No. 14.
Two Brookings senior fellows argue that the supposed economic advantages of Social Security privatization require short-term economic sacrifices.

Mitchell, Daniel, "Creating a Better Social Security System for America," *Heritage Foundation Backgrounder*, April 23, 1997.
A senior fellow at the conservative Heritage Foundation details why Social Security is in trouble and is a bad deal for today's workers.

***Baby Boomers Look Toward Retirement,* American Association of Retired Persons, June 2, 1998.**
A Roper Starch Worldwide survey of 2,001 people born between 1946 and 1964 finds the vast majority expect to continue to work during retirement and are largely optimistic about their retirement years.

***Social Security: Why Action Should Be Taken Soon,* Social Security Advisory Board, July 1998.**
An independent, bipartisan board created by Congress and appointed by the president and Congress outlines reasons that prompt action is required to fix the retirement system.

6 Welfare Reform and Child Poverty

KATHY KOCH

It's boom time in America — but with a catch. While the rich are getting richer, the poorest Americans are getting poorer — and children are suffering the most, the Children's Defense Fund (CDF) says.

Despite the nation's economic prosperity, an American child is more likely to be poor now than at any time between 1966 and 1980 — the first 14 years of the War on Poverty.

Nearly one of every five American children lives in poverty — twice the adult-poverty rate and four times the child-poverty rate of Western European nations.

Child poverty in America actually began inching downward in 1993, about the time many states began overhauling their welfare programs, and last year the rate fell a full percentage point. Conservatives attribute the progress — including the lowest poverty rate for black children in U.S. history — to welfare reform, which forced unprecedented numbers of single mothers off welfare and into the work force.

But the CDF's latest annual report condemns as "immoral" the fact that 13.5 million American children are still poor "amidst unprecedented prosperity, huge federal and state budget surpluses, hundreds of billions of tobacco-settlement monies, eight years of continuous, unprecedented economic growth and a presidential boast that the state of the Union has never been better." [1]

Since the 1960s, child poverty has become increasingly concentrated in the inner cities, among minorities and families of single mothers. One of every three African-American and Hispanic children lives in a family with an income below the federal poverty level of $16,660 or less for a family of four. And kids under 6 whose mothers are not married are five times as likely to be poor as children whose parents are married.

From *The CQ Researcher*, April 7, 2000.

AP Photo/Morry Gash

Jenni McGlaun takes her children for dinner at the St. Vincent de Paul free meal program in Milwaukee. Thousands of welfare recipients must work under Wisconsin's groundbreaking welfare reforms.

In addition, nearly 6 million American children live in extreme poverty, with family incomes below $6,500 a year — less than $6 a day per person for a family of three. Meanwhile, the gap between rich children and poor children is the widest it has been in the 52 years since annual income statistics have been collected, according to the CDF. The average income of the top 5 percent of American families jumped $100,000 during the last 25 years while the average income of the poorest one-fifth of families was lower in 1998 — $12,526 — than it was in 1973. [2]

Partly because of the widening income gap, the number of children in working-poor families increased by 1.3 million during the last decade, which the Annie E. Casey Foundation calls "remarkable" given the current economic boom.

"The stock market has hit an all-time high, and the unemployment rate has hit a 25-year low, yet the number of children in working-poor families has grown by nearly a third since 1989," says a recent foundation report. [3]

In general, poor children perform more poorly in school and are more likely to end up in crime, sick, disabled or unemployed, child advocates say.

The CDF complained that despite "presidential and gubernatorial political spin about the success of ending welfare as we know it," families with children are increasingly showing up at homeless shelters and food banks. "Rampant child hunger, homelessness, insecurity and suffering persist." [4]

Welfare — the nation's primary anti-poverty program — was overhauled in 1996 in a sweeping measure that House Republicans recently called "one of the most successful pieces of social legislation in American history." [5] Instead of paying poor citizens cash payments, or entitlements, the new law required that recipients work in exchange for benefits, and limited them to five years.

But architects of welfare reform chafe at implications that somehow welfare reform should have dramatically reduced child poverty, because they say that wasn't the law's primary goal. They say the measure was primarily designed to reduce illegitimacy and welfare dependence.

"Of those three goals, material poverty is largely inconsequential," says Robert Rector, a senior research fellow at the conservative Heritage Foundation and a leading authority on wel-

Poor Children in America

Nearly one of every five children under age 18 in the United States lives in poverty. The poverty rate of black and Hispanic youths is twice the rate of whites, and nearly half of all the poor children live in a female-headed household. Nearly one-third of all poor American children live in poverty even though a family member worked full time, year-round.

	Number of poor children (in thousands)	Percent
Under age 18	13,467	18.9%
White	8,443	15.1
Black	4,151	36.7
Asian/Pacific Islander	564	18.0
Hispanic	3,837	34.4
In female-headed household	7,627	46.1
Family member works full time, year-round	4,302	7.8
In central city	5,836	27.7
In suburb	4,404	12.2
In rural area	2,605	19.7

Source: Children's Defense Fund, based on Census Bureau data from Current Population Reports and Current Population Survey, March 1998 and March 1999.

fare. "It has very little direct effect on the well-being of a child. Family values and the work ethos espoused in the home are more important than family income in determining a child's future success in life." Material poverty is less important than the negative effects of welfare dependency, he says, which is far more damaging to a child than loss of income.

Thus, he says, children are better off thanks to welfare reform because it has prompted the greatest exodus from the welfare rolls in the nation's history. State welfare caseloads plummeted an astonishing 51 percent nationwide since 1993, as thousands of former welfare recipients, mainly single mothers, entered the work force, some for the first time.

Partly as a result, Rector adds, America's child-poverty rate, which had reached 22.7 percent in 1993, began inching downward in 1994 — the year most states began reforming their welfare systems in anticipation of the federal reforms. Since 1994, the child-poverty rate dropped 3 percentage points, from 21.8 percent to 18.9 percent in 1998.

But critics say the nation can do better during a booming economy and record low unemployment rates. "Even with these small advances, there are still 3 million more children in poverty today than in 1970," said former Sen. Bill Bradley, D-N.J., who made eliminating child poverty the cornerstone of his recent unsuccessful campaign for the Democratic presidential nomination. "Only in an indifferent moral universe can we feel satisfied with ourselves for lifting a small percentage of children out of poverty." [6]

Rather than suffering from welfare dependency, child advocates say, children are suffering because wages are too low and housing prices too high for their working parents to get ahead.

They also are suffering because states have been sitting on unprecedented amounts of unspent federal welfare funds, critics say. Because caseloads have fallen so fast, states had $7.4 billion in federal welfare money sitting unspent in the U.S. Treasury last year, left over from fiscal 1997 and 1998. *

Meanwhile, states have dramatically cut the amount they spend on programs for the poor, according to a study by the Rockefeller Institute of Government. Some states have even used federal welfare funds to offset their own state welfare spending so they could give property tax relief to wealthier citizens. [7]

In February, the National Campaign for Jobs and Income, a coalition of grass-roots activists from 35 states, unleashed a blistering condemnation of state spending patterns since welfare reform. It singled out six states — Connecticut, Kansas, Minnesota, New York, Texas and Wisconsin — for cutting state spending on key assistance programs and replacing the difference with federal dollars.

For instance, in 1999 Minnesota decided to use $100 million from federal welfare funds over the next two years to supplant state spending on child care and other social services. Meanwhile, the state cut personal income taxes by $785 million.

"Money originally intended for poor kids [got] transferred into tax cuts for upper-income folks," said Jason Walsh of the Affirmative Options Coalition in St. Paul. "In my mind, that's not just bad policy, it's immoral."

The federal government, the National Conference of State Legislatures and the National Governors'

* The Congressional Budget Office has predicted that at their current level of spending, the states will have $12 billion in surplus federal welfare funds by 2002.

Association have all urged state lawmakers to use the unspent funds to extend services to the working poor and expand services to help the hard-to-employ find jobs.

As states and the federal government debate how to reduce child poverty, here are some of the questions they are asking:

Has welfare reform helped reduce child poverty?

Child advocates complain that while welfare caseloads have fallen a dramatic 44 percent since welfare was overhauled in 1996, child poverty fell by only 7.8 percent, nowhere near as dramatically. In fact, the rate of progress in reducing child poverty actually slowed markedly after welfare reform, and many of the poorest families became poorer, say welfare reform opponents.

During the two years before welfare reform was initiated, the number of poor children in America fell by 2.4 million. But during the two years immediately following reform, only 360,000 children — about one-sixth as many — were lifted out of poverty, according to a report by the Center on Budget and Policy Priorities (CBPP), a liberal research institute. In addition, the percentage of children living in extreme poverty went up between 1995 and 1997, and there was a substantial increase in extreme poverty among working families with children during the same period. [8]

"Amid the good news of economic growth, it is troubling that those children who remain poor have slipped somewhat deeper into poverty," said Kathryn Porter, co-author of the CBPP report. "While the robust economy is helping many families, others are being affected adversely by the contraction in some parts of the safety net." [9]

Much of the decline was caused by substantial cutbacks in so-called safety-net programs, said another CBPP report, released in December. Large numbers of working-poor families that qualify for food stamps, child-care subsidies and subsidized health insurance are not receiving those supports. Had the safety nets been as effective in removing children from poverty in 1997 as they were in 1995, the study concluded, 700,000 fewer children would have been poor in 1997. The negative effects of the cutbacks outweighed the positive impact of concurrent increases in employment, wages, and tax credits for the working poor, said the latest study. [10]

Child advocates complain there is an "information gap" about the benefits — either former recipients don't know they are still eligible for the non-cash benefits, or some state caseworkers are turning eligible candidates away. For instance, New York and Michigan erected barriers to food-stamp applicants that federal courts subsequently ruled were illegal. And according to an Urban Institute report, former welfare families who are among the poorest of the poor stopped receiving food stamps at twice the rate of other families. In fact, two-thirds of families who leave welfare are still eligible for food stamps, the institute said. [11]

Still another CBPP study, released last August, found that the poorest single mothers and their children have lost ground since welfare reform. The incomes of the poorest 20 percent of single-mother families — a group consisting of about 6 million people — fell by nearly $600 between 1995 and 1997. The study counted food stamps, housing subsidies, the earned-income tax credit (EITC) and similar benefits as income.

But even with those benefits, the families' incomes were still well below the poverty line, the report said, and the poorest 10th of female-headed families lost about one-seventh of their incomes. The decline wiped out all of the income gains the

Children in Working-Poor Families

The number of children living in working-poor U.S. families increased from 4.3 million children in 1989 to 5.6 million in 1997, a 30 percent increase during the economically booming 1990s.

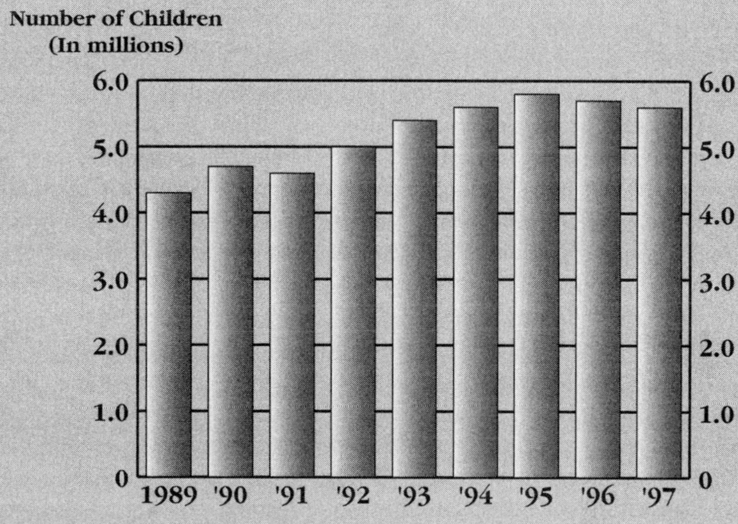

Source: Census Bureau, Current Population Surveys

families had secured between 1993 and 1995 and returned their average income to 1993 levels, when unemployment was high. [12]

"It is disturbing that substantial numbers of children and families are sinking more deeply into poverty when we have the strongest economy in decades and when substantial amounts of funds provided to states to assist these families are going unused," said Wendell Primus, the study's lead author. [13]

According to the CDF, more than 70 percent of working adults who had been on welfare in 1997 earned below-poverty wages. And most state surveys tracking former welfare families found that 40 to 50 percent had no earnings at all, the group said.

Most working former welfare parents remain one crisis away from returning to cash assistance because their jobs are often temporary, pay only minimum wage and don't provide sick leave, health benefits or vacation pay. Then, once the women start working, many states raise the rent on their subsidized housing, in some cases doubling it, advocates say.

"Most of these women have less than $100 left over at the end of the month to pay for food, clothes and incidentals," says Harriet Dither, deputy director of Philadelphia Citizens for Children and Youth, a private group that has been tracking 50 former welfare mothers for the past two years.

Others point to increasing requests from families with children for emergency food and shelter as evidence that child poverty is increasing as a result of welfare reform. The U.S. Department of Agriculture says that the number of children without enough food increased by 3.7 million children from 1997 to 1998.

Critics of welfare reform say its success should be judged according to whether the well-being of poor children has improved, not simply by how much state caseloads have declined

Rector couldn't agree more. But he says a child's well-being should not be measured by the family's income. "The Left's obsession with constantly giving people things to try to bolster their material living standards" has only increased welfare dependence and illegitimacy, Rector says. "And those two things, without question, have extremely negative effects on child outcomes."

Rector cites a 1994 study in the *Journal of Human Resources* that compared children with identical social and economic factors, such as race, income, family structure, neighborhood and mothers' IQ and education.

"The authors make it clear that it is not poverty but welfare itself that has a damaging effect on the child," Rector writes. "The longer a child spent in the welfare system, the lower the child's IQ." [14]

A similar study at the University of Michigan showed that welfare reduces the long-term employment and earnings capacity of young boys. "The more welfare income received by a family while a boy was growing up, the lower the boy's earnings as an adult," Rector writes. For instance, he writes, a $1,000 increase in welfare benefits directly coincides with a 10 percent decrease in a boy's future earnings. [15]

Instead of asking whether welfare reform has reduced child poverty, he says, "We should be asking if it reduced the culture of dependence and illegitimacy. In both cases, the answer is 'Yes.' And by reducing dependency and illegitimacy, we have improved child well-being."

Finally, Rector reiterates, "The Left's paramount goal of trying to artificially boost people's incomes" deals with a symptom, not the root cause of poverty. "Child poverty is as high as it is in this country because we've had an astronomical increase in illegitimacy over the last 30 years," he says. "A child born outside of marriage will spend seven times more time in poverty than one born in an intact family, and a child is born out-of-wedlock every 25 seconds in the United States."

But Timothy M. Smeeding, director of the Center for Policy Research at Syracuse University, says more children are born out-of-wedlock in Scandinavia and Holland than in the United States, "and their child-poverty rate is less than half of ours."

Amy Sherman, an adjunct fellow at the Manhattan Institute and director of urban ministries at Trinity Presbyterian Church in Charlottesville, Va., rejects the complaint that welfare reform has merely transformed families from the welfare poor to the working poor.

"This tedious perspective erroneously assumes that the welfare poor could miraculously reach the middle class without a stopover in the ranks of the working poor," she wrote in *Family Policy*, published by the conservative Family Research Council. "The working poor are almost always better off materially [than those on welfare]; their self-respect rises, their children's self-esteem improves and they are better-positioned to receive help from charitable institutions who view them as the 'deserving poor.' " [16]

Indeed, Rector contends that today's poor are better off than most people think. He says the Census Bureau overestimates poverty in America by setting an artificially high poverty threshold level ($16,660 for a family of four), ignores accumulated family assets and undercounts by about $2 trillion the total economic resources received each year by the American public.

"Some welfare mothers have a lot more sources of income than the government knows about," Rector says. "I've sat in welfare offices in Wisconsin and New York City, and I've seen them turn around and walk right out the door when they were told that they would have to go to work to receive benefits. So they must have some other income — from boyfriends, parents or public housing and food stamps — that they can rely upon."

Other reform proponents argue that government measures of child poverty do not take into account major increases in other benefit programs since the mid-1980s, specifically the EITC and food stamps. "We spend $28 billion a year for EITC and $30 billion in food stamps, and none of it is counted toward income for the poor," complained a House Republican staffer who has worked on welfare reform for years.

A House Republican white paper on welfare reform said analyses of both national and state data on caseload declines "fail to provide a shred of evidence for the claim that declines in welfare benefits inevitably lead to increases in poverty." [17]

Instead, the paper said, states that have reduced their welfare caseloads the most (25 percent or more) have seen their child-poverty rates fall faster than states with only moderate caseload declines. Child poverty dropped an average of 1.8 percentage points between 1995 and 1997 in high-reduction states, according to the paper, compared with 0.3 percentage points in states with less dramatic caseload reductions.

"Nevertheless, welfare reform has led to an unprecedented increase in employment of single mothers, which has helped reduce child poverty," Rector says. Opponents are "struggling to somehow put a dark picture" on the lowest child-poverty rate since 1980 and the lowest poverty rate for black children in history, down to 36.7 percent from 47.6 percent in 1982. And the 47.5 percent poverty rate for single mothers is the lowest in history, he adds.

To paint a dark picture, he says, opponents "found some little subgroup that is not doing well," which he says is an "expected short-term effect" of welfare reform. "When you make people accountable for their actions, they will suffer if they don't behave in a constructive manner," he says. "You can't have accountability without having that kind of result."

But eventually, that group will probably benefit the most in the long term, he says, "because they are the ones who need a change in behavior the most."

Would increasing the minimum wage help alleviate child poverty?

Sharon Daly, vice president for social policy at Catholic Charities USA, bristles at the Heritage Foundation's argument that "behavior causes poverty rather than low wages and a lack of affordable housing." The wages of some poor parents are so low that they spend 50 to 80 percent of their income on rent, she points out.

One solution proposed by the Clinton administration has been to raise the $5.15 federal minimum wage by $1 an hour to $6.15 an hour. Both the House and Senate have voted to raise the rate, but not without heated debate.

Rep. Cass Ballenger, R-N.C., argued during House floor debate on March 9 that raising the minimum wage is an ineffective way to target child poverty because most minimum wage earners are teenagers living with their parents. (*See "At Issue," p. 111.*)

"Few workers actually support families under the minimum wage," he said. "The minimum wage is typically paid to individuals who are just entering the work force, the overwhelming majority of whom are young, single and childless."

According to the Census Bureau, he says, 37 percent of those who ben-

Children in Poverty

More than half the children of East St. Louis, Ill., lived in poverty in 1990 — the highest percentage of any U.S. city.

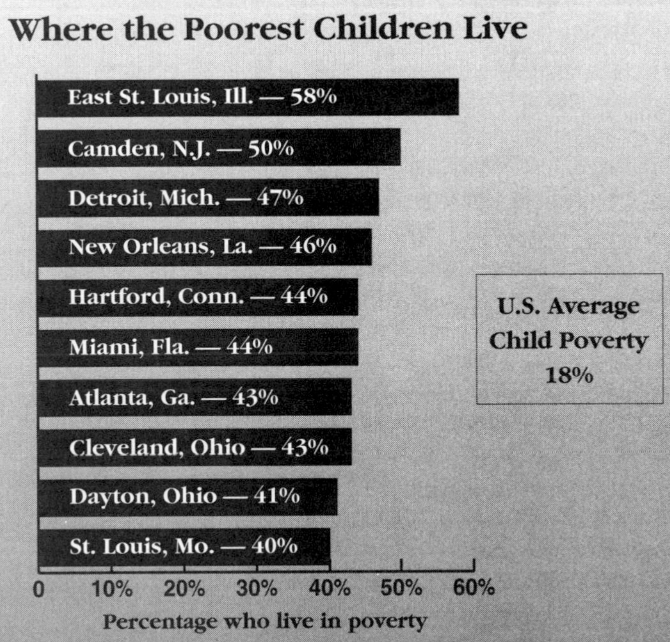

Source: Education Week; *1990 U.S. Census data*

U.S. Child-Poverty Rate the Highest

*Despite its enormous wealth, the United States has the highest child-poverty rate in the developed world, according to a study of 17 selected industrialized nations.**

Children in Poverty in Developed Nations

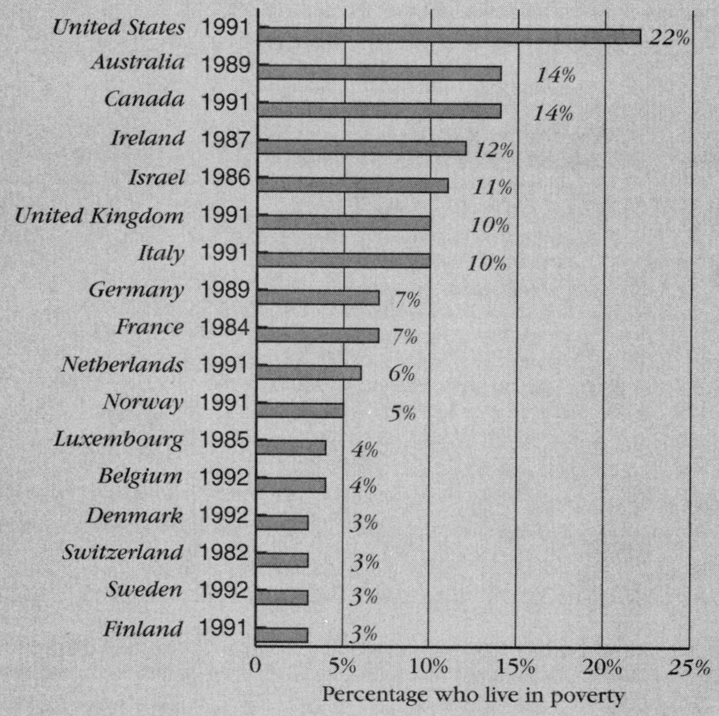

** The data are based on current federal poverty levels.*

Sources: The Annie E. Casey Foundation, "1999 Kids Count"

efited from the last minimum wage increase were young people living with their parents. And 85 percent either live with their parents, or are single and childless, or live alone, or have a working spouse. "Only one in 10 minimum wage earners is trying to support a family," Ballenger said.

In addition, he said, studies show that increasing the minimum wage will shift many jobs from low-skilled adults to teenagers and students. "While it benefits some individuals," he said, "it will clearly harm others by lessening employment opportunities . . . and causing price increases that disproportionately affect the poor."

Other critics argue that raising the minimum wage would lead to job losses and create wage pressure. "It would be inflationary," said Rep. Tom Tancredo, R-Colo.

Moreover, he said, economists had admitted under questioning in committee hearings that there was no sound economic study justifying the increase. "We do not know if a dollar is right over a year, over two years, over three, over four [years]; we have no idea," Tancredo said. "It is just a good, round number."

But during Senate debate, Sen. Edward M. Kennedy, D-Mass., said more than 11.4 million workers earn less than $6.15 an hour and that a $1 increase would enable more people to share in the nation's economic well-being.

A full-time minimum wage worker earns only $10,700 a year, Kennedy said, while the median salary and bonus for American chief executive officers in 1997 was $770 an hour. "At that rate," he said, "it takes an average CEO less than two days to earn what a minimum wage worker earns in an entire year."

Raising the wage would enable poor workers to better afford housing, he said. At $5.15 per hour, it would take a worker 80 hours per week to afford the fair market rent set by the federal government for assisted housing in 195 metropolitan areas in the United States, he said.

Some low-wage workers often must decide between paying rent or buying groceries, Kennedy said. "The price of prosperity should not be unfair wages for those who tend the sick, care for our children, clean offices and serve food," he said.

Robert Kuttner, co-editor of *The American Prospect*, disputes the argument that raising the minimum wage would cause employers to eliminate some low-wage jobs. When the minimum wage was last raised, in two stages, in 1996 and 1997, opponents made similar dire predictions of job losses, he wrote. During this period, the restaurant industry and its think tank, the Employment Policies Institute, "put out repeated reports shedding crocodile tears for all the jobs that would be lost, especially among the very-low-income people the legislation was intended to help," he wrote.

"But of course, during that period unemployment came steadily down, and most dramatically among the very groups most affected by the minimum wage — minorities, teenagers, and people without college degrees." [18]

Jared Bernstein, an economist at the liberal Economic Policy Institute and co-author of *The State of Working America*, says the minimum wage debate often needs "a statistical arbiter to make sure people aren't playing fast and loose with the facts."

First of all, he says, it's a "red herring" to say that a minimum wage increase only reaches a small percent of the poor, because 49 percent of the poor are children and only 41 percent of the poor who are old enough to work are working.

"So you really should look at how it affects the low-wage workers," he says. "That's who you are targeting." About 60 percent of the benefits from a minimum wage increase goes to households with an average income "in the $20,000 range," he says, or above the official poverty line of $16,600 for a family of four. "That's not poverty, but they are certainly worthy beneficiaries of a wage increase," he says.

"So most of the water gets to the fire, but it's not nearly as well-targeted as the earned-income tax credit is."

In addition, those who argue that mostly teenagers will be helped because most working parents don't make the minimum wage are ignoring the total population of workers who would be helped by an increase, he says.

"They are only looking at those who are making exactly $5.15 an hour. But raising the minimum wage will also help everyone who is making between $5.15 and $6.16 an hour," he says. And 70 percent of those folks are adults over 20, he points out. Only 30 percent are teenagers, 60 percent are female and about 10 percent are female heads of household.

"So this is really a women's issue," he says.

Bernstein admits that he could easily see a minimum wage increase that would be high enough that it would actually hurt the very people it was trying to help. "But a moderate increase like this," he says, "which still leaves you about 15 percent below the real value of what the minimum wage was in 1979, won't do that."

Should faith-based solutions be relied on more to solve the child-poverty problem?

A little-known provision of the welfare-reform law, called Charitable Choice, made it easier for the government to contract with religious organizations to provide social services to the poor.

KRT Photo/Gayle Shomer

Gunter Early and DeMarkus White attend an after-school program run by the All God's Children United Methodist Church in Aulander, N.C. Under the Charitable Choice provision of the 1996 welfare-reform law, local governments can contract with religious organizations to provide social services for the poor.

The new rules prohibit public officials from discriminating against religious agencies when awarding contracts for social services. They also allow faith-based organizations (FBOs) accepting government funds to retain a religious atmosphere in their facilities. Under the old rules, religious organizations accepting taxpayer money had to keep their social service books separate from their regular church accounts, and make sure religious paraphernalia was not displayed wherever they offer social services. They also had to avoid promoting religion when counseling clients.

During the current presidential election campaign, both Vice President Al Gore and Gov. George W. Bush, R-Texas, have promised to rely on faith-based organizations to deliver more government services.

In a speech last May 24 at the Atlanta headquarters of the Salvation Army, Gore said FBOs are often more effective than government agencies because their workers are motivated by service instead of institutional allegiance. To FBO workers, "the client is not a number, but a child of God," said Gore.

"Most Americans are hungry for a deeper connection between politics and moral values, many would say spiritual values," said Gore. And while he strongly believes in the separation of church and state, "freedom of religion need not mean freedom from religion," he insisted.

Gore vowed to clear bureaucratic hurdles preventing FBOs from being awarded government contracts, and said he would extend Charitable Choice to other vital services — such as drug treatment, homelessness and youth violence prevention.

Bush agrees that faith-based organizations are more effective at solving social problems at a fraction of

Living-Wage Movement Gaining Strength . . .

While Congress is deadlocked over raising the $5.15 federal minimum wage by $1 an hour, grass-roots organizers are convincing local officials around the country to set minimum wages for government contractors, which sometimes are twice the federal rate.

Over the last six years, such so-called living-wage ordinances have been passed in at least 44 localities, including Los Angeles, San Jose, New York, Chicago, Boston and Milwaukee. Similar campaigns are under way in at least 69 more. Living wages — ranging from $6.25 to $11 an hour — are calculated to ensure that a worker can bring home enough money to support a family above the poverty level without having to work two jobs. Currently, a family of three with one full-time worker earning $5.15 has 30 percent less income than the official federal poverty level for a family that size. [1]

Living-wage campaigns are gaining momentum during these robust economic times, aided by community, church, student and labor groups, says Jen Kern, director of the National Living Wage Resource Center in Washington, D.C.

"It's more shameful to argue against modest wage increases and health benefits when the economy is doing so well," she says.

Kern says several other economic factors are making this an opportune time to press for a living wage:

- Low-end wages have stagnated during most of the 1990s, so even if Congress does raise the minimum wage by $1, it will still be worth 15 percent less than its real value was in 1979.
- Welfare reform has sent thousands of low-skilled mothers into the work force, potentially depressing the wages of other low-paid workers.
- The fastest-growing job sector, the service industry, typically is among the lowest-paid.
- Many city and county governments have begun contracting out services once provided by unionized city employees to non-union contractors.
- Companies have been reaping billions of dollars in tax breaks and economic-development subsidies over the last two decades as cities and counties have stepped up competition with each other to attract what often turn out to be only minimum wage jobs.

The movement for what Kern calls "economic justice" is also gaining popularity because people are frustrated when they see Congress squabbling over whether to phase in the $1 increase over two years or three years, "as they propose giving businesses $120 billion in tax breaks."

When Baltimore passed the nation's first living wage in 1994, it required certain city contractors to pay workers at least $7.70 per hour by 1999. But more recent ordinances also require them to provide benefits and incentives to unionize. Now supporters are demanding that any company receiving a tax exemption or government subsidy be covered by the living-wage requirements.

"Taxpayers see companies double-dipping — negotiating huge economic-development tax breaks and subsidies that exempt them from paying for good schools or revitalizing their communities," says Nathan Smith, an organizer with the Association of Community Organizations for Reform Now (ACORN), which supports living-wage campaigns across the country. "Then those companies turn around and pay such low wages that taxpayers must shell out even more money for food stamps and Medicaid to bring those workers' incomes up to the poverty line."

ACORN says studies of the impact of living-wage ordinances in Baltimore and Los Angeles show that they do not adversely affect business, the local economy or city spending. In Los Angeles, for instance, the ordinance caused a 1 - 1.5 percent increase in total expenses for affected companies, according to one study. Another study, by researchers at Johns Hopkins University, found that Baltimore's living-wage ordinance resulted in a 1.2 percent increase in the cost of city contracts, less than the rate of inflation. [2]

But business groups, once relatively indifferent to the

Continued from p. 292

the cost of a bureaucracy. "Often when a life is broken, it can only be rebuilt by another caring, concerned human being," Bush said last July 22 in Indianapolis, Ind. "It is not an isolated act — it is a personal relationship. And it works," he said, citing the Big Brothers/Big Sisters mentoring program, which he said cuts first-time drug use by 50 percent and violent behavior by a third.

Bush promised that, if elected, when serving the poor his government would first look to faith-based organizations, charities and community groups, because they "have shown their ability to save and change lives." His administration would wage war against poverty by rallying "armies of compassion," he said, rather than the "failed compassion of towering, distant bureaucracies."

Bush also promised to establish an "Office of Faith-Based Action" in the White House, to expand Charitable Choice to other services and to provide $8 billion in new tax incentives for individual and corporate giving during his first year in office.

Proponents of Charitable Choice can cite many "very appealing" anecdotes about how effective these programs are, says Barry Lynn, executive director of Americans United for Separation of Church and State. "But we don't know how widespread the success really is, because no serious longitudinal studies have looked at what happens, for example, five years out."

. . . As Grass-Roots Groups Seek 'Economic Justice'

ordinances because they covered so few workers, are vigorously opposing them now that they are affecting more companies. They oppose living-wage laws on the same grounds that they oppose federal minimum wage legislation. They contend they hurt the intended beneficiaries by forcing businesses to employ fewer workers, especially fewer unskilled workers, or to relocate to avoid living-wage cities.

The laws also will damage local governments' competitiveness, they say, because some firms will refuse to bid on city contracts. "If local governments attract fewer bidders, it could mean they have fewer choices and possibly be forced to pay higher prices," says Ronald Bird, chief economist for the Economic Policy Foundation, a think tank funded in part by major corporations.

Bird admits that the impact of living-wage ordinances has been minor so far, but that's because until now fewer than 50,000 workers nationwide have been covered by them. "But if these ordinances were adopted on a national or statewide level, which is the ultimate objective," Bird says, "it could have a really bad impact."

However, advocates point out that in 1997, the last time the federal minimum wage was raised, business predicted they would have to lay off workers, but the robust economy sent unemployment to historic lows instead.

Higher wages also boost productivity because they lower absenteeism and turnover, economist Robert Pollin wrote last April. [3]

Business groups also complain that the ordinances are tools for union organizing, which appeared to be borne out by a comment from Los Angeles labor organizer Miguel Contreras. A union complaint about wage inequity is likely to be dismissed as self-serving, he said, "but if it has the cloak of religious leaders and community activists, then it becomes a community issue." [4]

Bird also says supplementary aid programs, like food stamps, Medicaid or the earned-income tax credit, are more effective at targeting the working poor than minimum and living-wage ordinances. Most people who make minimum wage, he says, are teenagers.

But Jared Bernstein, a labor economist at the liberal Economic Policy Institute, says raising the minimum wage targets not only those making $5.15 an hour but also anyone making a wage that falls between $5.15 and whatever the new "livable" wage is — a group that includes many low-wage breadwinners.

ACORN's Smith argues that relying on government handouts "just shifts the burden back to the taxpayers, who end up indirectly subsidizing the companies to pay below-poverty wages."

Kern says the living-wage debate is part of a larger controversy over what kind of economic development public officials are buying with their tax breaks. "Do we really need to subsidize another shopping mall that provides only minimum wage jobs?" she asks.

Bird contends that when public officials grant businesses tax abatements to attract jobs, they believe the new jobs will generate enough additional sales and income taxes to offset the lost business taxes — an assumption that is increasingly being challenged.

"Now that we have record low unemployment in much of the country, the time to stop this bidding war between the states is long past," Bernstein says. "Often, these corporate subsidies are being granted for business growth that would have happened anyway."

---

[1] The Census Bureau sets the poverty threshold for a family of three at $13,003 and at $16,660 for a family of four.

[2] Christopher Niedt, et al., "The Effects of the Living Wage in Baltimore," Johns Hopkins University, February 1999.

[3] Robert Pollin, "Living Wage Gives a Boost to Demand," *Los Angeles Times*, April 1, 1999.

[4] Louis Uchitelle, "Minimum Wages, City by City," *The New York Times*, Nov. 19, 1999.

Those promoting Charitable Choice take an "astonishing leap of faith" by ordering that millions of public dollars should be directed to religious groups, without any compelling studies to show that they work, he says.

"They don't even ask if such studies exist," says Larry Brown, director of the Center on Hunger, Poverty and Nutrition Policy at Tufts University School of Medicine. "It's just not part of the debate." Yet the same politicians will demand accountability from public education and other social-service agencies, he says. "It's such a double standard."

Yet since 1996, Charitable Choice provisions have been attached to pending juvenile justice and education bills. And Sen. John Ashcroft, R-Mo., has vowed to introduce a similar amendment to every piece of social legislation that passes through Congress, Lynn points out.

Lynn's group claims that Charitable Choice violates the U.S. Constitution by promoting "excessive entanglement" between government and religion and by using public funds to promote religion. Further, he says, it allows FBOs to use public funds to discriminate in hiring based on religion. "There is literally no other federal program that allows hiring discrimination with tax dollars," Lynn says.

Lynn suggests that by approving Charitable Choice, Congress is setting the stage for allowing federal education funds to be used for school vouchers — to be given to students or their parents to pay for education at religious schools.

In fact, one of Bush's proposals — a new "charitable state-tax credit" — sounds a lot like school vouchers. The credits would "allow individuals to give a part of what they owe in state taxes directly to religious institutions fighting poverty in their own communities," Bush said in Indianapolis. "Individuals will choose who conducts this war on poverty — and their support won't be filtered through layers of government officials."

Joseph Loconte, a Heritage Foundation fellow, also favors publicly funded social-service vouchers going directly to families and individuals. Such a system would prevent government agencies from co-opting the religious organizations that accept their money.

Loconte says religious organizations accepting public money risk "mission creep," which occurs when government rules and regulations "bog down, paralyze and dehumanize care-giving groups." [19]

But Deborah Weinstein, director of the CDF's Family Income Division, warns that religious organizations could never provide enough resources to completely replace government programs. "Religious leaders will tell you they still need the active role of the public sector in providing cash assistance, job training, food stamps and tax credits for the working poor," she says. "The whole range of supports is still essential."

Along with more assistance from the religious community, Daly of Catholic Charities says, "We still need the federal government to invest in affordable housing for families and in child care during non-traditional working hours and in transportation subsidies to help urban commuters get to suburban jobs."

Carol Devita, a senior research associate at the Urban Institute's Center on Nonprofits and Philanthropy, says that except for a few megachurches, the average U.S congregation has fewer than 100 members. "Do we really want to base our public policy on such limited capacity?" she asks.

Both proponents and opponents admit faith-based organizations could never replace government welfare programs because they are just too large. According to Rector, federal and state governments spend $430 billion a year to run more than 75 major interrelated and overlapping welfare programs, including cash aid, food, medical aid, housing aid, energy aid, jobs and training, targeted and means-tested education programs, social services and urban and community development programs.

Brown points out that when Congress passed welfare reform, it cut $27 billion worth of food stamps from federal programs over the 1997-2002 period. That translates into a shortfall in food for the hungry of 23 billion pounds, he says.

To provide that much food, Brown says, a nonprofit would need a convoy of trucks, each carrying 5,000 pounds, stretching, literally, "from here to the moon and back." ■

BACKGROUND

War on Poverty

Broadly defined, welfare includes any government-assistance program that is means tested, or one in which eligibility is determined on the basis of need.

Only about one-fourth of federal, state and local welfare money is distributed as cash aid to the poor. The rest is delivered as "in-kind assistance," such as Medicaid, food stamps and reduced-price school lunches, housing benefits or student aid. [20]

However, most of the welfare reform debate during the 104th Congress focused on cash-assistance programs, specifically the former Aid to Families with Dependent Children (AFDC), which made up about 1 percent of the federal budget and only 1 percent of state and local revenues.

AFDC's origins lie in turn-of-the-century widows' pension laws, which allowed widows with children to stay home to raise them rather than going to work or placing the children in a foster home or institution. Missouri passed the first such law in 1911, and by 1935 all but two states had them. By that time, most of the laws had been broadened to extend coverage to all needy mothers, including women with illegitimate children.

The federal government did not get involved in welfare policy until the Great Depression brought demands for more federal help for the needy. Title IV of the Social Security Act of 1935 established the precursor to AFDC, then called Aid to Dependent Children, which gave states matching federal funds "to assist, broaden and supervise existing mothers' aid programs."

Postwar prosperity in the 1950s gave families unprecedented job security and increasing benefits. In the 1960s, however, the civil rights movement brought growing awareness of the stark contrast between prosperity and relentless poverty in the South, Appalachia and industrial Northern cities. In 1964, in his first State of the Union address, President Lyndon B. Johnson declared an "unconditional war on poverty." A succession of new programs followed, including Job Corps, Head Start and Medicaid.

As a result of these programs and growing economic prosperity, the poverty rate dropped 9 percent dur-

Chronology

1960s *Presidents John F. Kennedy and Lyndon B. Johnson push initiatives to help the poor.*

1964
Johnson declares "unconditional war on poverty" in his first State of the Union address. Congress approves Economic Opportunity Act, establishing anti-poverty programs.

1967
Congress establishes Work Incentive Program (WIN), which cuts off benefits to adults receiving welfare unless they accept jobs or job training.

1969
The burgeoning economy and the "War on Poverty" help raise the median family income by 38 percent over 1959 and cut unemployment, especially among black men.

1970s *The energy crisis stalls America's postwar boom, widening the gap between rich and poor. Income-support programs urged by Presidents Richard M. Nixon and Jimmy Carter die in Congress, but some federal welfare programs are expanded.*

1974
Aid programs for elderly, blind and disabled persons are consolidated into the federal Supplemental Security Income (SSI) program. The earned-income tax credit (EITC) is enacted to provide tax refunds for the working poor.

1980s *The decline in manufacturing eliminates thousands of jobs. President Ronald Reagan presides over deregulation, tax breaks for the wealthy and cuts in programs to help the poor. Most states establish welfare-to-work programs. Median family income is 6 percent below the 1973 level, and a record 14.4 percent of Americans are living in poverty.*

July 31, 1981
Congress cuts cash benefits for the working poor and allows states to require welfare recipients to work.

Oct. 13, 1988
Reagan signs the Family Support Act of 1988 requiring states to implement education, job training and placement programs for welfare recipients.

1990s-2000s *Congress passes the first increase in the minimum wage since 1981. Many states receive waivers from federal welfare rules to experiment with using incentives or penalties to try to modify welfare recipients' behavior.*

Jan. 28, 1992
President Bush, in State of the Union address, says it's "time to . . . help reform the welfare system" and promises to ease federal review of welfare-reform initiatives by the states.

1993
Newly elected President Bill Clinton extends the EITC to include low-income workers without children and raises the amount paid to working families.

1994
Republican majority takes over Congress and begins debating ways to reform welfare.

1995
President Clinton proposes increasing the minimum wage to $5.15 an hour. Republican lawmakers propose massive spending cuts in programs that help poor workers.

1996
Clinton signs the Personal Responsibility and Work Opportunity Act, forcing welfare recipients to find work, cutting off welfare benefits from noncitizens and cutting back on the food stamp program. Congress increases the minimum wage from $4.25 to $4.75 an hour.

Sept. 1, 1997
The minimum wage is increased again, to $5.15 an hour. States begin amassing a $7 billion surplus in unspent federal welfare funds.

1998
Census Bureau reports that income levels are the highest ever recorded, as poverty drops to 12.7 percent nationwide. Child poverty drops to 18.9 percent, lowest level since 1989.

2002
The states will have $12 billion in surplus federal welfare funds, according to the Congressional Budget Office.

ing the 1960s. "The 1960s was probably the decade in which there was the most sustained economic progress for all segments of society, but especially for people at the bottom," says Gary Burtless, an economist at the Brookings Institution. "The elderly poor got much fatter Social Security checks, the poor with children got fatter welfare checks and poor workers got fatter paychecks." [21]

For many Americans, the dream began to unravel when Western Europe and Japan, newly recovered from World War II, began producing affordable, quality goods. As demand for U.S. goods faltered, the economy slowed, generating less wages and tax revenues to fund social programs. Public support of welfare plummeted, especially as the number of unmarried, black mothers receiving benefits skyrocketed. When Ronald Reagan arrived in the White House in 1981, he promised to cut welfare for the unemployed.

During the 1980s, American corporations retrenched and restructured to improve productivity and remain competitive in the new global marketplace. Thousands of workers lost their manufacturing jobs, often switching to lower-paid, non-union jobs in the service sector. By the mid-1980s, four in 10 displaced manufacturing workers were unemployed or had stopped looking for work altogether, causing a sudden increase in poverty rates. And it wasn't only the unemployed who were poor. By 1986, there were about 9 million working poor.

Reform Movement

By the late 1980s, politicians were becoming increasingly adamant that welfare recipients should be required to work. Reagan and the Democratic-controlled Congress crafted a welfare reform law in 1988 that combined some of the social-service concepts of the 1960s with tougher work requirements. The Family Support Act required that adult welfare recipients be "encouraged, assisted and required" to work to support their children.

In return, the government would provide support for education, training, health care and child care. But the reforms were poorly enforced and unevenly administered by the states. To make matters worse, the whole system was swamped by a recession that sent welfare rolls surging 25 percent from 1989 to 1992. The weakened national economy also drained state coffers, further undermining the new law.

But starting in 1988, the Reagan administration had begun allowing states to experiment with alternative ways of using welfare policy to change behavior. Wisconsin led the way, reducing welfare benefits for parents who failed to prevent truancy among their teenagers. Later, President George Bush allowed Ohio to require all teen parents receiving welfare to attend school.

In 1992, Bush espoused the idea of allowing states to waive traditional AFDC rules to promote positive behavior. "States throughout the country are beginning to operate with new assumptions: that when able-bodied people receive government assistance, they have a responsibility to seek work, education or job training; a responsibility to get their lives in order; a responsibility to hold their families together and refrain from having children out-of-wedlock," Bush said in his State of the Union address. "We are going to help this movement." [22]

Requests for waivers from federal welfare rules flooded in, gaining added momentum when Bill Clinton — a former Arkansas governor and vigorous welfare-reform advocate — took office in 1993. Most states, hoping to increase incentives to work, received permission to allow families to earn more before their AFDC benefits were reduced. Others imposed time limits on benefits or used welfare funds to subsidize wages, employ recipients to rehabilitate public housing, help welfare families set up their own small businesses or to create subsidized jobs. A handful also tried imposing "family caps," which cut or eliminate benefits if recipients have additional children while on welfare.

By 1996, the waivers had become so widespread that states effectively had seized the welfare-reform initiative from the federal government, and most had abandoned the concept of unconditional entitlements for the poor.

By the time the 104th Congress overhauled the AFDC program in 1996, two powerful political trends — devolution and deficit cutting — were driving the agenda. They propelled the new Republican majority to transfer power from the federal to the state level and cut spending.

The 1996 law partially satisfied both agendas. It trimmed federal spending by a projected $55 billion over six years and shifted primary responsibility for the welfare program to the states, giving the nation's governors their first, best chance to prove that devolution works.

After vetoing two earlier Republican proposals in 1995 and early '96, President Clinton finally signed a welfare-reform bill on Aug. 22, 1996. Noting that the administration had lost control of the issue after the Republicans took over Congress in 1994, David Ellwood, a Harvard University welfare expert and a former Clinton administration welfare official, said glumly, "We got hit by a freight train, in part because our own train moved too sluggishly." [23]

To the dismay of many liberals, the new law ended the government's 61-year commitment of entitlements, or open-ended assistance. Under the new law, the federal government pays about half the cost of cash aid, called Temporary Assistance for Needy Families (TANF), but it is now "capped" at about $17 billion a year, with no guarantee that funding will rise if the number of families in need increases.

While AFDC had offered training and education, the new law demanded "work first." In general, states must move recipients into "work activities" within 24 months or stop using federal funds to support them. States were also required to move 30 percent of single parents into jobs by 1998 and 35 percent by 1999. Recipients could not receive aid for more than 60 months total (five years) during their lifetime, but states were allowed to exempt 20 percent of their caseloads from that requirement. Finally, each state had to spend at least 75 percent of what it spent in 1994 from its own coffers or risk losing its federal funds.

Within these guidelines, states could design and run their programs as they saw fit. They could turn recipients away, and raise or lower benefit levels. Now benefits range from less than $200 a month for a family of three in Alabama, Louisiana, Mississippi, Texas and Tennessee to a high of $923 per month in Alaska. The average monthly payment per case in 1998 was $402. States could end benefits before the 60-month deadline or demand that recipients start work sooner than 24 months. Recipients who didn't comply with program rules could be "sanctioned," or have their benefits reduced or terminated.

In taking on the welfare system, states are facing some of the most wrenching changes in state government in decades. To identify and help the hardest-to-employ, welfare bureaucrats must become quasi-social workers. Clerks accustomed to filing paperwork and cutting checks must learn to judge whether a person can successfully hold down a job and, if not, direct her to appropriate help.

But in most states, those support services — including child care, drug treatment, transportation, mental counseling and tutoring — are still largely unavailable to welfare families, either because space is limited or families don't know they exist. ■

CURRENT SITUATION

Unspent Funds

With welfare caseloads plummeting, most states have enjoyed a windfall in their federal welfare payments, which have remained constant. But they receive widely differing amounts of federal block grants because the grants are calculated on the basis of each state's welfare spending in 1994. So states that were more generous before the new law went into effect are better off than others are. Vermont, for instance, collects $2,761 for every poor child in the state while Texas, which was considerably less munificent in the past, gets just $339 per child.

According to the Center on Budget and Policy Priorities, 26 states spent all of their 1999 federal welfare funds and began to tap into the surpluses accumulated since 1997. But eight states sat on large surpluses in 1999. New York, with a child-poverty rate of about 25 percent, had $1.1 billion in unspent welfare funds. Three other states with high child-poverty rates — Mississippi, Georgia and West Virginia — had a total of nearly $200 million.

Last year, numerous proposals sought unsuccessfully to raid some of the $7.4 billion in unused 1997 and '98 TANF funds sitting in the federal Treasury. The Senate considered cutting TANF funds to pay for disaster assistance in Central America and military aid to Jordan. The House suggested cutting TANF funds or transferring them to general education programs.

Congress also was chagrined to discover an unintended result of the 1996 law: Because caseloads are down so much, states had dramatically cut back on their own spending on welfare, leaving the federal government shouldering a larger share of the nation's welfare costs.

The CDF and other child advocates have urged the states to use the money to offer more job training and improve access to child care, transportation, drug treatment and mental-health counseling to help the hard-to-employ move more easily from welfare to work. They also want such services extended to the working poor.

The CDF argued further that if Congress cut TANF surpluses — which many states are holding in reserve in case leaner economic times cause caseloads to go up — it would discourage states from investing in innovative programs to help families get and keep good jobs. "State policy-makers must be assured that the TANF funds already committed by the federal government will be there to sustain needed services," said an April 2, 1999, CDF position paper. [24]

The group is further concerned that former welfare recipients are underutilizing available support services like day care, food stamps and transportation subsidies. Child advocates suggest that either caseworkers are discouraging eligible recipients from applying for such subsidies or former recipients don't realize that they are still eligible for them.

In San Francisco, for instance, when welfare officials returned more than $6 million in day-care funds to the federal government, claiming mothers leaving welfare were not interested in subsidized child care, some outraged eligible mothers said they were never told about the program.

Jack Frech, director of the Department of Human Services in Athens County, Ohio, has another theory to explain why former welfare users are ignoring programs for which they are eligible. "Our system is so coercive and controlling that people are really anxious to get out from under all the red tape," he says.

Minimum Wage Bills

Private social-service agencies say that the upsurge in families using food banks and homeless shelters suggests that parents leaving welfare are still having a tough time. A Kansas group found that half the families leaving welfare had stayed recently in a homeless shelter, and half had moved in with friends to share expenses. About half had not gotten needed medical care during the previous six months, and only 25 percent were using Medicaid. A third were receiving food stamps, but only 4 percent were receiving child-care subsidies.

One of the more controversial provisions of the 1996 law allowed states to deny additional benefits to welfare mothers who had more children while on welfare. At least 21 states have imposed such "family caps."

Deborah Frank, director of the Grow Clinic for malnourished babies at Boston Medical Center, says the policy is having "unanticipated consequences for children's health." Since Massachusetts adopted a family cap provision in 1996, she says, a third of her severely underweight patients are either family cap children or siblings of family cap children.

During the last three years, the clinic has seen a surge in underweight patients, including both welfare babies and children of working-poor families. In 1997, the clinic had 30 new cases; in 1999, a record 74 new cases were referred for treatment, she said. [25]

Frank suggested that perhaps the high cost of housing was forcing families to spend more of their incomes on rent instead of food. Whatever the cause, she said, "We are systematically disabling a whole generation of children." [26]

Meanwhile, legislation to increase the federal minimum wage by $1 an hour, even though it has passed both houses of Congress, is deadlocked in the Senate, where it is procedurally entangled with a controversial overhaul of personal bankruptcy law and multibillion-dollar tax cuts.

Republican and Democratic leaders in the Senate agree that the bankruptcy provisions should be separated from the wage and tax package, but they could not agree on how. [27]

Generally, Republicans want to set aside the wage and tax proposals for now and move forward with a bankruptcy conference. But Democrats don't want to endanger ultimate enactment of a minimum wage increase. Lobbyists for restaurants and retailers say the tax breaks Congress has drafted as compensation for the minimum wage increase — $122.7 billion in the Senate bill and $103 billion in the House version — are insufficient.

"We believe an increase is bad policy, and we're going to try to work to defeat an increase," said Lee Culpepper, senior vice president of government affairs and public policy for the National Restaurant Association. "I appreciate the attempts at tying this to tax relief, but at this point tax relief does not outweigh the negative of an increase." [28]

President Clinton has promised a veto if the bill comes to him containing "irresponsible" tax cuts. Senate Minority Leader Tom Daschle, D-S.D., has said the House cuts were too expensive and tilted toward the rich. Republicans contend the cuts are aimed at small-business owners to offset the costs of the mandatory wage increase. ■

OUTLOOK

The Hard-to-Employ

Next year, Congress will begin re-examining the impact of welfare reform as it prepares to reauthorize the TANF program in 2002. Lawmakers are expected to look at three problem areas: eligible families who are not using food stamps and Medicaid and children who fell into "extreme poverty" after their mothers left welfare but didn't go to work.

State and federal welfare officials also will be focusing more money and attention on those still left on welfare — the "hard-to-employ." Historically, the easiest to employ — people with high school diplomas and some work experience — move off welfare most readily, leaving the least educated and the chronically unemployed as a bigger percentage of the caseload. Many of those left behind lack a high school education or have emotional, mental or substance-abuse problems preventing them from working.

At Issue:

Would raising the minimum wage help alleviate child poverty?

yes

JARED BERNSTEIN

Economist, Economic Policy Institute and co-author of* The State of Working America, 1998-99 *(Cornell University, 1999).

WRITTEN FOR *THE CQ RESEARCHER*

Each time a minimum wage increase is introduced, opponents raise the same arguments, and each time our experience with the wage hike shows these arguments to be false. This time around, Rep. [Cass] Ballenger [R-N.C.] returns to the familiar arguments that the policy is poorly targeted, leads to job losses and creates wage pressure.

The targeting question: We know the minimum wage reaches low-wage workers, but do those workers live in low-income households? In fact, most of the benefits from recent minimum wage increases have gone to the intended recipients: low-wage workers in low-income, working households. If the minimum wage were increased by $1 today, 63 percent of the benefits would go to low-income working families

Rep. Ballenger also criticizes the minimum wage as an anti-poverty tool, but this, too, is unfair. Even in this era of welfare reform, many poor people have only marginal connections to the labor force, and non-workers cannot be expected to benefit from minimum wage increases. Half of the poor in this country are children or elderly. Furthermore, less than half (41 percent) of the working-age poor (16 or older) held jobs in 1998. However, once poor people do go to work, they are most likely to enter low-wage occupations and will thus be helped by an increased minimum wage.

The job-loss argument is a tough sell for opponents this time around, given the exceptional performance of the low-wage labor market since the last minimum wage increase. Since the minimum was last raised, from $4.25 to $5.15, the employment rates for low-wage workers have hit a 30-year high, and their unemployment rates have hit a 30-year low. Yet, without evidence, Rep. Ballenger asserts that increasing the minimum wage will "clearly harm" low-wage workers by "lessening employment opportunities."

Finally, Rep. Ballenger raises the possibility the minimum wage will lead to wage inflation and force the Fed to raise interest rates. In fact, wages have risen as a result of the minimum wage increase, but there is no evidence of price pressures coming from these recent wage gains.

The evidence is clear that modest increases in the minimum wage benefit low-wage workers in low-income families without generating job losses or price pressures. The minimum wage is an important policy for connecting low-income families to our growing economy.

no

REP. CASS BALLENGER, R-N.C.

Chairman, Education and the Workforce Subcommittee on Workforce Protections

FROM STATEMENT IN THE HOUSE, MARCH 9, 2000.

We have heard so much discussion today . . . about a higher minimum wage lifting the working poor out of poverty. But the proposed increase will have little impact on low-income families because few workers actually support families under the minimum wage. The minimum wage is typically paid to individuals who are just entering the work force, the overwhelming majority of whom are young, single and childless.

According to . . . the data that we get from the U.S. Census Bureau, 37 percent of those who benefited from the last minimum wage increase were young people living with their parents. Some 85 percent either live with their parents, or are single and childless, or living alone or have a working spouse. Only one in 10 minimum wage earner is trying to support a family. In reality, the minimum wage is a poorly targeted issue for anti-poverty as a tool.

The proponents of a higher minimum wage increase seem to suggest that entry-level employees work for years without a wage increase. But according to recent research, the vast majority of those who start at the minimum wage do not remain there long. Nearly two-thirds of minimum wage workers move above the minimum wage within one year of working. The majority of minimum wage workers use entry-level positions to gain experience and acquire the skills necessary to move ahead in better-paying jobs.

Those employees who do not quickly advance beyond the minimum wage tend to be the least skilled, the least educated and the least experienced workers. Typically, those are the most vulnerable in terms of losing their jobs or having their hours of work reduced. Research has shown that the minimum wage increases shift many jobs from low-skilled adults to teenagers and students.

Increasing the minimum wage is an ineffective way of helping those in need. It is not well-targeted at poor families. And while it benefits some individuals, it will clearly harm others by lessening employment opportunities.

For the 25 percent of low-wage workers whose families are poor, hiking the minimum wage too quickly may do more harm than good. Minimum wage increases cause price increases that disproportionately affect the poor. . . .

The hallmark of the economic good times we enjoy today has been low inflation. Raising the minimum wage will contribute to raise inflation at the same time as the Federal Reserve is raising interest rates to contain the deleterious effects of wage inflation.

Michelle Crawford Got Off Welfare . . .

Machine operator, mother of three and former welfare recipient Michelle Crawford became a symbol of Wisconsin's groundbreaking welfare-to-work program last year when she joined Republican Gov. Tommy G. Thompson at his annual State of the State address.

"My kids see a difference in me. They see their mother making it," Crawford told state lawmakers, describing her success under the Wisconsin Works program, or W-2. "W-2 gave me a chance, and I feel good about myself."

After thanking her employers and everyone else involved, she asked other employers to take a chance on W-2 workers. "We won't let you down," she said. [1]

W-2, which has reduced Wisconsin's welfare rolls by 90 percent and its child-poverty rate by half, is widely considered as a model for welfare reform.

"Wisconsin is by far the leader in the nation in reducing dependency," says Robert Rector, senior research fellow at the conservative Heritage Foundation and an authority on welfare. "I've been in this debate for 25 years, and the Left always told us that we could not make welfare recipients work because there aren't enough jobs, child care or transportation — and some people were just unemployable." But in Wisconsin, he says, even the bottom 10 percent are working. "That was a surprise to everyone, even in Wisconsin."

Now, most counties outside Madison have no one receiving cash benefits, he says. "Basically, welfare dependence is gone," he says. Even in Milwaukee, the caseload has dropped by more than two-thirds and is still going down, he says. Because the caseload was cut so dramatically, Thompson was able to increase monthly benefit levels for those still receiving cash benefits.

Meanwhile, the strict requirement that anyone receiving cash assistance must work has transformed W-2 staffers from check-writers into employment counselors and mentors. They help parents address the sometimes overwhelming personal and family problems preventing them from working, said J. Jean Rogers, administrator of the Wisconsin Department of Workforce Development.

She told the House Ways and Means Human Resources Subcommittee last May 27 that Wisconsin offers people who leave welfare a package of support services, such as job retention, food stamps, Medicaid, child-care assistance and the state earned-income tax credit. Thompson has recently called for increasing the income-eligibility limits and reducing the copayment for child-care assistance, expanding education and training opportunities for parents already in the work force and helping strengthen work-force retention and advancement among low-income working parents.

Wisconsin also offers immediate, intensive work-training services to help participants find work within the state's strict, 60-month time limit, Rogers said.

A 1999 Urban Institute study found that Wisconsin had the lowest child-poverty rate — 11.4 percent — of 13 states studied; the national rate was 20.5 percent at the time. [2]

Wisconsin also has the third-highest incidence of children living in two-parent families, according to the study, which researchers say reduces the likelihood that a child will grow up poor. And the state had the highest rate of employed parents, with 74.4 percent of its low-income parents and 86.9 percent of all parents working. [3]

"Anecdotal evidence supports the belief that children are thriving in the era of welfare-to-work," Rogers said. Caseworkers report that home life is more structured for the children when their mothers must abide by a work schedule, the children have a newfound respect for their mothers and more dads are getting involved in their children's lives, she said.

Advocates for the poor say many of those still unemployed may be having a hard time finding child care, because many low-wage jobs are for night and weekend-shift work, when most day-care centers are closed. Some also fear that as the states' one-year deadline passes for transitional child-care benefits, some working mothers will have to leave their minimum wage jobs because they won't be able to afford child care on their own.

But welfare-reform advocates say there is scant evidence that lack of child care is keeping mothers from working. The General Accounting Office is studying the problem.

Initial reports indicate that those who remain on welfare are also increasingly likely to be blacks, Hispanics and Native Americans, because whites have left the welfare rolls faster than minorities have. Those who remain are also more likely to live in the inner city. According to the Brookings Institution, urban counties saw their share of state welfare caseloads climb from 45 percent to 53 percent from 1994 to 1998.

Of the 6.8 million people still on welfare, anyone who was on the rolls in August 1996 — when welfare reform was passed — will lose federal benefits as of August 2001, when the law's five-year lifetime limit expires. In New York, for instance, 226,000 welfare families are facing the five-year cutoff.

But most families will not be cut off entirely, reformers say, because the law allows states to exempt 20 percent of their caseloads from the five-year limit. In addition, some states have set up fallback plans, such as New York's "Safety Net" program, if those remaining on welfare exceed the 20 percent limit.

. . . Thanks to Wisconsin's Welfare-to-Work Program

"W-2 is pulling families together and teaching them how to rely on themselves and their larger communities for support," Rogers said.

A January 1999 Wisconsin study found that 69 percent of those who have left W-2 were employed at an average wage of $7.42. And 21 percent who were not employed at the time of the study had worked since leaving the program. Ninety-four percent of those who were unemployed were receiving other family or government support. Finally, the report found, 68 percent said getting a job was easier than being on welfare, and 60 percent said they probably would not need welfare again.

Larry Mead, a welfare expert at New York University, said the study showed that the Wisconsin program is the "greatest achievement in anti-poverty policy since the Great Society." [4]

But others found disturbing news in the study. For example, despite Wisconsin's booming economy, some of those pushed off welfare by the program's universal work requirement are having problems paying for utilities, housing and food.

"This supports advocates who say the program has serious problems," said Pamela Fendt, a researcher at the University of Wisconsin in Milwaukee. [5]

Rogers admitted that those remaining on welfare have more severe barriers to work. "Our efforts must be focused on strategies to help remove those barriers," Rogers said. The state will seek community-based partner organizations with expertise in such areas as substance abuse and domestic violence, she said. And with more than half of the remaining welfare recipients lacking a high school or equivalency diploma, more emphasis is being put on basic education.

Rogers urged Congress to resist proposals to cut welfare block grants and funding for child-support enforcement. "We strongly object to such proposals," she said. "We have kept our part of the bargain, we urge you to keep yours."

Wisconsin started its reform in 1988 and had a fairly liberal reform program that focused on job training and job-search assistance. The state was able to cut its caseload by 20 percent, and it stayed flat throughout the recession of the early 1990s, when caseloads were rising by about a third in other states, Rector says.

Then in 1994, Wisconsin became the first state to impose universal work requirements. [6] "It's a safety net with a work requirement," Rector says. "When a single mother loses her job, she goes into a sheltered work program. Then when she gets another private-sector job, she moves out of the program."

The transition from welfare into a full-time job will not by itself alleviate all the personal problems these families face, Rogers said. "But, it's the first step," she said. "As individuals increase their level of confidence in their personal abilities, they develop positive strategies for dealing with their personal problems. And they no longer view welfare as their panacea."

[1] Quoted in testimony by J. Jean Rogers, administrator of the Wisconsin Department of Workforce Development, before the House Ways and Means Human Resources Subcommittee on May 27, 1999.

[2] Urban Institute, "Snapshots of America's Families," January 1999.

[3] Nationally, only 65 percent of low-income parents and 79.8 percent of all parents are working.

[4] Quoted in Jason DeParle, "Wisconsin Welfare Overhaul Justifies Hope and Some Fear," *The New York Times*, Jan. 15, 1999.

[5] *Ibid.*

[6] See Susan Kellam, "Welfare Experiments," *The CQ Researcher*, Sept. 16, 1994, pp. 793-816.

States that spent less of their own money on welfare in recent years by relying more on federal funds could get burned. Congress historically links its contributions to spending by each state. So states that have been spending less could receive fewer federal dollars and end up paying a greater percentage of their own money for existing programs.

Rep. Nancy L. Johnson, R-Conn., chairman of the Ways and Means Subcommittee on Human Resources, also warned governors in a March 15 letter that Congress could assume that it has provided states with too much money if it finds that states are supplanting their own welfare funds with federal welfare funds and using their own money for non-welfare purposes like tax cuts or building roads.

"Jurisdictions that do so will become widely known and criticized" she wrote, and "could provoke Congress to take actions that would hold serious consequences for every state."

Many states say they have been reserving their own state welfare funds in case the economy flounders. But Rector doubts that caseloads will automatically increase if the economy takes a downturn.

"It's quite clear from the data that caseload declines are tied overwhelmingly to the toughness of a state's workfare program, not to the robustness of a state's economy," he says.

Douglas Besharov, an expert on welfare at the American Enterprise Institute, doubts that child poverty can ever be eliminated. "The two largest causes of child poverty in this country are immigration and family breakdown," he says. "As long as we have a constantly replenishing source of child poverty through immigration, and until we reduce the rate of out-of-wedlock births, we won't see child poverty decline."

"Reducing illegitimacy and encouraging marriage is the one place where reform has really fallen short," Rector says. "The principal effort should never have been just to make single mothers work hard, but to restore the culture of marriage."

But, Syracuse University's Smeeding points out, "Canada has a lot more foreign-born immigrants than the United States does, and their child-poverty rate is two-thirds what ours is." Other countries with higher illegitimacy rates also have lower poverty rates, he says. Moreover, U.S. poverty rates among married, two-parent white families are the highest of the major industrialized nations, he says, because the U.S. offers fewer safety-net benefits.

Primus, of the Center on Budget and Policy Priorities, agrees. "Our safety net doesn't remove as many kids from poverty as it used to, or as it should. We as a country ought to be embarrassed about that," he says. "I would hope we will enact policies over the next few years that will ensure that our child-poverty rate ends up a lot lower than it is now." ■

FOR MORE INFORMATION

Center on Budget and Policy Priorities, 820 First St. N.E., Suite 510, Washington, D.C. 20002; (202) 408-1080; www.cbpp.org. This nonpartisan research group analyzes federal, state and local government policies affecting low- and moderate-income Americans.

Center for Law and Social Policy, 1616 P St. N.W., Suite 150, Washington, D.C. 20036; (202) 328-5140; http://epn.org/clasp.html. This public-interest law firm engages in educational activities, policy research and advocacy on behalf of low-income families.

Economic Policy Institute, 1660 L St. N.W., Suite 1200, Washington, D.C. 20036; (202) 775-8810; www.epinet.org. This research organization analyzes income distribution and other economic data with a focus on the impact of the income gap on American workers' living standards.

Heritage Foundation, 214 Massachusetts Ave. N.E., Washington, D.C. 20002; (202) 546-4400; www.heritage.org. This conservative think tank promotes free enterprise, limited government and "traditional" American values.

Notes

[1] Children's Defense Fund, *The State of America's Children: Yearbook 2000 (2000).* States had $33.4 billion in surplus funds in 1999, largely due to the robust economy and the $246 billion tobacco settlement.

[2] *Ibid.*

[3] The Annie E. Casey Foundation, "Kids Count," 1999.

[4] Children's Defense Fund, *op. cit.*

[5] Quoted from a House Republican white paper, "Welfare Reform Has Already Achieved Major Successes," issued May 27, 1999, by members of the House Ways and Means Human Resources Subcommittee.

[6] Quoted from a speech last October 21 at Concord Baptist Church in Brooklyn, N.Y.

[7] See "Since Welfare Reform, States Spend Less on Poor," stateline.org, Feb. 17, 2000.

[8] See Wendell Primus, et al., "The Initial Impacts of Welfare Reform on the Incomes of Single Mother Families," Center on Budget and Policy Priorities, Aug. 22, 1999.

[9] News release, Dec. 23, 1999.

[10] Kathryn Porter and Wendell Primus, "Recent Changes in the Impact of the Safety Net on Child Poverty," Center on Budget and Policy Priorities, Dec. 23, 1999.

[11] Shelia R. Zeldlewski and Sarah Brauner, "Are the Steep Declines in Food Stamp Participation Linked to Falling Welfare Caseloads?" Urban Institute, November 1999.

[12] Wendell Primus, et al., "The Initial Impacts of Welfare Reform on the Incomes of Single Mother Families," Center on Budget and Policy Priorities, Aug. 22, 1999.

[13] Press release, Aug. 22, 1999.

[14] Robert Rector, "Welfare: Broadening the Reform," Candidates Briefing Book, Heritage Foundation, p. 9.

[15] *Ibid.* Rector was quoting from Mary Corcoran, et al., "The Association Between Men's Economic Status and Their Family and Community Origins," *Journal of Human Resources,* fall 1992, pp. 575-601.

[16] Amy L. Sherman, "The Changing Face of Welfare," *Family Policy,* Family Research Council, November-December 1999.

[17] House Republican white paper, *op. cit.*

[18] Robert Kuttner, "A Living Wage Without Inflation," *The American Prospect,* Sept. 19, 1999.

[19] Joseph Loconte, "Seducing the Samaritan: The Downside of Public Funding of Nonprofits," *Pioneer Paper No. 13,* Pioneer Institute for Public Policy Research, July 1997.

[20] For background, see Kenneth Jost, "Welfare Reform," *The CQ Researcher,* April 10, 1992, pp. 313-336.

[21] Quoted Mary H. Cooper, "The Working Poor," *The CQ Researcher,* Nov. 3, 1995, pp. 969-992.

[22] Quoted in Christopher Conte, "Welfare, Work and the States," *The CQ Researcher,* Dec. 6, 1996, p. 1069.

[23] David Ellwood, "Welfare Reform as I Knew It: When Bad Things Happen to Good Policies," *The American Prospect,* May-June 1996, pp. 22-29.

[24] Children's Defense Fund Web site, March 16, 2000.

[25] Robin Estrin, "Clinic questions social policy of 'family cap,'" The Associated Press, March 19, 2000.

[26] *Ibid.*

[27] For background, see James C. Benton and Alan K. Ota, "Leaders Fail to Untangle Bankruptcy Law Rewrite, Minimum Wage Increase," *CQ Weekly,* March 25, 2000, p. 669.

[28] Quoted in James C. Benton and Sumana Chatterjee, "Leaders Will Try to Disentangle Bankruptcy Overhaul From Minimum Wage and Tax Package," *CQ Weekly,* March 18, 2000, p. 602.

Bibliography

Selected Sources Used

Books

Bryner, Gary C., *Politics and Public Morality: The Great American Welfare Reform Debate*, W.W. Norton, 1998.
A professor of political science at Brigham Young University traces how welfare reform is intertwined with racism, crime, sexism and urban decline.

Harris, Fred R., and Lynn A. Curtis, *Locked in the Poorhouse: Cities, Race and Poverty in the United States*, Rowman and Littlefield, 1998.
This update of the landmark 1968 Kerner Commission *Report on Poverty in America* concludes that child-poverty rates are higher now than at any time from 1966 to 1980.

Articles

DeParle, Jason, "Leftover Money for Welfare Baffles, or Inspires, States," *The New York Times*, Aug. 29, 1999.
With welfare rolls plummeting, states are awash in federal welfare money because federal financing remains fixed at historic highs.

Kuttner, Robert, "A Living Wage Without Inflation," *The American Prospect*, Sept. 19, 1999.
Kuttner disputes business claims that raising the minimum wage will cause companies to lay off workers.

Loconte, Joseph, "Seducing the Samaritan: The Downside of Public Funding of Nonprofits," *Pioneer Paper No. 13*, Pioneer Institute for Public Policy Research, July 1997.
Loconte, a fellow at the Heritage Foundation, argues that religious organizations accepting public money risk having their message neutralized by government rules and regulations that come attached to government dollars.

Sherman, Amy L., "The Changing Face of Welfare," *Family Policy*, Family Research Council, November-December 1999.
Sherman, an adjunct fellow at the Manhattan Institute, extols the changes that have occurred since the 1996 welfare-reform bill was passed.

Reports and Studies

"Poverty in the United States," U.S. Census Bureau, September 1999.
The March 1999 "Current Population Survey" gives information on household income and shows that in 1998 child poverty dropped statistically below 20 percent for the first time since 1980.

The Annie E. Casey Foundation, "Kids Count," 1999.
Partly because of the widening income gap, the number of children living in working-poor families increased by 1.3 million during the last decade.

Children's Defense Fund, *The State of America's Children: Yearbook 2000*, March 24, 2000.
The child-advocacy group's annual report finds that, despite the booming economy, America still has the highest child-poverty rate in the industrialized world.

Corcoran, Mary, et al., "The Association Between Men's Economic Status and Their Family and Community Origins," *Journal of Human Resources*, fall 1992, pp. 575-601.
University of Michigan researchers show that, all other factors being equal, receiving welfare reduces the long-term employment and earnings capacity of young boys.

House Ways and Means Human Resources Subcommittee, "Welfare Reform Has Already Achieved Major Successes," May 27, 1999.
This House Republican white paper calls the 1996 welfare-reform law "one of the most successful pieces of social legislation in American history."

Porter, Kathryn, and Wendell Primus, "Recent Changes in the Impact of the Safety Net on Child Poverty," Center on Budget and Policy Priorities, Dec. 23, 1999.
Cutbacks in child safety-net programs slowed progress in lifting children out of poverty in 1997.

Primus, Wendell, et al., "The Initial Impacts of Welfare Reform on the Incomes of Single Mother Families," Center on Budget and Policy Priorities, Aug. 22, 1999.
Progress in reducing child poverty slowed markedly after welfare reform, and many of the poorest families became poorer, says this group of welfare-reform opponents.

Rainwater, Lee, and Timothy M. Smeeding, "Doing Poorly: The Real Income of American Children in a Comparative Perspective," August 1995.
Professors at Harvard and Syracuse universities conclude that both poverty and inequality have increased in the United States since the late 1970s.

Rector, Robert, "Welfare: Broadening the Reform," *Candidates Briefing Book*, Heritage Foundation.
Rector cites a 1994 study that found it is not poverty but welfare itself that most damages children.

7 Death Penalty

MARY H. COOPER

It has been more than three years since Rolando Cruz was cleared of the charges that landed him on death row, but there's still bitterness in his voice. "I did 12 years, three months and three days," he told a recent conference on capital punishment. "They did kill me. I am who I am now because this is who they made." [1]

Cruz and another man, Alejandro Hernandez, were sentenced to death for the 1983 abduction, rape and murder of 10-year-old Jeanine Nicarico of Naperville, Ill. It was the kind of high-profile crime that prompts communities to demand quick action by law enforcement officers. DuPage County authorities complied by charging Cruz and Hernandez with Jeanine's murder.

Both men were tried, convicted and sentenced to death in 1985. Their convictions were based largely on the testimony of jailhouse informants and a deputy sheriff who said Cruz's description of a dream included details about the murder that only the killer would have known.

In 1995, after more than 10 years on death row, Cruz and Hernandez were released from prison after DNA testing proved that another man had raped Jeanine. At the time of the murder, Brian Dugan, a repeat sex offender and confessed murderer, had told authorities that he alone had committed the crime — a fact that the Cruz and Hernandez juries weren't told. Three prosecutors and four law enforcement officers have since been charged with obstruction of justice for concealing evidence that would have exonerated the men a decade earlier. [2]

The Cruz and Hernandez cases may be dramatic, but they're hardly unique. Five hundred people have been executed in the United States since the Supreme Court reinstated the death penalty in 1976. Over that same period, 75 condemned inmates have been released after evidence showed they had been wrongfully convicted. That equates to roughly one exoneration for every seven executions.

From *The CQ Researcher*, January 8, 1999.

"If you had to go to a hospital for a life-and-death operation and found that hospital misdiagnosed [one out of every seven] cases, you'd run," said lawyer Barry Scheck, a member of O.J. Simpson's defense team. "It's an intolerable level of error, regardless of your views on the death penalty." [3]

Scheck spoke at a recent national conference on wrongful conviction and the death penalty at Northwestern University Law School. (*See story, p. 122.*) "We don't have a position on the ultimate morality of the death penalty," says conference participant Richard C. Dieter, executive director of the Death Penalty Information Center in Washington. "It's how the death penalty is applied in the United States that we are critical of. We say that there's a lot of unfairness and that mistakes are made, and that at least we should attempt to change and correct those things."

Indeed, no one is predicting the death penalty will be abolished anytime soon in the United States. Capital punishment is on the books in 38 states, plus the federal government and the military. There are now 3,517 prisoners around the country awaiting execution.

A large majority of Americans still support capital punishment, and that support seems unlikely to wane in the wake of several horrific crimes in the past few years. Few protested the death sentence meted out to an unrepentant Timothy J. McVeigh for his role in the 1995 bombing of the Alfred P. Murrah Federal Building in Oklahoma City, which killed 168 people. And many Americans were angered when Susan Smith was sentenced in South Carolina to life in prison rather than death after drowning her two young children in 1994 and charging a mysterious black man with the crime. Similarly, many thought "Unabomber" Theodore Kaczynski deserved the death penalty for mailing letter bombs that left three people dead and 22 others injured. (*See "At Issue," p. 131.*)

Death penalty advocates say leniency in some of these cases shows that the system works by sparing mentally ill or mentally retarded criminals. But many legal experts point to flaws in the death penalty's application that open the criminal justice system to charges of pervasive unfairness. Recent studies have documented longstanding allegations of racial discrimination in capital cases. Statistics show that prisoners of all races are more likely to be executed if the victim was white than some other race. Although about half the homicide victims are people of color, more than 80 percent of the prisoners executed were convicted of killing whites. [4] A study this year also suggests that blacks are the most likely to receive the death penalty, regardless of the victim's race. [5]

"These studies are trying to determine whether race discrimination accounts for the race disparities in sentencing," says Dieter, author of the latest such study. "The odds of getting the death penalty are much higher if you're black than if you're white."

Defenders of capital punishment counter that any racial discrimination that may exist in its application argues for expanding the use of capital punishment, not abolishing it. "If it is true that people who kill black victims are less likely to get sentenced to death, that doesn't show the death penalty is discriminatorily imposed," says Kent S. Scheidegger, legal director at the Criminal Justice Legal Foundation in Sacramento, Calif. "It shows the death penalty is discriminatorily withheld. And the answer to that is more death sentences, not fewer, for the same kinds of crime in black-victim cases."

Another area of concern has been the death penalty's application to mentally retarded or mentally ill prisoners. The U.S. Supreme Court ruled in 1986 that the Eighth Amendment prohibits the execution of insane prisoners, but the definition of insanity varies widely among jurisdictions. Although evidence of mental illness led courts to spare Kaczynski and Smith, many less notorious killers have been executed despite evidence that they were unable to discern the seriousness of their crimes. In fact, 12 mentally retarded people have been executed since 1976; only 12 states prohibit the death penalty for the mentally retarded. [6]

Much of the current criticism of capital punishment concerns recently implemented restrictions on habeas corpus, a procedure for challenging a state conviction or sentence in federal court on constitutional grounds after normal appeals have been exhausted. The Constitution enshrines this right in Article 1, Section 9, and forbids the suspension of habeas corpus except in cases involving rebellion or invasion that threaten the public safety.

The mounting crime rates of the late 1980s prompted Congress to pass the 1996 Anti-Terrorism and Effective Death Penalty Act. Among other things, the sweeping measure not only set a one-year deadline for submitting a habeas corpus petition after state appeals are exhausted but also limited prisoners to one appeal in most cases. Supporters of the measure wanted to deter prisoners from launching repeated and groundless petitions to stall their executions.

Critics say the 1996 law fails to recognize the importance of the appeals process, compounding the unfairness of capital punishment. Most defendants in capital cases cannot afford experienced defense attorneys, and many don't receive adequate counsel, critics say, either at trial or during the appeals process.

In 1997, the American Bar Association (ABA) called for a moratorium on executions, citing "a haphazard maze of unfair practices with no internal consistency." But public support for the death penalty continues to run high, making the prospects doubtful for substantive reform in the near future.

As the debate over the fairness of the death penalty continues, these are some of the questions being asked:

Should recent restrictions on the right to appeal be rolled back?

One of the main complaints of death penalty advocates has been the growing delay between sentencing and execution. From 1977 to 1996, the average stay on death row increased from 51 months to 125 months, as prisoners appealed their sentences at the state level and, if those failed, at the federal level, all the way to the Supreme Court. [7] Critics claimed that most of the appeals were without merit and intended only to stall for time, and they called on Congress and the courts to do something.

Over the last decade the Supreme Court and Congress have responded, restricting men and women on death row from seeking habeas corpus review of their convictions. Chief Justice William Rehnquist has led the high court's efforts to streamline the handling of death row appeals. In 1991, for example, the Supreme Court ruled that an appeal filed three days late is not entitled to federal court review. Last April, it made it harder for appeals court judges to delay executions, ruling that a federal court had committed a "grave abuse of discretion" when it halted the execution of convicted rapist and murderer Thomas Thompson in California (*p. 129*).

Congress also ratcheted up the effort to curtail death row appeals. The 1996 Anti-Terrorism and Effective Death Penalty Act set a limit of one year for state prisoners to petition to the federal level after exhausting their appeals in state courts. But in states that meet the law's standards for providing adequate counsel to defendants, the limit is only six months. The law also made it difficult to file more than one habeas petition by requiring federal judges to defer to state court rulings on constitutional and other issues unless the state rulings were deemed "unreasonable."

"If a second or successive habeas petition raises the same claim that has been raised and decided adversely to the petitioner, then it must be dismissed," says Ira Robbins, a law professor at the American University's Washington College of Law and an expert on capital appeals. "There is no discretion there."

Even if a new claim is presented in a second or successive appeal, under the 1996 law the petition cannot be filed without authorization by a federal appeals court. Such courts have only limited discretion in authorizing the filing because they must examine a combination of reasons why the new claim was not presented earlier, including possible changes in the law, as well as evidence of innocence. "The court of appeals must look at that combination, which is

Capital Punishment in the United States

Since the Supreme Court declared the death penalty constitutional in 1976, 29 of the 38 states with death penalty statutes have held executions. Texas, Virginia and Florida conducted more than half of the 500 executions since 1976. Sixty-eight people were executed nationwide in 1998.*

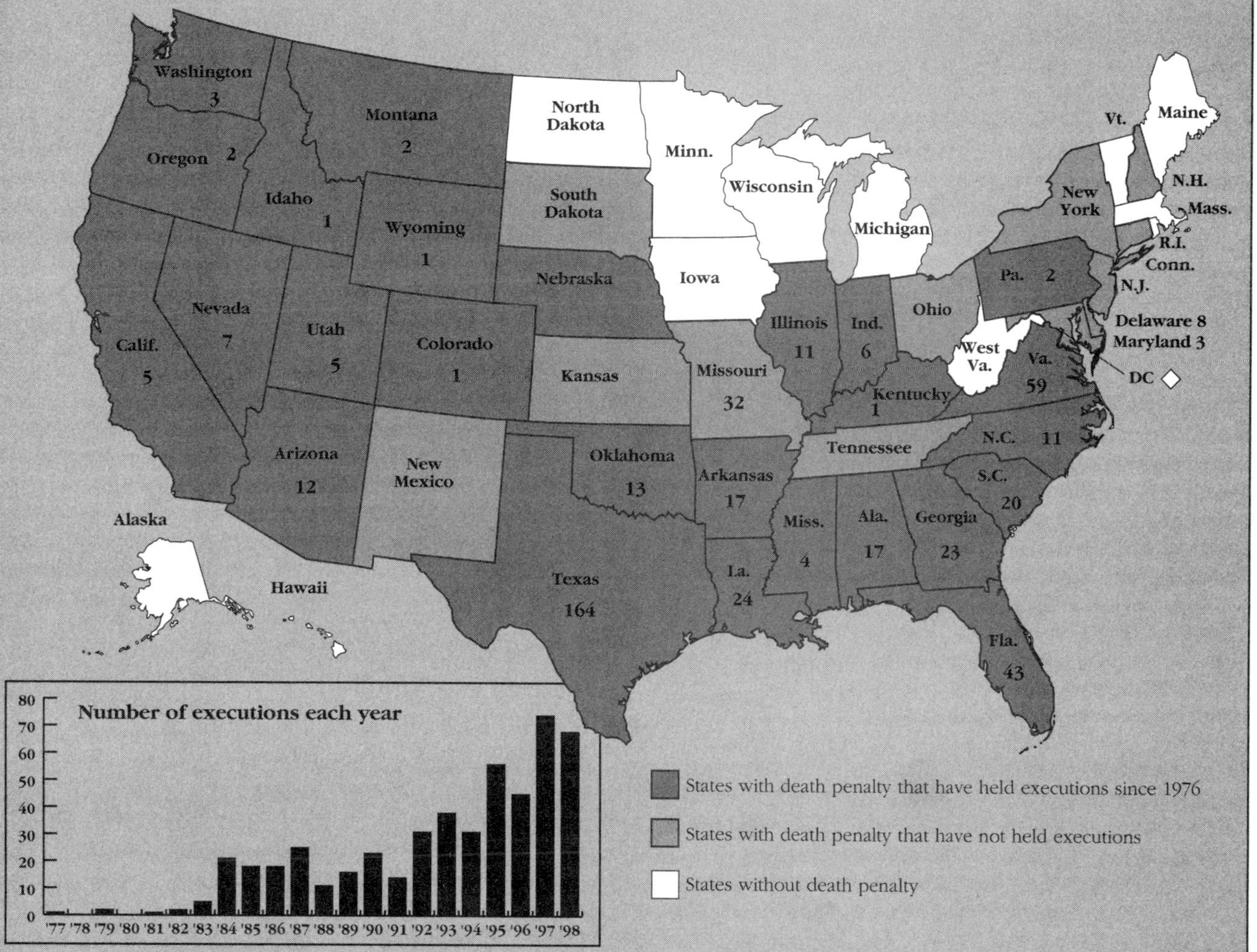

** Numbers on the map indicate the number of executions held in each state since 1976.*

Source: Death Penalty Information Center

a very hard test to satisfy," Robbins says. "So there has been a striking limitation on the ability to file second or successive petitions in the district court because of this gatekeeping provision that has to be ruled on by the court of appeals."

The other main restriction to death row appeals, the one-year statute of limitations on habeas petitions, marks a clear departure from previous law. "There was no statute of limitations prior to April 24, 1996, when the law was passed," Robbins says.

Critics say the new combination of restrictions could make it harder for innocent prisoners to make their case in time to avoid execution. "The restrictions impinge right at the point where these kinds of cases might run into trouble," Dieter says. "Some of the evidence of DNA doesn't show up until a number of years later. Not everybody needs 20 years to make their case, but there needs to be an exception for credible claims of innocence that allows that door to be open. These restrictions make it more likely not only that innocent people will be sentenced to death but that some will be executed."

In Dieter's view the federal restrictions on death row appeals are especially onerous in light of obstacles that already block appeals at the state level. In most states, a death row appeal goes from the trial court straight to the state supreme court. "These cases are reviewed at the state level, and that's where the mistakes should be found," Dieter says. "But what you find on the state level are comparable or even worse restrictions on appeals. The standard to get a review in some states is almost insurmountable. A lot of states have passed measures to limit the state part of the appeal, and when you tack on the federal limitations, you have a very difficult situation for anybody who has evidence of their innocence to get anywhere."

But other legal experts say the appeals process needs more, not fewer, restrictions. "Successive petitions," Scheidegger says, "are almost always without merit." He cites the 1997 *Lindh v. Murphy* case, in which the Supreme Court held that the 1996 law's provisions could not apply to petitions that were pending before the law was passed. "This was a quite wrong decision, in my opinion, that has postponed most of the law's benefits by eliminating a very large class," he says.

With 513 prisoners on death row and only five executions since 1976, California has the biggest backlog of death penalty cases in the country. "As far as the existing backlog goes," Scheidegger says, "the new law is doing us no good at all."

Critics say the anti-terrorism act has failed to streamline the appeals process in large part because it gave federal judges the authority to decide whether states qualify for the six-month deadline by providing competent legal counsel to indigent prisoners. "Congress gave this critical responsibility to the very federal judges whom the act was meant to control," writes Andrew Peyton Thomas, a former assistant attorney general for Arizona. "Not surprisingly, they have been in no hurry to declare the states in compliance. To date, not a single state has been permitted to opt in to the [anti-terrorism act's] system of expedited capital appeals. Two years after passage of the [law], death penalty appeals in the federal courts remain as protracted as ever." [8]

Critics of the anti-terrorism act cite studies suggesting that innocent people have already been executed in the United States and predict that the law makes such mistakes more likely to occur. A landmark 1987 study concluded that 23 innocent prisoners were executed from 1900 to 1987. [9] But some supporters of streamlining the appeals process for death row inmates question the findings and even suggest that executing the occasional innocent may be an acceptable price to pay.

"There is no proof that an innocent has been executed since 1900," affirms Justice for All, a Houston-based victims'-rights group. "In the context that hundreds of thousands of innocents have been murdered or seriously injured, since 1900, by criminals improperly released by the U.S. criminal justice system (or not incarcerated at all!), the relevant question is: Is the risk of executing the innocent, however slight, worth the justifications for the death penalty — those being retribution, rehabilitation, incapacitation, required punishment, deterrence, escalating punishments, religious mandates, cost savings, the moral imperative, just punishment and the saving of innocent lives?" [10]

Should behavior in prison be considered in decisions to carry out executions?

In 1983, Karla Faye Tucker and a male companion broke into a Houston apartment to steal some motorcycle parts. But they encountered two occupants and brutally killed them with a pickax. Both were convicted and sentenced to death. Tucker's codefendant died in prison of natural causes, but as Tucker's date with the executioner neared last January, Pope John Paul II and other religious leaders urged Gov. George W. Bush, R-Texas, to spare her life.

"She is not the same person who committed those heinous ax murders," said televangelist Pat Robertson on "The 700 Club." "She is totally transformed, and I think to execute her is more of an act of vengeance than it is appropriate justice." [11]

To Tucker's supporters, she had earned clemency throughout her 14 years of incarceration. Soon after arriving on death row, she became a born-again Christian. Prison guards attested to her exemplary behavior over the years, including her efforts to help other prisoners learn from her experience. By all accounts, Tucker appeared to have been completely rehabilitated.

Governors in Texas, which leads the country in executions — 164 since 1976 — have offered clemency to about a fifth of the prisoners scheduled for execution. Despite the appeals and the protesters outside the Huntsville prison complex calling for mercy, Bush allowed the 38-year-old Tucker to be executed by lethal injection on Feb. 3. But the controversy over what role post-conviction behavior should play in carrying out the death penalty continues.

Males typically commit capital crimes. Of the total U.S. death row population of 3,517, only 48 are women. Before Tucker, only two women had been executed in the United States since 1976, and only one in Texas since the Civil War. (A fourth woman, Judi Buenoano, was executed March 30 in Florida.)

Tucker's conversion to an evangelical form of Christianity also made her attractive to conservative religious leaders like Robertson, who normally support the death penalty.

"We believe that to not have the death penalty on the books would lower the value of life itself by suggesting that there is no crime worthy of the penalty of death," says Richard Cizik, acting director of the National Association of Evangelicals. "But that position does not suggest that the death penalty is appropriate in any particular case. We weren't arguing for Karla Faye Tucker's release. We were arguing for commutation of her death sentence on the grounds she would do much greater good to society alive in prison than she could dead."

Death penalty critics say Tucker's execution forces society to examine what it is trying to accomplish with capital punishment. "Are we trying to prevent future crime, or are we trying to punish because someone is so horrible?" Dieter asks. "If we look at the reasons for the death penalty and then try to see if it still makes sense, then I think it is worth looking at whether a person has changed in prison."

This is especially true in Tucker's case, Dieter says, because the key standard Texas jurors must use in deciding whether to apply the death sentence is whether the convicted person poses a future danger to society. "From that perspective, Tucker — like some other prisoners — was not much of a danger to anyone in prison," Dieter says. "She wasn't knifing guards or fellow inmates. She seems to have been a lovable person. If a prisoner's future danger is one of the criteria for the death penalty — and Texas isn't the only state where that applies — then we should re-evaluate it if we have the chance. Rehabilitation should make a difference in clemency proceedings."

But by its very nature, clemency is outside the judicial process. After all appeals have been exhausted through the courts, the final decision on execution rests solely with the governor of the state. This is as it should be, in Scheidegger's view. "Post-conviction behavior is something a governor may choose to consider," he says. "The clemency proceedings have, by and large, gone the way they should. There hasn't been the kind of abuse of the process that would get us concerned."

"She is not the same person who committed those heinous ax murders. She is totally transformed, and I think to execute her is more of an act of vengeance than it is appropriate justice."

— Televangelist Pat Robertson, "The 700 Club," speaking about Karla Faye Tucker

Other death penalty advocates say post-conviction behavior should not be taken into account because it does not accurately predict a person's behavior upon release. "Death row is a very cloistered, structured environment," says Diane Clements, president of Justice for All. "I don't believe that behavior on death row is a barometer as to how we would measure someone's behavior outside death row. That is why in Texas we sentence people to death, not only because of the crime they have committed, but also whether the individual is a future threat."

Ultimately, supporters of Bush's decision to deny Tucker clemency say the crime is more important than any subsequent change of heart. "Capital punishment is the redemption of a contract society owes to all human beings," writes William F. Buckley Jr. "To protect them and to guard posthumously their dignity, by taking the life of those who took their lives." [12]

Should minors be subject to capital punishment?

Shareef Cousin was just 16 when he was arrested, tried and convicted of fatally shooting Michael Gerardi in the face during a holdup outside a restaurant in New Orleans' French Quarter. In 1996, Cousin became the youngest death row inmate in the country when he began awaiting execution by lethal injection. He was 17. Cousin continued to proclaim his innocence, and last spring the Louisiana Supreme Court granted him a new trial. Justices determined that prosecutors had failed to disclose that Gerardi's date, an eyewitness to

Conference Highlights Incredible Journey . . .

Conferences on legal issues rarely attract public attention, given their dry discussions of arcane legal matters. But a recent meeting in Chicago drew worldwide press coverage. Among the lawyers and professors attending the conference on wrongful convictions and the death penalty were more than 30 former death row inmates.[1] They were among 75 people who have been sentenced to death in the United States since 1976 and later released from prison after being declared innocent or after charges against them were dropped due to overwhelming evidence of innocence. The wrongfully convicted include:

Brochure from the Conference on Wrongful Convictions and the Death Penalty. According to more recent data, 75 death row inmates have been exonerated.

James Richardson — The migrant farmworker was convicted in 1968 of poisoning seven of his children with pesticide. Prosecutors claimed he had bought life insurance policies for the children the day before they died and presented testimony of two jailhouse informants who said they had heard Richardson incriminate himself. Lawyers who later took on the case discovered that Richardson had not bought life insurance and that a babysitter who was with the children the night they died had been convicted of poisoning her husband. She later confessed to killing the children. Richardson was released in 1989 after a review of his case by then Dade County State Attorney Janet Reno. Richardson spent 21 years on death row, the longest for a wrongfully convicted person.

Sabrina Butler — She was sentenced to death in 1990 in Mississippi for murdering her 9-month-old baby. One of two women on the list of wrongfully convicted people, Butler said she performed CPR on her child when she found him not breathing and then took him to the hospital. The Mississippi Supreme Court overturned the conviction in 1992, and in 1995 Butler was acquitted on evidence that the baby had died of kidney disease or sudden infant death syndrome.

Dennis Williams and Verneal Jimerson — They were convicted along with two others for the 1978 murder of a young Illinois couple and spent 18 years on death row before three journalism students gathered new evidence showing that all four men had been wrongly convicted. The students interviewed suspects seen leaving the crime scene by a witness whose testimony police had ignored after charging the four with the crime. Two of the suspects confessed. DNA tests indicated that none of the four were involved in the crime. After charges were dropped, the Cook County state's attorney apologized

. . . From Death Row to Freedom

to the four men, calling the case a "glaring example" of the justice system's fallibility.

Jonathan Treadway — Convicted in 1974 of sodomizing and killing a 6-year-old boy in Arizona and sentenced to death, Treadway was granted a retrial by the state Supreme Court based on the incompetence of his trial counsel. He was acquitted of all charges after five pathologists testified that there was no evidence of sodomy and that the child had probably died of natural causes.

Joseph Green Brown — Sentenced to death in 1974 for murder, rape and robbery, Brown spent 13 years on Florida's death row before the 11th U.S. Circuit Court of Appeals ruled that prosecutors had knowingly allowed false testimony to be introduced at trial. The key evidence used against him was testimony of Ronald Floyd, whom Brown had turned in to police for an unrelated crime. Floyd later admitted that he had lied at trial and that he had testified in return for not being prosecuted himself for the same murder. After state courts rejected Brown's appeals, Brown filed a habeas corpus petition, and a federal court overturned his conviction. He came within 13 hours of execution.

AP Photo/Michael S. Green

Five years after being convicted in Mississippi of murdering her 9-month-old child, Sabrina Butler, here with her husband, was acquitted in a new trial.

Opponents of capital punishment took heart from the conference and the media coverage it attracted. "Certainly the American people are not in favor of executing innocent people," says Richard C. Dieter, executive director of the Death Penalty Information Center, who attended the Chicago conference. "People don't always realize that there are people on death row who don't have lawyers. They see the federal cases, which are well-represented and take weeks. They don't see the quick trial in Alabama, where they pay attorneys $2,000 maximum to take a death penalty case. If more people realized this, they would accept a greater requirement of fairness, and many would be more open to applying a sentence of life without parole."

Other legal experts are less sanguine about the conference's impact. "People who want to abolish the death penalty get energized by these kinds of conferences," says Victor Streib, dean of Ohio Northern University Law School and an opponent of capital punishment for juvenile offenders. "They think something like this will end support for the death penalty. I think people are concerned about wrongfully convicted people, but if you keep your finger on the public pulse with the polls, you'll find that support for the death penalty remains strong."

For their part, supporters of capital punishment are skeptical about the innocence of former death row inmates. "Of the 75 exonerated prisoners that they highlighted at the conference, even the conference organizers said they could not prove innocence," says Diane Clements, president of Justice for All, a Houston victims' rights group. "Along with everybody else in the United States, Justice for All does not want to see innocents wrongly convicted. But were these people really innocent?"

---

[1]The conference was held at Northwestern University Law School, Nov. 13-15, 1998.

the crime, had initially told authorities she was not wearing her glasses at the time and could see only patterns and shapes. At the trial, however, she positively identified Cousin as the murderer.

Dwayne Wright was not so lucky. Like Cousin, Wright was black, and he grew up in a poor, crime-ridden neighborhood of Washington, D.C. His father was imprisoned when Dwayne was 4; his mother was mentally ill and often unemployed. When Dwayne was 10, his older brother was murdered. As a teenager, Dwayne was hospitalized for major depression and psychosis and was held in juvenile detention facilities. He was evaluated as borderline retarded. A month after his 17th birthday, Dwayne went on a two-day crime spree that culminated in the robbery, attempted rape and shooting death of a 33-year-old woman in Virginia. He confessed after his arrest and was tried and sentenced to death in 1991. [13]

In his appeal, Wright contended that his defense attorney had failed to discover that an expert witness for the prosecution, a psychologist, had once concluded in a study that mental illness and environment are not responsible for a criminal's behavior. The appeal was rejected, however, and Gov. James Gilmore III, R-Va., a former prosecutor and a death penalty advocate, declined to stop the execution by lethal injection. On Oct. 14, 1998, Wright, then 26, became the 12th person to be executed in the United States since 1976 for a crime committed as a minor.

Few other countries in the world have executed juvenile offenders in recent years. Iran, Nigeria, Pakistan, Saudi Arabia and Yemen are the only other countries since 1990 known to have executed people for crimes they committed as minors. The United States has executed more juvenile offenders — 160 — than any nation since 1973. [14]

"We are literally the only country in the world that does this now," says Victor Streib, dean of Ohio Northern University's law school and an expert on condemned teens. "It was very rare in other countries until recently, and then because of some international treaties other countries have stopped it altogether."

"We believe that the death penalty is appropriate because it is a deterrent. We also believe it is the ultimate punishment for the ultimate crime. We must respect life."

—Diane Clements, President, Justice for All

The United States signed the International Covenant on Civil and Political Rights in 1992 but reserved the right to ignore the treaty's stipulation that "sentence of death shall not be imposed for crimes committed by persons below 18 years of age."

Supporters of harsher treatment of juvenile offenders point to the recent spate of schoolyard killings by teenagers and even preteens as evidence that a crackdown is needed to protect society from its youngest predators. Last March, a 13-year-old and his 11-year-old schoolmate were arrested for killing four students and a teacher at a Jonesboro, Ark., school.

In several states, no child is too young to be charged as an adult for certain violent crimes. [15] Federal law allows defendants as young as 13 to be tried as adults. U.S. Sen. Orrin G. Hatch, R-Utah, last year sponsored legislation that would require all states to lower the threshold to 14 for violent crimes. "Kids all over America are laughing at the juvenile courts," said Sen. Jeff Sessions, R-Ala., one of the bill's 25 cosponsors, all Republicans. "We're having more kids commit murder, armed robbery, the most serious offenses." [16]

Schoolyard shootings also have generated support for lowering the minimum age when a defendant can receive the death penalty. Of the 39 jurisdictions (38 states and the federal government) with capital punishment, 15 set the minimum age at the time of the crime at 18; four set it at 17; and the other 20 set it at 16. [17]

In Mississippi, where a high school student killed two classmates in October 1997, lawmakers are considering a bill that would allow prosecutors to seek the death penalty for juveniles when slayings occur on school grounds.[18] Other lawmakers went further, proposing death for younger offenders no matter where the killings occur.

"These children are not like they were when you and I were growing up," said Texas state Rep. Jim Pitts. In the wake of the Jonesboro shootings, Pitts proposed lowering the age at which juveniles are eligible for the death penalty in Texas from 17 to 11. "They're not what I call the Beaver Cleavers of the world," he said. "These kids are different. And, yes, I do feel that an 11-year-old should be . . . accountable for what they commit."[19] While Texans overwhelmingly support death for adults, only 25 percent of the respondents to a recent poll supported lowering the age of eligibility to 11.[20]

A rise in juvenile crime in the mid-1980s sparked a nationwide crackdown. But critics of the death penalty for juveniles point to statistics showing a fall in violent crime among teenagers since 1993 and suggest that the juvenile justice system does not need to be made tougher. "A tremendous amount of publicity has been given to a few, terribly horrific crimes, but the fact is that youth crime has gone down," says Brian Henninger, program coordinator for the National Coalition to Abolish the Death Penalty. "Instead of looking at this fact, as well as what has been working to get the youth crime rate down and doing more of that, we're looking at our gut instinct, at how we can punish more and make clear that these crimes can't happen again."

Some legal experts and child advocates say that any benefits the death penalty may have for adult offenders in deterring crime are utterly lost on juveniles. "Mostly, we know that kids don't think before they act," Streib says. "So threatening them with any kind of consequences doesn't seem to work. If you stopped a kid in a parking lot as he went into a store with a gun and warned him what would happen to him, it wouldn't work," Streib says.

"They're often high, they're excited and hormones are flying around," he continues. "So someone who says we need to increase the punishment for these crimes as a way to somehow prevent these kids from doing this, I say that's somebody who doesn't understand kids. It will not work." ■

BACKGROUND

Early Reforms

The death penalty arrived in America with the English, whose laws ruled the Colonies for a century and a half. Public hanging was mandatory for a number of crimes, and the first colonist executed, George Kendall, died in 1608 at Jamestown.[21]

After the Revolution, English common law remained the basis of the U.S. justice system. Neither the Bill of Rights nor the Eighth Amendment to the Constitution prohibiting "cruel and unusual punishment" were construed to prohibit executions. But modifications to English legal precedents soon distanced the U.S. criminal justice system from the English model.

Bowing to Quakers and other opponents of the death penalty, Pennsylvania in 1793 introduced the distinction between first-degree and second-degree murder. Capital punishment was reserved for offenses that were deemed more brutal because they involved premeditation. Most other jurisdictions also adopted this distinction.

The United States also ended the spectacle of public executions that were the rule in England. Rioting was not uncommon at hangings, especially when the condemned, rather than dying instantly of a broken neck, slowly strangled or was decapitated. Philadelphia physician Benjamin Rush, a vocal opponent of the death penalty, criticized the circuslike atmosphere at hangings. In 1835, New York began conducting hangings in enclosed yards before official witnesses only. The other states eventually followed New York's example, though Kentucky and Missouri continued public hangings until the late 1930s.

English law mandated the death sentence for capital offenses. But American jurisdictions, bowing to populist sentiment, allowed trial juries to make binding sentence recommendations of either death or life in prison. Introduced in 1841 in Alabama and Tennessee, jury sentencing discretion spread to other jurisdictions in the 19th century and has applied to virtually all capital cases as a result of Supreme Court rulings in the 1970s.

American criminal law also reduced the number of offenses punishable by death under the English system. However, a variety of capital offenses other than homicide, including kidnapping, treason, rape and armed robbery, remained on the books in many jurisdictions until recently. In 1977, for example, the Supreme Court abolished the death penalty for rape. Homicide is the only crime punishable by death that the Supreme Court has upheld as constitutional. But the 1994 Federal Death Penalty Act authorizes the death penalty for some federal crimes that do not involve homicide, such as espionage and treason.

Abolition Movement

The movement to abolish the death penalty made its greatest headway early in the 20th century. Nine states repealed capital punishment, joining Michigan, Rhode Island and Wisconsin, which had abolished the death penalty in the mid-1800s.

By the late 1920s, the abolition movement had lost its momentum. Partly as a result of public anxiety over "crime waves" during Prohibition and the Great Depression, the number of executions rose sharply in the 1930s and '40s.

This period saw two important changes in capital punishment. The first was the widespread adoption of the electric chair as an alternative to hanging. Developed in the late 1880s as a more humane method of execution, electrocution itself came under attack as cruel and barbaric and was replaced in some jurisdictions by the gas chamber and later by lethal injection. Today, all but four states provide lethal injection as at least an alternative for execution.

The other major change during the 1930s and '40s was the involvement of federal appeals courts in reviewing state court death sentences. Until then, death sentences had almost always been carried out without review of any kind, state or federal. A few landmark cases, such as the Scottsboro Boys rape case (*Powell v. Alabama*, 1932), set precedents for federal review of appeals based on charges that state courts had violated the federal Bill of Rights. *

Delaware's repeal of capital punishment in 1958 revived the abolition movement. The movement peaked in 1966, the only time that Americans opposed to the death penalty outnumbered advocates, though by a narrow margin of 47 percent to 42 percent. Also in the mid-1960s, three states abolished the death penalty, bringing the number of states without capital punishment to 12, plus the District of Columbia. (*See map, p. 119.*)

The growing sentiment against capital punishment was accompanied by a steady decrease in executions from a peak of 199 in 1935 to just one in 1966. Between 1968 and 1976, while the constitutionality of the death penalty was tested in the courts, no executions were held in the United States. The courts continued to sentence prisoners to death, however, and the decline in executions was accompanied by the growth of the death row population from just over 500 in 1970 to more than 3,000 by 1995.

Two landmark cases decided the fate of capital punishment in the United States. In June 1972 the Supreme Court ruled in *Furman v. Georgia* that the death penalty as administered by 35 states at the time was unconstitutional. Because the ruling essentially nullified the sentences of the more than 600 prisoners on death row, state courts were required to resentence them. The court later made several important changes to capital punishment — prohibiting mandatory death penalties, limiting death sentences to some form of criminal homicide and requiring each death sentence to undergo review by a state appeals court.

Although the Supreme Court placed restrictions on certain aspects of the death penalty in *Furman*, the decision marked the end of the most recent drive to eliminate capital punishment in the United States. Within months of the ruling, state legislatures had overhauled their capital punishment laws to comply with the new guidelines. In the mid-1970s, the court ruled in *Gregg v. Georgia* (1976) and other cases that the death penalty as applied under revised state laws did not violate the Eighth Amendment's prohibition of "cruel and unusual punishment." Executions resumed in 1977.

Support for Executions

The resumption of executions coincided with a surge in violent crime that began in the late 1960s and continued for two decades. Popular support for the death penalty rose rapidly during this period, surpassing 70 percent of Americans by the early 1990s. At the same time, victims' rights advocates fought for, and obtained, the right of families of homicide victims to participate in the sentencing process. [22]

In campaigns for public office, including Ronald Reagan's successful bid for the California governorship in 1966 and George Bush's presidential campaign of 1988, candidates won votes by presenting themselves as tough on crime and supportive of capital punishment. Accordingly, governors and presidents alike have refrained from granting clemency. The average number of clemency awards each year fell from 18 in the 1960s to one a year in the decade ending in 1994.

Meanwhile, evidence of unfairness in the administration of capital punishment prompted a renewal of the death penalty debate. Beginning in the 1980s, a number of studies concluded that racial discrimination was common in meting out death sentences. [23] The first was a study by Iowa researcher David C. Baldus showing that killers of white victims in Georgia were more likely to receive the death penalty than killers of black victims. Based on Baldus' study, the Supreme Court ruled in *McKleskey v. Kemp* (1987) that defendants could not use evidence of racial disparities in death sentences as evidence of racial discrimination in their own sentences. Subsequent studies have found such evidence stemming from the overall number of black inmates on death row and the overwhelming prevalence of white prosecutors in capital cases. [24]

The vast majority of death sentences have been handed out by state

* The rape convictions and death sentences of the defendants in the Scottsboro case were overturned because the state failed to provide adequate defense counsel.

Chronology

1970s Executions are suspended in the United States pending court review of capital punishment's constitutionality.

1972
The U.S. Supreme Court holds in *Furman v. Georgia* that the death penalty, as administered by 35 states, is unconstitutional. The court later prohibits mandatory death penalties, limits death sentences to some form of criminal homicide and requires that each death sentence undergo review by a state appeals court.

1976
The Supreme Court reinstates the death penalty in *Gregg v. Georgia,* holding that it does not violate the Eighth Amendment's prohibition of "cruel and unusual punishment" as applied under revised state laws. Executions resume the next year.

1980s The incidence of violent crimes punishable by death rises rapidly.

1986
The Supreme Court rules that the Eighth Amendment prohibits the execution of insane people.

1987
The Supreme Court rules in *McKleskey v. Kemp* that defendants may not use evidence of racial disparities in death sentences as evidence of racial discrimination in their own sentences.

1990s Horrific crimes bolster public support for the death penalty amid concerns about the fairness with which it is applied.

1992
The United States signs the International Covenant on Civil and Political Rights but reserves the right to ignore the treaty's ban on executing individuals for crimes committed when they were under age 18.

1994
Susan Smith is sentenced to life in prison in South Carolina for drowning her two young children. Congress authorizes the death penalty for numerous federal crimes. Supreme Court Justice Harry Blackmun reverses his earlier support for the death penalty.

1995
Timothy J. McVeigh and Terry Nichols are convicted of blowing up the Alfred P. Murrah Federal Building in Oklahoma City, killing 168 people. McVeigh is later sentenced to death; Nichols receives a life sentence.

April 24, 1996
Congress passes the Anti-Terrorism and Effective Death Penalty Act restricting convicted criminals' rights to file habeas corpus appeals of their sentences. The measure sets a one-year deadline for submitting such petitions after state appeals are exhausted and limits prisoners to one such hearing in most cases.

1997
Citing due-process questions raised by the 1996 law and other concerns, the American Bar Association calls for a moratorium on executions in the United States. The Supreme Court holds that the Anti-Terrorism Act does not apply to petitions pending before the law was passed, excluding a number of backlogged cases in California and other states.

February 1998
Gov. George W. Bush, R-Texas, refuses to grant clemency to Karla Faye Tucker, a condemned murderer who became a born-again Christian on death row.

April 1998
The Supreme Court rules that a federal appeals court committed a "grave abuse of discretion" by halting the execution of a convicted rapist and murderer in California; the high court makes it harder for appeals court judges to delay executions. The court also rules that an appeals court may change a death sentence handed down by a state court only if presented with "clear and convincing evidence" of the defendant's innocence. Kentucky passes the Racial Justice Act, becoming the first state to allow defendants to challenge a death sentence on grounds of racial disparity in sentencing.

May 4, 1998
"Unabomber" Theodore Kaczynski is sentenced to life in prison for mailing letter bombs that killed three people and injured 22 others.

Nov. 13-15, 1998
Northwestern University Law School holds a conference on wrongful convictions, featuring more than 30 former death row inmates whose sentences were overturned.

Despite Global Trend, U.S. Executions Continue

Last Nov. 12, while attempting to pass through Italian customs on a false passport, Abdullah Ocalan was arrested and detained in Rome. Ocalan, leader of the Kurdish Workers' Party, had led a bloody campaign for Kurdish self-rule in southeastern Turkey for 14 years. He asked for political asylum in Italy. But the Turkish government holds Ocalan responsible for the deaths of 30,000 citizens and demanded his extradition to face charges of terrorism and treason. Ocalan also was wanted on terrorism charges in Germany.

If convicted in a Turkish court of law, Ocalan would almost certainly receive a death sentence. But Italy, which does not have the death penalty, is barred by its constitution from extraditing foreigners to countries with capital punishment. Outraged over Italy's refusal to hand over its most wanted criminal, the Turkish government threatened economic retaliation. The incident became a major diplomatic crisis between the two NATO members that escalated in late December, when Italian Premier Massimo D'Alema announced that Ocalan had been released following Germany's cancellation of its warrant.

The controversy swirling around Ocalan's treatment in Europe stands in stark contrast to the death penalty debate in the United States. As Kurdish and Turkish protesters clashed outside the Rome building where Ocalan was held, the American criminal justice system quietly executed its 500th prisoner since 1976, when the Supreme Court upheld the constitutionality of capital punishment.

Of course, the United States is hardly alone in executing its most vicious criminals. Since 1996, when China launched its "Strike Hard" anti-crime campaign, more than 6,000 people have been sentenced to die in China, of whom more than 4,000 were executed in 1997. [1] In the past couple of years, a number of Caribbean countries, including Jamaica and Trinidad and Tobago, have taken steps to increase capital punishment in an attempt to curb rising violent crime rates linked to the region's thriving drug traffic. [2]

But more than half the countries in the world have abandoned capital punishment, either by statute or in practice. Today, the United States is one of 90 countries that have the death penalty; 63 have abolished capital punishment, while another 25 — including Turkey — are considered to be de facto abolitionists because they haven't executed anyone for at least 25 years or since gaining independence. Of the 90 countries with the death penalty, 16 reserve it for "extraordinary crimes," such as treason and espionage. [3] Among the countries with capital punishment, only a handful apply it frequently: Only China, Iran and Saudi Arabia are known to have executed more prisoners than the United States in 1997. [4]

But over the past several decades, as the pace of executions picked up in the United States, there has been a global trend to abandon capital punishment. The Universal Declaration of Human Rights adopted in 1948 by the United Nations does not specifically ban capital punishment, but many critics say the document does so implicitly. "The Declaration proclaims each person's right to protection from deprivation of life, and it categorically states that no one shall be subjected to cruel or degrading punishment," states Amnesty International USA. "The death penalty — the premeditated and cold-blooded killing of prisoners in state custody — violates both of these rights." [5]

Other international agreements address specific issues related to capital punishment. The 1992 International Covenant on Civil and Political Rights forbids the execution of offenders younger than 18. Upon ratifying that agreement, the U.S. reserved the right to carry out such executions. In May 1989, the United Nations Economic and Social Council recommended "eliminating the death penalty for persons suffering from mental retardation or extremely limited mental competence." In 1997, the U.N. Commission on Human Rights passed a resolution calling for all states with capital punishment to consider suspending executions with a view to abolishing the death penalty.

Last April the commission released a report condemning the application of capital punishment in the United States. Specifically, the report says that some of the states carry out executions in an arbitrary and discriminatory manner that does not spare juveniles, the mentally retarded or the mentally ill.

Congressional conservatives, including longtime critics of the United Nations and U.S. support of the institution, quickly responded to the report. "With all the abuses in places like Burma, China, Cuba and Iraq, to be wasting time and money to investigate the freest country in the world shows what a strange and distant planet the United Nations inhabits," said Marc Thiessen, a spokesman for Senate Foreign Relations Committee Chairman Jesse Helms, R-N.C. "I hope the U.N. will send this report to every single U.S. citizen so they can see how their money is being spent by an institution so badly in need of top-to-bottom reform." [6]

---

[1] "China's Crimes and Punishments" *Harper's*, November 1997.

[2] Larry Rohter, "In the Caribbean, Support Growing for the Death Penalty," *The New York Times*, Oct. 4, 1998.

[3] Data from Amnesty International USA.

[4] Amnesty International USA, "United States of America: 'A Macabre Assembly Line of Death,'" *Death Penalty Developments in 1997*, April 1998.

[5] Amnesty International USA, "A Violation of Human Rights," *U.S. Death Penalty Fact Sheet #10*, September 1998. For background, see Kenneth Jost, "Human Rights," *The CQ Researcher*, Nov. 13, 1998, pp. 977-999.

[6] Quoted in John M. Goshko, "U.N. Panel Calls On U.S. To Halt Death Penalty," *The Washington Post*, April 4, 1998.

courts. But in 1994, Congress responded to public anger over terrorism and drug-related killings by passing a massive crime bill that authorized the death penalty for several dozen federal crimes, including drug trafficking by "drug kingpins," treason, espionage or causing a death by mailing explosives. Since the law took effect, the death penalty has been sought in about 70 federal cases, up from just seven in 1994, the year before the law took effect. [25] ■

CURRENT SITUATION

Questions of Fairness

While Congress and the Supreme Court have acted to speed executions in recent years, concerns about the death penalty's fairness have led several prominent jurists who had not opposed the death penalty to reverse course. "From this day forward, I no longer shall tinker with the machinery of death," declared then Supreme Court Justice Harry Blackmun in 1994. "For more than 20 years I have endeavored — indeed, I have struggled — along with a majority of this Court, to develop procedural and substantive rules that would lend more than the mere appearance of fairness to the death penalty endeavor. Rather than continue to coddle the Court's delusion that the desired level of fairness has been achieved and the need for regulation eviscerated, I feel morally and intellectually obligated to concede that the death penalty experiment has failed." [26]

The victims' rights movement has broadened the debate over the death penalty beyond concern about fair treatment of defendants and capital punishment's effectiveness in deterring future crimes. It is only right, many victims' advocates say, that murderers pay for their crime with their lives. Until an inmate is executed, they say, victims' families are unable to reach "closure," to reconcile themselves to the crime that has torn apart their lives. "We believe that the death penalty is appropriate because it is a deterrent," says Clements of Justice for All. "We also believe it is the ultimate punishment for the ultimate crime. We must respect life."

The author of *Dead Man Walking*, Sister Helen Prejean, came to understand the need for retribution through her work as a spiritual consultant to prisoners on death row in Louisiana. As Prejean recounted in her book, later made into a popular movie, the family of a young man who had been brutally murdered desperately wanted his murderer, Robert Willie, to be executed. Moreover, they had been angered by Prejean, who had ministered to Willie but had ignored the victim's family.

The victim's girlfriend, who had been kidnapped and raped by the same man, was more ambivalent about the execution's role in enabling her to get on with her life. "Robert Willie's death . . . definitely reduced the fear I had to live with, [and] while I wasn't at all sure that was justification enough to execute a man, I couldn't help the fact that I simply felt better knowing Robert Willie was dead," wrote Debbie Morris. "But I do know this: Justice didn't do a thing to heal me. Forgiveness did." [27]

Death penalty opponents decry the focus on retribution, no matter what the crime. "To say that unless we get the death penalty for this person we are depreciating the value of the lost victim is simply a basic sickness," says juvenile crime expert Streib. "If somebody, God forbid, were to kill my child, I would not measure the value of my child's life on this Earth by whatever happened to the guy who killed her. But society to some degree has bought into the notion that you can put a price on the victim's pain by the punishment given the offender. That puzzles me because it has absolutely nothing to do with crime control. It has to do with satisfying the victim's family by killing yet somebody else by feeding that appetite we have for violent revenge."

Streib acknowledges that his views are not widely shared. "Between 75 and 80 percent of Americans support the death penalty," he says, "and that hasn't changed very much in the last 10-15 years."

There are some signs that recent studies tracking racial disparities in sentencing are beginning to influence the administration of capital punishment, however. In April 1998, Kentucky became the first state to allow defendants to challenge a death sentence on grounds of racial disparity in sentencing. "Under Kentucky's Racial Justice Act," says Dieter of the Death Penalty Information Center, "a defendant in whose case the death penalty is being sought no longer must prove purposeful racial discrimination, but may challenge the decision by simply introducing evidence of a pattern of racial bias or disparity in death sentencing against whatever minority group he or she belongs to."

But most statutory changes in recent years have made it easier, not harder, for prosecutors to seek the death sentence. In 1996, for example, a number of states added to the list of aggravating circumstances* in death penalty cases, including murder of a witness (South Carolina), murder of a firefighter, paramedic or emergency rescue worker engaged

* Aggravating and mitigating circumstances in capital cases are facts that can be weighed during the sentencing phase in deciding whether to sentence a defendant to death or a lesser sentence, such as life in prison without parole.

AP Photo/Michael S. Green

Many of the 75 people freed from death row after their convictions were overturned attended the recent National Conference on Wrongful Conviction and the Death Penalty in Chicago.

in official duties when the defendant had reason to know the victim's occupation (Tennessee), and mutilation or torture of a murder victim while still alive (Indiana). [28] After the November slashing death of a 9-year-old boy in Oceanside, Calif., legislators called for a change in the law to allow the death penalty in the murder of a child under 14. [29]

The pace of executions also has quickened. In 1997, 17 states executed 74 prisoners — 29 more than in 1996 and the highest number since the 1950s. Texas led the way, with 37 executions. Last year's total was 68 executions, down slightly from 1997. Andrew Smith, 38, convicted of the 1983 stabbing deaths of two elderly relatives, died by lethal injection on Dec. 18 in South Carolina. He was the last person to be executed in 1998, and the 500th since capital punishment was reinstated in 1976.

Anti-Terrorism Law

Passage of the Anti-Terrorism and Effective Death Penalty Act in 1996 was greeted enthusiastically by conservatives, who had long opposed the repeated filing of habeas corpus petitions to delay executions. At isssue was what conservatives called prisoners' meritless claims that their constitutional rights had been violated during the trial or appeals phase.

Capital punishment advocates were soon disappointed, however, as attorneys for death row prisoners took advantage of a rarely used avenue to pursue their cases, asking federal appellate courts to review death sentences based on procedural flaws at trial or on new evidence.

In April 1998, the Supreme Court shut the door on this type of petition by ruling that an appeals court can only change a state court's death sentence if presented with "clear and convincing evidence" of the defendant's innocence. That decision paved the way for the execution in California of Thomas Thompson, a convicted rapist and murderer scheduled to die the previous August.

"The Thompson execution could not go forward until the Supreme Court jumped in to enforce the law," says Scheidegger of the Criminal Justice Legal Foundation. With the Supreme Court ruling, he says "The law has already had the effect of cutting off repeated petitions in all but the most rare cases." Thompson was executed on July 14, 1998.

Some conservatives say the 1996 law does not go far enough, however, in restricting the authority of federal appellate courts to defy state court decisions by prolonging the appeals process. A frequent target of such criticism is the 9th U.S. Circuit Court of Appeals in San Francisco, which ruled on the Thompson case.

"The [anti-terrorism law] seemed a reasonable, studied response to the seemingly interminable delays in executions of first-degree murderers across the land," writes Thomas, the former assistant attorney general for Arizona. "But it already seems clear that [it] is an abject failure, a metaphor for the very problem it was meant to help remedy: an out-of-control federal judiciary, impervious to the claims of the rest of the political system, or even of simple justice."

Thomas wants Congress to repeal the law's requirement that

At Issue:

Should the death penalty be abolished?

yes

Amnesty International USA,
Program to Abolish the Death Penalty

FROM FACT SHEETS, SEPTEMBER 1998.

Extensive evidence shows that death sentencing continues to be arbitrary in the United States. The death penalty is applied neither fairly nor consistently. Several thousand defendants are convicted of murder each year, and less than 1 percent of them receive death sentences.

Gravity of crime and culpability are not always factors in determining the sentence. Race, social and economic status, level of education, location of crime and pure chance play significant roles in the legal processes which send some defendants to prisons, others to death. Offenders who commit similar crimes under similar circumstances have received widely differing sentences.

In almost all jurisdictions throughout the United States, the prosecutor is an elected official. It is the prosecutor who decides whether to seek the death penalty. Some prosecutors rarely seek the death penalty; some seek it whenever possible. Some prosecutors call for capital punishment only if a case is widely publicized, a focus of community pressure or an issue among defense attorneys or local police. Some prosecutors demonstrate racial bias in their decisions to seek the death penalty. Prosecutors settle many cases through plea bargaining. More culpable defendants at high risk of receiving a death sentence often plea bargain in return for a reduced sentence. Their less culpable accomplices, however, may receive the death penalty.

In addition, prosecutors seek the death penalty far more frequently when the victim of the homicide is white than when the victim is black. . . .

In most states prosecutors may reject potential jurors who oppose the death penalty. Potential black jurors are often removed by peremptory challenge — that is, without any stated reason — in cases involving black defendants. Since reinstatement of the death penalty in 1976, only five white persons have been executed for killing a black person.

Jury interpretations of aggravating or mitigating circumstances also cause discrepancies in death sentencing. In Texas a defendant's life or death may depend on a jury's prediction of his or her future conduct. In Alabama, Delaware, Florida and Indiana, trial judges may override the jury's sentencing recommendation. . . .

Even with the costly safeguards required by the United States judicial systems, gross miscarriages of justice occur. Innocent people have been executed in the past and statistics show that several innocent people are convicted of capital crimes in the United States each year.

no

David Gelertner
A professor of computer science at Yale University who was letter-bombed and nearly killed in June 1993

FROM "WHAT DO MURDERERS DESERVE?" **COMMENTARY,** *APRIL 1998.*

Why execute murderers? To deter? To avenge? Supporters of the death penalty often give the first answer, opponents the second. But neither can be the whole truth. If our main goal were deterring crime, we would insist on public executions . . . . If our main goal were vengeance, we would allow the grieving parties to decide the murderer's fate. . . . In fact, we execute murderers in order to make a communal proclamation: that murder is intolerable. A deliberate murderer embodies evil so terrible that it defiles the community. . . .

When a murder takes place, the community is obliged, whether it feels like it or not, to clear its throat and step up to the microphone. Every murder demands a communal response. Among possible responses, the death penalty is uniquely powerful because it is permanent and can never be retracted or overturned. . . .

Of course, we could make the same point less emphatically if we wanted to — for example, by locking up murderers for life (as we sometimes do). The question then becomes: Is the death penalty overdoing it? Should we make a less forceful proclamation instead?

The answer might be yes if we were a community in which murder was a shocking anomaly and thus, in effect, a solved problem. But we are not. Our big cities are full of murderers at large. . . .

Granted (some people say), the death penalty is a communal proclamation; it is nevertheless an incoherent one. If our goal is to affirm that human life is more precious than anything else, how can we make such a declaration by destroying life? . . . [But] the point of capital punishment is not to pronounce on life in general but on the crime of murder. . . .

A newer objection grows out of the seemingly random way in which we apply capital punishment. . . . We can grant that, on the whole, we are doing a disgracefully bad job of administering the death penalty. After all, we are divided and confused on the issue. The community at large is strongly in favor of capital punishment; the cultural elite is strongly against it. Our attempts to speak with assurance as a community come out sounding in consequence like a man who is fighting off a choke-hold as he talks. But a community as cavalier about murder as we are has no right to back down. That we are botching things does not entitle us to give up.

states provide competent counsel to indigent defendants in capital cases.

"The states should be trusted once again to hire qualified counsel for capital appeals without supervision by the same federal judges the [anti-terrorism law] is meant to curb," he writes. "[H]ardened murderers on death row have been able to avoid execution for more than a decade on average, in large part because their advocates are quite competent indeed — seated on the bench, with gavels in hand." [30]

But other legal experts say the law exacerbates longstanding flaws in the death penalty's administration. The ABA has long criticized the death penalty for people who committed crimes as juveniles or who are mentally impaired. In August 1997, in response to concerns about the anti-terrorism law, the ABA finally called for a moratorium on executions altogether.

"The anti-terrorism statute was really the impetus for getting this done now," says Kenneth Goldsmith, staff counsel for the ABA's criminal justice section. Because the ABA represents practitioners of all branches of the law, including criminal prosecutors, Goldsmith says, there had not been enough support to pass a moratorium resolution until the new law raised due-process concerns. "The anti-terrorism statute created an atmosphere which otherwise would not have been conducive to the ABA's taking on the death penalty."

Anti-death penalty advocates see another danger in the law. "In states like Missouri, this law has actually been applied retroactively, which is disturbing in its own right," says Henninger of the National Coalition to Abolish the Death Penalty. "Missouri doesn't by a long shot meet the requirements that are necessary to fall under the act, yet they're processing appeals faster than any other state in the country right now."

Henninger says the 8th U.S. Circuit Court of Appeals, which presides over Missouri, has not looked at the fact that three Missouri inmates have been executed since passage of the anti-terrorism law without recourse to the federal appeals process.

'That is very disturbing, and if we see other circuits follow suit, we could have a real problem on our hands," he says. ■

OUTLOOK

Piecemeal Reforms?

The courts have yet to grapple with a key issue raised by the 1996 Anti-Terrorism and Effective Death Penalty Act.

"When you enact a statute of limitations to cut off habeas cases — or you enact such a strict gatekeeping provision as for second or successive habeas petitions and you say they can't be filed if they are same-claims successive petitions — does that violate the [Constitution's] suspension clause?" asks Robbins of the Washington College of Law. "A good argument could be made that it does, but a good argument could also be made that it doesn't."

At the time the clause was written, Robbins points out, habeas corpus relief was available only to federal prisoners. State prisoners, the vast majority of death row inmates, were not allowed to file habeas claims until passage of the Habeas Corpus Act in 1867.

"So you could argue that what Congress gave in 1867 Congress can take away, and say that habeas for state prisoners is not a constitutional matter," Robbins says. "You could also argue that it is a constitutional matter because habeas corpus has become the primary vehicle for testing constitutional criminal procedures for state prisoners for more than 130 years now. There is a nice argument on both sides. Ultimately, as with all nice questions, the answer is whether you can get five votes at the Supreme Court level, and that would be an uphill battle."

Meanwhile, death penalty opponents are pushing for piecemeal reforms in an effort to lessen the 1996 law's impact.

"We're not going for abolition or even a moratorium on executions," Henninger says. Instead, his group wants to prevent a lowering of the minimum age for death sentences and eliminate them for the mentally retarded. "We are just trying to scale back the law in ways that legislatures can see it more as a fairness issue rather than deciding whether the death penalty in and of itself is right or wrong."

At the same time, death penalty supporters are backing proposals to extend capital sentencing to yet more crimes. Murder alone is not enough to bring down a death sentence in many states. In Texas, for example, capital punishment is reserved for cases in which murder is accompanied by another felony crime such as burglary or rape.

Clements of Justice for All advocates mandatory application of the death sentence to murderers of senior citizens, a provision recently adopted by the Washington state legislature. She also would like to see killers in domestic violence cases subject to the death penalty.

"Most often these horrible crimes involve a woman with a protective order against an assaultive, stalking ex-boyfriend or husband," she says. "They've done everything they can to protect themselves — they've moved, changed jobs, gone to the courts, gone to the police, and nobody can do anything for them. All they can do is hope and pray that whoever the protective order is against has enough respect for the fact that there is a protective order not to assault, stalk or murder them, but very, very often they do." ■

FOR MORE INFORMATION

American Bar Association, 740 15th St. N.W., Washington, D.C. 20005; (202) 662-1501; www.abanet.org. The leading organization of lawyers has called for a moratorium on executions, citing inconsistencies and unfairness in its application.

Criminal Justice Legal Foundation, P.O. Box 1199, Sacramento, Calif. 95812; (916) 446-0345; www.cjlf.org. The public interest law organization seeks to "enhance public safety and victims' rights" and provides the media with a "balancing perspective to the well-publicized advocates of criminals' rights."

Death Penalty Information Center, 1320 Eighteenth St. N.W., Fifth Floor, Washington, D.C. 20036; (202) 293-6970; www.essential.org/dpic. This nonprofit organization provides information on issues concerning capital punishment.

Justice for All, P.O. Box 55159, Houston, Texas 77255; (713) 935-9300; www.jfa.net. This victims' rights organization supports the death penalty and aids victims of violent crime and their families.

National Association of Evangelicals, 1001 Connecticut Ave. N.W., Suite 522, Washington, D.C. 20036; (202) 789-1011; www.nae.net. The leading membership group of conservative Christian churches and individuals recently raised questions about capital punishment, citing inequities in its application.

National Coalition to Abolish the Death Penalty, 1436 U St. N.W., Suite 104, Washington, D.C. 20009; (202) 387-3890; www.ncadp.org. This advocacy group opposes the death penalty and calls it an instrument of racial oppression against minority groups.

Notes

[1] Quoted in the *Chicago Sun-Times*, Nov. 15, 1998, p. 15.

[2] Amnesty International USA, "Fatal Flaws: Innocence and the Death Penalty," Nov. 12, 1998.

[3] Quoted in Vince Beiser, "Lucky to Be Alive," *Maclean's*, Nov. 30, 1998, p. 49.

[4] U.S. General Accounting Office, "Death Penalty Sentencing," February 1990.

[5] Richard C. Dieter, "The Death Penalty in Black & White," Death Penalty Information Center, 1998.

[6] Death Penalty Information Center, "Facts About the Death Penalty," Nov. 20, 1998.

[7] Tracy L. Snell, "Capital Punishment 1996," U.S. Department of Justice, Bureau of Justice Statistics, Feb. 6, 1998.

[8] Andrew Peyton Thomas, "Penalty Box: A Much-Needed Reform Seemed Poised to Hasten Executions Until Federal Judges Got Their Hands on It," *National Review*, May 4, 1998, p. 40.

[9] H. A. Bedau and Michael L. Radelet, "Miscarriages of Justice in Potentially Capital Cases," *Stanford Law Review*, November 1987.

[10] Justice for All, "Death Penalty and Sentencing Information in the United States," Oct. 1, 1997.

[11] Quoted in "Conservatives Rethink the Death Penalty," *Christianity Today*, April 6, 1998, p. 19.

[12] William F. Buckley Jr., "Miss Tucker's Plea," *National Review*, March 9, 1998, p. 71.

[13] Amnesty International USA, *On the Wrong Side of History: Children and the Death Penalty in the USA*, October 1998.

[14] National Coalition to Abolish the Death Penalty, "The U.S. Leads the World in Killing Kids," NCADP Fact Sheet #3.

[15] See Patrick Griffin, Paticia Torbet and Linda Szymanski, "Trying Juveniles as Adults in Criminal Court: An Analysis of State Transfer Provisions," U.S. Department of Justice, December 1998.

[16] Quoted by Arlene Levinson, "States Steadily Lower Age When Child Becomes Adult in Eyes of Law," The Associated Press, March 27, 1998.

[17] Victor L. Streib, "Another Kind of Innocence: The Death Penalty for Children," paper presented at the National Conference on Wrongful Convictions and the Death Penalty, Nov. 14, 1998.

[18] Arlene Levinson, "States Steadily Lower Age when Child Becomes Adult in Eyes of Law," The Associated Press, March 27, 1998.

[19] Speaking April 20, 1998, on NBC's "Today" show.

[20] John W. Gonzalez, "Many in Poll Want Stiffer Laws on Juvenile Criminals; Support Growing to Punish Parents," *The Houston Chronicle*, June 21, 1998.

[21] Information in this section is based on Hugo Adam Bedau, *The Death Penalty in America: Current Controversies* (1997), pp. 3-24. See also Richard L. Worsnop, "Death Penalty Debate," *The CQ Researcher*, March 10, 1995, pp. 193-216.

[22] For background, see Charles S. Clark, "Crime Victims' Rights," *The CQ Researcher*, July 22, 1994, pp. 625-648.

[23] The results of the study were published later in David C. Baldus, Charles Pulanski and George Woodworth, *Equal Justice and the Death Penalty* (1990).

[24] Dieter, *op. cit.*

[25] Roberto Suro, "How a Federal Case Becomes a Capital Case," *The Washington Post*, Jan. 11, 1998.

[26] From a dissenting opinion by Blackmun in *Callins v. Collins* (1994).

[27] Debbie Morris, *Forgiving the Dead Man Walking* (1998), pp. 232, 251.

[28] Snell, *op. cit.*

[29] Tony Perry, "Boy's Slaying Sparks Call for Expansion of Death Penalty Law," *Los Angeles Times*, Dec. 3, 1998.

[30] Thomas, *op. cit.*

Bibliography

Selected Sources Used

Books

Bedau, Hugo Adam, ed., *The Death Penalty in America: Current Controversies,* Oxford University Press, 1997.
A noted legal scholar presents 40 essays by legal experts that examine various elements of the debate over capital punishment in the United States.

Jackson, Rev. Jesse, *Legal Lynching: Racism, Injustice and the Death Penalty,* Marlowe, 1996.
Jackson presents the findings of numerous studies of racial disparity in sentencing and concludes that black Americans, as well as the poor and residents of Southern states, are discriminated against in capital cases.

Morris, Debbie, *Forgiving the Dead Man Walking,* Zondervan Publishing, 1998.
The author survived kidnapping, rape and her boyfriend's shooting at the hand of Robert Willie, one of the inmates portrayed in the book and film entitled *Dead Man Walking.* After suffering severe emotional distress, Morris forgave her assailant and remained ambivalent about the death penalty.

Prejean, Helen, *Dead Man Walking: An Eyewitness Account of the Death Penalty in the United States,* Random House, 1993.
Sister Prejean's account of serving as spiritual adviser to death row inmates in Louisiana was portrayed in a popular film of the same title. The experience galvanized her opposition to capital punishment while forcing her to sympathize with the frustration and anger of victims' families who supported capital punishment.

Weinglass, Leonard, *Race for Justice,* Common Courage Press, 1995.
The author served as chief defense counsel for Mumia Abu-Jamal, a black activist condemned to death for murdering a Philadelphia police officer. He describes numerous discrepancies in the case that prompted an international appeal for Jamal's release.

Articles

Buckley, William F. Jr., "Miss Tucker's Plea," *National Review*, March 9, 1998, p. 71.
A conservative supporter of capital punishment justifies the February 1998 execution of Karla Faye Tucker as a possible deterrent to future crime and the fulfilling of society's need for retribution.

Farley, Christopher John, and James Willwerth, "Dead Teen Walking," *Time,* Jan. 19, 1998, pp. 50-57.
This account of the trial and conviction of Shareef Cousin helped draw attention to the case involving a juvenile condemned to death for murder under questionable evidence. Cousin was subsequently granted a retrial.

"The Lesson of Karla Faye Tucker: Evangelical Instincts Against Her Execution Were Right, but Not Because She Was a Christian," *Christianity Today,* April 6, 1998, pp. 15-16.
With this editorial, the leading magazine of conservative Christians broke with tradition by calling for the abolition of the death penalty. "The death penalty as it is practiced in this country is unfair and discriminatory," the editorial states. "It has not made the United States a safer country or a more equitable one."

McCormick, John, "The Wrongly Condemned," *Newsweek,* Nov. 9, 1998, pp. 64-66.
A recent conference in Chicago highlighted the cases of 75 former death row prisoners who were released after evidence of innocence or of procedural flaws at trial prompted courts to overturn their death sentences.

Schlosser, Eric, "The Prison-Industrial Complex," *The Atlantic Monthly,* December 1998, pp. 51-77.
To house the nearly 2 million Americans who are currently behind bars, a vast industry has emerged involving architectural firms, Wall Street banks and an array of contractors providing goods and services to prisons.

Reports and Studies

Amnesty International, *The United States of America: Rights for All,* Amnesty International Publications, 1998.
This report on the status of human rights in the United States includes a chapter on the death penalty, which Amnesty opposes as "cruel, inhuman and degrading" punishment.

Dieter, Richard C., *Innocence and the Death Penalty: The Increasing Danger of Executing the Innocent,* Death Penalty Information Center, July 1997.
Of the 69 prisoners sentenced to death and later released on evidence of their innocence described in this report, the average time spent on death row was about seven years. With recent steps to shorten the appeals process, the author predicts that more innocent prisoners will be executed.

Streib, Victor L., *Another Kind of Innocence: The Death Penalty for Children,* Nov. 14, 1998
This paper, presented at the Chicago conference on wrongful convictions by an expert on juvenile crime, examines the application of capital punishment to prisoners who committed their crimes before age 18.

8 Prison-Building Boom

David Masci

The inmates quietly file into the room and begin emptying their pockets — cigarettes, lighters, pens — onto a big table. As a guard reads out their names, they step through a metal detector, then pick up their possessions and go into an adjacent room to wait.

"Twenty-eight!" the guard in the next room calls out, confirming the count after the last man has been checked in. Then an automatic iron door between the rooms clangs shut, and a new group of inmates enters.

It's lunchtime at the Maryland Correctional Institution in Hagerstown, Md., and inmates returning from their jobs in the prison's factories are hungry. But the check-in process can't be rushed. After passing through the metal detector, they will be searched and counted again. Then they must wait in another locked room until they are finally allowed into the cafeteria.

"This is a totally controlled environment," says Lloyd "Pete" Waters, warden of the medium-security institution. "We tell them where to sleep, what to eat and when to work. Everything."

The entire 2,000-inmate facility is designed to give Waters and his staff of 660 complete control at every moment. No prisoner can travel more than a few hundred feet down any hallway without running into a gate or guard. "We need to know where these people are at all times," Waters says, "or we would lose control."

Though he runs the prison with tough and determined efficiency, Waters is not considered a harsh taskmaster. As he walks among the men, many greet him with a "Good morning, sir" or a "How's it going, warden?"

Waters proudly points out that he has reduced the level of tension and

violence at the facility during his eight years there, in part by greatly increasing the number of activities and opportunities available to prisoners.

"I don't give up on any of these men," he says. "I try to make a difference with each of them."

Making a difference isn't always easy, he admits. For one thing, Waters says, the offenders who come to Hagerstown are often "broken men." Many were drug abusers, and some are unable to read. A large percentage had long juvenile records.

Indeed, Waters says, more needs to be done to ensure that there are fewer broken men in the future. "Prevention is always better than reaction," he says, "and I don't think we do enough of that. Every time I hear that states like California or Florida spend more on prisons than on education, it makes me cringe."

The warden's views are widely shared by liberal criminal justice experts and others, who say the United States has gone on a prison-building binge at the expense of education, drug treatment and other programs that might help prevent crimes. They say that over the last 25 years the states and the federal government have spent billions of scarce tax dollars to build hundreds of new correctional facilities. As a result, the United States now has four times as many people behind bars as it did in 1975 and has the world's second-highest incarceration rate.

Opponents of increased prison building argue that while locking up violent criminals makes society safer, the current policy is akin to drift-net fishing: Also scooped up with the truly bad actors are many less dangerous felons, who could be more inexpensively and effectively punished without resorting to incarceration.

"We have 1.8 million people in prisons today, and I think we reached a point a while ago where there is nothing but diminishing returns for continuing this policy," says Marc Mauer, assistant director of The Sentencing Project, a criminal justice think tank.

Mauer and others contend that community-based solutions like parole and probation are being underutilized in favor of the so-called get-tough approach. As a result, many men who have committed lesser, non-violent offenses are being removed from their neighborhoods, unable to work and support their families. "People in these communities are often already struggling," he says, "and this just makes it worse."

In addition, critics like Mauer argue that at least some of the billions directed toward prison building each year should be reallocated to programs proven to prevent crime, like after-school and drug-treatment programs.

"The bottom line is we need more social workers and fewer policemen on the street," says Jamie Fellner, associate counsel at Human Rights Watch in New York.

But while Waters would like to

From *The CQ Researcher*, September 17, 1999.

U.S. Criminal Justice Census at a Glance

Nearly 6 million Americans were in jail or prison, or on probation or parole in 1998 — 2.8 percent of all U.S. adults. The number of inmates in state and federal prisons increased more than fivefold from 1970 to 1998.

Status of Inmate Populations 1998

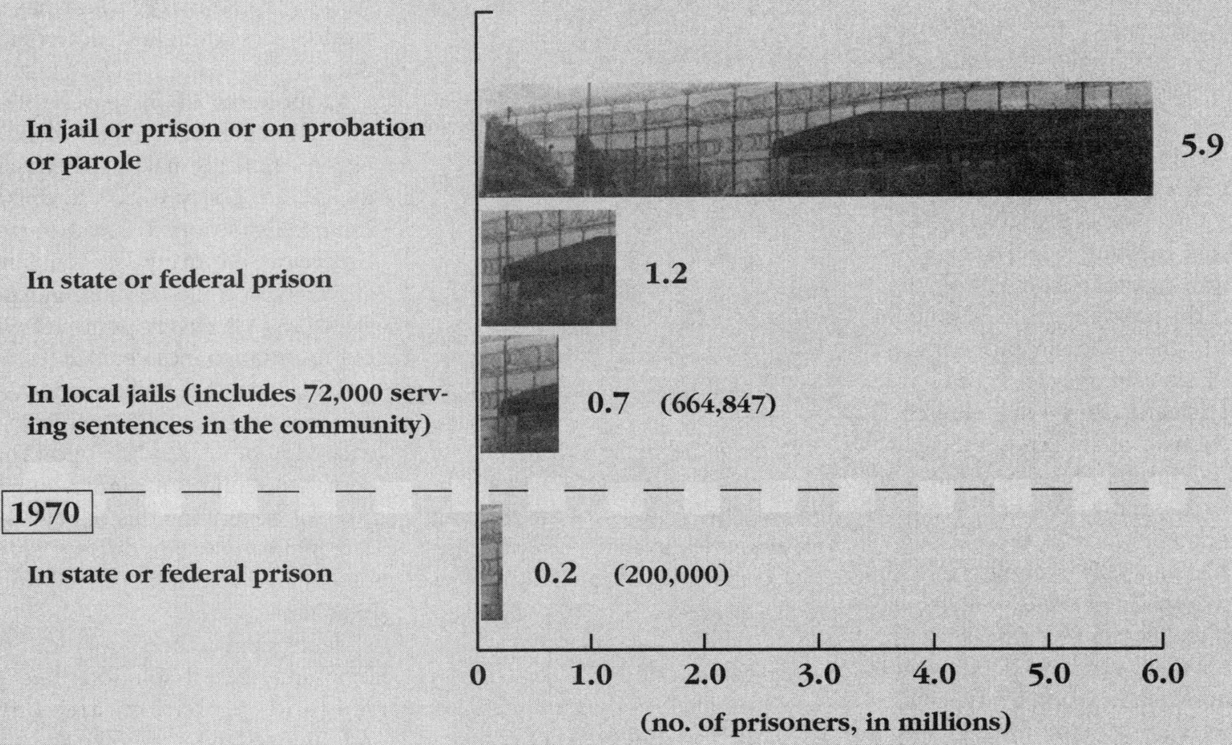

Source: Department of Justice, Bureau of Justice Statistics, Sept. 7, 1999

see more money directed at prevention programs, he doesn't necessarily believe, as do many on the left, that society has become too punitive or overly reliant on prisons. "Prison does prevent crime," he says. "It's common sense: If you lock up the bad guys, crime will go down."

Waters' view of prison as a crime deterrent coincides with the views of many conservatives, who argue that the most effective way to fight crime is to put a substantial portion of the criminal element behind bars.

"Prisons work to prevent crime by simply isolating criminals from the rest of society," says Morgan Reynolds, director of the Criminal Justice Center at the nonprofit National Center for Policy Analysis in Dallas. "Prison, while unpleasant and expensive, is effective."

In addition, Reynolds and others say, increased incarceration sends a message to criminals that the system is capable of meting out adequate punishment when the law is broken. Indeed, they say, during the 1960s and '70s, the crime rate increased, in part because lenient judges and overcrowded jails often meant less or even no prison time for those who had committed serious offenses. "The system lost its credibility," Reynolds says, "and things got much worse."

But building additional prisons does more than just give the system the wherewithal to protect the public. It also improves community life by reducing the power of the criminal element in a given area. This, conservatives argue, can be more effective in preventing future crime than new spending on social programs because it takes offenders out of the vicinity of children and other law-abiding citizens.

At the same time that the number of prisons has been growing, there has been a parallel increase in the amount of time inmates serve. Many states accomplished this through mandatory minimum sentences for certain crimes and so-called truth-in-sentencing laws, which require an inmate to serve out most of his sentence before being released. Half the states have enacted "three-strikes" laws, which usually require a judge to sentence a defendant to life in prison after a third felony, generally for violent offenses.

Here too, conservatives say, the trends have largely been positive. They argue that tough sentencing laws assure the public that criminals will serve "real time for real crimes." "Sure there are exceptions, but most of these people are dangerous criminals who need to be put away for a long time," says Washington lawyer Richard Willard, a former assistant U.S. attorney general.

Willard and others also see tough sentencing laws as an antidote to the trend toward small sentences for big crimes, which began in the 1960s.

"It used to be if you got lucky and drew the right judge, you could get a low sentence, which basically meant getting away with it," says Kurt Scheidegger, legal director of the Criminal Justice Legal Foundation, a conservative think tank in Sacramento, Calif.

But liberals and others say that mandatory minimums and similar laws are a simpleminded and brutish weapon in the war against crime. The biggest problem, they say, is that tens of thousands of mostly young, black men are going to prison for a long time for what are, in many cases, minor drug crimes. "I don't think people realize how many tragic stories there are because of these laws," says Julie Stewart, president of Families Against Mandatory Minimums.

Stewart and others contend that taking sentencing discretion away from judges and imposing a one-size-fits-all solution to the problem has created a system that is both unfair and ineffective. In addition to imposing Draconian sentences on minor criminals — and taking up space needed to hold more serious offenders — the new laws have clogged the nation's jails and prisons with inmates who could probably be better dealt with through supervised release and access to drug treatment.

"We've chosen an expensive way to deal with these kids," Stewart says.

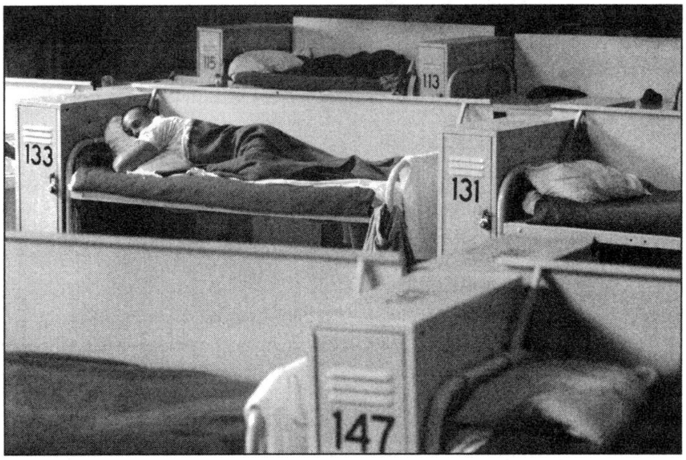

AP Photo/Steve Yeater

Due to overcrowding, a converted gymnasium is used to house California prisoners at the Deuel Vocational Institute in Tracy.

Right now, it's an expense most people seem willing to bear. But polls show that while most Americans have little sympathy for adult criminals, they don't give much thought to the penal system and how many lives it touches. According to the most recent figures released by the Justice Department's Bureau of Justice Statistics (BJS), 5.9 million persons, or almost 3 percent of the nation's adult population, are in prison or jail or on probation or parole. Almost all of these people, it's safe to assume, have family members and friends who must also cope with their incarceration.

As experts and others ponder these and other statistics, here are some of the questions they are asking:

Should some of the resources being devoted to building prisons be redirected to educational and other social spending?

In 1983, federal District Judge William Wayne Justice assumed direct control of the state prison system in Texas. Overcrowding had caused such bad conditions, Justice said, that prisoners' constitutional rights were being violated — specifically the Eighth Amendment prohibition on cruel and unusual punishment. [1]

Texas responded to the ruling with a massive prison-building campaign. In the last two decades, the state penal system has grown nearly tenfold — from about 15 prisons housing 18,000 inmates to 110 facilities incarcerating 150,000 inmates. [2]

Many other states also went on prison-building sprees in recent years, though none grew as fast as Texas. From 1990 to 1995 alone, Texas and the other states spent almost $15 billion on prison construction, adding almost 400,000 new beds. The federal government also was busy, building 45 new prisons during the same period. [3]

As in Texas, prison construction around the nation was the result of overcrowding caused by increased crime and harsher sentencing laws enacted since the 1980s.

"We've built more prisons because we've needed to take more criminals off the streets," says Todd Gaziano, a senior fellow in legal studies at the Heritage Foundation, a conservative think tank. "It's as simple as that."

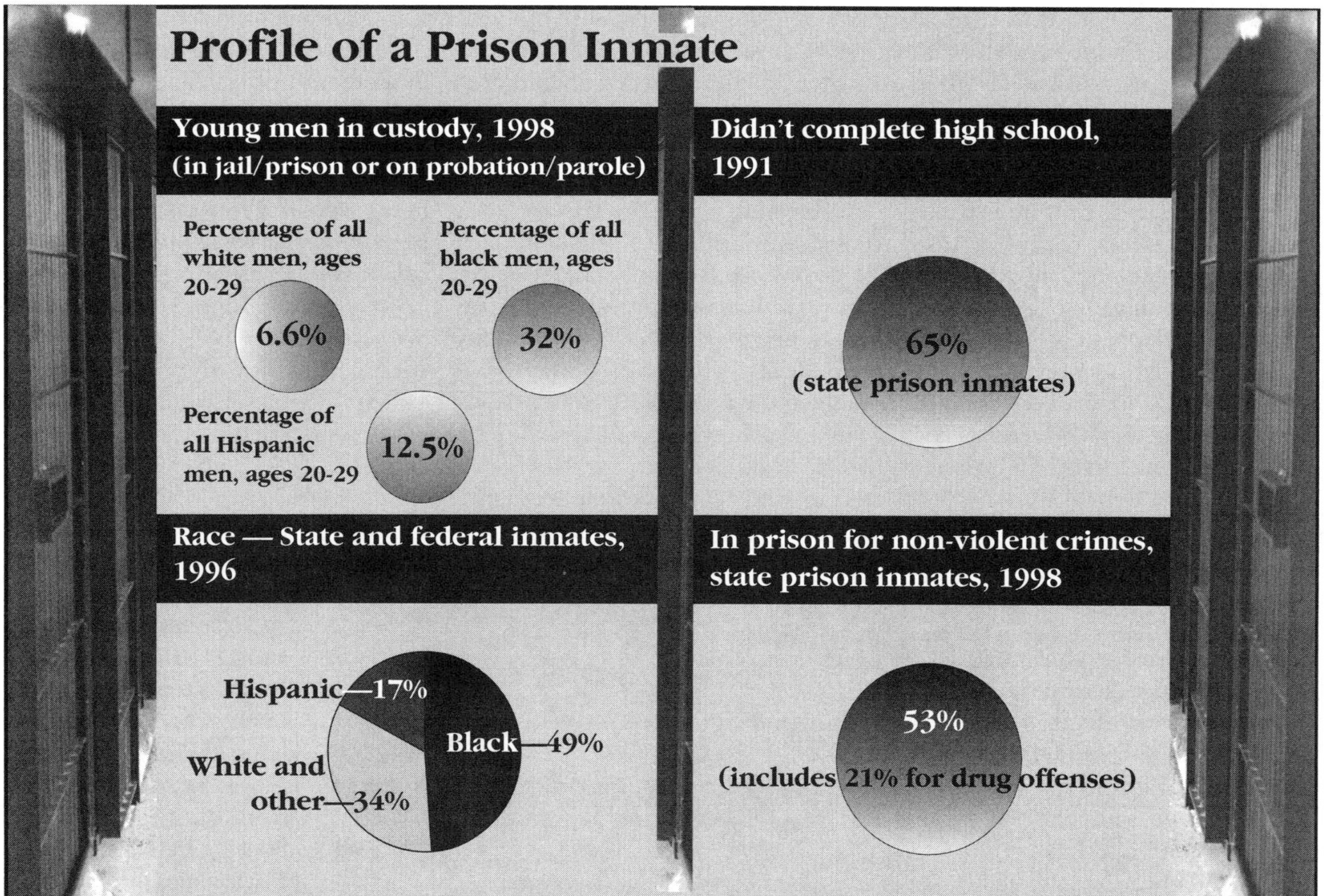

Sources: Department of Justice, Bureau of Justice Statistics, "Corrections Compendium"; The Sentencing Project

But liberals and others contend that it is actually not so simple. They say the prison-building boom itself has been an overly simplistic way of dealing with the complex societal problems that are associated with crime. "We've taken the easy and expedient way out by saying that we'll deal with these problems by locking people up," says Jenni Gainsborough, communications director for the Campaign for an Effective Crime Policy.

The Sentencing Project's Mauer agrees, pointing out that the current wave of prison construction will inevitably lead to more and more prisoners, regardless of whether the crime rate rises or falls. "We've made a serious commitment to long-term imprisonment," he says. "And that means that as we build more and more prisons the number of prisoners inevitably increases, because the prison population always expands to fill the extra space."

Moreover, Mauer and others argue, policies that rely on incarceration are having a devastating effect on many communities around the country, particularly inner-city neighborhoods. "In some places, kids see more people go to prison than they do leave for work every morning," Mauer says. "What kind of message is that sending?"

In addition, critics say, creating more convicts will likely lead to a larger criminal class. "Going to prison makes getting a job much harder when you get out," says Human Rights Watch's Fellner. "So you have these people, many of whom are already on the edge, returning to society with the odds even further against them." And that makes them more likely to return to crime, she adds.

Finally, critics of the construction boom say, all the money being spent on prisons is diverting scarce resources from programs that focus on preventing crime without putting people behind bars. "What's really tragic about this whole thing is that it has sucked so much money away from important things that could really make a difference," Gainsborough says.

Tonya McClary, research director for the Criminal Justice Project at the NAACP Legal Defense Fund, agrees. "We've become a throwaway society, throwing people away in prison as an alternative to trying to genuinely help them and their communities."

For instance, McClary and others

argue, society would be better served by funding more drug treatment programs, both in prisons and in neighborhoods. "Every study we have has shown that dollar for dollar drug treatment is more effective [at deterring crime] than prison," Mauer says.

In addition, critics say, more funding should be directed to community-based sanctions like parole and probation, which could be both more effective and infinitely cheaper than incarceration. "Right now, these programs are so underfunded that they are thought of as a joke," Gainsborough says.

Gainsborough and others also argue that money needs to be put into programs that strengthen the family and community. "There's so much we can do, like after-school programs to keep kids busy and off the street," she says. "Studies show that most juvenile crime occurs between the time children leave school and when mom and dad come home."

But many conservatives say that while some programs aimed at preventing crime might help a little, prison will remain a key component of society's crime-fighting strategy as long as felons walk the streets. "No matter what they might say, we haven't discovered a magic bullet, be it drug treatment or something else, to solve the crime problem," Willard says.

And, Willard and others argue, society is unlikely to find a "magic bullet" any time soon, no matter how much money is spent on drug treatment and after-school programs.

"The whole idea that a lot more social spending can reduce the crime rate is a Great Society pipe dream," says the Criminal Justice Legal Foundation's Scheidegger, referring to the programs championed by President Lyndon B. Johnson.

Scheidegger points out that earlier in the century, when poverty and racism were much more prevalent, the incidence of criminal behavior was actually much lower. "The problem [today] is a general cultural rot, a decline in attitudes, that has led people to feel alienated from society and justified in breaking its rules," he says.

Putting more criminals in prison counters this trend, according to Scheidegger and others, by making would-be criminals think twice about breaking the law. "The criminal element on the outside needs to fear and respect the [criminal justice] system or it's meaningless," says Reynolds of the National Center for Policy Analysis.

In addition, many conservatives say, taking criminals off the street improves communities in general and the prospects for children in particular. "Crime begets more crime," Willard says. "One reason young people in some areas commit crimes is that they are surrounded by criminals."

Finally, supporters of prison building say, incarcerating more criminals is simply the most effective means of fighting crime. "It's pretty obvious that the best way to deal with crime is to lock up the criminals," Willard says. "Prisons are the best form of prevention we have."

Not surprisingly, proponents of prison building credit the recent construction boom for at least part of the drop in violent and other types of crime over the last seven years. "There's no question that it's played a significant part in reducing crime in America," Gaziano says.

Gaziano and others argue that the crime rate rose in the 1960s, '70s and '80s in part because the penal system was not big enough to incarcerate the number of criminals being processed through the courts. "It's helpful to go back 10 or 15 years and find out what prompted this movement to build prisons," he says. "Things had gotten so bad, prisons so overcrowded, that some states were letting people convicted of serious crimes go free after only serving a tenth of their sentences."

Reynolds agrees. "Many on the left believed and still do that punishment was outmoded and ineffective," he says. "But the bottom line is, it works, and you can see that in the statistics."

Today, Gaziano and others say, most states have the facilities to keep the worst offenders off the streets for significant periods of time. In addition, they say, criminals know that they're unlikely to be released after serving only a small fraction of their sentence. "Criminals today know that they're going to get hammered pretty badly if they get caught," Reynolds says. "Don't think that doesn't make a difference."

But liberals and others question the correlation between prison building and falling crime rates. "This is a pick-your-statistics game," Gainsborough says, noting, for example, that while violent crime has declined, drug use is up, in spite of the fact that drug arrests have skyrocketed.

According to Fellner, the real impetus behind prison building has more to do with attitudes than statistics. "They've transformed mean-spiritedness into public policy under the guise of cracking down on crime," she says.

But conservatives counter that building more prisons is nothing more or less than a necessary evil. "When liberals talk about the rising numbers" of prisoners, Scheidegger says, "they never mention that we're incarcerating more people because the crime rate has risen so dramatically in the last 30 years."

Conservatives think that liberals should shift some of their concern away from those in prison and toward law-abiding citizens. "We need to care more about innocent victims of crime than we do about convicted criminals," Gaziano says. "So if we're faced with a difficult policy question,

U.S. Has Second-Highest Incarceration Rate

*The United States has the second-highest incarceration rate (after Russia) among 59 other nations in Asia, Europe and North America. The U.S. rate is generally six to 10 times the rate for most nations in Western Europe.**

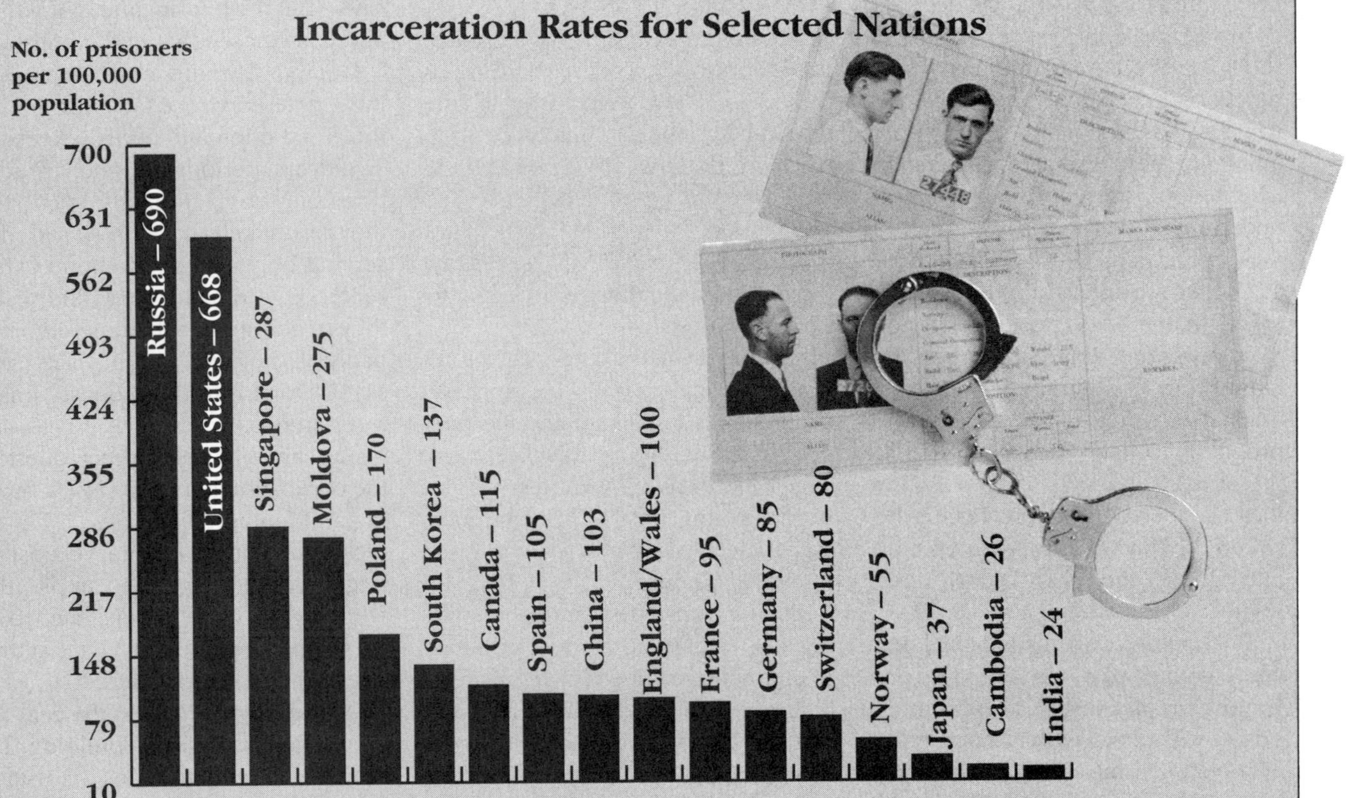

Available data do not generally include countries in Africa and South America.

Source: The Sentencing Project, June 1997

we need to err on the side of public safety."

Should mandatory sentencing, three-strikes statutes and similar laws be repealed or scaled back?

On March 11, 42-year-old Odalis Harris was sentenced to life in prison for robbing a shoestore in Roanoke, Va. Harris, who had served time twice before for robbery, was sentenced under the state's "three-strikes" law. The 1994 statute requires juries to sentence convicted felons to life if they had two prior felony convictions, at least one involving violence. [4]

To opponents of three-strikes laws, mandatory minimum sentences and truth-in-sentencing acts, Harris' case is just one of the many miscarriages of justice that have occurred since legislatures began passing such statutes in the 1970s and '80s.

"It's really amazing how many of these horror stories there are," says Stewart of Families Against Mandatory Minimums. "These cases are not the exception, but the rule." Critics like Stewart say that life terms and other long sentences should be reserved only for the most serious offenders.

Supporters of mandatory minimums challenge Stewart's contention that "horror stories" are common. But all sides agree that mandatory minimums and similar laws have become widely used during the last 25 years. In fact, a majority of states as well as the federal government impose mandatory minimums for crimes ranging from drug offenses to weapons violations.

Also increasingly popular in recent years are truth-in-sentencing laws, which require persons convicted of certain crimes to serve out a large portion of their sentence in prison. Less common are "three-strikes" laws, such as the one used in the Harris case. In addition to Virginia, only a few states have such laws, most notably California.

As many opponents see it, the problem with such laws is that they try to impose a one-size-fits-all solution to individual cases that are all very different. The result, they say, is a system that regularly sentences relatively minor felons to unnecessarily long and cruel jail terms.

"We have tens of thousands of people in prison serving unjust sentences," says Eric Sterling, who helped write federal mandatory minimum laws while working as a counsel for the House Judiciary Committee during the 1980s. Now president of the Criminal Justice Policy Foundation, he is vehemently opposed to the laws he helped draft.

Calling his work on the issue "the greatest tragedy of my professional life," Sterling says that mandatory minimums destroy the entire concept of what is a just sentence. Human Rights Watch's Fellner agrees, "There are a whole host of factors that go into deciding a sentence," he says, "but this boils it down to one or two."

"When it comes to sentencing, you have to look at each individual to determine what the best sanction is," Gainsborough says. "The problem with mandatory minimums is that judges can't do that."

Many judges, in fact, are among the most vehement critics of mandatory minimums, arguing that it takes away their ability to find a punishment to fits the crime. "Judges hate them because they don't allow them to do what they were appointed to do," Stewart says.

Opponents contend that the new laws have, in essence, given the prosecutor primary authority for imposing sentence. "Because your sentence often depends on what you're convicted of, the real decision-maker in this process becomes the prosecutor," Fellner says, "because he or she decides what you'll be charged with."

Critics of mandatory minimum sentences say they clog the prison system with low-level drug offenders. Supporters say that most offenders convicted under tough sentencing laws are hardened criminals with long records who need to be taken off the street.

The power wielded by prosecutors is particularly troublesome, Fellner says, because prosecutors make their charging decisions behind closed doors, without any real information about the defendant's background. "They're not like judges, who have the defendant's whole record, their life history, in front of them," she says. "And a judge's decisions can be reviewed and reversed by higher courts."

In addition, critics of mandatory minimum laws argue that they end up clogging the prison system with low-level drug offenders and other non-violent criminals who could be dealt with in less expensive and more effective ways.

"We've decided that it's better to warehouse these people rather than try other things like drug treatment and community-based sanctions like parole or probation," Fellner says. "I mean, they say these laws are meant to put drug kingpins away, but most of the time its low-level kids, usually poor, usually minority, that end up serving these sentences."

As evidence, Fellner and others point to a recent study by the Justice Policy Institute, which shows that the new, tough sentencing laws have increased the number of inmates convicted of non-violent offenses in the nation's prisons and jails to more than 1 million, or more than half of all people behind bars. [5]

And in New York state, which has some of the toughest mandatory minimum sentencing laws in the nation, a March 1999 report from Human Rights Watch said that one in four felons recently sent to a state prison had been convicted of a low-level, non-violent drug offense. [6] Opponents of mandatory minimums often point to the five-year prison sentence that must be imposed on anyone convicted in federal court of selling five or more grams of crack cocaine.

But conservatives argue that mandatory minimums and similar laws are an effective way of fighting crime.

"Most of the people who are sentenced under these laws are hardened criminals with long criminal records who need to be taken off the street for a long period of time," says former Assistant U.S. Attorney General Willard.

Take drug dealers, for instance, says Gaziano. "Liberals always talk about 'low-level drug dealers,' but what does that mean? What's a low-level drug dealer? What if it's someone who provides drugs to little kids? They may not be a so-called kingpin, but these are bad people we're talking about."

Moreover, conservatives say, the new, tough sentencing laws are largely fair and are not putting away good kids who have made one small mistake. "Most of the people in prison today are hardened criminals, with long histories of criminal activity, not some kid caught with a small amount of drugs," Willard says.

Reynolds agrees, arguing that liberals have found the occasional example where the sentence might not have fit the crime in order to give the impression that these laws are too Draconian. "You can find horror stories if you look for them, but this isn't some sort of problem that's run amok," he says.

Indeed, he and others say, it was horror stories of another kind that led to the enactment of mandatory minimums, truth-in-sentencing and three-strikes laws. According to conservatives, many judges in the 1960s and '70s were meting out laughably light sentences for very serious crimes.

"There's no question that some judges were not handing down stiff enough sentences," Scheidegger says. "A lot of them didn't take some crimes, especially drug crimes, seriously enough."

Another problem, they say, was that many inmates who had been given appropriate sentences were being released after serving only a small portion of their time. "You had people serving a tenth of their sentences, and for serious crimes," Gaziano says. "In Texas, for instance, you had rapists doing a year or two."

But liberals argue that while a few judges might have been too lenient, the vast majority were handing down appropriate sentences. "It's a myth that people were getting short sentences for rape and murder," Gainsborough says. "What do they think, that judges don't care about public safety? That's ridiculous."

In addition, many liberals say, politicians have fostered the misperception that judges are lenient and out of touch in order to score easy political points with voters. "The 'tough on crime' stand is a winner for [politicians] because unlike almost every other issue, such as the environment, there's no powerful interest on the other side," Sterling says.

But conservatives dispute the notion that support for these tough sentences was whipped up by politicians looking for easy campaign issues. "I don't think politicians created this opinion," says John Lott Jr., a professor of law at the University of Chicago. "They followed the voters, and the voters innately realize that deterrence works." ■

BACKGROUND

A Rising Population

The United States incarcerates more people than any other country in the world. Even China, with more than four times America's population, has fewer total inmates.[7] And, of those countries that report the size of their inmate populations, only Russia has a greater percentage of its citizenry in prison. (*See graph, p. 140.*)

According to the Bureau of Justice Statistics, the United States currently incarcerates 1.8 million of its citizens and residents. The majority of these inmates, about 1.1 million people, are held in state prisons. Another 100,000 reside in federal facilities. The remaining 650,000 are held in local jails, which are used to incarcerate those awaiting trial or convicts serving short sentences. (*See graph, p. 136.*)

To put these numbers in a different perspective, Eric Schlosser writes in *The Atlantic*, "imagine the combined populations of Atlanta, St. Louis, Pittsburgh, Des Moines and Miami behind bars."[8]

The high U.S. rate of incarceration is a relatively recent phenomenon. Until the early 1970s, the incarceration rate was only about 110 inmates per 100,000 people in the United States. But beginning in the mid-to-late '70s, the numbers began to increase, doubling in the '80s and again in the '90s. Today, there are approximately 668 inmates for every 100,000 persons in the United States.[9]

But in the last few years the rise in the incarceration rate has slowed down a bit. In 1998, the total number of inmates increased by 59,900, or 4.8 percent, below the 6.7 percent average growth rate since 1990.[10]

The makeup of the nation's prison population bears little resemblance to the country's overall demographics. The vast majority of people currently in prison and jail tend to come from low-income households and often have a history of substance-abuse problems. In addition, prisoners tend to be poorly educated — only a third are able to read and write when they arrive.[11]

The overwhelming majority of inmates are men, though the country itself is roughly divided in half by gender. Only 78,000 persons, or 6 percent of all jail and prison inmates,

Chronology

1970s *Rising crime rates set off a debate about the best way to protect society.*

1971
Gov. Nelson A. Rockefeller, R-N.Y., proposes the toughest anti-drug laws in the nation.

1972
There are 330,000 local, state and federal prisoners in the U.S.

1976
After serving time in connection with the Watergate burglary, Charles Colson founds the Prison Fellowship Ministry.

1979
Texas Judge Wayne Justice takes control of the state's prisons after declaring that the overcrowded system was violating prisoners' constitutional right to protection from cruel and unusual punishment.

1980s *Increasing drug use and other crimes prompt many states to pass tougher sentencing laws. The inmate population begins to climb dramatically.*

1980
There are nearly 500,000 people incarcerated in the United States.

1984
The Corrections Corporation of America opens the nation's first privately run prison in Texas.

1985
There are 750,000 people incarcerated in the United States.

1986
Congress passes the Anti-Drug Abuse Act, which includes 28 new mandatory minimum sentences for drug-related crimes.

1987
Parole is abolished in the federal system.

1988
The infamous Willie Horton advertisement used by George Bush during his race for the presidency helps to make crime a top campaign issue. Horton, a convicted murderer, raped a Maryland woman while on furlough from a Massachusetts prison.

1989
Sixty-seven new prisons are built by the states and federal government, adding 31,642 new beds.

1990s *Incarceration rates reach record levels as the crime rate's rise begins to slow down.*

1991
The U.S. Supreme Court upholds a Michigan law imposing a mandatory life sentence without the possibility of parole to anyone convicted of possessing more than 650 grams of cocaine.

1992
The Bush administration releases a report entitled "The Case for More Incarceration," arguing that longer prison terms will lower the crime rate.

April 1993
Riot in the Lucasville, Ohio, prison kills nine inmates and a corrections officer.

November 1993
Washington state voters approve the first so-called "three-strikes" law, mandating life without parole for third-time serious offenders.

March 1994
California enacts a tough three-strikes law.

August 1994
The Omnibus Crime Bill authorizes almost $8 billion in prison-building grants to the states. The legislation also includes tough federal sentencing laws.

September 1994
Virginia passes a truth-in-sentencing law that requires convicted felons to serve 85 percent of their sentences.

1995
One of every three black men in the United States between the ages of 20 and 29 is either in prison, jail, on parole or probation at any given moment.

1997
Riots at the newly opened Northeast Ohio Correctional Facility in Youngstown spark a debate on the merits of private prisons. Twenty-five new state prisons (including six in North Carolina alone) and six federal facilities are built, adding 25,248 new beds.

1999
There are 1.8 million Americans behind bars.

Losing the Vote

Ten states disenfranchise felony ex-offenders for life. Only four states allow offenders in prison to vote. Forty-six states and the District of Columbia do not allow convicted felons in prison to vote.*

Allow convicted felons in prison to vote

Maine
Massachusetts
New Hampshire
Vermont

Disenfranchise ex-felons

Alabama	*Mississippi*
Delaware	*Nevada*
Florida	*New Mexico*
Iowa	*Virginia*
Kentucky	*Wyoming*
Maryland	

** Arizona and Maryland disenfranchise offenders for life after a second felony conviction; Tennessee and Washington deny the vote to those convicted before 1986 and 1984, respectively.*

Sources: The Sentencing Project, Human Rights Watch, October 1998

are female. Still, the number of women in prison has tripled since 1980. Many have been sentenced under the tougher state drug laws.[12] Most, about 75 percent, also leave children behind when they enter prison.

There is an equally big disparity between the nation's racial makeup and its prisons. Although African-Americans make up 12 percent of the general population, they comprise 49 percent of the nation's jail and prison inmates. By contrast, whites and Hispanics make up 33 percent and 17 percent of the inmate population, respectively.[13]

As things stand, one in three black men ages 20-29 has some contact with the criminal justice system on any given day. To many, this statistic shows a terrible bias in the way justice is administered in the United States. "If you're black and poor, your chances of running afoul of the police are good, regardless of what you do," the NAACP's McClary says. "It's simply a question of skin color."

According to McClary, the incarceration of so many African-American men is having a tragic ripple effect throughout black America. In addition to the obvious problems that come with imprisonment — like broken families — there is a set of less visible concerns associated with the fact that so many young, black men are currently in jail. "A lot of these young people won't have children because they'll spend much or all of their young-adult years in prison," she says. "It's almost genocidal."

McClary also laments the fact that many states now prohibit convicted felons from voting. "These rules disenfranchise a whole generation," she says. "There are now many people who will never be able to participate in our political process, and that's not right." *(See "At Issue," p. 149.)*

But others argue that, as tragic as the racial disparity in incarceration is, it is not based on some overarching bias on the part of the criminal justice system. Instead, they say, young, black men in inner-city areas are simply much more likely to be committing the kinds of drug-related offenses that put people in jail today.

"If you want to question the incarceration of blacks, you need to question the whole notion of locking people up for drug offenses, because that's what's causing this" says the University of Chicago's Lott.

Lott also points out that just as a substantial number of inmates are black, so are many victims of crime, whether they are harmed by violence or drugs. "You can't separate this fact out from the rest of the debate," he adds.

Rehabilitation

Four inmates stand on the stage of the prison auditorium in Hagerstown, harmonizing their way through

Despite Low Pay, Inmates Covet Prison Jobs

The scene could be a furniture factory anywhere in the country. Some men are welding unfinished filing cabinets; others work on pressing machines, turning sheets of metal into tubular legs and other components.

But this isn't anywhere: It's the medium-security Maryland Correctional Institute (MCI) in Hagerstown. The factory, one of three at the prison, makes metal furniture for various state institutions.

"We're currently working on an order for 4,500 beds for the University of Maryland," says Warden Lloyd "Pete" Waters, pointing to a string of unfinished bed frames hanging from a long cable.

Waters is among many prison officials who view prison jobs as one of the best rehabilitation tools they have.

"This teaches them responsibility and to behave properly," Waters says, pointing out that inmates can lose their coveted — if low-paying — jobs if they're not good workers or if they get into trouble. "And besides, it gives them a trade that they can use after they're released."

"I think it has tremendous rehabilitative value," says Kent Scheidegger, legal director of the Criminal Justice Legal Foundation, a conservative think tank in Sacramento, Calif. "People have to learn to obey the rules and finish the job."

Timothy Brown, an inmate at MCI who operates a pressing machine, says that the program is helping him to turn his life around. "This has taught me to be a responsible person, to work hard and show up on time." It also gives Brown, who has served 10 years of a 35-year sentence for second-degree murder, an opportunity to help his family. "I'm able to send money home to my mother and to my kids, and that's wonderful."

MCI's three factories — there is also a meat-processing plant and another furniture operation — are among 30 factories operated in 26 Maryland prisons by State Use Industries (SUI). The state-run manufacturing operation employs 1,300 inmates, bringing in more than $30 million in revenue each year by supplying the state with office furniture, food products and, of course, license plates.[1]

David Masci

Warden Lloyd "Pete" Waters views prison jobs as an effective rehabilitation tool.

But SUI only employs 5.7 percent of the states 22,500 inmates.[2] "There's quite a waiting list of people wanting to get in here," Waters says. "We wish we could do more."

To a large extent, Maryland and other states that manufacture products used by state institutions deliberately limit the number of inmates they put to work, and hence limit their output. That's because the use of prison labor draws opposition from both unions and businesses, who complain that the very low wages typically paid to inmates makes profit-making firms unable to compete with prison products. At MCI for instance, inmates usually earn up to $2.50 a day, working from 7:30 a.m. to 3:30 p.m.

"This is a problem, especially for [organized] labor, since inmates make a small fraction of what workers outside do," says Marc Mauer, assistant director of the Washington-based Sentencing Project, which promotes sentencing reform. "I think everyone would feel better about this if prisoners were paid close to the prevailing wage."

Similar concerns attach to proposals for using prison labor in the private sector. Existing federal law bans the interstate sale of products produced by prisoners for private industry. As a result, only about 2,000 prisoners nationwide work for private businesses.[3]

But others say that using more prisoners in the private sector will not negatively impact the economy. "We have a labor shortage in this country right now," says Morgan Reynolds, director of the Criminal Justice Center at the National Center for Policy Analysis in Dallas. "At the same time, we have more than a million able-bodied men who are literally doing nothing and would benefit tremendously from a steady job. It's a no-brainer."

[1] Paul Valentine, "Productive Program in Md. Prisons; State Says Giving Jobs to Inmates Pays Off," *The Washington Post*, March 22, 1999.

[2] *Ibid.*

[3] The National Center for Policy Analysis, "Factories Behind Bars," October, 1996.

"The Road Is Long." When they finish, to enthusiastic applause, Brad Keller, the prison's education director, addresses the audience of about 100 prisoners and two-dozen family members and other visitors. "I want to extend my congratulations to everyone here," he says. "A lot of hard work went into making this day happen."

It's graduation day at the institution, and the men in attendance have either earned their high school equivalency diplomas (GED) or a vocational certificate for proficiency in a trade.

The graduation ceremony has many of the usual trappings, including a commencement speaker. On this day, it's Robert Harleston, a retired Army general who currently chairs the Criminal Justice Department at the University of Maryland's Eastern Shore campus. "Studies have shown that success in such programs is consistent with good feelings about oneself and success in further endeavors once you leave this place," he tells the inmates.

Harleston is among many in the criminal justice community who say that educational and similar programs can give at least some inmates a better chance at becoming law-abiding and productive citizens once they are released.

For much of the 20th century, penologists and others have focused on how best to rehabilitate inmates. Only in the 1970s did the pendulum swing more toward using punitive measures as a way to fight crime. During the last few decades, many programs aimed at improving or rehabilitating inmates have been eliminated or scaled back. In one well-publicized example, in 1994, Congress eliminated Pell grant eligibility for those incarcerated.[14] The cash stipends had allowed some inmates to earn university degrees without ever leaving prison.

"We've abandoned the notion of rehabilitation in prison, cutting back on counseling, drug treatment and education programs," says the NAACP Legal Defense Fund's McClary. "And that's a shame because I believe that a lot of these [inmates] could be turned around because we know what works."

What "works," according Stephen J. Steurer, executive director of the Correctional Education Association, is a combination of programs both in and out of prison. "There are three linchpins in this equation: education, drug programs and help finding a job and other support after they're released," he says. "If we did these three things, we could drop the recidivism rate like a stone."

Still, while efforts at rehabilitation might have slackened in some prison systems, they have not ended. At Hagerstown, for instance, prisoners can take reading and math classes, participate in psychological and substance-abuse counseling, receive vocational training and even work and earn money. There is also a transition program to help ex-inmates find work and readjust to their new lives.

"Most prisoners are going to be released at some time," Warden Waters says, "so anything that will give them a better chance of meeting their responsibilities in the community is worth trying." In addition, he says, these activities are important because keeping the inmates busy makes things easier on themselves and on the staff charged with watching them.

Still, Waters says, some inmates, for one reason or another, can't change for the better. "You've got guys who just won't move forward, no matter what we do," he says. "For some inmates the only form of rehabilitation that works is age," he says, referring to the fact that older inmates are much less likely to commit a crime after release than a younger prisoner.

Others go much further, arguing that rehabilitation is oversold as a solution. "We really don't know how to rehabilitate people, so I'm very skeptical about a lot of these ideas," Scheidegger says. "Take counseling. I really don't think it does any good."

Lott agrees. "A lot of these guys are gaming the system," he argues. "If you tell someone that you'll reduce their sentence if they get their GED, then you may be giving them an incentive, but what good is it doing?"

He also disputes the studies showing that certain rehabilitative efforts reduce rates of recidivism, arguing that many of the inmates who try out these programs are already determined to go straight. "My concern is that these studies don't take into account the [self-selection] that occurs in prison." ■

CURRENT SITUATION

Prisons for Profit

The fledgling Northeast Ohio Correctional Center in Youngstown has had a rocky startup. In the first 10 months after it opened in 1997, 20 inmates were stabbed, two fatally. Soon afterward, six inmates, including four murderers, escaped. (All were caught.)[15]

While it is not the first prison to have violence and security problems, Youngstown garnered more than its share of headlines because it is part of a small but growing national ex-

Saving Souls in a Texas Prison

A unique experiment in rehabilitation is being tried at Jester II, a minimum-security prison in Sugarland, Texas. The hope is that an intensive program of Bible study and other religious activity can turn offenders away from crime.

"We believe that only through the grace of our Lord Jesus Christ can [prisoners] transform their lives and truly turn themselves around," says Pat Nolan, president of Justice Fellowship, the public policy arm of Prison Fellowship Ministries, which developed the InnerChange Freedom Initiative program at Jester.

The 100 inmates who have enrolled in the 18-month program divide their time between Bible study, prayer and worship and more traditional rehabilitative activities such as counseling, educational classes and job training. Television-watching and other recreational activities are kept to a minimum.

The hope, according to Nolan and others, is to get lawbreakers to acknowledge that they are sinners, repent for what they've done and commit to a life based on Judeo-Christian values and teachings. "We believe that crime isn't a legal problem, but a moral one," says Nolan, an ex-offender. "Until they understand that there are moral laws set down by God that we are all bound to obey, they won't change."

Charles Colson, who served time in prison for the Watergate burglary, founded Prison Fellowship Ministries in 1976. "There has to be something in people that makes them want to do the right thing," he said. "That's what Christian conversion does that nothing else does."[1]

Prison Fellowship Ministries

Prison Fellowship Ministries founder Charles Colson

Of course, using religion to rehabilitate criminals is not a new idea. The word penitentiary is derived from penitent, which has obvious religious overtones. In addition, the first major penal reforms in the United States were initiated by Quakers in Pennsylvania. The so-called Philadelphia system kept inmates in solitary confinement to allow them to think about what they had done and repent.[2]

Faith-based programs are already being offered in almost every prison in America, but they are not as comprehensive as InnerChange. They do, however, touch the lives of hundreds of thousands of prisoners, with prayer, counseling, Bible study and other religious activities. Prison Fellowship Ministries alone has 50,000 volunteers and a paid staff of 300.

Although a few Jester II inmates who enrolled in InnerChange have dropped out, most who begin the 18-month program finish. One participant, James Peterson, even successfully petitioned the Texas Department of Criminal Justice to delay his scheduled release so that he could complete InnerChange.[3]

After a year in the program inside the prison, inmates who participate take part in a six-month post-release program that matches them with a church and a mentor and helps them find a job. "This is vitally important," Nolan said, "because most prisoners who leave don't have help making the transition to life on the outside."

The jury is out as to the program's effectiveness. It's only been in operation since April 1997, and a Princeton University study gauging its effectiveness is not yet complete.

Meanwhile, Prison Fellowship Ministries is currently setting up two new programs at prisons in Iowa and Kansas. In addition, 25 other states have expressed interest in establishing similar programs, the group says.

Growing interest in InnerChange has led its supporters to predict that intensely focused, faith-based programs will become the rule rather than the exception in prisons in the future.

"It's like welfare reform — it will begin in a few states and then spread to the rest of the nation once it's shown to work," says Joe Loconte, a fellow at the Heritage Foundation.

"The fact that Texas, with its 'lock 'em up and throw away the key' attitude, is willing to embrace [InnerChange], shows a growing openness among those in law enforcement to something like this," he says. "It may take a generation for this to go mainstream, but it will happen."

---

[1] Quoted in Joe Loconte, "Jailhouse Rock of Ages," *Policy Review*, July 1997.

[2] Peter N. Carroll and David W. Noble, *The Restless Centuries: A History of the American People* (1979), p. 224.

[3] William R., Mattox Jr., "Prison Program Uses Faith to Transform Lives," *USA Today*, March 15, 1999.

periment in the use of privately owned and operated correctional facilities.

Some saw the trouble in Ohio as an inevitable result of government abrogating its responsibility to incarcerate criminals. Others, who see the growth of private prisons as a positive trend, viewed the Youngstown incidents as regrettable, but not unusual.

Until recently, incarceration was entirely the provenance of the government. But the explosion in the nation's inmate population during the 1980s forced some states to seek alternatives. As a result, the number of private prisons has skyrocketed in recent years, rising from just a few in the mid-1980s to more than 168 in early 1999.

Almost half of the nation's privately run facilities, including the prison in Youngstown, are operated by the Corrections Corporation of America (CCA). With 74 prisons in 26 states and Puerto Rico, Nashville-based CCA is the nation's fourth-largest corrections system, public or private.

As Schlosser points out, private prisons operate much like motels. They often take in inmates from other states, which usually pay between $25-$60 per inmate per day.[16]

Twenty-seven states currently have arrangements for inmate incarceration with for-profit prison companies. About 90,000 inmates, or 6 percent of the national total, are currently held in private facilities. But experts expect the number of private correctional facilities to continue to rise in the coming years, noting that dozens of new, private prisons are currently being constructed or being planned. "It's already a big business," Mauer says.

Critics of the private prison trend, liberals and conservatives alike, argue that the rush to privatize correctional services should at least be slowed and possibly stopped. For one thing, they say, none of the facilities are adequately supervised by governmental authorities. Nor are they always required to meet minimum standards before receiving inmates.

"What is different and unfortunate about private correctional facilities is their lack of accountability," writes Nancy Mahon, director of the Center on Crime, Communities and Culture at the Open Society Institute in New York.[17] Mahon and other critics also point to a slew of incidents, ranging from severe prisoners beatings to escapes to misuse of inmate labor.

Others worry that for-profit prisons will try to keep inmates incarcerated longer than necessary in order to keep their facilities full and boost earnings. "I could see a situation where fewer people might be paroled due to the profit motive," Mauer says.

Still others argue that the private sector isn't suited to carry out some crucial government functions, like public safety, under any circumstances. "I generally support the free market," says Scheidegger, "but prisons are like the military and police in that they should always be under the control of the state."

But supporters of privatizing correctional services counter that for-profit prisons are generally cheaper and at least as effective as their public counterparts. "The rate of violence, escapes and similar incidents is no higher in private prisons than in the public system," says Pat Cannan, a spokesman for Florida-based Wackenhut Corrections Corp., the second-largest operator of private prisons in the nation with 45 facilities.

He also counters the charge that the profit motive will prompt private prisons to keep inmates longer than is necessary. "The ultimate decision as to who goes and who stays rests with the state, not us."

Cannan admits that some states have not adequately regulated private prisons. "Private corrections is a new phenomenon and some states just haven't caught up with it yet," he says. But "as the industry continues to grow, so will [government] oversight and regulation."

Parole Under Fire

Many more people processed through the criminal justice system walk the streets than are in prison. At the end of 1998, 3.8 million Americans convicted of a crime were either on parole or probation, more than twice the number of people incarcerated.

The idea behind parole is simple: If a convicted offender, after a certain amount of time in prison, no longer seems to be a threat to society, the criminal justice system should at least consider a supervised release. Prisoners are usually eligible for parole after serving a certain portion of their sentence. Likewise, probation, usually given in lieu of a prison sentence, is often intended for first offenders and others deemed less likely to repeat their crimes or threaten people or property.

But particularly since the 1970s, the concept of supervised release has come in for much criticism. Critics contend that allowing early release from prison for good conduct does little or no good. "There's no evidence to suggest that sorting through prisoners and trying to choose the ones who won't commit crimes works," says the University of Chicago's Lott.

In fact, Lott and others say that parole might lead to an increase in the crime rate since it allows many hardened criminals out of prison early. "Most inmates know how to play the

At Issue:

Should convicted felons be allowed to vote after they leave prison?

yes

Jamie Fellner and Marc Mauer

Fellner is associate counsel, Human Rights Watch; Mauer is assistant director, The Sentencing Project

WRITTEN FOR *THE CQ RESEARCHER*, APRIL 1999.

Millions of Americans went to the polls last November, but Lawrence Tyrone Hill was not one of them. A computer programmer in New Mexico, Hill spent a few years in prison in the 1980s. Since his release in 1986, he has worked, paid taxes and led an unblemished life. He has the right to acquire property, travel, get married, sign contracts, surf the Web, buy beer, run up his credit card — everything any other adult can do with one remarkable exception. He can't vote. Hill is one of more than 1.4 million Americans who is barred from the ballot box for life because he was once convicted of a crime.

In *Losing the Vote*, a report issued last November, Human Rights Watch and The Sentencing Project documented the impact of disenfranchisement laws in the United States. Few Americans were shocked upon learning that 46 states deny prisoners the vote and 32 deny the vote to felons on probation or parole. But even the most ardent "tough-on-crime" advocates were stunned to death to learn that 14 states deny the vote to former lawbreakers even after they have been released from the criminal justice system.

In these states, the right to vote can be permanently lost upon conviction of even relatively minor crimes, such as passing a bad check or selling marijuana. In most cases, the only way to get the vote back is through gubernatorial action.

Disenfranchisement laws have dramatically curtailed the black vote in several states. Nationwide, disenfranchisement because of felony convictions bars an estimated 13 percent of all black men from voting. In eight states, one in five black men is permanently denied the right to vote because of a felony conviction. At current rates, 30 to 40 percent of the next generation of black men in these states will be disenfranchised as adults. With the exception of certain Southern states, disenfranchisement laws were enacted without any express racist intent. Whatever the intent, however, the current impact clearly disproportionately affects African-Americans.

Denying ex-offenders the vote does not fight crime or have any practical deterrent effect. Some have argued that ex-offenders should be denied suffrage because they lack the judgment needed to vote responsibly. But in a democracy the vote is not reserved for the virtuous or wise.

At the edge of the millennium, it's time to remove disenfranchisement laws and get on with the tough business of deepening democracy by encouraging those who have the right to vote to do so.

no

John R. Lott Jr.

***John M. Olin law and economics fellow, University of Chicago School of Law, and author of* More Guns, Less Crime: Understanding Crime and Gun Control Laws**

WRITTEN FOR *THE CQ RESEARCHER*, APRIL 1999.

Society imposes many penalties on convicted criminals after they leave prison. They face difficulties in joining unions, securing public employment, obtaining business licenses and obtaining the licenses necessary to practice occupations regulated by the government. Ex-convicts face many other forms of penalties, such as being prevented from inheriting property, suffering partial or complete divestment of assets, losing life and automobile insurance and losing pension funds (even if they are already retired). Depending upon the state one lives in, conviction affects parental rights, divorce, the ability to hold public office, ownership of firearms and the ability to serve as a juror. In addition, ex-convicts can lose the right to vote.

It is not obvious why only losing the right to vote is generating serious objections. The loss of many other rights, such as parental rights or the right to own a firearm for self defense, may well impose a much greater penalty on the ex-convict. Surely many of these collateral penalties impose a much greater financial hardship on the ex-convict. Yet, just as ex-convicts are deemed unqualified to be a parent or untrustworthy to have a firearm, it is surely just as reasonable that we might consider an ex-convict to lack the proper social concerns when exercising the decision to vote.

For society to function well, there are benefits to having voters who care about the well-being of others. Those who have committed violent crimes have provided information on how little they value other people. States have also claimed that important information about a person's character is obtained from other types of drug or property crimes. A criminal may have served his debt to society by serving out his prison term, but that does not imply that society must accept that prison has corrected his judgment or his values.

Because certain groups of citizens are incarcerated at higher rates than others, many are concerned about the discriminatory impact of denying ex-convicts the right to vote. Even if conscious discrimination were involved and even if different groups of the population were not committing crimes at relatively high rates, it is still not obvious why voting rights are somehow distinct from other lost rights. The most direct approach to solving such problems would seem to be eliminating the discrimination taking place at conviction and sentencing.

game and use the system to their advantage. So a lot of bad people get out early."

Such concerns have prompted 15 states, including California, Illinois, Arizona, Ohio and Mississippi, to abolish their parole boards, which review inmates' records and decide whether early releases are warranted. The federal government has also done away with parole.[18]

Other states are considering eliminating parole. On Jan. 6, Gov. George E. Pataki, R-N.Y., announced that he would push to end his state's use of parole entirely. Instead, Pataki said, prisoners would not only serve out their full sentences but also be required to have their DNA on file in order to make it easier to link them to future crimes and, hopefully, deter criminal activity.

Even in states that retain parole, its use has dropped significantly due in part to the passage of mandatory minimum and truth-in-sentencing laws. In Texas, for instance, the number of inmates eligible for parole fell from 57 percent in 1988 to 20 percent last year.[19] And according to a recent report by the Bureau of Justice Statistics, the average time served by inmates in states that still have parole boards has increased from 23 months in 1990 to 25 months in 1996.[20]

Supporters of parole bemoan the trend away from supervised release, arguing that it hurts public safety as well as inmates. For one thing, they say, parole boards have the authority not to release dangerous convicts on parole but to hold them to the full maximum of their sentences. So, eliminating these boards reduces a state's "ability to keep very dangerous offenders in prison," said Joan Petersilia, a professor of criminology at the University of California at Davis.[21]

Supporters of parole argue that it allows prisons to discharge those inmates who are clearly not a threat to society and whose cells could be filled by more dangerous felons. "It's so stupid because prison is extremely expensive, and so we're paying all this money to keep these less dangerous people off the streets," says the Sentencing Project's Mauer.

In addition, Mauer argues, parole or probation after prison can help transition an inmate back into society. "Research shows that if you guide and supervise an inmate, get him some counseling, help him get a job, he'll be less likely to commit another crime," Mauer says. "I mean, it's better than letting him serve his entire sentence, giving him a bus ticket home and forgetting about him."

Mauer and others would like to see more money put into making parole work. "The caseloads of parole officers are almost always too large," Sterling says. "So supervision instead of prison is never really given a chance to work." ■

OUTLOOK

Shift in Priorities?

Conservatives and liberals may disagree over how increased incarceration affects the nation's crime rate. But most agree that the growth in prison building and in the prison population is likely to slow or even stop in the near future.

For many conservatives, the prison-building boom of the last two decades was necessary to correct the imbalances brought about by the mistaken, liberal judicial policies of the 1960s and '70s. In other words, they say, now that a more appropriate balance between punishment and crime has been restored, there will be less need to continue incarcerating more and more people.

"We lost control back then, and the crime rate grew and was able to overwhelm the system," says Morgan of the National Center for Policy Analysis. "Now the system is overwhelming crime."

Scheidegger agrees. "As the crime rate comes down, I think we'll realize that we have it right and won't continue to increase or decrease sentences."

Other conservatives go a step further, predicting that if the crime rate continues to fall, so will spending on prisons. "If things continue going the way they are, we'll start to see a drop in the number of prisoners," says Chicago's Lott. "Soon, the amount of resources people will be willing to spend on [imprisonment] will begin to fall, and it's not clear that that will be wrong."

Liberals generally embrace the shifting of resources away from imprisonment. And many are confident that national policy will begin to turn away from what they see as the overly punitive measures enacted over the last two and a half decades, including mandatory sentences.

"I'm optimistic because some people who were tough-on-crime types are reconsidering their positions," Mauer says. "There's a growing consensus among police and others in the criminal justice community that things are out of balance here and need to be reexamined."

Others agree, but cite different reasons. "I think they'll reconsider this incarceration boom because financial pressure will force them to," says Sterling, the former House Judiciary Committee staffer. "The cost of keeping so many people behind bars will eventually counterweigh the political pressure to put and keep people away."

In addition, Sterling argues, as prison touches more and more people, either directly or indirectly, the sentiment against widescale incarceration will increase. "As more people are related to or know someone in jail, they may become more sensitive to the absurdity of what we've been doing."

But other liberal thinkers, while cautiously optimistic that incarceration rates will begin falling in sync with the crime rate, warn that the national mood is very fickle when it comes to crime.

"People think we're more unsafe than we actually are, and so it's easy to exaggerate the dangers out there," says Gainsborough of the Campaign for an Effective Crime Policy. "All it takes is one well-publicized and heinous crime, and things can shift and we could very quickly undo a lot of progress." ■

FOR MORE INFORMATION

American Correctional Association, 4380 Forbes Blvd., Lanham, Md. 20706; (301) 918-1800; www.corrections.com/aca. The association conducts and publishes research on correctional standards and related issues.

Families Against Mandatory Minimums, 1612 K St., N.W., Suite 1400, Washington, D.C. 20006; (202) 822-6700; www.fammm.org. This organization lobbies for the repeal of mandatory minimum sentences.

Prison Fellowship Ministries, P.O. Box 17500, Washington, D.C. 20041; (703) 478-0100; www.pfm.org. This Christian organization ministers to prisoners, ex-prisoners and victims of crime.

The Sentencing Project, 918 F St., N.W., Suite 501, Washington, D.C. 20004; (202) 628-0871; www.sentencingproject.org. Promotes sentencing reform that reduces reliance on incarceration and conducts research on criminal justice policy.

Notes

[1] Rick Lyman, "Judge Rules That Despite Improvements, Prisons in Texas Still Need Federal Oversight," *The New York Times*, March 2, 1999.

[2] Figures cited in Christy Hoppe, "Judge Keeps Supervision of Prisons," *The Dallas Morning News*, March 2, 1999.

[3] Figures cited in Carl M. Cannon, "America: All Locked Up," *The National Journal*, Aug. 15. 1998.

[4] Laurence Hammack, "Third Strike Gets Robber Life in Prison," *The Roanoke Times*, March 12, 1999.

[5] "America's One Million Non-violent Prisoners," Justice Policy Institute, March 1999.

[6] Cited in "Who Goes to Prison for Drug Offenses," *Human Rights Watch*, March 18, 1999.

[7] Marc Mauer, "Americans Behind Bars: U.S. and International Use of Incarceration, 1995," The Sentencing Project, June 1997.

[8] Eric Schlosser, "The Prison-Industrial Complex," *The Atlantic*, December, 1998.

[9] *Ibid.*

[10] Figures cited in "More Than Any Other Democracy," *The Economist*, March 20, 1999.

[11] Data provided by The Sentencing Project.

[12] Ron Stodghill II, "Unequal Justice: Why Women Fare Worse," *Time*, Feb. 1, 1999.

[13] Figures provided by the Bureau of Justice Statistics.

[14] Jan Austin (ed.), *Congressional Quarterly Almanac* (1994), p. 288.

[15] Pam Belluck, "As More Prisons Go Private, States Seek Tighter Controls," *The New York Times*, April 15, 1999.

[16] Schlosser, *op. cit.*

[17] Nancy Mahon, "The Problem with Private Prisons," *The Washington Post*, Nov. 1, 1998.

[18] Fox Butterfield, "Eliminating Parole Boards Isn't a Cure-All, Experts Say," *The New York Times*, Jan. 11, 1999.

[19] Cited in Fox Butterfield, "Inmates Serving More Time," *The New York Times*, Jan. 11, 1999.

[20] *Ibid.*

[21] Quoted in Butterfield, *op. cit.*, "Eliminating Parole Boards Isn't a Cure-All, Experts Say."

Bibliography

Selected Sources Used

Books

Christianson, Scott, *With Liberty For Some: 500 Years of Imprisonment in America*, Northeastern University (1999).
Christianson details the history of penal life in America, from its role as a dumping ground for British criminals during the Colonial period to the recent prison building boom of the 1980s and '90s. He argues that the high rate of incarceration in the United States today is not just the result of the rising rate of crime but also reflects the mean-spirited side of the American character.

Articles

Belluck, Pam, "As More Prisons Go Private, States Seek Tighter Controls," *The New York Times*, April 15, 1999.
Belluck details the debate currently raging over the utility of privately run prisons, focusing on well-publicized problems with certain private facilities.

Butterfield, Fox, "Eliminating Parole Boards Isn't a Cure-All, Experts Say," *The New York Times*, Jan. 10, 1999.
The article examines efforts around the country to abolish parole boards and severely limit supervised release. Butterfield quotes some experts who say the parole system is in such disarray that abolishing parole won't have a significant positive or negative impact on crime.

Clark, Charles S., "Prison Overcrowding," *The CQ Researcher*, Feb. 4, 1994.
This dated but thoroughly researched piece details the debate over whether building more prisons in the future will reduce crime.

Cloud, John, "A Get-Tough Policy That's Failed," *Time*, Feb. 1, 1999.
Cloud argues that mandatory minimum sentences for non-violent offenders are overly harsh and ineffective. The good news, according to Cloud, is that the law enforcement community is slowly coming to believe "that mandatory minimums are foolish."

Loconte, Joe, "The Remarkable Second Career of Chuck Colson," *The Weekly Standard*, June 28, 1999.
Loconte, a fellow at the Heritage Foundation, chronicle's Colson's journey from Watergate felon to the leader of Prison Fellowship Ministries, which aims to rehabilitate inmates through Christian conversion.

Miller, Lisa, "Inside the Competitive New World of Prison Ministries," *The Wall Street Journal*, Sept. 6, 1999.
Miller examines the growing faith-based movement in corrections, detailing the competition that often ensues between Muslim and Christian groups operating inside prisons.

Schlosser, Eric, "The Prison Industrial Complex," *The Atlantic*, December, 1998.
Schlosser takes an in-depth look at the economic pressures that drive prison construction. He concludes that the interest groups and businesses that build and run the nation's prisons — and by definition define many of our criminal-justice policies — are driven by self-interest, not public service.

Swope, Christopher, "Truth and Consequences," *Governing*, April, 1999.
Swope surveys the impact of truth-in-sentencing laws around the nation. While some states have seen their prison population boom as a result of these laws, others have been more cautious in locking up inmates for a long time.

Valentine, Paul W., "Productive Program in Md. Prisons; State Says Giving Jobs to Inmates Pays Off," *The Washington Post*, March 22, 1999.
The article detail's Maryland's efforts to put inmates to work in fields ranging from food processing to furniture making.

Will, George F., "A Jail Break for Geriatrics," *Newsweek*, July 20, 1998.
The conservative columnist decries tough laws that are keeping older prisoners behind bars. He argues that studies showing low rates of recidivism for older inmates make it a waste of their time and taxpayer money to keep many of them in prison.

Reports

***Losing the Vote: The Impact of Felony Disenfranchisement Laws in the United States*, Human Rights Watch and The Sentencing Project, October, 1998.**
A 50-state survey of felony disenfranchisement laws concludes that they are "unreasonable" as well as "racially discriminatory."

9 Racism and the Black Middle Class

DAVID MASCI

By any measure, Wanda Alexander is a success. Just 39, she has built her own real estate consulting business and lives in Upper Marlboro, Md., a comfortable suburb south of Washington.

But Alexander's journey to reach the American dream wasn't easy. As a black woman, she faced obstacles that she believes were placed in her way because of her race. Before striking out on her own, for example, she watched her less experienced white colleagues receive training and promotions ahead of her. "I got tired of people telling me in subtle and sometimes overt ways that I would never do better than I had because of my race and gender," she says.

Stories like Alexander's are common among black professionals. Many feel anger and frustration even as they achieve personal and professional success. Indeed, polls show that a solid majority of well-off African-Americans still feel that racism is an obstacle to their advancement. A 1995 poll commissioned by *The Washington Post*, the Kaiser Family Foundation and Harvard University found that 84 percent of all black Americans with an annual household income of between $30,000 and $75,000, believed that "past and present discrimination is the major reason for the economic and social ills blacks face." Perhaps surprisingly, only 66 percent of poor and working-class blacks felt the same way. [1]

The sense that discrimination is still a problem for middle-class blacks is hard for many Americans to understand. By all accounts, the post-civil rights era has been a time of great growth for the black middle class. Today, more than one-third of all Afri-

can-Americans meet the fiscal definition of middle class: They reside in households that earn the median national income of $35,000 per year or more. In the 1960s, fewer than 10 percent of black Americans fit this description. Moreover, the number of black doctors, lawyers and engineers has grown exponentially since World War II. Indeed, the percentage of African-Americans in white-collar jobs has jumped from under 6 percent in 1940 to roughly half today. [2]

Blacks also have made great strides in the business world. The number of successful black entrepreneurs is increasing every year in fields as diverse as finance, software and manufacturing. Blacks serve as the presidents of several big U.S. corporations, including American Express and Maytag, putting them just one rung below CEO.

And yet, in the minds of many well-to-do African-Americans, all is not well. "Despite its evident prosperity, much of America's black middle class is in pain," writes *Newsweek* reporter Ellis Cose in his 1993 book, *The Rage of a Privileged Class*. The reason, according to Cose, is that white America has broken its "covenant" with blacks. The idea, he writes, "that if you work hard, get a good education and play by the rules you will be allowed to advance and achieve to the limits of your ability" has never been fully realized. [3]

For many middle-class African-Americans, the "pain" is felt most keenly in the workplace, where they say their race is still a factor in hiring and promotion. "Discrimination still exists, even if it's masked well," says Joanne Dowdell, an African-American who is vice president for new product development at Washington Business Information Inc.

Many scholars of race relations echo such sentiments, arguing that while some businesses — especially large corporations — have become more open to blacks and other minorities, racism is still a big problem. "It's still an obstacle. It just takes a more subtle form," says Bart Landry, an associate professor of sociology at the University of Maryland at College Park.

Some white managers mean well and don't know that they are discriminating, Landry and others say. But they feel that many managers still view African-Americans as lazy or less capable than whites, or both. And so, they say, even at companies that pride themselves on hiring and promoting minorities, few African-Americans ever rise to the top or even to positions of real responsibility. "People in control want to work with people who look like them," says Ronald Walters, a professor of government at Maryland. As a result, Walters and others point out, there are no black CEOs at America's largest, most powerful corporations.

But other observers argue that discrimination is no longer a great stumbling block for African-Americans. In fact, says Shelby Steele, a research fellow at the Hoover Institution, universities, companies and

From *The CQ Researcher*, January 23, 1998.

How Are Blacks Doing?

African-Americans don't think they are faring as well as whites think they are, according to a comprehensive Gallup Poll in early 1997. But the poll also showed substantial improvement over time in blacks' satisfaction with their lives.

How are blacks treated in your community?

Answered by blacks | **Answered by whites**

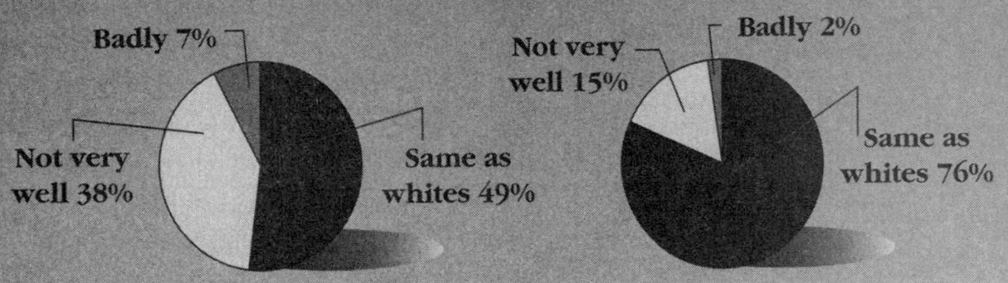

How do you feel about affirmative action?

	Answered by Blacks	Answered by Whites
Increase affirmative action	53%	22%
Keep affirmative action the same	29%	29%
Decrease affirmative action	12%	37%

Blacks in your community have as good a chance as whites to:

	Answered by Blacks	Answered by Whites
Get a job	46%	79%
Get housing	58%	86%
Get an education	63%	79%

Percent who think blacks are treated the same as whites in your community:

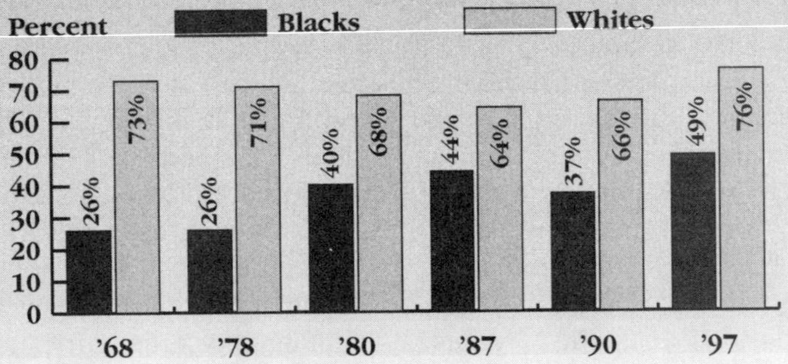

Source: The Gallup Organization conducted a telephone poll of 3,076 black and white Americans between Jan. 4 and Feb. 28, 1997.

the government are working hard to find, hire and promote blacks. "This is the new spirit of corporate America," says Steele, who is black.

Steele and others argue that the problem for African-Americans on the job isn't racism, but lack of progress in education and training. For instance, they point out, blacks — even from middle-class backgrounds — don't score as well on standardized tests and are more likely to drop out of college than whites, even poor whites.[4] "The fact is that in many [occupational] areas there is a very small pool of qualified black applicants, and that's the problem," says Gerald Reynalds, president of the Center for New Black Leadership.

According to Steele, Reynalds and others, the view that racism is still the primary obstacle to black advancement on the job and elsewhere has hurt African-Americans by shifting the emphasis from self-improvement to fighting discrimination. "People put too much stock in discrimination today," says Walter Williams, chairman of the Economics Department at George Mason University in Fairfax, Va. Blaming discrimination, says Williams, has undercut blacks' advancement by leading them to rely on racial preferences instead of their own efforts.

To begin with, Williams and other black conservatives say, preferences created by the policy known as "affirmative action" are damaging to society as a whole because it is fundamentally unfair to judge someone based on race, regardless of the reason. Such efforts lead to resentment among whites and bolster stereotypes of black inferiority.

But, Williams argues, the policy does the greatest harm to those it is intended to help because it lowers the standards by which African-Americans are judged. Giving someone a preference "doesn't do them any favor," he says, because people who don't have to work as hard to get ahead, won't. In other words, by lowering standards for African-Americans, companies, universities and others are giving them a disincentive to achieve on their own.

The net result of such assistance, Williams says, is that it produces problems when the beneficiaries of affirmative action are eventually forced to compete head to head with everyone else. It also makes blacks "passive," in Steele's view. "It makes me into someone who cannot move forward unless white people are benevolent and help me move forward," he says.

But supporters of affirmative action counter that it is necessary simply to give African-Americans a chance to succeed in the face of past and present racism. The bottom line, they say, is that there is no level playing field when it comes to competition between blacks and whites. White men have controlled all the levers of power in American society from the beginning, they say, conferring upon them an advantage that did not go away when the Civil Rights Act of 1964 was passed.

"The effects of discrimination linger," says Cecilia Conrad, a research associate at the Joint Center for Political and Economic Studies, which focuses on issues of interest to blacks. "Whites are still benefiting from Jim Crow," she adds.

But vestiges of traditional discrimination have been felt far beyond the workplace. For instance, until recently, many suburban areas were virtually off-limits to African-Americans. And while housing discrimination has not been entirely eliminated, most neighborhoods that were, in effect, reserved for whites are now open to black homeowners. Not surprisingly, the number of African-Americans living in the suburbs has risen dramatically in the last three decades. [5]

But some black thinkers argue that "black flight" from the inner cities has hurt African-Americans. As the best and the brightest have left for the suburbs, many formerly segregated communities, usually in cities, have degenerated into neighborhoods characterized by high crime, little economic opportunity and hopelessness. "Talented individuals and stable families have left, and left a vacuum," says Roy Brooks, a law professor at San Diego State University.

Brooks is among the blacks who urge middle-class African-Americans to move into black urban areas in order to revitalize them. They argue that black professionals can serve as role models for members of the underclass. In addition, they say, by living and shopping in these areas, professionals and other residents will increase economic opportunities in the neighborhood as businesses are established to serve them.

But many black professionals reject the notion that they should feel obliged to live in a poor, crime-ridden area in order to serve the less fortunate. "I want to live where I'm most comfortable," Alexander says. Elijah Anderson, a professor of ethnography at the University of Pennsylvania, agrees. "The bottom line is that people should be able to do what they want."

Anderson and others argue that there is no sense in working hard and succeeding if you can't live where you want to. In addition, he doubts that an influx of the black middle class back to the cities would make a big difference in the lives of poor African-Americans. Instead, he argues, the underclass needs training and jobs, not role models.

Besides, they contend, one does not have to live next door to someone in order to help them. "There are other ways that you can give back to the community," Dowdell says. Alexander and Dowdell, who lives in a predominantly white part of Washington, both work to help other African-Americans get ahead. Alexander, for instance, helps to finance scholarships for young, black women.

But others are torn over the issue. "You need good role models so that kids can see that there are legitimate alternatives to poverty," says Gavin Jackson, a human resources specialist at the Department of the Treasury, who lives in suburban Burtonsville, Md., with his wife and two children. At the same time, Jackson admits that he is not ready to move out of suburbia. "I can't sacrifice my children. I mean, we moved [to the suburbs] because the schools were better." [6]

Like many black professionals, Jackson feels the tug of group identity even as he strives to build a life for himself and his family. As Jackson and other African-Americans look toward the future, these are some of the questions they are asking:

Is racism still a big obstacle to advancement for many black professionals?

In November 1996, oil giant Texaco agreed to pay $176.1 million to settle a discrimination suit filed by 1,400 current and former black employees. Many of the workers who sued alleged that they had repeatedly lost out on promotions and raises because of their race. They also claimed that they were subjected to racial slurs and other indignities. [7]

For many black Americans, the Texaco case is simply the tip of a very large iceberg. According to recent polls, fully two-thirds of middle-class blacks think that discrimination is still a real problem in their lives. Racism, most of these professionals say, is a fact of life in corporate America, a fact that puts African-Americans at a serious disadvantage as they try to compete with whites in the workplace.

Many whites and others wonder how their black colleagues can still feel discriminated against. After all, they say, the days of Jim Crow, of overt, institutionalized racism, are over.

"It's not a nationwide problem," said Michael Losey, president and CEO of the Society for Human Resource Management. According to

Blacks in White-Collar Occupations

In stark contrast to 1940, when most blacks did manual labor, more than half the black women and a third of the men had white-collar jobs in 1990.

	1940	1970	1990
		(Percentage)	
Men			
Professionals	1.8	7.8	9.4
Proprietors, managers and officials	1.3	4.7	6.7
Clerical and sales	2.1	9.2	15.9
Total white-collar	5.2	21.7	32.0
Women			
Professionals	4.3	10.8	15.9
Proprietors, managers and officials	0.7	1.9	7.6
Clerical and sales	1.4	23.4	35.4
Total white-collar	6.4	36.1	58.9

Sources: Stephan and Abigail Thernstrom, America in Black and White: One Nation, Indivisible, *1997, based on U.S. Census Bureau,* "Money Income in the U.S.: *1995."*

Losey, who is white, when a case like Texaco does occur, there is a reason people are shocked. He says that "many people recognize this as inconsistent with what they see in their community, what they see as their company policy where they work, what they see as a practice." [8]

But many black thinkers argue that discrimination encountered by minorities today is harder to recognize because it is much different from the obvious examples of past prejudice. "We are dealing not with overt racism, but a subtler form," says Professor Robert Hill, director of the Institute for Urban Research at Morgan State University in Baltimore.

Hill argues that many white managers don't know that they are discriminating against their black colleagues. "They are doing their best," he says, "but they don't realize that their best is not adequate." For instance, Hill says, whites exclude blacks from their network of close co-workers ("the buddy system"), which in effect excludes African-Americans from important decisions and promotions.

Others argue that many whites still view blacks as their intellectual inferiors. "A lot of white people have not really viewed black people close-up," says the University of Pennsylvania's Anderson, "operating instead on stereotypes."

And so, even at companies that try to hire and promote a lot of minorities, there are few black professionals in any important slots, says Sharon Collins, an associate professor of sociology at the University of Illinois in Chicago. "Black managers tend to go in the personnel or public relations departments," she add. "These don't tend to be the most career-enhancing jobs."

Moreover, says Conrad of the Joint Center for Economics and Politics, African-Americans are excluded from key posts because whites don't trust blacks to do the most important work in the corporation. "They tend not to be in the company's profit centers, like sales or product development," she says.

As a result, Collins and Conrad say, the very top of the corporate hierarchy includes very few black executives. In addition, they say, there are no black CEOs at *Fortune* 500 companies, with the exception of Beatrice Foods Inc., which is black-owned.

But other African-American thinkers reject the idea that black professionals are being held back in large numbers by discrimination. In fact, many say, large companies and government agencies are working overtime to hire and promote minorities. "Every major company is busting its ass looking for brown faces," says Reynalds of the Center for New Black Leadership.

The Hoover Institution's Steele, author of the best-selling treatise on race *The Content of Our Character*, agrees with Reynalds, pointing out that "in corporations, universities and the government, people are looking for ways to encourage and mentor blacks."

Steele, Reynalds and other thinkers are not saying that America is a color-blind society. "People have lost their minds if they think they can do away with prejudice," Reynalds says. But he believes that racism today is not a powerful enough force in our society to hold back minorities who want to succeed.

The problem, Reynalds, Steele and others say, isn't discrimination, but a lack of education and training. For instance, they point out, blacks do score significantly lower on standardized tests and are much more likely to have been involved in the criminal-justice system than whites. "If you've been convicted of a felony or don't have a proper education, that will be a much greater obstacle to job advancement than your race," Reynalds says.

Steele agrees, arguing that poverty and other social factors have "brought us to a point where we're not as competitive as other groups are."

But what about polls showing middle-class blacks' concern over discrimination and anger over the way society is treating them? Some, like Ward Connerly, the

California businessman behind Proposition 209, the ballot initiative ending affirmative action programs in California, say that African-American anger is due to outmoded attitudes about race. "I think part of our racial problem is that my fellow black Americans are so sensitive to the issue of racism that it almost becomes a self-fulfilling prophecy," he says. "You look for it, and by golly, it's there — whether it's real or not." [9]

Others are less forgiving. Steele, for instance, believes that African-Americans, either consciously or unconsciously, often cry racism because it produces results. "If I'm black and I'm angry, I'm more likely to get attention and get preferential treatment than if I'm black and not angry," he says. In short, the accusations of racism and the anger are tools that give black employees leverage over their white managers, who do not want to be accused of racism.

"This [behavior] trips white guilt and obligation and gets [blacks] preferential treatment, like a promotion or an all-black lounge at the office," Steele says. In many cases these African-American professionals convince themselves that they are victims. "We all tend to believe in what serves us, even if it's wrong," he says.

Lou Denatteis/Reuters

Marchers protesting Proposition 209 cross the Golden Gate Bridge led by Jesse Jackson, San Francisco Supervisor Mabel Teng and Mayor Willie Brown.

Do members of the black middle class have an obligation to other blacks to live in predominantly African-American neighborhoods, especially in poorer areas in the inner city?

Buying a home in the suburbs is the quintessential right of passage for middle-class Americans. But before the civil rights movement of the 1950s and '60s, African-Americans were not welcome in most suburban areas.

Today, the situation is different, although housing discrimination is far from eradicated. A recent study in the Washington, D.C., area, for instance, showed that many real estate agencies still "steer" minorities away from certain areas. But by and large, suburban enclaves that were once segregated are now open to African-Americans.

Statistics bear out this new interracial reality. Polls show that since 1960 the number of African-Americans living in suburban areas has more than doubled. Today roughly 32 percent of all black Americans live in the suburbs. [10] And in some areas, blacks comprise the majority of suburbanites. For instance, Prince George's County, Md., outside Washington, is now 62 percent African-American. [11]

For a member of the black middle class, the suburbs have the same allure that they do for their white counterparts: better schools, lower crime rates and bucolic settings usually not found in cities.

But some African-Americans view the middle-class exodus with dread and call for black professionals to move back to the urban areas where they grew up.

"Integration has resulted in a depletion of human and economic resources from the black community," says San Diego State's Brooks. "We need to find a way to reintegrate the black middle class into inner-city areas," Walters adds.

The problem, Brooks, Walters and others say, is that middle-class migration to the suburbs has drained traditionally black areas of some of their most productive and valuable citizens. In the past, when segregation forced all blacks to live together regardless of class, professionals and other accomplished African-Americans served as leaders and role models in the community. Today, they say, there is a void in many areas created by the absence of successful people. "They need to reconnect with their roots and serve as role models to the rest of the community," Walters says.

Walters also argues that "the middle class leaves behind a much weaker institutional base and a citizenry denuded of resources." For example, he says, the presence of middle-class residents gives the areas greater political clout, which in turn could lead to better city services, like police and sanitation. In addition, he says, middle-class children and par-

Blacks Flocked to the Suburbs

Many black Americans moved to the suburbs following the civil rights movement of the 1950s and '60s. From 1960 to 1995, the number of suburban blacks tripled, and the percentage of blacks who were suburbanites doubled.

Blacks in the Suburbs

	Number *(in millions)*	Percent of total black population	Percent of total suburban population
1950	2.2	15	5.5
1960	2.9	15.2	4.8
1970	3.6	16.1	4.8
1980	5.9	22.3	5.9
1995	10.6	31.9	8.1

Sources: Stephan and Abigail Thernstrom, America in Black and White: One Nation, Indivisible, *1997, based on data from* Statistical Abstract of the U.S.: 1974 *and U.S. Bureau of the Census.*

ents "raise the standards at schools, which benefits everyone."

Finally, Walters and Brooks argue, the presence of a large group of people with disposable income will give blighted areas an economic shot in the arm, which in turn will create needed jobs. "Businesses will be created to serve them, and they will start businesses of their own in the community," Brooks says.

The idea that the presence of a middle class is necessary for healthy community development has prompted a number of cities, including Philadelphia and Cleveland, to offer tax and other incentives to lure professionals back to inner-city neighborhoods long abandoned by all but the poor. Cleveland, for instance, is offering lots in rundown areas for as little as $100 to anyone willing to build a house and live there. The city also offers mortgage assistance and will waive property taxes for up to 15 years. "Cities cannot survive if they are full of old and poor people," says Cleveland Mayor Michael White, an African-American. [12]

The city's plan seems to be working. Since 1990, 2,400 new homes have been built in the special areas, almost all by African-Americans. More broadly, the percentage of black households nationwide with an income of $75,000 or more that have stayed in cities has remained at 48 percent throughout the 1990s. [13]

But while many thinkers on race applaud the back-to-the-city trend, others argue that middle-class African-Americans should not feel obligated to stay in or move back to inner cities. "I like the idea that people have choices . . . and if I want to move to a certain area because it's, say, close to work, I should be able to do that," says Conrad, who grew up in a segregated neighborhood. "If you have the money and wherewithal, you should live where you want to, period," agrees George Mason's Williams.

Others say that trying to push middle-class blacks back into their old, largely African-American neighborhoods is bad for both them and the country. To begin with, they argue, more blacks and whites should be living together, not trying to stay with their own kind. "What we're talking about here is resegregation, plain and simple," Anderson says. "We will lose the idea of making America into a universalist, egalitarian society," he says.

Anderson and others also argue that the middle-class African-Americans who move into inner-city neighborhoods are making a sacrifice in the name of racial unity. For one thing, he says, blacks are financially penalized when they go to sell their city houses because the only people who will want to purchase a home in these areas are other African-Americans. "This is a limited housing market because whites, Asians and other folks aren't interested in these neighborhoods," he says. "That's a bad way to play the capitalist game."

Finally, opponents of efforts to lure professionals back to cities argue that the presence of some middle-class African-Americans in the neighborhood isn't a solution to the real problems of the black underclass. "What inner-city blacks need is not the middle class but a real job base," Landry says. According to Landry and others, the presence of middle-class residents might improve local government and create a few new service jobs, but it won't generate the kind of employment, such as a factory work, that allows poorer residents the opportunity to make a decent living.

Landry also rejects the notion that black professionals will make a difference by serving as role models for their less fortunate brethren. "Black kids don't need these role models in that sense," he says, "because in our media age the role models and avenues to success are well-known."

Do middle-class African-Americans need affirmative action to have equal opportunities at school and work?

On Nov. 5, 1996, proponents of

affirmative action suffered a stunning blow when voters in California passed Proposition 209, a ballot measure that outlawed the use of racial or gender preferences at all state government institutions. A year later, on Nov. 3, Prop. 209 went into effect when the Supreme Court refused to review an earlier Court of Appeals decision upholding the referendum's constitutionality. [14]

The success of Proposition 209 has inspired similar efforts in other parts of the country. Voters in Colorado and Ohio, among others, will have a chance to eliminate gender and racial preferences in the upcoming 1998 elections.

Meanwhile, recent court challenges to affirmative action programs also have proven successful. For instance, in 1996 the Supreme Court refused to review (and hence effectively upheld) a 5th Circuit Court of Appeals decision prohibiting the University of Texas from using race or gender in admissions. In New Jersey, a discrimination suit brought by a white teacher was settled before it went to the Supreme Court. Settlement was prompted by the likelihood that the court would rule that the affirmative action policy that led to the teacher's dismissal was unconstitutional. She had been laid off and a black teacher retained, although both had equal tenure and qualifications, because the school system wanted to maintain racial diversity.

To many black professionals, the success of efforts to eliminate or scale back affirmative action is both disheartening and misguided. "A lot of white people say: 'We've solved racism, so just get on with [life] already,'" says the University of Pennsylvania's Anderson.

But the reality, according to Anderson and others, is that affirmative action is still needed to give African-Americans simply a fighting chance of competing in a world where the odds are still stacked against them, even three decades after the successes of the civil rights movement.

Blacks in College Steadily Increased

Four times as many blacks had attended college for at least four years in 1995 as in 1960.

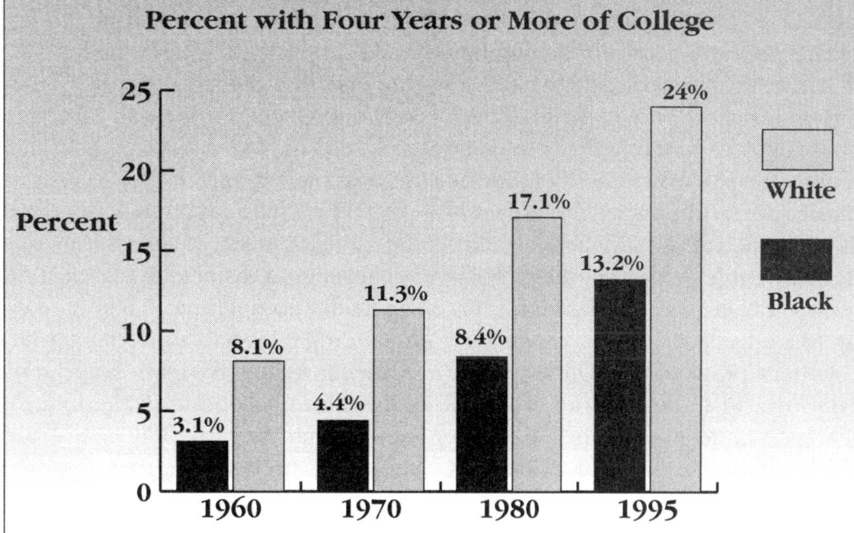

Sources: Stephan and Abigail Thernstrom, America in Black and White: One Nation, Indivisible, *1997, based on U.S. Census Bureau,* "Money Income in the U.S.: *1995.*"

"You cannot do in 30 years what [America has] done with great success for 300 years — that is, give affirmative action to white people," says historian John Hope Franklin, who heads the advisory panel on race relations established in June by President Clinton. [15]

Wade Henderson, executive director of the Leadership Conference on Civil Rights, agrees that whites have enjoyed such great advantages historically that attempts to rectify past injustices require more than a level playing field. He points out, for example, that African-Americans graduating from college and looking for work might not have either the financial resources or "connections" that their white counterparts may enjoy thanks to their families. "The roots of racism run deep," he says.

In fact, Henderson and others argue, it's not possible to have a level playing field, and so it's counterproductive to pretend otherwise. "Nepotism and favoritism, that's white affirmative action, and it determines a lot of hiring and promotion decisions," says the University of Maryland's Landry. "Blacks don't have those kind of connections, and so they shouldn't feel apologetic if they substitute affirmative action instead," he adds.

Finally, supporters of affirmative action say, the evidence to support the policy is in the numbers. To begin with, they point out, blacks are still woefully underrepresented, both as students in universities and as white-collar workers. For example, according to 1995 Department of Education statistics, only 44.9 percent of African-Americans had attended at least some college, compared with 55.4 percent of whites. [16] In addition, as of 1994, only 14.7 percent of black men and

20.1 percent of black women held what would be considered managerial or professional jobs. By contrast, 27.5 percent of white men and 29.9 percent of white women worked in such jobs.[17] (*See graph, p. 156.*)

The disparity between the number of African-Americans and whites in higher learning and executive-level jobs would be much higher if it were not for affirmative action, say supporters of race and gender preferences. "If you ended affirmative action, many of the people who run these businesses wouldn't give a fig about hiring black people," Anderson says.

Others point to the University of California at Berkeley as an example of what would happen in university admissions of blacks nationwide if affirmative action were totally abolished. At the university's law school, for instance, admission of African-American students dropped 81 percent the year after racial preferences were eliminated. "Imagine if we had Proposition 209 nationwide," Anderson says. "We'd have institutionalized segregation again."

But opponents of affirmative action argue that the policy — far from helping African-Americans — actually has had a detrimental impact on the black middle class. To begin with, they say, affirmative action lowers standards by which black Americans are judged, at school or on the job. This in turn creates what Reynalds calls "perverse incentives" for African-Americans to expect more for less. "If you don't have to work as hard, you won't," he says. "That's just human nature."

The problem, Reynalds argues, comes when black students or workers have to compete head to head with their white counterparts. "Once they get into the real world, they're in for a rude awakening because most folks run into the higher standard sooner or later and often don't know how to handle it." This leads to higher rates of black failure, Reynalds contends. For instance, he says, many more black than white students who get into good colleges and universities drop out before they graduate.

By accepting unqualified candidates, opponents like Reynalds say, universities, companies and other institutions help to mask the real problem in the black community: poor achievement.

"Affirmative action has suppressed the development of black America because it is a disincentive to becoming more competitive," Steele says. According to Steele and others, preferences make African-Americans much more accepting of the inferior educational system that many are subjected to because they look to white America and affirmative action for uplift, not themselves.

Lower standards also fuel false stereotypes of black inferiority, opponents say, because people will always wonder whether African-Americans owe their success to hard work and intelligence or affirmative action. "If you have a white who has graduated from an Ivy League school, you know something about that kid and the work he's had to do to get there," Steele says. But "if someone has been getting a preference since high school, you don't know much about his true worth, regardless of his credentials on paper." In the end, Steele argues, "the big tragedy is that many blacks have high SAT scores, but they're tarred with the same brush." In other words, affirmative action distorts the connection between your credentials and your ability, regardless of the reality of the situation.

Others say that preferences also create white resentment, which in turn leads to race-based anger. "In many places, they'll kick the white guy's butt if he does shoddy work, but not the black guy's," Williams says. "This, of course, creates ill will among the races."

Most important, opponents say, affirmative action is simply immoral in a society that claims to be working toward true equality. "If you believe in equality before the law, you have to be offended by an institution that uses racial preferences," Williams says. ■

BACKGROUND

The Migration North

Until the turn of the century, most black Americans lived in rural areas of the South. Even in 1940, a majority of African-Americans were still working in agriculture below the Mason-Dixon line.

The concentration of blacks in the South retarded African-American progress. On purely economic grounds, few blacks, even after Emancipation, benefited from the industrialization and urbanization taking place in the North and other parts of the country. In the decades following the Civil War, most blacks stayed in the areas where they had been slaves, many working as sharecroppers on land owned by whites.

Meanwhile, throughout the country, but especially in the South, government institutions and businesses treated African-Americans like pariahs. From restaurants to universities to the local Woolworth's, the list of indignities was endless. In many parts of the country, African-Americans were effectively barred from voting or sitting on juries. Public facilities were often segregated, and many businesses refused to serve blacks. Well-funded state universities attended by whites didn't admit blacks.

Chronology

1940s-1950s

World War II and its aftermath presage big changes for African-Americans as the migration north intensifies and the civil rights movement takes off.

1941
U.S. entry into World War II causes an immediate shortage of industrial labor at home, increasing the migration of African-Americans from the South to Northern urban areas.

1946
President Harry S Truman orders an end to racial segregation in the armed forces.

1947
Jackie Robinson joins the Brooklyn Dodgers, becoming the first African-American to play Major League baseball.

1954
The Supreme Court's landmark *Brown v. Board of Education* ruling overturns the previous "separate but equal" policy in public education.

1955
Rosa Parks refuses to give up her seat on a city bus to a white man, sparking the Montgomery, Ala., bus boycott. The Rev. Martin Luther King Jr. emerges as a civil rights leader.

1960s

The civil rights movement becomes a national crusade. Congress enacts a raft of legislation aimed at ending discrimination.

1961
President John F. Kennedy uses the term "affirmative action" for the first time, ordering federal contractors to take affirmative action not to discriminate in hiring, but does not set numerical quotas.

1963
Martin Luther King Jr. gives his stirring "I Have a Dream" speech at the Lincoln Memorial in Washington.

1964
Congress passes the sweeping Civil Rights Act, which prohibits discrimination by employers on the basis of race, sex or national origin.

1965
In August President Lyndon B. Johnson signs the Voting Rights Act, which outlaws unreasonable barriers to voting. In September he issues Executive Order 11246 requiring federal contractors to actively recruit minorities.

1966
The Black Panthers, a group advocating "black power," is founded.

1968
Civil Rights leader Martin Luther King Jr. is assassinated, touching off race riots in many American cities.

1970s-present

In the post-civil rights era, new policies like affirmative action are adopted, sparking a backlash among whites.

1970
President Richard M. Nixon expands upon Executive Order 11246 to require contractors to set goals for minority employment.

1978
In *University of California Regents v. Bakke*, the Supreme Court rules that universities can use race as a factor in admissions, but may not impose quotas.

1980
Affirmative action foe Ronald Reagan is elected to the presidency. The Justice Department begins attacking racial quotas.

1995
Middle-class blacks are widely represented among the hundreds of thousands of people at the Million Man March in Washington, D.C.

1996
Voters in California approve Proposition 209 outlawing the use of race or gender preferences at all state government institutions.

1997
President Clinton names an advisory panel on race relations as part of a "national dialogue on race."

1998
Referendums in Colorado, Ohio, Washington and Florida will give voters a chance to strike down racial preferences in hiring and college admissions.

Still, even in this harsh economic and social environment, a small black middle class slowly grew. The process was aided in the early part of the century by a migration of African-Americans to Northern industrial areas. The first great wave of this movement occurred during World War I. The conflict cut off the flow of immigrants from Europe, forcing American factories to look for cheap labor elsewhere. By 1920, most Northern cities had sizable black communities.

World War II also played a key role in black population shifts. While heavy industry was expanding almost exponentially to produce weapons and other war materiel to fight the Axis powers, many of the nation's white factory workers were in uniform. Blacks, on the other hand, were not inducted into the armed forces at as great a rate as whites, making them prime candidates to fill the void. As a result, African-Americans moved in large numbers to the industrial North and would continue to do so for the next three decades.

This second great migration ballooned black populations in cities from Los Angeles to New York. By the end of the war, more than one-quarter of all African-Americans lived outside the South. By 1960, the number had risen to 40 percent.[18]

As more and more black Americans shifted from agricultural to factory work, income levels began improving. More money meant more power for blacks, as consumers and voters. It also — along with the GI Bill and other factors — led to a significant increase in black educational attainment. As a result, the number of African-Americans with at least a high school diploma jumped from 12.3 percent in 1940 to 38.6 percent in 1960. During the same period, the percentage of black men doing white-collar work jumped from 10 percent to nearly one-quarter.[19]

But the Second World War altered more than income and education levels. Many blacks, and a few whites, saw the irony of more than 300,000 young, black men fighting — in segregated units — for freedom around the world. By the end of the war, black Americans felt that they had done their part and deserved to be treated accordingly by the broader society. More important, black leaders and liberal, white politicians began to forcefully and openly campaign against the nation's overtly racist policies.

"The Second World War altered more than income and education levels. Many blacks, and a few whites, saw the irony of more than 300,000 young, black men fighting — in segregated units — for freedom around the world."

Their efforts produced some startling results. The armed forces, and, more slowly, professional sports, were integrated. Some colleges and universities began accepting African-Americans, albeit in small numbers. Ten years after the war ended in 1945, however, many barriers to full integration remained.

Civil Rights Era

Still, the winds of change were blowing. In 1954, the Supreme Court's historic *Brown v. Board of Education* decision declared state-sponsored segregation in schools to be unconstitutional. At the same time, the civil rights movement was beginning to attract the attention of white America. Just a year after the *Brown* ruling, Rosa Parks was arrested on a city bus in Montgomery, Ala., for refusing to give up her seat to a white passenger.

The arrest united Montgomery's black community and led to the Montgomery bus boycott. The Parks incident also catapulted a young Atlanta clergyman into the leadership of the boycott and, eventually, the national spotlight. His name: the Rev. Martin Luther King Jr.

After almost a year, the boycott ended when a federal court ruled that segregation on the city's buses was unconstitutional. But the incident had an impact far beyond the city's boundaries. King built on the victory in Montgomery to found a national civil rights organization, the Southern Christian Leadership Conference (SCLC). Run largely by black clergymen, it was dedicated to non-violence as an agent of change. Throughout the late 1950s and early '60s, the SCLC and other civil rights groups scored a number of stunning victories in the fight against racial segregation. From the sit-in at Woolworth's in Greensboro, N.C., to the business boycott in Birmingham, Ala., blacks, sympathetic whites and civil rights groups made slow but steady gains in the struggle for equality.

Outside the South, white America had awakened to the realities of Jim Crow. Television networks regularly broadcast the indignities suffered by

At the NAACP, a Challenge to Integration

The unthinkable occurred at the NAACP's annual meeting in Pittsburgh last July. As the nation's oldest and most respected civil rights organization gathered to chart a course for the coming year, a sizable and vocal minority of members were calling for reconsideration of the group's longstanding support for integration.

The proposal caused a fire storm both within the organization and around the country. After all, the NAACP had been founded on the principle that "separate but equal" was an unworkable fallacy and had to be ended.

Indeed, integration has been the bedrock of mainstream civil rights philosophy for decades. Black leaders ranging from Supreme Court Justice Thurgood Marshall to the Rev. Martin Luther King Jr. to Jesse Jackson have all supported the idea that blacks and whites should strive toward a society where all peoples work, learn and live together. In addition, most of the great grass-roots victories of the civil rights movement involved integrating institutions from universities to lunch counters.

NAACP President Kweisi Mfume

The NAACP's new chairperson, Myrlie Evers-Williams, the widow of slain civil rights leader Medger Evers, led the fight to beat back the anti-integration effort. "We're doing what we have always done, and our position remains the same," she said at the time. [1]

It was not the first time that integration has come under black attack. Scientist Booker T. Washington believed that the races could work better together by working separately. Others, from black nationalist Marcus Garvey to the Nation of Islam's Louis Farrakan have called for black separatism as the only way to encourage African-American advancement.

But the fact that so strong and public a challenge occurred on such a fundamental issue was seen as telling. For a growing number of African-Americans, the question isn't whether to integrate, but how to build prosperous, stable black communities. Many of these critics are not opposed to blacks and whites living and working together. Instead, they argue, civil rights groups should end their quest for integration above and beyond all other concerns. "Integration hasn't served African-Americans well, especially poorer ones," says Roy Brooks, a law professor at San Diego State University.

Brooks and others argue that instead of trying to push people into a broader society that may not fully accept them, groups like the NAACP should work to foster black self-help. "African-Americans, like Italians, Jews and Cubans, must pull together," Brooks says. "These groups were able to succeed within their own segregated communities and used that as a springboard to the wider community."

Such sentiments are especially strong with regard to schools. Critics of integration argue that the civil rights community has focused on busing at the expense of quality education. For one thing, they argue, busing black students to white schools leads to white flight, which in turn leads to resegregated schools. In fact, two-thirds of all black students already attend schools where a majority of the pupils are from minority groups. And if integration as an ideal is sacrificed on the altar of good education, so be it, say these critics. "Our biggest concern now is whether our schools will be equal. Separate but equal would not be too bad," says Amos Quick, an African-American who is a member of a citizens' committee redrawing school boundaries in Greensboro, N.C. [2]

But civil rights leaders, including NAACP President Kweisi Mfume, argue that separating the races will not improve the quality of schools. In addition, Mfume says, "most parents want their children to have the most diverse, comprehensive educational experience they can have. And they want them to have it with different races." [3]

Mfume and other civil rights advocates say that recent talk of ending the fight for integration is a result of African-American frustration after years of trying to gain acceptance by whites. According to Theodore Shaw, associate director-counsel of the NAACP Legal Defense and Education Fund, this frustration is natural in the current environment in which most blacks live. "You're beating your head up against the wall until it's bloody. At some point you have to ask, 'Should I continue to beat up against this wall?' " [4]

But others argue that the civil rights groups are reaping what they have sown by pushing for racial preferences in hiring and education at the expense of the colorblind society. According to Shelby Steele, a research fellow at the Hoover Institution, the growing rejection of integration is "an outgrowth of the same incentive system that created affirmative action."

Black people, he says, have been encouraged to think of themselves in largely racial terms, making integration harder. "They have been rewarded for saying their black identity is their first identity, " he says, "so it's not surprising" that their group identity overrides all other concerns.

---

[1] Quoted on National Public Radio, "Weekend All Things Considered," July 12, 1997.

[2] Quoted in Nat Hentoff, "The Undercutting of Thurgood Marshall — by the NAACP," *The Washington Post*, July 12, 1997.

[3] Quoted on National Public Radio, *op. cit.*

[4] Quoted in James S. Kunen, "Integration Forever?" *Time*, July 21, 1997.

African-Americans who were jailed, beaten and abused for protesting segregation. The dramatic media coverage helped effect a tremendous shift in public opinion in favor of civil rights. By 1963, 83 percent of all whites said they favored equality in the workplace, almost double the number who responded to the same question 19 years earlier.

The campaign for equality culminated in the Civil Rights Act of 1964, which prohibited discrimination based on race. The following year, Congress passed the Voting Rights Act, which put an end to literacy tests and other tactics used by Southern states to prohibit blacks from registering to vote. These two laws, and others that followed, did not end institutional discrimination overnight. But they did reflect the federal government's commitment to rooting out the race-based policies that had long been a part of American life.

Affirmative Action

By the 1970s, most historians agree, the worst excesses of the past had been eliminated. Meanwhile, black Americans were making great strides in catching up to white America. By 1969, median income for a black family was $22,000, a far cry from the white average of almost $36,000 but a significant improvement over the previous decades. Other factors also showed that the gap was closing. For instance, by 1970, 36.1 percent of African-Americans were in white-collar jobs, up from 6.4 percent in 1940. And the percentage of blacks attending college rose by a factor of five, from 7.2 percent in 1960 to 37.5 percent in 1995. [20]

During the civil rights battles of the 1950s and '60s, the vast majority of white Americans came to believe in the justness of the struggle against discrimination. But in the post-civil rights era, this relative consensus broke down. Part of this schism grew out of the "Black Power" movement in the late 1960s and early '70s. Black power represented the repudiation of the civil rights movement. First, it explicitly rejected cooperation between races, which had been a hallmark of the struggle. It also advocated acquiring power "by any means necessary," including violence. Hence, it rejected King's strategy of non-violent action.

At the same time, America's cities experienced a sharp increase in crime and an explosion of race-related riots. All of this made white America, as well as many blacks, highly uncomfortable.

In addition, new initiatives aimed at fighting poverty and fostering black advancement in general have proven much more controversial than the original anti-discrimination laws of the early 1960s. The new initiatives, part of President Lyndon B. Johnson's "Great Society" program, did not entirely achieve their goals. Many of these programs have since been altered or eliminated.

One policy from this era that has become increasingly controversial is affirmative action. President John F. Kennedy first used the term in 1961, when he issued an executive order requiring federal contractors to take "affirmative action" to ensure that they did not discriminate. In 1965, President Johnson put teeth into the policy, issuing an executive order that required federal contractors not merely not to discriminate, but to actively recruit minorities. During the Nixon administration, the mandate was strengthened to require contractors to establish and meet specific minority-hiring goals.

By the end of the 1970s, affirmative action had spread to most sectors of society. Colleges and universities were using it in admissions. The federal government had expanded it to "set aside" a certain percentage of contracts for minority-owned businesses. [21] And corporations were voluntarily setting up minority-recruitment and other affirmative action programs.

But even as affirmative action was becoming more commonplace, it was coming under attack. During the 1970s, the Supreme Court heard a number of challenges to the policy, including the landmark 1978 case, *University of California Regents v. Bakke.* The case involved a white law school applicant, who claimed that he had been rejected in favor of less-qualified blacks under the university's affirmative action program. The justices agreed, outlawing the use of numerical racial quotas in university admissions. The court also ruled, however, that while quotas were unconstitutional, race could still be a *factor* in making admission decisions.

Attacks against affirmative action intensified in the 1980s. President Ronald Reagan and his successor, George Bush, were opposed to race-based preferences, and the Justice Department in their administrations worked to eliminate quotas and other race-based hiring programs. In addition, the six new justices chosen for the Supreme Court during this period either opposed or had serious reservations about the policy. In the 1990s, as a result, the high court has handed down several decisions striking down affirmative action programs. [22]

At the same time, the policy has been attacked at the grass-roots level. In 1996, Californians voted to approve Proposition 209, the first statewide repeal of affirmative action programs. Similar referenda are slated for votes this year in Washington, Ohio, Florida and Colorado.

Today, according to recent polls, roughly 60 percent of whites and 40 percent of blacks oppose affirmative action. [23] It has become a litmus test in most debates over race. For instance, the recent GOP opposition to Bill Lann Lee, President Clinton's nominee to head the Civil Rights Division at the Justice Department, revolved around Lee's support for preferences. And at the president's recent "town hall" meeting in Akron, Ohio, part of his national dialogue on race, affirmative action sparked the fiercest debate. [24]

For members of the black middle class, affirmative action is often a difficult issue. But, regardless of their position, many blacks worry that it will lead whites to devalue all achievement by African-Americans, be it in the workplace or the classroom.

"You know, I just want the opportunity to succeed, nothing more," says Alexander, who supports the policy. ■

Blacks' Income and Assets Lag

The median income of white families was 65 percent more than that of blacks in 1995. White households had 10 times the material assets of black households in 1993.

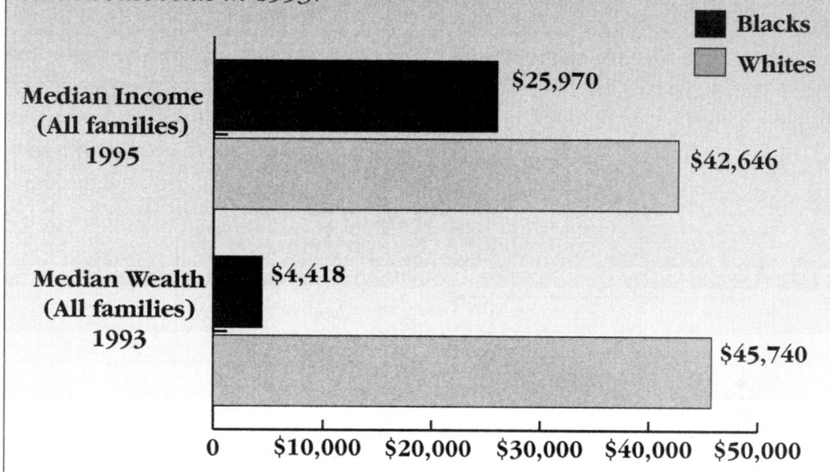

Sources: Stephan and Abigail Thernstrom, America in Black and White: One Nation, Indivisible, *1997, based on U.S. Census Bureau,* "Money Income in the U.S: *1995."*

CURRENT SITUATION

Economic Gains

As the list of CEOs at the nation's 500 largest companies confirms, white men still run corporate America. But in the last 30 years African-Americans have made progress in their quest to join the country's business elite. Some gains, of course, were inevitable given the fact that until the civil rights movement, there were virtually no high-ranking black executives. "We really had nowhere to go but up," says Morgan State's Hill.

Today, the situation is somewhat different. At many of the nation's biggest corporations, African-Americans are near the very top of the corporate totem pole, including Kenneth Chenault and Lloyd Ward, the presidents of American Express and Maytag. Other corporations, among them General Motors, Walt Disney and Morgan Stanley, have African-Americans in top-level slots. According to Richard Parsons, president of entertainment giant Time Warner, "people of color are achieving corporate positions that their parents never dreamed of reaching, and in unprecedented numbers." [25]

But according to many blacks, the fact that some African-American executives have managed to climb most of the way up the corporate ladder should not be taken as a sign that racism has been eliminated from the boardroom. For one thing, none of the big corporations has ever been run by a black person. "You'd think over the last 30 years someone would have made it to the top" says Collins, author of the recent book *Black Corporate Executives.* In addition, Collins notes, since the 1970s, there have always been a few black executives who were touted as the next CEO. "But all of them were moved to less important positions or they left," he says.

Many black executives who cut their teeth in large corporations have gone on to start their own businesses. Some just want to go it alone. Others go into business for themselves, at least in part, because of the frustration they felt in largely white corporate America. Alexander started her own business because she was tired of being mistreated and taken for granted while at the same time working diligently. "I thought: 'I've made so much money for [my white boss] over the years, why shouldn't I do it for myself?' " she says.

Alexander is far from alone. The number and size of black-owned businesses have grown significantly in the last few decades. According to *Black Enterprise* magazine, the 100 largest black-owned companies generated $14.1 billion in revenue in 1996. In 1973, the top 100 produced less than a half-million. [26]

Still, as with African-American executives, the success of black-owned businesses, while notable, is not staggering. For instance, if the top 100 black businesses today merged into one company, it would only be the 83rd-largest corporation in the United States as ranked by annual revenue. [27]

The Asset Gap

While a significant disparity in income exists between whites and blacks, the difference in total worth is even more profound. In 1993, the median net worth of the average white household was $45,740; the average black household was worth only $4,418.

Even among households with equal income levels, net worth among African-Americans is still much lower. According to the new book *America in Black and White* by scholars Stephan and Abigail Thernstrom, the asset gap, even among high-earners, largely is determined by inherited wealth. They write that "only within the past few decades have any but a handful of black people had the opportunity to acquire substantial property; few of their parents and grandparents, living under slavery and then Jim Crow, bequeathed significant estates to their descendants." [28]

The impact of the asset gap is significant, scholars say. For instance, it is not uncommon for young middle-class whites to ask their parents for financial help for everything from their education to buying their first home. This option is available to far fewer black people. "It puts you at a disadvantage early on," Hill says. It also contributes to segregation, since many black professionals do not have the financial backing to afford as expensive a house as their white counterparts.

Not having the assets to buy a nice house, or any house, tends to make the net-worth disparity self-perpetuating. That's because a house, for most middle-class people, is the primary asset. And for those African-Americans who own a home, it is more likely to be a greater source of total wealth than having a house is for whites. According to 1991 statistics, the house makes up 63 percent of the total wealth of the average black homeowner compared with 41 percent for the average white homeowner, who is more likely to have other financial assets. [29] (*See graph, p. 165.*) ■

"In 1993, the median net worth of the average white household was $45,740; the average black household was worth only $4,418."

OUTLOOK

Guarded Optimism

A recent CNN/*Time* magazine poll showed that only 18 percent of black teens think that the problems faced by African-Americans today are caused by whites. Similarly, only 23 percent said that they had ever been the victim of discrimination. [30]

Some scholars say that statistics like these confirm their optimism about the future. Children, they say, are not as hobbled by America's segregated past as are their parents. "If you go to a suburban mall and look at groups of kids, you'll see a girl from India, three WASPs, a Jew and two blacks," says the University of Pennsylvania's Anderson. "That's the future."

But, Anderson and others point out, middle-class blacks are struggling with their children's willingness to mix with whites. "On one hand, they know it's good to have all different kinds of friends," he says. "But on the other, they feel their kids should know what it means to be black — so that you know where it comes from when you're kicked."

How best to raise black children in today's America is part of a larger question that middle-class African-Americans are asking: How far should I assimilate? The question is different for blacks than it has been for many other groups. Long after the Civil War and Emancipation, the idea of African-American assimilation was absurd to both blacks and whites, although for different reasons. But the advent of the civil rights movement and the rise of the black middle class make the proposition much less unrealistic.

Some, like Reynalds, say that the death of Jim Crow and the birth of economic opportunity will slowly push blacks into the mainstream. One particularly telling sign of this change, he argues, is that younger blacks have turned their backs on government as the prime engine of oppor-

At Issue:

Is affirmative action still necessary?

HILARY SHELTON

Deputy Director, Washington bureau, National Association for the Advancement of Colored People

yes

Opponents of affirmative action have distorted the meaning of the principle, rewritten history and clearly ignored present realities in their eagerness to eliminate present programs. Since the end of slavery, African-Americans, as well as other ethnic minority groups and women, have struggled for economic justice, an equal opportunity to enter the workplace to earn equal pay and equal access to higher education.

Dr. Mary Frances Berry, U.S. Commission on Civil Rights chairperson, has stated: "Some progress in job opportunities for African-Americans was made during World War II and beyond. But it was limited. In grocery and department stores, clerks were white and janitors and elevator operators were black. Generations of African-Americans swept the floors in factories, while denied the opportunity to become higher paid operators on the machines."

The reality of life in America before affirmative action included thousands of towns and cities in which the police departments and fire departments were all white males. . . .

Detractors of affirmative action use the battle cry of "merit" over any racial or gender considerations. They seem to forget there were no merit standards for employment for white males who occupied the best jobs. . . . Men with the privilege of white skin, whether their granddaddies ever owned slaves or not, whether they were early or late immigrants, had the good-job pie all to themselves.

To be sure, women and minorities have been the major beneficiaries of affirmative action over the past three decades. Few realize, however, that white males are also beneficiaries. Before affirmative action, the "old-boys' network" way of doing things prevailed.

Because of affirmative action, fairness is now the rule, guaranteeing more opportunities for white males as well as minorities and women to compete for jobs. Indeed, the purpose of affirmative action has always been to create an environment where merit can prevail.

On July 19, 1996, President Bill Clinton delivered an address on affirmative action at the National Archives in Washington, D.C., while standing in front of the original U.S. Constitution. He said:

"If properly done, affirmative action can help us come together, go forward and grow together. It is in our moral, legal and practical interest to see that every person can make the most of his [or her] life. In the fight for the future, we need all hands on deck, and some of those hands still need a helping hand."

GERALD REYNALDS

President, Center for New Black Leadership

no

Race-based affirmative action policies harm many of their intended beneficiaries, as well as better-qualified white and Asian competitors. For example, data from elite public colleges clearly demonstrate that double standards in admissions policies have harmed many of the black beneficiaries of preference policies. College administrators are quick to point out any increase in minority enrollment. However, they never mention that a disproportionate number of these students never graduate. . . .

By shielding blacks from unfettered competition in college admissions, contracting and employment, proponents of preference polices have placed too many middle-class blacks in a protective cocoon. Many of these blacks have no incentive to work hard enough to meet or exceed "real world" standards since they are not penalized for a substandard performance. Preference policies also cheapen the accomplishments of those blacks who meet or exceed the same standards met by whites and Asians.

Recently President Clinton implied that Gen. Colin Powell owed his success to racial-preference policies. President Clinton is not alone. Many supporters of preference policies believe that the tremendous gains achieved by the black middle class are due, in large part, to preference policies and that these policies are still needed. They are wrong. The data do not support the assertion that preference policies were the primarily cause behind the growth of the black middle class. In fact, the data suggest that the groundwork for the growth of the black middle class was in place prior to the implementation of racial preference policies.

The confluence of black migration from the South to the North, a strong work ethic, enhanced employment opportunities, the enactment and enforcement of anti-discrimination statutes and improved educational opportunities enabled black strivers to reach the middle class. Racial preference policies merely accelerated the advancement of those blacks who possess middle-class values. These policies have never been prerequisites for advancement.

For much of our history black Americans lived under a racial caste system. Prior to the civil rights revolution, one's chances of economic, social and political advancement were not determined by talent, initiative and industry. The prospects of the majority of blacks were severely limited by state-sponsored segregation and a hard-core white racism. However, racial discrimination is no longer an insurmountable obstacle for black Americans. My grandmother use to argue that because of racism, blacks had to be twice as good their white competitors. While the level of racism has waned substantially, the need to strive for excellence has not.

Are Black Conservatives on the Rise?

Thomas Sowell once joked that if you put all African-American conservatives in one room there wouldn't be enough people for a game of pinochle.

Sowell, the much-quoted Hoover Institution scholar, would have plenty of card players to sit down with nowadays. In the last decade, the number of black conservatives in the public eye has jumped dramatically. From Supreme Court Justice Clarence Thomas and Rep. J.C. Watts, R-Okla., to talk-show host Armstrong Williams and anti-affirmative action crusader Ward Connerly, more and more black conservatives are entering the limelight.

Indeed, Alan L. Keyes, a Harvard-educated radio talk show host and former Foreign Service officer, ran for the GOP presidential nomination in 1996. Another black Republican, retired Gen. Colin Powell, is considered his party's front-runner for the 2000 presidential nomination, although he has said he's not interested.

These new faces come at a time when black support for the Democratic Party endures. Since the Great Depression of the 1930s, the vast majority of blacks have voted for Democrats in presidential and congressional elections. Today, fewer than 10 percent of all African-Americans identify themselves as Republicans. Black Republicans hold just one seat in Congress (Watts). Furthermore, as of 1997, only 11 of the 550 African-Americans in state legislatures were members of the GOP. [1]

Conservatives explain these statistics by arguing that there is a tremendous pressure within the black community to conform politically. "Black America is a one-party system," says Shelby Steele, another black research fellow at Hoover and author of the best-selling book on affirmative action *The Content of Our Character*. "Black conservatives are immediately labeled as 'Uncle Toms' and as traitors to their race," he says.

The "one-party system," as Steele labels it, is perpetuated by more than just loyalty to race. It is built, he says, on adherence to an overriding belief. "As a black man, I am judged on [my attitude about] one issue: whether victimization is black America's biggest problem. If I say 'yes,' it's OK. If I say 'no,' I'm a black conservative, period."

The reality, Steele and others say, is that African-Americans are much more conservative than their Democratic political affiliation would indicate. Gavin Jackson, a human relations specialist at the Department of the Treasury and a self-described conservative, agrees. "I think black folks are inherently conservative," he says, "especially when you look at our attitudes toward religion, family and money."

Indeed, according to a 1996 poll commissioned by the Joint Center for Political and Economic Studies, a black-oriented think tank, 30 percent of all African-Americans identified themselves as "conservative." By contrast, only 31 percent of the blacks polled said that they were "liberal." [2]

Why, then, does the GOP fare so poorly with black Americans? The answer, according to black liberals, is tied directly to the hostility the Republican Party and conservatives in general have shown toward African-Americans and their priorities. "It is not even close to think that the assault on government that [House Speaker] Newt [Gingrich] and company are leading is in the interest of the vast majority of black people in this country," says famed civil rights activist Julian Bond. [3]

In addition, many black Democrats accuse the GOP of using wedge issues like affirmative action to scare white voters into supporting them. While this tactic has helped Republicans capture the Congress, they say, it has alienated African-American voters.

But black conservatives are optimistic about the growth of their movement. "It's going to keep expanding," Steele says. He and others compare the black community today with Jewish Americans, a traditionally liberal group that has begun to diversify ideologically. "During the 1980s, we started to see Jewish Republicans," Steele says. He predicts a similar trend in black America as the old, liberal mantras begin to ring hollow. "There's no other way for us to go," he says.

Yet some black conservatives are not convinced that the expansion of conservatism is inevitable. According to Gavin Jackson, the GOP can't just wait for African-Americans to come to them. "I think more black folks will vote Republican when [the GOP] focuses some attention on black issues."

[1] Stephan and Abigail Thernstrom, *America in Black and White: One Nation, Indivisible* (1997), pp. 302-303.

[2] *Ibid.*, p. 303.

[3] Quoted in Eric Alterman, "The Right Brothers," *The Nation*, March 4, 1996.

tunity. "Young folks tend to look to themselves more than the government," he says. "The folks wedded to government solutions tend to be older ones, and that's understandable since it was government that broke the back of Jim Crow."

If there is a problem, conservative African-Americans and others say, it is the influence of many black leaders, who are pushing for greater dependency on the government. According to Thomas Sowell, a fellow at the Hoover Institution: "Too many black 'leaders' today have a vested interest in the application of old myths. They are like Moses in reverse — leading their people back into the welfare state, to a self-imposed isolation from the growing opportunities all around them." [31]

But others are less sanguine, arguing that racism is still causing a lot of middle-class African-Americans to feel ostracized and angry. And, they say, these negative feelings multiply when whites show impatience with the lack of black progress. "You know, it's like, 'After 30 years, haven't we done enough for you people,' " says Collins of the University of Illinois.

Henderson agrees, arguing that attacks on affirmative action and other programs have left many well-to-do blacks suspicious of white America's motives. "Some people feel like refugees in their own country," he says. According to Henderson and others, blacks have done all they can to integrate into American society, and now just need to be welcomed.

"African-Americans are among the most patriotic of citizens, " Henderson says. "We ascribe to core American values and see ourselves as part of the mainstream of America." ■

FOR MORE INFORMATION

Hoover Institution, Stanford University, Stanford, Calif. 94303; (650) 723-1754; www.hoover.org.
The Hoover Institution is a public-policy think tank that has attracted a large number of conservative scholars.

Joint Center for Political and Economic Studies, 1090 Vermont Ave., N.W., Suite 1100, Washington, D.C. 20005; (202) 789-3500; www.jointctr.org.
This think tank researches issues that are of concern to black Americans.

Lincoln Institute for Research and Education, 1001 Connecticut Ave., N.W., Suite 1135, Washington, D.C. 20036; (202) 223-5112.
The Institute studies issues that impact middle class African-Americans. Topics include education, employment and health.

National Association for the Advancement of Colored People (NAACP), 1025 Vermont Ave., N.W., Suite 1120, Washington, D.C. 20005; (202) 638-2269; www.nvi.net/naacp_washington_bureau/.
The NAACP works for civil rights in all sectors of society. Efforts include lobbying, legal action and education.

National Urban League, 1111 14th St., N.W., Suite 1001, Washington, D.C. 2005-5603; (202) 898-1604; www.nul.org.
This federation of affiliates is concerned with the welfare of African-Americans and other minorities.

Notes

[1] Kevin Merida, "Worry, Frustration Build for Many in the Black Middle Class," *The Washington Post,* Oct. 9, 1995.

[2] Cited in Stephan and Abigail Thernstrom, *America in Black and White: One Nation, Indivisible* (1997),. p. 185.

[3] Ellis Cose, *The Rage of a Privileged Class* (1993), p. 1.

[4] For background, see "Intelligence Testing," *The CQ Researcher,* July 30, 1993, pp. 649-672.

[5] For background, see "Housing Discrimination," *The CQ Researcher,* Feb. 24, 1995, pp. 169-192.

[6] For background, see "Racial Tensions in Schools," *The CQ Researcher,* Jan. 7, 1994, pp. 1-24.

[7] See Connie Aitcheson, "Corporate America's Black Eye," *Black Enterprise,* April 1997.

[8] Quoted on "The NewsHour with Jim Lehrer," Nov. 12, 1996.

[9] Quoted in Eric Pooley, "Fairness of Folly," *Time,* June 23, 1997.

[10] Thernstrom, *op. cit.,* p. 211.

[11] Lisa Frazier, "Pr. George's is 62% Black, Study Finds," *The Washington Post,* Dec. 7, 1997.

[12] Quoted in Haya El Nasser, "In Cleveland, Dream Homes Displace Decline," *USA Today,* Oct. 23, 1997.

[13] Haya El Nasser, "Growing Middle-Class Isn't Fleeing to the Suburbs," *USA Today,* Oct. 23, 1997.

[14] See Carol Morello, "Controversial Measure Proves Difficult to Enforce," *USA Today,* Nov. 17, 1997.

[15] Quoted in Susan Page, "Race Panel Head Sees Progress, Backsliding," *USA Today,* Nov. 17, 1997.

[16] Thernstrom, *op. cit.,* p. 391.

[17] Doris Warriner, Joint Center for Political and Economic Studies, "African Americans Today: A Demographic Profile," 1996, p. 32.

[18] Thernstrom, *op. cit.* p. 80.

[19] *Ibid.,* p. 84.

[20] *Ibid.,* p. 192.

[21] For background, see, "Rethinking Affirmative Action," *The CQ Researcher,* April 26, 1995, pp. 369-392.

[22] *Ibid.*

[23] Pooley, *op.cit.*

[24] Warren P. Strobel, "Forum Finds No Consensus on Race Issues," *The Washington Times,* Dec. 4, 1997.

[25] Quoted in Roy S. Johnson, "The New Black Power," *Fortune,* Aug. 4, 1997.

[26] Cited in *Ibid.*

[27] *Ibid.*

[28] Thernstrom, *op. cit.* p. 198.

[29] Warriner, *op. cit.* p. 53.

[30] Christopher John Farley, "Kids and Race," *Time,* Nov. 24, 1997.

[31] Thomas Sowell, "Yes, Blacks Can Make It on Their Own," *Time,* Sept. 8, 1997.

Bibliography

Selected Sources Used

Books

Cose, Ellis, *The Rage of a Privileged Class,* HarperCollins, 1993.
Cose, a writer at *Newsweek*, tries to answer the question: Why are successful black professionals so angry? The answer, he says, is that many African-Americans who have "made it" still do not believe they are operating in a system that will fully reward them for their intelligence, education and effort.

D'Souza, Dinesh, *The End of Racism: Principles for a Multiracial Society,* The Free Press, 1995.
D'Souza, a fellow at the American Enterprise Institute, argues that civil rights advocates are fighting against a largely non-existent enemy. One reason, he says, is that fighting racism has become an industry, one that is self-perpetuating.

Shipler, David K., *A Country of Strangers: Blacks and Whites in America,* Alfred A. Knopf, 1997.
A journalist and Pulitzer Prize-winning author, Shipler looks at how Americans are dealing with the issue of race. By combining history and statistics with literally hundreds of anecdotes and stories, Shipler paints a picture of a nation and a people that are not close to achieving any kind of racial harmony.

Thernstrom, Stephan and Abigail, *America in Black and White: One Nation, Indivisible,* Simon & Schuster, 1997.
Stephan Thernstrom, a professor of history at Harvard University, and his wife Abigail, a fellow at thc Manhattan Institute, have produced a sweeping portrait of black America as it was and is. The Thernstroms argue that blacks have made much more progress during the 20th century than is generally acknowledged. They also make the case that race relations are better than many people think.

Articles

Biskupic, Joan, "On Race, a Court Transformed," *The Washington Post,* Dec. 15, 1997.
Biskupic describes the transformation of the Supreme Court from "the salvation of civil rights advocates" to "a place to be avoided." The reason, she writes, is that Presidents Ronald Reagan and George Bush appointed justices who were generally less friendly to affirmative action and some other programs favored by the civil rights community.

El Nasser, Haya, "Growing Middle Class Isn't Fleeing to Suburbs," *USA Today,* Oct. 23, 1997.
El Nasser details a growing trend among middle-class blacks: suburban flight. Many African-Americans who can afford to live in the suburbs are choosing instead to move to inner-city areas, many of which have high crime and other problems. Some are lured by cheap land, an opportunity made even sweeter in certain cities through tax breaks and cheap loans. Other blacks found the largely white suburbs "isolating" and want to live with people of their own race.

Johnson, Roy. S, "The New Black Power," *Fortune,* Aug. 4, 1997.
Johnson's piece is the lead-off to several articles on African-Americans and business. He argues that while blacks have made substantial progress in the business world, both as corporate executives and entrepreneurs, "people of color still confront huge obstacles in the workplace."

Merida, Kevin, "Worry, Frustration Build for Many in the Black Middle Class," *The Washington Post,* Oct. 9, 1995.
Merida looks at middle-class black attitudes and discovers a surprising amount of anger and fear. Black professionals are plagued by the same problems that affect their white counterparts, such as the fear of being downsized out of a job. But African-Americans also say they have problems that are unique to minorities, like feeling devalued at work by their white colleagues.

Pooley, Eric, "Fairness or Folly?" *Time,* June 23, 1997.
Pooley does a good job of describing the players and dynamics in the debate over affirmative action. In particular, he focuses on Ward Connerly, the African-American businessman who successfully led the fight for Proposition 209, the California ballot initiative that eliminated the use of preferences at all state agencies and institutions.

Reports

Doris Warriner, "African Americans Today: A Demographic Profile," Joint Center for Political and Economic Studies, 1996.
This report from the black-oriented think tank contains a wealth of statistical data on the state of black America. Topics include education, income, wealth and political participation.

10 Gay Rights

KENNETH JOST

The three couples who sought the right to same-sex marriage in Vermont are Holly Puterbaugh and Lois Farnham, front, and rear, from left, Stacy Jolles and Nina Beck and Stan Baker and Peter Harrigan.

After Nina Beck and Stacy Jolles met and fell in love, they pledged themselves to each other in a commitment ceremony. That was nearly 10 years ago. But despite what she calls "our spiritual union," Beck worries that she and Stacy have no legal bonds to each other.

For the past three years, Beck and Jolles have been trying to win legal recognition of their relationship in Vermont, their adopted state. And on March 22, their ninth anniversary, they went to the Statehouse in Montpelier to plead their cause.

Benefits automatically enjoyed by married heterosexual couples are simply unavailable to gay or lesbian couples, Beck told the Senate Judiciary Committee. "Civil marriage is currently the only construct by which these benefits are granted in our society," she said.

"Without access to this system, we are denied any legal recognition of our unions and of our families," Beck continued. "Without legal recognition, we are vulnerable." [1]

But the Vermont senators also heard from one of their colleagues who opposes legal recognition for same-sex couples. "Civil rights should not be judged by lifestyle or sexual behavior," Sen. Julius Canns, a Republican, told the committee. "The vast majority of my constituents support traditional marriage and feel threatened by level recognition of same-sex legal unions."

Pastoral Vermont might seem an unlikely battleground for same-sex marriage. But it's on the verge of becoming the first state to grant a full complement of marriagelike rights and benefits to gay and lesbian couples — including property rights, insurance coverage and child custody.

The Vermont House has already passed a bill allowing "civil unions" between lesbians or gay men, and the state Senate is expected to give its approval by the end of the month. The legislature is acting under orders from the Vermont Supreme Court, which ruled on Dec. 20 that gay and lesbian couples are entitled to the same legal benefits as heterosexual, married couples.

Beck and Jolles were among three couples who challenged state laws after local officials rejected their applications for marriage licenses. The state high court's ruling in *Baker v. State* said the legislature had to allow same-sex couples either to marry or to form a "domestic partnership" or some alternative relationship. [2] The decision was based on an interpretation of a provision in the Vermont Constitution and therefore could not be appealed to the U.S. Supreme Court, which cannot override a state court's interpretation of state law. [3]

Same-sex marriage is one of several gay-rights issues that have risen to the top of the national agenda in recent months. Gay-rights advocates have been pressing their efforts to modify or repeal the military's "don't ask, don't tell" policy on homosexuality ever since the murder of a gay soldier at an Army base in Kentucky in June 1999. [4] They renewed their arguments last March following a Defense Department report that found evidence of widespread harassment of gay and lesbian servicemembers (*see p. 182*).

Vice President Al Gore, campaigning for the Democratic presidential nomination, has vowed to repeal the policy if elected; Texas Gov. George W. Bush, the presumptive Republican nominee, favors the existing policy.

Gore also has called for federal legislation prohibiting job discrimination based on sexual orientation. Gay-rights groups have won passage of anti-discrimination legislation in 11 states and more than 100 municipalities, but they have failed to get a federal bill through either the House or the Senate. Bush opposes such legislation (*see p. 183*).

Meanwhile, the U.S. Supreme Court is set to consider a New Jersey case testing whether the Boy Scouts of America can bar open homosexuals as leaders. The state Supreme Court ruled that the policy violated the state's anti-discrimination law, but the Scouts contend the ruling infringes on their First Amendment rights (*see p. 181*).

In addition, some school districts are debating whether to allow high school students to form so-called gay-straight alliance clubs. Proponents say the clubs help promote tolerance and combat harassment of gay and lesbian students; critics say they promote homosexuality. (*See story, p. 186; see "At Issue," p. 185.*)

In Vermont, the state legislature quickly turned to the same-sex mar-

From *The CQ Researcher*, April 14, 2000.

Laws Prohibiting Discrimination

Legislation prohibiting discrimination in private employment based on sexual orientation is in force in 11 states, the District of Columbia and some 124 municipalities and counties. Similar federal legislation has failed in the House and Senate.

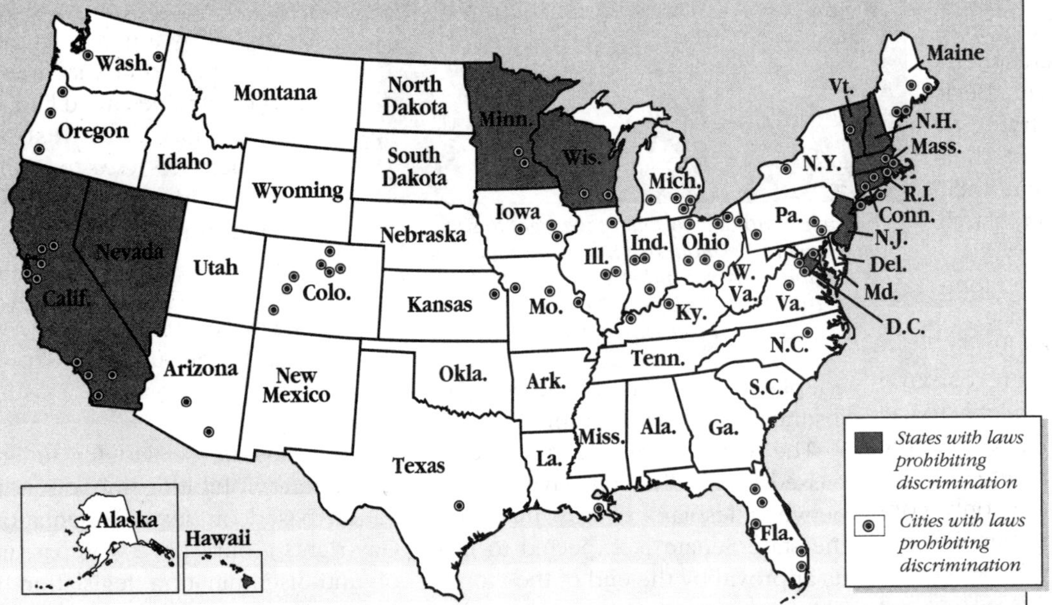

Source: Wayne van der Meide, "Legislating Equality: A Review of Laws Affecting Gay, Lesbian, Bisexual, and Transgendered People in the United States," National Gay and Lesbian Task Force

riage issue in January, a month after the state high court's ruling. Most lawmakers rejected marriage for same-sex couples in favor of allowing homosexuals to form a "civil union" with essentially all the legal rights of marriage. The Vermont House narrowly approved the bill in March; the more liberal Senate is expected to follow suit. The state's Democratic governor, Howard Dean, has said he will sign the bill, which would take effect in September.

Opponents nonetheless are still mounting arguments against legal recognition for homosexual couples. "I disagree with the concept that they're entitled to the same things that heterosexual couples are entitled to," says Michele Cummings, president of the ad hoc lobbying group Take It to the People. "We do not believe that benefits should be awarded on the basis of sexual activity."

Cummings, a mother of seven with no previous experience in politics or lobbying, considers homosexuality immoral and says the Vermont Supreme Court's ruling "is changing the fabric of what makes the world what it is."

National groups make similar arguments. "If you say two men constitute a marriage, you are creating a counterfeit," says Robert Knight, director of cultural studies for the Family Research Council. "Homosexual relationships are not a facsimile of marriage. They are entirely different."

Gay-rights advocates, however, contend that the reasons for refusing to recognize same-sex relationships are outdated. "Our social context of marriage has changed so much," says Paula Ettelbrick, director of the Family Law Project of the National Gay and Lesbian Task Force (NGLTF). "It's really about economic benefits and the support systems that government provides to families. It's much less about being a proper procreative form or having a male head of household."

The opposing advocacy groups also clash on the role of the courts in dealing with the issue. "We feel that it needed to be taken to the people, that five judges shouldn't make that decision for all of us," Cummings says.

"The judicial branch's very reason for being is to protect the rights of the minority," counters Susan Murray, one of the attorneys for the same-sex couples in the Vermont case. "If we waited for the majority to grant rights that they're not interested in thinking about granting, it would take a heck of a longer time."

If enacted, the Vermont measure would represent a major victory for the gay-rights movement. But a leading gay-rights advocate says the civil unions to be recognized under the bill can also be viewed as a "second-best" status. "The glass is still at least half-empty," says William Rubenstein, a law professor at UCLA. "No same-sex couple can be married anywhere in the United States."

Rubenstein, formerly director of the American Civil Liberties Union's National Lesbian and Gay Rights Project, says gay-rights advocates have comparable records in other areas. "There has been enormous progress in the last 30 years," he says, "but there is still an enormous amount of work to go." Only a minority of states have enacted anti-discrimination laws, he notes, while some 19 states have retained anti-sodomy laws once widely used to prosecute homosexuals for consensual sexual behavior. (*See map, p. 176.*)

Nonetheless, a new *Newsweek* poll shows that Americans' level of comfort with homosexuality is improving: In 1998 54 percent said homosexuality was a sin compared with 46 percent today.

Critics and opponents, however, accuse the gay-rights movement of fostering legal and social changes that are undermining traditional morality.

"When you have corporations promoting open homosexuality, when you have ordinances on the books of many cities adding sexual orientation to civil rights laws, you are well on the way to suppressing dissent on the issue," Knight says. "But like any good activist, they say they are never satisfied. Just a few years ago, they were demanding tolerance. Now they're demanding gay marriages and homosexual curriculums in the schools. That's quite an advance, particularly for such a tiny segment of the population."

The debate — part political, part legal, part cultural — will move to center stage at the end of April, when gay-rights groups are planning a major march in Washington to highlight their agenda. Here are some of the major questions they and their opponents are debating:

Should same-sex relationships be legally recognized?

Over the past five years, attorneys Murray and Beth Robinson talked to dozens of church and civic groups in Vermont as they made the case for legal recognition of same-sex relationships. Audiences were skeptical initially, Murray recalls, but most people ended with greater sympathy for their position.

"If we can talk to Vermonters about the tangible benefits that married couples obtain simply by obtaining a marriage certificate, fair-minded Vermonters sit back and say, 'Wow, I've never thought of it that way; of course, gay couples deserve that,' " she says.

By the time Vermont lawmakers took up the issue last month, a poll — commissioned by the Vermont Freedom to Marry Task Force — found that most people supported allowing homosexual partners either to marry (30 percent) or to form "civil unions" (25 percent). Only 40 percent opposed either legal recognition for same-sex couples.

Across the nation, however, same-sex marriage still draws fire. National polls consistently show solid majorities opposed to homosexual marriages.[5] And Congress and some 30 states have passed laws to block recognition of same-sex marriages.

Gay-rights advocates view the government's refusal to recognize same-sex relationships as outright discrimination. "The issue is not so much marriage, it's a denial of equal benefits," Ettelbrick says. "That's the constitutional problem. That's where the state most fundamentally treats same-sex partners differently."

Opponents, however, insist that recognizing same-sex relationships would lead to myriad practical problems. "Marriage is about more than the two individuals involved," the Family Research Council's Knight says. "It's how kinship develops and family names are passed down and the generations are linked and property is distributed and where new life is created."

Advocates of same-sex marriage say legal recognition would benefit homosexuals as well as society at large. "Same-sex marriage is good for gay people and good for America," writes Yale Law School Professor William Eskridge Jr., "and for the same reason: It civilizes gays, and it civilizes America."[6]

Eskridge argues that recognizing same-sex marriage would encourage the broad social trend toward tolerance for homosexuality while reducing promiscuity among homosexuals, especially gay men. Other gay-rights advocates, however, back away from any such claim.

"I see the issues as different," UCLA's Rubenstein says. "There's the question of legal recognition, and there's the question of sexual practices."

Indeed, some gay-rights advocates are less than enthusiastic about marriage for homosexual couples. Ettelbrick, for example, has previously denounced marriage as a "patriarchal" institution. "I don't think marriage should be the only way that we describe or support families," she says. "Good public policy will accept and provide economic support for people who are caring for each other whether they're married or not."[7]

In any event, opponents are unconvinced that recognizing same-sex marriage would reduce the incidence of multiple sexual partners among homosexuals. "That is a disingenuous argument," says Lynn Wardell, a law professor at Brigham Young University in Provo, Utah. "I'm waiting to see the evidence."

Given the strong opposition to same-sex marriage, gay-rights organizations began working in the 1980s for a less ambitious goal: winning workplace benefits such as health insurance for same-sex couples. On that front, there has been what Ettelbrick calls "tremendous success." Thousands of employers, including many of the country's biggest businesses, today allow unmarried employees — homosexuals as well as heterosexuals — to designate their partners for health insurance coverage.

Military Discharges for Homosexual Conduct

President Clinton was forced to back away from a post-election promise to lift the strict Pentagon ban on homosexuals and in 1993 fashioned a compromise known as "don't ask, don't tell." Despite the seeming liberalization of the policy, the number of servicemembers discharged for homosexuality has increased since 1993 along with the reported incidence of anti-gay harassment.

Source: Department of Defense

Anti-gay-rights groups, however, also object to domestic partnerships — though perhaps not as fiercely. "If you want the benefits of marriage, you have to meet the qualifications," Knight says, "the first of which is that you have to open your life to a person of the opposite sex and make a lifelong commitment."

Wardell agrees, though he says he would allow some recognition for same-sex couples — for example, in hospital visitation. "Hospital visitation ought not depend on a marital relationship," he says.

Vermont's civil union bill goes further than any previous law or employer policy in providing same-sex couples the rights enjoyed by heterosexuals. After the Vermont House vote, the Family Research Council called the measure "nothing short of an endorsement of 'same-sex marriage.' "

For her part, though attorney Murray says the bill does not go far enough. "Marriage, of course, is the only thing that gives gay and lesbian couples true equality," she says. "This is a very good bill, but it is a first step, not the end of the road."

Should the military's "don't ask, don't tell" policy be changed?

Pfc. Barry Winchell suffered through four months of taunting, harassment and anti-gay epithets from fellow soldiers at Fort Campbell in Kentucky before his murder on July 5, 1999. Two soldiers have been convicted in the killing: Pvt. Calvin Glover, who shattered Winchell's skull with a baseball bat, and Spec. Justin Fisher, who gave Glover the bat.

Gay-rights groups, however, believe the real culprit in the Winchell case is the Army itself — for tolerating anti-gay harassment — as well as the military's "don't ask, don't tell" policy — for forcing homosexual servicemembers to conceal their identities in order to serve their country.

"There is no safe haven for military members to turn to if they are harassed or threatened," says Michelle Benecke, co-director of the Servicemembers Legal Defense Network (SLDN). "How many people have to be harassed or murdered before people take this problem seriously?"

SLDN says that despite the seeming liberalization of "don't ask, don't tell," the number of servicemembers discharged for homosexuality has increased since 1993 along with the incidence of anti-gay harassment. (*See graph, p. 174.*) Winchell's murder did prompt the Defense Department to adopt more explicit anti-gay-harassment policies. But the "don't ask, don't tell" policy remains in effect, seven years after its adoption as a compromise of sorts following President Clinton's failure to win support for lifting the ban on homosexuals in the military altogether.

The Winchell episode did renew debate in Washington and across the country over the military's policy. But some opponents of homosexuals in military say that the harassment issue has been exaggerated, and they remain convinced that homosexuality is "incompatible" with military service — just as Congress declared in 1993 in a Defense Department authorization bill that Clinton signed into law.

"There are no doubt incidents in which drill sergeants and platoon leaders have used derogatory language, and they're wrong," says Robert Maginnis, a retired Army lieutenant colonel and now director of national security and foreign affairs at the Family Research Council. "But I don't think that it's part of the dominant culture."

Maginnis calls Winchell's killing "a terrible situation." But he discounts SLDN's statistics on anti-gay harassment and considers the new anti-harassment policy an overreaction. "Why are we getting so bent out of shape about a group of people that we've decided ought to be excluded?" he asks.

Gay-rights advocates continue to regard "don't ask, don't tell" as unfair to gay and lesbian servicemembers. The policy "discriminates against lesbian, gay and bisexual servicemembers," Benecke says. "Gay people are kicked out for saying and doing the same thing straight people do every day."

In addition, Benecke and other critics say the policy is bad for the military at a time when the services are having difficulty recruiting and retaining personnel. "This law is forcing commanders to kick good people out of the military," she says.

Supporters of the policy continue to defend the restrictions on open expressions of homosexuality as necessary to protect the rights of straight servicemembers forced to live with fellow soldiers and sailors in close quarters.

"You're talking about the privacy rights of straights as well as gays," says Charles Moskos, a professor of sociology at Northwestern University in Evanston, Ill., and an adviser to the administration at the time of the policy's adoption. "It might be that in the future people won't mind," he says, "but that's not the era we live in right now."

Maginnis cites other reasons for opposing homosexuals in the military, including the risk of sexually transmitted diseases and what he says is an adverse effect on the morale of individual units. "When we throw the ingredient of sex in, whether it's heterosexual or same-sex attraction, it undermines the confidence and trust we must have in these teams," he says.

Gay-rights advocates say they want the military to honor the "don't ask, don't tell" policy by ensuring that commanders do not investigate servicemembers suspected of being homosexual and that they crack down on anti-gay harassment. In the long term, though, they believe the policy should be replaced by one that permits homosexuals to serve openly.

"Ultimately, this law should be replaced with a principle of nondiscrimination where everyone is evaluated according to their merit rather than a characteristic that has nothing to do with their performance," Benecke says.

Maginnis, on the other hand, wants to reinstitute an outright ban on service by homosexuals — the policy that he says is prescribed by law but circumvented by the Clinton administration's regulations. "The law is very clear: it's an exclusion policy," Maginnis says. The administration, he says, "has forced something on the military that is not in the best interest of the service."

Moskos, however, sees no better alternative than the current policy. "It's much like what Winston Churchill said about democracy," Moskos says. "It's the worst system possible, except for any other."

Are additional laws needed to prohibit discrimination on the basis of sexual orientation?

Dwayne Simonton claimed in a federal civil rights suit that his co-workers at the Farmingdale, N.Y., post office mercilessly ridiculed him because of his homosexuality. A federal judge last June found their conduct "offensive" but dismissed Simonton's sexual-harassment lawsuit. The reason: The federal Civil Rights Act does not prohibit discrimination on the basis of sexual orientation. [8]

Gay-rights advocates have been pushing for two decades for passage of laws to prohibit discrimination against homosexuals in the workplace, in housing and in public accommodations. "There's a tremendous amount of individual bias against gay people," says Beatrice Dohrn, legal director for the Lambda Legal Defense and Education Fund. "Some people want us to continue having second-class status."

Polls show that a substantial majority of Americans — more than 80 percent — believe that homosexuals should not be discriminated against in the workplace. (*See poll, p. 180.*) But efforts to enact anti-gay-discrimination laws have fallen short in Washington and in most state capitals in the face of a swirl of arguments raised by conservative advocacy groups.

They warn of a parade of horribles that would result, in particular, from a proposed federal law, the Employment Non-Discrimination Act (ENDA): job quotas, heavy-handed federal enforcement, invasive questioning about employees' sexual orientation and intrusions on the religious liberties of faith-based employers. Most broadly, opponents say the law would undermine traditional morality and give "special rights" to a group that neither needs nor deserves special legal protections.

ENDA "requires the federal government to abandon its commitments to the traditions of marriage and family and to declare that all sexual preferences are equally valid," says a Family Research Council position paper. The bill "affords special protection to a group that is not disadvantaged," the paper continues. "Homosexuals, as a group, outpace most other Americans economically and educationally, and no one can dispute their political power and savvy."

Lobbyists insist the opponents are exaggerating or misstating the provisions of the federal bill. "This is a very modest piece of legislation," says Winnie Stachelberg, po-

Sixteen States Still Have Anti-Sodomy Laws

Anti-sodomy laws historically have been used to prosecute homosexuals for oral and anal sex, although they also typically apply to heterosexuals. The laws are rarely enforced today but are still used, according to gay-rights advocates, to deny employment and child custody and visitation rights to gays. Supporters say that even if the laws are rarely enforced, they help to safeguard the legal and moral status of the family and to contain sexual conduct that is a factor in sexually transmitted diseases.

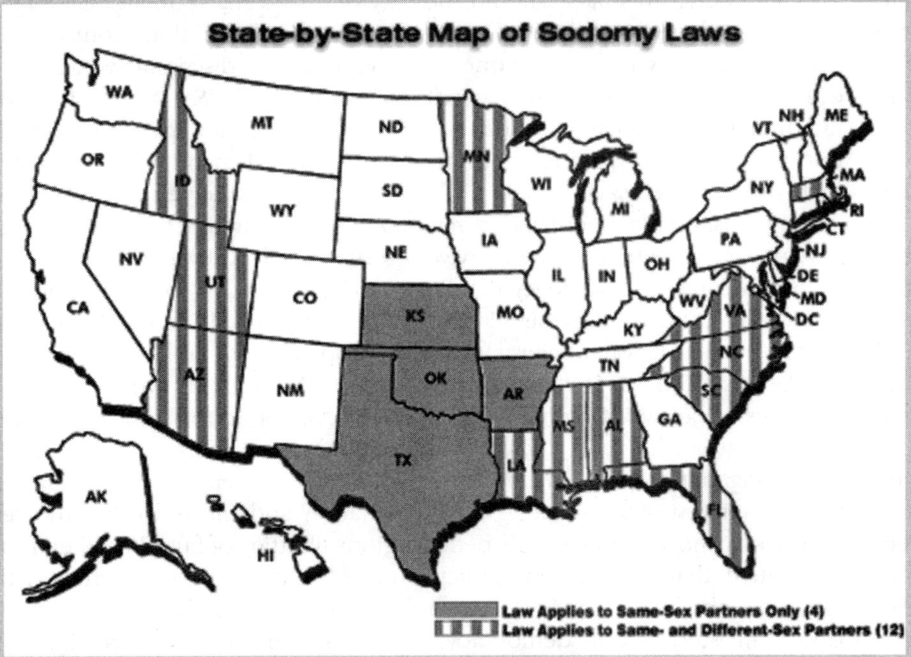

Lambda Legal Defense and Education Fund

Source: Lambda Legal Defense and Education Fund, March 4, 2000

litical director of Human Rights Campaign (HRC), a gay-rights organization. "All it would say is you can't be fired from your job for sexual orientation — because of a factor that has nothing to do with your job performance."

Opponents acknowledge that the bill bars the use of quotas or preferences for homosexuals. But they contend that administrative enforcement and litigation will pressure employers into adopting such schemes anyway. "Employers will be forced to learn more about their employees' sex lives," the Family Research Council warns, "in order to defend themselves against possible lawsuits."

Supporters of the bill dismiss such fears as groundless. "I don't think there's any reason to believe that having laws [in some states] has injected all sorts of sexual-orientation questions into the workplace," Dohrn says. "The laws provide an incentive for employers to leave the subject out." In any event, the notion of quotas is "kind of ridiculous," she says. "There is no way in the world to count how many people are gay."

Opponents also warn that the bill could force religious organizations to hire homosexuals despite religious convictions against homosexuality. They acknowledge the bill includes an exemption for religious organizations but say it does not extend to individuals and might not apply to some church-sponsored social services. Supporters again say the warnings are off base. The bill "has a religious exemption so big you could push the National Cathedral through it," Dohrn says.

Despite the failure of the federal bill, some 11 states, the District of Columbia and 124 municipalities and counties have passed gay-rights measures — almost all of them with employment-discrimination provisions. Gay-rights advocates say, somewhat regretfully, that the laws have not generated the kind of rush of litigation that opponents have warned about.

"The laws are underused, and that's because using them is an expensive, uphill battle," Dohrn says. "Coming out is still a dangerous proposition in many parts of the country, and litigating against your employer is always a risky proposition."

Congress has had only one recorded vote on the federal bill: in the Senate in September 1996. The measure failed 49-50, with one senator absent. The vote was largely symbolic since the House would have had no time to act on the measure late in the session. Since that time, Stachelberg says, the Republican leadership in the House and the Senate has kept the bill "bottled up."

The Family Research Council's Knight acknowledges that more states and municipalities are likely to pass such laws, though he doubts Congress will. But he also sees a likely backlash. "You're going to see more of these laws challenged," he says. "People will say you shouldn't create a sweeping new category" for civil rights laws.

But Dohrn thinks the movement to enact such laws will continue. "It's remarkable how many people think that discrimination on the basis of sexual orientation is already illegal," she says. "Eventually, the law will conform to people's expectations about the law." ■

BACKGROUND

Birth of a Movement

Homosexuals were largely invisible, politically unorganized and legally vulnerable from the founding of the United States until the early 20th century. When homosexual subcultures started becoming more visible, the social pressures against homosexuality turned into legal strictures with expansively written "crime-against-nature" laws.

The legal crackdown on homosexuals increased from the 1920s through the decades after World War II. Ironically, the crackdown spawned the gay-rights movement, as homosexuals organized first to protect themselves from prosecution and then to demand legal recognition and equal rights. [9]

The legal crackdown on homosexuality was multifaceted. Under the 1917 Immigration Act, the government barred "sexual perverts" from entering the country, much as a 1921 Army regulation permitted exclusion for "sexual perversion." Homosexual organizations were shut down through the use of disorderly-conduct laws. Gay bars found their licenses suspended or revoked. Most dramatically, homosexuals were subject to criminal prosecution for sodomy, lewd conduct or other offenses. On the eve of World War II, Yale's Eskridge writes, "a homosexual with an active social life had a good chance of spending time in jail." [10]

The pursuit of homosexuals intensified after World War II, when Eskridge estimates that as many as 100,000 gays per year, mostly men, were arrested for consensual sexual behavior. Some states moved to bar homosexuals as teachers or as lawyers. Thousands of soldiers and sailors were discharged on grounds of homosexuality, proven or suspected.

The crackdown finally engendered resistance — and the first stirrings of the gay-rights movement. The leading resistance group was the Mattachine Society, formed in Los Angeles in 1951. Taking its name from a medieval Italian court jester who expressed unpopular truths from behind a mask, the group vowed to unify homosexuals and to assist "our people who are victimized daily as a result of our oppression." [11]

The Mattachine Society and the Daughters of Bilitis — the first lesbian organization, founded in San Francisco in 1955 — both adopted assimilationist strategies. Mattachine wanted to educate homosexuals and heterosexuals alike to an "ethical homosexual culture," while the Daughters advocated "a mode of behavior and dress acceptable to society."

The non-confrontational approach combined with liberalizing trends in politics, law and society to produce some tangible gains. Illinois became the first state to decriminalize sodomy in 1961. The California Supreme Court acted to protect gay bars from arbitrary closures, and the U.S. Supreme Court limited the Post Office's power to censor male physique magazines.

The number of gay organizations increased in the 1960s — from 15 in 1966 to nearly 50 three years later — and the groups became both more visible and more aggressive. [12] Then in 1969, two days of disturbances touched off by a police raid at a dilapidated — and unlicensed — gay dance bar in New York City gave new impetus and militancy to the gay-rights movement. [13] Plainclothes officers ordered patrons out of Greenwich Village's Stonewall Inn on June 28 and loaded three men dressed as women into paddywagons. When the crowd threw cans and bottles, the police retreated and reinforcements arrived to clear the streets.

The next night, as hundreds of protesters gathered, the mood was camp rather than revolution. But a milestone had been reached. Gay people, author Eric Marcus writes, "were finally pushed to the point where they'd had enough, and they fought back." A month later, activists in Greenwich Village organized what they called the city's "first gay-power vigil.

"Do you think homosexuals are revolting?" a leaflet asked, capturing the movement's new sense of pride and militancy. "You bet your sweet ass we are," it answered in capital letters. [14]

Successes and Setbacks

The gay-rights movement made fitful advances over the next two decades. Anti-sodomy statutes were repealed or invalidated in many states, while a few states and many municipalities prohibited discrimination against homosexuals. But social conservatives — the so-called New Right — responded with lobbying and citizen initiatives to block gay-rights measures or in a few cities to repeal ordinances already enacted.

The Supreme Court also dealt the movement a setback, upholding state anti-sodomy statutes. Meanwhile, same-sex marriage made no headway in the courts, although some cities enacted domestic partnership laws. And the Pentagon actually toughened its policy on homosexuality, explicitly excluding homosexuals from the military. [15]

The movement's broadest success came in eradicating sodomy laws. Connecticut followed Illinois' lead in repealing its anti-sodomy statute in 1971. By 1992, similar laws had been repealed in some 19 other state legislatures and nullified by court rulings in four others.

Nonetheless, the U.S. Supreme Court in 1986 voted 5-4 to uphold the constitutionality of enforcing sodomy statutes against private, consensual homosexual conduct. Writing for the majority in *Bowers v. Hardwick*, Justice Byron White said Georgia's law could be justified on the basis of "the presumed belief of a majority of the electorate in Georgia that homosexual conduct is immoral and unacceptable."

Gay-rights advocates began winning enactment of anti-discrimination laws at the local level in the 1970s and then in a handful of states in the '80s. Generally, the laws prohibited discrimination in government or private employment on the basis of sexual orientation; some also barred discrimination in housing or public accommodations.

Opponents succeeded in several cities in overturning ordinances through the referendum process — notably in Miami-Dade County, Fla., in a 1977 campaign led by pop singer Anita Bryant and fueled by conservative religious groups. At the state level, opponents succeeded in stalling bills or — for example, in California in 1985 — in persuading the governor to veto a measure approved by lawmakers. Despite the difficulties, by 1992 gay-rights laws were on the books in seven states and some 90 municipalities — mostly large cities or university towns.

Advocates of same-sex marriage made no headway before the 1990s. A few couples brought suits, but courts rejected their constitutional claims almost out of hand. None of the major gay and lesbian organizations supported their efforts. The community was, in fact, divided on the issue, with many gay and lesbian activists viewing marriage as the kind of hierarchical institution that the movement should seek to displace.

In the 1980s, gay-rights groups did support the emerging effort to win workplace equality through recognition of domestic partnerships. The San Francisco Board of Supervisors passed a domestic partnership bill in 1981, but it was vetoed by then-Mayor Dianne Feinstein. A year later, Berkeley, Calif., became the first city to enact such an ordinance. By 1991, another two dozen cities had followed suit — including San Francisco.

Gay-rights advocates suffered one clear setback — in the military. Regulations dating back to World War II had prohibited service by homosexuals, but they were often ignored. Pentagon officials began rewriting the regulations in the late 1970s, under President Jimmy Carter; the revamping was completed in the first year of President Ronald Reagan's administration in 1981.

The new regulations reiterated the description of homosexuality as "incompatible with military service" but expanded the definition to include anyone who "engages in, desires to engage in or intends to engage in homosexual acts."

As author Randy Shilts put it, "The military had, in effect, banned homosexual thoughts." [16] The new regulations were more rigorously enforced: nearly 17,000 servicemembers were discharged for homosexual conduct during the 12 years of Reagan's and George Bush's presidencies.

"A Seat at the Table"

Despite continuing resistance, the movement made remarkable strides in the 1990s, legally and politically. Gay rights became a focus of national debate for the first time during the 1992 presidential election. The Clinton administration and the Democratic Party aligned themselves for the rest of the decade with many of the issues on the gay-rights agenda.

Still, there were setbacks: the "don't ask, don't tell" policy; Congress' failure to pass a gay civil-rights law; and the adoption of defense of marriage laws by Congress and a majority of states.

Clinton signaled his support for the cause by appearing at a 1992 Los Angeles fund-raiser organized by gay activists. [17] The Clinton campaign netted $100,000 — and the gay community showed it could flex its considerable financial muscle to further its aims. For his part, Clinton said gay Americans represented "a community of our nation's gifted people that we have been willing to squander." He pledged to undo the Pentagon's policy, crack down on anti-gay hate crimes and include an HIV-positive speaker at the Democratic National Convention.

In office, Clinton proved unable to deliver on his promises. Most dramatically, his effort to open military service to homosexuals fell short in the face of a strong backlash from military leaders, members of Congress from both parties and the public. [18]

Clinton was forced to back away from a post-election promise to lift the ban on homosexuals by executive order and then fashioned a short-term compromise — soon known as "don't ask, don't tell." Gay servicemembers derisively termed it "don't tell, don't touch."

Chronology

Before 1945

Homosexuals are politically unorganized, legally vulnerable.

1945-1970 ***Initial stirrings of gay-rights movement.***

1951
Mattachine Society is founded in Los Angeles to provide support for male homosexuals. Four years later, Daughters of Bilitis is founded in San Francisco as first U.S. lesbian organization.

1961
Illinois becomes first state to remove penalty for consensual homosexual relations between adults.

June 1969
Police raid on the Stonewall Inn, a popular gay bar in New York City, becomes defining moment for modern gay-rights movement.

1970s ***Gay rights becomes national issue, but gains are limited.***

1977
Miami-Dade County, Fla., adopts ordinance prohibiting discrimination against gay men and lesbians; ordinance overturned by referendum six months later.

1979
First national gay-rights march held in Washington.

1980s ***Gay rights advances, but social conservatives stiffen opposition; AIDS becomes an epidemic.***

1981
Wisconsin becomes first state to bar discrimination against homosexuals in employment, housing and public accommodations.

1984
Berkeley, Calif., becomes first city to provide domestic-partner benefits for gays and lesbians.

1986
U.S. Supreme Court upholds state laws against consensual homosexual sodomy.

1990s ***Gay-rights movement combines political clout and legal initiatives to make significant gains against continuing resistance.***

1992
Democratic presidential candidate Bill Clinton promises support for several gay-rights proposals; after his election, Clinton repeats vow to end military policy excluding gays.

1993
Congress forces Clinton to accept "don't ask, don't tell" policy on gays in military; Hawaii Supreme Court says state must justify law prohibiting same-sex marriages; third gay-rights march on Washington.

1994
Massachusetts becomes first state to outlaw discrimination against gays in public schools.

1996
Colorado initiative prohibiting legal protections for homosexuals nullified by Supreme Court.

July 5, 1999
Pfc. Barry Winchell is beaten to death by a fellow soldier after being taunted for being gay; Defense Secretary William Cohen announces policy against harassment of gays a month later.

Aug. 4, 1999
New Jersey Supreme Court says Boy Scouts' exclusion of gays violates state anti-discrimination law; U.S. Supreme Court to hear case April 26, 2000.

Dec. 20, 1999
Vermont Supreme Court says state must allow same-sex couples to enjoy legal benefits accorded to heterosexuals; legislation to create "civil union" status moves toward final approval early in 2000.

2000s ***New decade opens with gay-rights issues high on political, legal agendas.***

January 2000
Gay-rights measures backed by Democratic presidential candidate Al Gore, opposed by Republican George W. Bush.

April 30, 2000
Organizers hope to draw record crowd for Millennium March on Washington, but planning is marred by disorganization and disagreements.

How Americans Feel About Gay Rights

Public opinion polls indicate solid majority support for giving homosexuals "equal rights in terms of job opportunities." Most Americans, however, believe that sexual relations between two adults of the same sex are "always wrong," though the disapproval rate has fallen significantly in the last decade.

- Do you think homosexuals should have equal rights in terms of job opportunities? In 1996, Yes — 84%
- Do you think homosexuals should be accepted into the armed forces? In 1996, Yes — 66%
- Do you think homosexuals should be hired as elementary school teachers? In 1996, Yes — 60%

- Do you think sexual relations between two adults of the same sex is always wrong, almost always wrong, wrong only sometimes or not wrong at all?

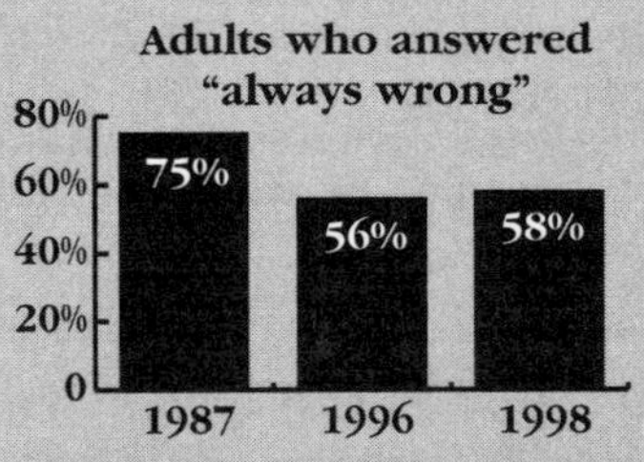

Source: Alan Yang, "From Wrongs to Rights, 1973-1999: Public Opinion on Gay and Lesbian Americans Moves Toward Equality," National Gay and Lesbian Task Force, 1999

Congress kept at the issue, however, and eventually approved a provision in the Defense Department authorization that codified the ban on homosexuals while leaving intact the administration's decision not to ask recruits about their sexual orientation and not to initiate investigations except after receiving "credible information" of homosexual conduct. Clinton signed the bill.

Seven years later, the administration also has been unable to win support for a gay civil rights bill or special federal penalties for anti-gay hate crimes. The 1990 Hate Crime Statistics Act, signed by President George Bush, does include anti-gay offenses as one category in an annual data compilation by the Justice Department. [19]

Gay-rights advocates continued to press their efforts both in Washington and before state and local legislative bodies. By the end of the decade, the number of gays was still increasing, two states had domestic-partnership schemes and the number of states with anti-sodomy statutes had dwindled to 19. [20]

Opponents tried to thwart gay-rights advocates with initiatives in several states aimed at blocking state or local governments from enacting laws to prohibit discrimination on the basis of sexual orientation. Colorado voters approved such a measure in 1992, but voters in three other states rejected similar initiatives: Idaho and Oregon in 1994 and Maine in 1995.

Then in 1996, the U.S. Supreme Court appeared to bar the tactic by ruling that the Colorado initiative violated the U.S. Constitution's Equal Protection Clause. The law had no rational basis, Justice Anthony Kennedy wrote in *Romer v. Evans.* It was, instead, a "status-based enactment" born out of "animosity toward homosexuals." [21]

The Hawaii Supreme Court's ruling on same-sex marriages in 1993 provoked a similar but stronger backlash. Opponents lobbied Congress and state legislatures to pass laws aimed at barring recognition of same-sex marriages. Congress cleared the federal Defense of Marriage Act on Sept. 10, 1996, just two months before the presidential election. [22]

The measure — which Clinton signed almost surreptitiously at 12:50 a.m. on Sept. 21 — said that states were not obligated to recognize same-sex marriages from other states and defined marriage for purposes of federal law as a union between people of opposite sexes. By decade's end, 30 states had similar laws — including Alaska and Hawaii itself, where voters approved constitutional amendments to ward off recognition of homosexual marriages. ■

CURRENT SITUATION

Debating 'Civil Unions'

The Vermont Supreme Court's ruling in the same-sex marriage case touched off a wide-ranging debate from one end of the state to another.

Can the Boy Scouts Exclude Gays?

James Dale became a Cub Scout at age 6 and graduated to Boy Scouts four years later. He went on to earn 30 merit badges and achieve Scouting's highest honors: Eagle Scout and the Order of the Arrow.

As a young man, Dale wanted to continue as a Scout leader. But the Boy Scouts council in Monmouth, N.J., summarily expelled him in 1990 when it learned from a newspaper story that Dale is gay.

Today, Dale is locked in a high-profile legal dispute with the Boy Scouts of America (BSA) that pits anti-discrimination principles against freedom of speech and association. The U.S. Supreme Court will hear arguments on April 26 in the Boy Scouts' effort to overturn a New Jersey Supreme Court ruling that Dale's expulsion violated the state's law against discrimination on the basis of sexual orientation in "public accommodations."

Dale's attorneys say the case, *Boy Scouts of America v. Dale,* is important not only for Dale but also for gay youths generally. "Gay youths need the same opportunity for socialization and fun and community service as their non-gay brothers and sisters do," says Evan Wolfson, senior attorney with the Lambda Legal Defense and Education Fund.

But BSA national spokesman Greg Shields says homosexuality is inconsistent with Scouting. "The Boy Scouts of America have long taught traditional family values based on the Scout oath and law," Shields says. "The Boy Scouts of America believe that an acknowledged homosexual would not be a role model for those values."

Lambda Legal Defense and Education Fund/Bob Pileggi

Former Eagle Scout James Dale

Dale, now 29, came out as a homosexual while attending Rutgers University in Newark, N.J. While co-president of the gay and lesbian student organization, he attended a seminar in July 1990 on psychological and health needs of homosexual teenagers. The local newspaper ran a story on the seminar along with Dale's picture and a caption identifying his role in the gay organization.

Days later, the Monmouth Boy Scouts council sent Dale a letter that revoked his membership. When Dale asked for a reason, BSA officials responded by saying the organization "specifically forbids membership to homosexuals." Two years later, Dale sued the Scouts under New Jersey's Law Against Discrimination.

The Boy Scouts have won five similar cases after courts decided that states' civil rights laws did not apply to private, membership organizations. A lower court in New Jersey reached the same conclusion in Dale's case. But in August the New Jersey Supreme Court unanimously ruled that the BSA is a "public accommodation" for purposes of the state's civil rights law and that forcing the organization to accept homosexuals as leaders would not violate its First Amendment right of freedom of speech or association.

In two rulings in the 1980s, the U.S. Supreme Court did uphold the enforcement of state civil rights laws to require private organizations — the Jaycees and Rotary clubs — to admit women. [1] In a concurring opinion in the Jaycees case, however, Justice Sandra Day O'Connor mentioned the Boy Scouts as an example of an organization that might have a First Amendment right to select its members without running afoul of anti-discrimination laws.

In his legal arguments, Wolfson relies heavily on those two decisions, stresses the Boy Scouts' broad membership policy and purposes and discounts O'Connor's passing reference to the Scouts. The Boy Scouts counters in its brief with a more recent Supreme Court decision that upheld the right of the organizers of Boston's St. Patrick's Day parade to exclude a gay group. [2]

The opposing briefs differ not only about legal precedent but even about the factual context of the Scouts' policy on homosexuality. In its brief, BSA contends that homosexual conduct is "not 'morally straight' under the Scout Oath, or 'clean' under the Scout Law." But Wolfson says there is "literally nothing" about homosexuality in the Scout Handbook's explanation of "morally straight."

Boy Scout officials and lawyers voice confidence that the Supreme Court will back their position. "We're confident that the court will find in our favor, and that we'll be done with these 20 years of litigation," Shields says.

Wolfson hedges on making a prediction, but other gay-rights advocates concede they are worried. "Most of us are feeling not so certain, to say the least, that the Supreme Court is going to uphold the New Jersey Supreme Court's ruling," says Paula Ettelbrick, director of the Family Law Project of the National Gay and Lesbian Task Force.

---

[1] The cases are *Board of Directors of Rotary International v. Rotary Club of Duarte* (1987) and *Roberts v. United States Jaycees* (1984).

[2] The case is *Hurley v. Irish-American Gay, Lesbian & Bisexual Group of Boston, Inc.* (1995).

Most Vermonters — lawmakers and citizens alike — appeared to oppose marriage for homosexual couples. But with little maneuvering room under the high court's ruling, the legislature inexorably moved toward approving a "civil union" bill giving gay and lesbian couples rights broader than homosexuals can enjoy in any other state.

The plaintiffs' lawyers — Robinson, Murray and Mary Bonauto of Boston-based Gay and Lesbian Advocates and Defenders (GLAD) — based their case on a provision of the Vermont Constitution known as the common-benefits clause. It provides that government is "instituted for the common benefit, protection and security of the people . . . and not for the particular emolument or advantage of any single person, family or set of persons."

They argued that a law allowing only heterosexual couples to enjoy all the legal benefits of marriage violated that provision. The state's lawyers offered one principal rationale for limiting marriage to heterosexuals: the government's interest in promoting the link between procreation and child-rearing.

In his 45-page opinion for the court, Chief Justice Jeffrey Amestoy pointed out that many heterosexual couples marry "for reasons unrelated to procreation." In addition, he noted that "a significant number of children" are now being raised by same-sex couples and that the state legislature had actually removed legal barriers for same-sex couples to adopt and raise children.

With the state's main argument rejected, Amestoy concluded: "We hold that the State is constitutionally required to extend to same-sex couples the common benefits and protections that flow from marriage under Vermont law."

Nationally, gay-rights advocates enthused about the ruling. "This decision marks the start of a tremendous sea change that will surely improve life for lesbian and gay families," Lambda's Dohrn declared. On the opposite side, the Family Research Council noted that the ruling fell short of mandating "gay marriage." But it called the decision "dangerously wrong" because it would "force the people of Vermont to support what is essentially a sin registry."

Opinion was similarly divided in Vermont.[23] Gay-rights advocates sported buttons reading, "I support the freedom to marry." Opponents had their own buttons: "God's plan — one woman, one man." Catholic and evangelical groups fueled the opposition, while leaders of other denominations supported the idea of gay marriage. A statewide poll conducted a month after the court's ruling found 38 percent in favor of the decision and 52 percent opposed. A near majority — 49 percent — favored a constitutional amendment to overturn the decision, with 44 percent opposed.

In the legislature, the House took first crack at the issue. The Judiciary Committee sent to the floor a detailed bill establishing "civil union" status for homosexual couples with virtually all the benefits and responsibilities of marriage. The bill declared the state's "strong interest in promoting stable and lasting families, including families based upon a same-sex couple."

After lengthy debate, the House passed the measure on March 16 by a narrow margin: 76-69. Afterward, the *Burlington Free Press* noted that female lawmakers provided the margin of victory, voting 35-9 in favor of the bill; men opposed it, 60-41.

Supporters and opponents viewed the House vote as critical. The Senate "is a little tougher picture," says Take It to the People's President Cummings. The Senate Judiciary Committee decided to hold a full round of hearings, with witnesses on all sides and even a hearing on interactive statewide television on April 3.

Senate Judiciary Committee leaders hoped to complete work on a civil union bill along the lines of the House measure during the week of April 10. Before marking up the bill, however, the committee voted on April 11 to send to the Senate floor without recommendation a proposed constitutional amendment aimed at overturning the Supreme Court's decision. The amendment — subject to voter approval after approval in two legislative sessions — would nullify any constitutional requirement to grant marriage benefits to homosexual couples.[24]

'Disturbing' Harassment

Anti-gay harassment is pervasive and widely tolerated in the U.S. military. That is the conclusion not only from gay-rights groups but also from the Pentagon itself.

A survey of some 71,500 servicemembers conducted by the Defense Department's Office of Inspector General and released on March 24 found that 37 percent had witnessed or experienced serious forms of anti-gay harassment, and 80 percent had heard offensive speech or jokes or derogatory names or remarks about homosexuals during the past year. Most of the harassment was not reported up the chain of command, the survey found, and no action was taken in three-fourths of those cases where senior officers were informed.[25]

"The report shows that military leaders must do more to make it clear that harassment based on sexual orientation violates military values," Defense Secretary William Cohen said. Pentagon spokesman Kenneth Bacon said the report showed a "disturbing" amount of harassment.

Gay-rights groups took satisfaction from the report. "This is the first time that the Pentagon has realized that it has a serious problem on its hands," said C. Dixon Osborne, co-director of the Servicemembers Legal Defense Network. But they also called for stronger action.

"Nothing is going to change until the uniformed military leadership, from the Joint Chiefs of Staff on down, send clear and unambiguous signals that this type of harassment will not be tolerated," said HRC Communications Director David Smith.

Opponents of military service by homosexuals questioned the survey's findings, noting that the report itself acknowledged that individual respondents were not randomly selected. "You can't paint the entire military with these results," the Family Research Council's Maginnis says. "That's political spin."

The survey's results suggested the limitations of the military's efforts to date to translate the "don't ask, don't tell" policy into actual practice. Most of the servicemembers surveyed — 57 percent — said they had received no training on the policy. About half — 54 percent — said they understood the policy, but only one-fourth of those correctly answered three questions designed to test their knowledge.

The military had already moved to make training in the policy universal. The Pentagon announced on Feb. 1 that every member of the armed forces would undergo training by the end of the year to prevent anti-gay harassment.[26] The hourlong training session is to include a slide presentation along with role-playing exercises and pamphlets. One of the slides reads, "Zero Tolerance for Harassment."

Reporters who watched some of the early training sessions observed instances of puzzlement among servicemembers taking part. At Fort Campbell — where Winchell was killed — an officer asked whether a gay soldier should be reported for asking another soldier on a date. "No, it's just associational behavior," the training officer, Maj. James Garrett, answered.[27]

At Fort Meade, Md., outside Washington, one of the soldiers attending a training session also worried about harassment of straight servicemembers, according to *The Washington Post*. "If I'm in the shower, and somebody comes up and starts groping me," the Post quoted the solider as saying, "my first instinct is not to go to the commander. My first instinct is, 'You better get off of me.'"[28]

The inspector general's survey found that a bare majority of the servicemembers surveyed — 50.1 percent — thought the "don't ask, don't tell" policy had been either moderately or very effective in preventing or reducing harassment. In his statement, Cohen detailed the steps taken so far to deal with the harassment issue — including the universal-training requirement. But he also acknowledged that "there is still more to do."

Toward that end, Cohen established a high-level working group with representatives from all four services to draft an "action plan . . . to address the problem of harassment based on perceived sexual orientation." Cohen gave the group a July 31 deadline.

Playing Politics

A week after Al Gore narrowly beat Bill Bradley in New Hampshire's Democratic presidential primary, the HRC Board of Directors met to consider making an endorsement in the race. Since both candidates had staked out pro-gay-rights positions, there was an argument to stay neutral. Nonetheless, with crucial primaries coming up in states with sizable gay voting blocs — California and New York — the board decided on Feb. 9 to back Gore.

"The vice president has toiled at our side over the last seven years," said President Elizabeth Birch. "We thought we better make a decision while it is valuable and relevant. Our candidate needs us."[29]

The competition between Gore and Bradley for gay votes and the HRC's explicitly political calculation in supporting Gore indicated both the changing political climate on gay-rights issues and the gay and lesbian community's increasing political sophistication.

"This is a community to be dealt with, and it can't be taken for granted," says Human Rights Campaign's Stachelberg.

The climate is different in the Republican Party. Gov. Bush snubbed the gay Log Cabin Republicans by refusing to meet with its leaders. He backed the "don't ask, don't tell" policy on gays in the military and opposed civil rights legislation. And during the crucial South Carolina primary he appeared to back away from previous statements that he would have no problem with appointing homosexuals to administration positions. "An openly known homosexual is somebody who probably wouldn't share my philosophy," Bush said.[30]

The Republicans' control of Congress has helped bottle up gay-rights legislation in Congress. "It is terribly disappointing that we still can't get a hate-crimes bill that includes sexual orientation, and we can't get the Employment Non-Discrimination Act passed," Stachelberg says. "Those two bills remain blocked by the leadership in Congress." At the same time, lawmakers in both parties rushed to approve the

Defense of Marriage Act in 1996 to try to ward off what they saw as the threat of same-sex marriage.

Gay-rights groups see the climate as more favorable at the state and local level. In an end-of-year review in December, the NGLTF said pro-gay-rights bills outnumbered "unfavorable" bills during the 1999 state legislative season, and "favorable" bills progressed in several states farther than in the past, even if they were not enacted. "The center of gravity is slowly shifting," said then Executive Director Kerry Lobel.

Still, the review pointed to only a handful of gay-rights measures actually enacted into law. Major victories came in California, where a new Democratic governor, Gray Davis, signed measures establishing domestic-partnership benefits for same-sex couples, prohibiting employment and housing discrimination on the basis of sexual orientation and protecting gay and lesbian students against discrimination. Other new gay-rights laws included an employment-discrimination act in Nevada and a hate-crimes measure in Missouri. In addition, New Hampshire repealed its ban on adoptions by gays and lesbians. [31]

Vermont's civil union bill seems likely to top the gay-rights movement's accomplishments for this year. In an offsetting defeat, however, Mississippi last month banned gay and lesbian adoptions, joining Florida as the only other state with a statutory ban.

For their part, anti-gay-rights groups blame what they call media bias and gay-rights "propaganda" for the support registered in public opinion polls for anti-discrimination legislation. The Family Research Council's Knight also says the poll results can be misleading.

"Most people don't want to see homosexuals singled out for discrimination, which isn't happening in widespread fashion anyway," Knight says. "But they don't want to see sexual behavior granted special rights either."

As for the presidential race, Knight praises Bush for "solid" positions opposing gay marriages and adoptions and gays in the military. He calls Gore's views on gay-rights issues "radical" but worries that Bush and other Republicans will not exploit the party's differences with the Democrats. "They don't seem to understand the issues themselves and are reluctant to engage it," the Family Research Council's Knight says. ■

OUTLOOK

Marching on Washington

For the past few weeks, patrons of Washington's gay bars have been interrupted in their dancing and drinking by activists passing out cards promoting the "Millennium March on Washington." The solicitations are part of a wide-ranging effort aimed at drawing hundreds of thousands of gay, lesbian, bisexual and transgendered people to Washington over the weekend of April 29-30 for a combination festival and political pep rally.

Organizers say the march — the fourth national event of its kind and the first since 1993 — is aimed in part at showcasing the gay community's growing political clout. "This is the first march in an election year, with the major goal of having a major voter turnout," says Dianne Hardy-Garcia, executive director for the march. "We have to show to the world how many people we are, what our voting bloc is and what we bring to the table."

The march has been marred, however, by organizational missteps and disagreements within the gay community over political priorities. [32] The principal sponsors of the march — HRC and the Metropolitan Community Church — announced plans for the event two years ago. They have been criticized for not getting more input in planning the event and failing to set clear goals. In February, one of the two original co-executive directors resigned, apparently in a dispute over the selection of a firm to produce the event.

Many gay activists have complained that the time and money being spent on the march — it's expected to cost $1.73 million and take in $1.95 million — would be better used at the state and local level. "Our folks need to be at home doing serious political work, not having a *tchotchke* sale on the mall," Rick Garcia, of Equality Illinois, told *The Washington Post.*

Hardy-Garcia, who is also executive director of the Lesbian and Gay Rights Lobby of Texas, dismisses the criticism. "I've spent my career fighting for lesbian and gay rights in Texas," she says. "That's really important to do. But there's nothing like coming to your national capital and realizing you're part of a larger movement."

Some gay scholars as well as gay-rights opponents are predicting that the march may not surpass the estimated 300,000 people who attended the 1993 event.

"It will be smaller than the '87 and '93 marches because there is no widely perceived need for a march on Washington right now," says John D'Emilio, a professor at the University of Illinois in Chicago and author of a history of the early gay-rights movement. "Most of the areas of advocacy that have a prospect of success and most of the advocacy energy have been focused on state and local issues, not on Washington."

Whatever the turnout, gay activists

At Issue:

Should high schools permit "gay-straight alliance" clubs?

yes

Jim Anderson
Communications director, Gay, Lesbian and Straight Education Network

WRITTEN FOR *THE CQ RESEARCHER*

Considerable media attention has been paid over the past few months, to gay-straight alliance (GSA) controversies in Utah, Louisiana and Orange County, Calif. In each instance, school boards either considered or took action to prevent students from exercising their federally protected right under the Equal Access Act.

While these battles and controversies have been intriguing, it is, perhaps, more interesting to consider the stories that have not made the news.

Little attention has been paid to the approximately 700 gay-straight alliances that are currently meeting in high schools from coast-to-coast. These school communities accepted or embraced the students and their efforts, and not as a result of judicial mandate. Instead, they recognized their professional, if not moral, responsibility to do so.

Should other high schools permit the creation of gay-straight alliances? To answer the question, we need to define gay-straight alliances and to discuss why students are forming them in such numbers. A gay-straight alliance is formed by lesbian, gay, bisexual and transgender (LGBT) students and their straight classmates. These students join together to support one another and to address concerns about the misinformation and ignorance that too often result in anti-gay harassment or violence at school.

Their concerns are well-founded. Studies by the federal Centers for Disease Control and Prevention (CDC) show that lesbian, gay and bisexual students are more than four times as likely as their heterosexual classmates to be threatened with or injured by a weapon while at school.

The Gay, Lesbian and Straight Education Network found similarly disturbing trends. In a recent national survey, we found that 61 percent of LGBT students experience verbal harassment, 27 percent physical harassment and 14 percent outright physical assault while at school.

This harassment and isolation may negatively affect students' self-esteem and school performance. Such experiences may explain why national mainstream organizations such as the American Counseling Association and the National Association of Social Workers have recently endorsed gay-straight alliances.

Every student is entitled to a supportive, safe and affirming learning environment. With this goal in mind, we urge schools not only to permit gay-straight alliances but also to encourage and foster their existence.

no

Peter LaBarbera
Senior analyst, Family Research Council

WRITTEN FOR *THE CQ RESEARCHER*

School districts should not allow the formation of gay-straight alliances on their campuses. These groups, where they already exist, have become de facto homosexuality booster clubs — causing unnecessary divisions and distractions and subjecting the entire student body to one-sided propaganda. Moreover, they are part of a movement that promotes radical identities and dangerous sexual practices to vulnerable, confused teens.

The gay-straight alliances are part of an ingenious strategy by pro-homosexuality and transsexuality groups like the Gay, Lesbian and Straight Education Network (GLSEN) to inject their unhealthy sexual and gender ideologies into the classroom. Students rally around the "rights" of gay, bi or even trans (transgender) classmates who, it is true, are ostracized and sometimes mistreated by their peers.

But while GLSEN and other groups have artfully "spun" the issue of youth homosexuality into one of "discrimination," it is really about behavior and parents' rights to guide their children's moral decisions.

In Massachusetts, taxpayers subsidize the formation of gay-straight alliances — there are now 185 — through state grants for GSA projects.

Across the country, educators are wasting valuable school time by allowing GSAs to promote extreme notions to the entire student body. Students rarely get to hear the other side of the debate, and they fear expressing their opposition to homosexuality because of the schools' politically correct embrace of homosexuality.

The National Education Association, the American Civil Liberties Union, GLSEN and their allies promote GSAs in the name of school "safety." But schools shouldn't promote homosexual identities to troubled kids when studies show that homosexual males have drastically shorter life spans. This is due to the risky sexual behavior that flourishes in the promiscuous "gay" world. At a March conference sponsored by GLSEN's Boston affiliate, speakers from the state's Education Department approvingly discussed "queer sex" acts to an audience made up mostly of students ages 14-21.

Parents must resist an agenda that uses schools' authority to confirm impressionable youth in harmful lifestyles. As one former homosexual has noted, "From every medical and health aspect — up to and including the probability of becoming infected with AIDS — it is tragic, even criminal, to lead a child into homosexuality because he or she showed some degree of confusion in adolescence."

Gay-Straight Club Divides California Community

Anthony Colin wanted to make his school in Orange, Calif., a better place for homosexual teenagers like himself. His efforts in founding a so-called gay-straight alliance club at El Modena High School have brought him national publicity and a local human rights award, as well as daily name-calling in school and a draining federal court battle with the local school board.

"I knew I was going to be facing a lot of opposition, but I didn't know just how far it would go," said Anthony, a 16-year-old sophomore. [1]

The controversy over the club — one of some 700 gay-straight alliances at high schools around the country — has divided the 2,000-student school and the community. Students opposed to the club appeared at an early school board meeting carrying signs that read, "Grades, Not AIDS."

Nationally, gay-rights groups and social conservatives sharply disagree over such clubs. Supporters say they are needed to give homosexual high school students a safe place to talk about issues affecting their lives and to promote tolerance among gay and straight students alike.

"Gay-straight alliances help one of most vulnerable populations feel a little safer, a little more accepted," says Kevin Jennings, executive director of the New York-based Gay, Lesbian and Straight Education Network (GLSEN).

"Gay youth are typically very unsupported in schools, unsupported in other aspects of their life, too," says Barbara Rienzo, a professor of health sciences at the University of Florida in Gainesville and co-author of a book on local gay-rights disputes. "Schools are one of the places where we could do a lot of things to intervene and help make schools a safe and healthy place for all youth."

But Robert Knight, director of cultural studies for the conservative Family Research Council, says the clubs promote homosexuality.

"Gay-straight school clubs are a method by which homosexuality is introduced into schools," Knight says. "This is dangerous because some kids are undoubtedly sexually confused and have intense feelings toward same-sex classmates, which is normal. They can be seriously damaged by taking their healthy emotional drives and detouring into homosexuality because they're told it's cool and that they have no alternative."

Anthony was moved to start the club by the killing of Matthew Shepard, the gay University of Wyoming student who was beaten, tied to a fence and left to die in October 1998. Anthony and high school senior Shannon MacMillan applied for recognition of the club to the school's principal, Nancy Murray, saying its mission was "to raise public awareness and promote tolerance by providing a safe

are hoping to make their impact felt in the November elections. "We're in a position now to show that we're a powerful voting bloc," says Hardy-Garcia. "We're 5 percent of the vote, on par with the Jewish and Latino vote. We've seen politicians respond to that."

The gay-rights movement has no assurance of tangible progress, however, even if the gay vote helps elect supportive candidates. President Clinton has gotten strong support from gay political groups but has been unable to get Congress to approve lifting the ban on gays in the military, barring discrimination against gays or passing a gay-hate-crimes measure.

If Gore is elected in November, he will face similar difficulties with those measures — with the Senate expected to remain in Republican control and the House likely to be narrowly divided whichever party has a majority. A Bush victory would leave gay groups worse off than today, with a president on record in opposition to most of their major legislative-agenda items.

Still, supporters and opponents acknowledge gays' growing strength. "The gay-rights movement has never been stronger, more influential, more diverse, more organized or better prepared for anything than it is today," says Eric Marcus, a New York writer and author of a post-World War II history of the movement.

From an opposing viewpoint, Knight credits the movement with "taking over" mainstream media and other organizations. "They have been successful at using what most Americans regarded as mainstream organizations to push a radical agenda," he says.

From its start, however, gay rights has been both a personal and a political struggle — a process of individual self-acceptance as well as collective mobilization. The gay community's growing visibility makes that process less difficult than in previous generations, but the process is no less important.

"These marches are like rites of passage," Hardy-Garcia says. "There's nothing like being somebody from Lubbock, Texas, and being on the Mall with hundreds of thousands of people and realizing you're not alone."

"The direction has been positive for a long time," Marcus says. "And there's no reason at this time to believe that we won't continue to make progress as long as gay and lesbian people come out and as long as those who love us support us in forum for discussion of issues related to sexual orientation and homophobia."

Contrary to normal policy, however, school administrators had instructed principals in 1998 to forward applications for gay-student clubs to the school board for decision. The seven-member Orange Unified School District school board held an open forum on the issue in November and then voted unanimously to deny the application.

Board member Kathy Ward, author of the resolution to reject the application, said the club's mission intruded on the school's sex-education curriculum. "Sex-based discussions have no place in a school club," Ward said. Other board members were harsher. The application, William Lewis said, "asks us to legitimize sin."

Colin and club co-president Heather Zetin responded by suing the School Board under the Equal Access Act. The 1984 federal law requires schools to be evenhanded in allowing use of school facilities by student groups.

"When a school allows one non-curricular club to meet at school during non-instructional times, they have to allow all groups that want to meet," says Myron Dean Quon, a lawyer with Lambda Legal Defense and Education Fund in Los Angeles, who is representing the club.

In February, U.S. District Judge David Carter agreed that the school board's action probably violated the law and issued a preliminary injunction allowing the club to organize and meet in school.

"Defendants cannot censor the students' speech to avoid discussions on campus that cause them discomfort or represent an unpopular viewpoint," Carter wrote in his 23-page ruling. The injunction remains in force until a full trial or other proceedings, expected this fall.

The club has met several times in the two months since, with as many as 50-60 members, according to Quon. But opposition persists.

"Parents say that there are things they don't want their children exposed to in high school," school board member Terri Sargeant says.[2]

Despite the controversy, the Orange County Human Relations Commission honored Anthony last month with one of its annual awards. He said the award validated his efforts. "It's going to let people know that this club is not bad [in the view of] the Human Relations Commission, that these people who say what is good and bad for us say this is good," he said.

[1] Quoted in *The Orange County Register*, March 26, 2000, p. B1. For background, see *The New York Times*, Feb. 10, 2000, p. A20; *Time*, Feb. 21, 2000, p. 52.

[2] Quoted in *The Orange County Register*, Feb. 11, 2000, p. A19.

ever greater numbers." ■

Notes

[1] Account drawn from *Burlington Free Press*, March 23, 2000. For extensive archived coverage of the same-sex marriage issue in Vermont since December 1999, see the newspaper's Web site: www.burlingtonfreepress.com.

[2] For background, see Richard L. Worsnop, "Gay Rights," *The CQ Researcher*, March 5, 1993, pp. 193-216, and Richard L. Worsnop, "Domestic Partners," *The CQ Researcher*, Sept. 4, 1992, pp. 761-784.

[3] For the full text of the opinion, see *ibid.* The decision can also be found on the Web site of the National Gay and Lesbian Task Force: www.ngltf.org. The text of the House-passed bill as well as other documents and background information can be found on the Vermont legislature's Web site: www.leg.state.vt.us.

[4] For background, see Craig Donegan, "New Military Culture," *The CQ Researcher*, April 26, 1996, pp. 361-384.

[5] See Alan Yang, "From Wrongs to Rights: Public Opinion on Gay and Lesbian Americans Moves Toward Equality," National Gay and Lesbian Task Force, 1999, p. 14. In the most recent poll cited, 29 percent of those surveyed in 1998 said marriages between homosexuals should be "recognized as legal by the law."

[6] William N. Eskridge Jr., *Gaylaw: Challenging the Apartheid of the Closet* (1999).

[7] For opposing views, see Thomas B. Stoddard, "Why Gay People Should Seek the Right to Marry," OUT/LOOK, *National Gay and Lesbian Quarterly*, No. 6 (fall 1989), and Paula L. Ettelbrick, "Since When Is Marriage a Path to Liberation?", *ibid.*, reprinted in Suzanne Sherman (ed.), *Lesbian and Gay Marriage: Private Commitments, Public Ceremonies* (1992), pp. 13-26.

[8] For background, see Sarah Glazer, "Crackdown on Sexual Harassment," *The CQ Researcher*, July 19, 1996, pp. 625-648.

[9] Background drawn from Eskridge, *op. cit.*

[10] *Ibid.*, p. 43.

[11] See Barry D. Adam, *The Rise of a Gay and Lesbian Movement* (rev. ed.) (1995), pp. 67-68. For background on the post-World War II decades, see John D'Emilio, *Sexual Politics, Sexual Communities: The Making of a Homosexual Minority in the United States, 1940-1970* (1983) and Dudley Clendinen and Adam Nagourney, *Out for Good: The Struggle to Build a Gay-Rights Movement in America* (1999).

[12] See Paul Varnell, "Stonewall: Get a Grip," *The Windy City Times*, June 10, 1999. The article appears on the Independent Gay Forum's Web site: www. indegayforum.org.

[13] Account drawn from Eric Marcus, "Stonewall Revisited" (www.indegayforum.org). The article was written for the defunct gay magazine *Ten Percent* to mark the 25th anniversary of Stonewall in 1994.

[14] Cited in Clendinen and Nagourney, *op. cit.*, p. 30.

[15] Background and data drawn from Will-

iam B. Rubenstein, Lesbians, *Gay Men and the Law* (1st ed.) (1993).
[16] Randy Shilts, *Conduct Unbecoming: Gays and Lesbians in the U.S. Military* (1993), p. 380.
[17] Account drawn from Clendinen and Nagourney, *op. cit.*, pp. 566-573. The authors note that Clinton's appearance was covered the next day in both *The New York Times* and, on the front page, in *The Washington Post.*
[18] For background, see Kenneth Jost, "Hate Crimes," *The CQ Researcher*, Jan. 8, 1993, pp. 1-24.
[19] See *1993 Congressional Quarterly Almanac*, pp. 454-462.
[20] See Wayne van der Meide, *Legislating Equality: A Review of Laws Affecting Gay, Lesbian, Bisexual, and Transgendered People in the United States*, Policy Institute of the National Gay and Lesbian Task Force (1999) (www.ngltf.org).
[21] See Kenneth Jost, *The Supreme Court Yearbook, 1995-1996* (1996), pp. 34-38.
[22] See *1996 Congressional Quarterly Almanac*, pp. 526-529.
[23] Some background drawn from *The New York Times*, Feb. 3, 2000, p. A1. The two major opposing advocacy groups in Vermont have Web sites: www.vtfreetomarry.org; www.takeittothepeople.org.
[24] See *Burlington Free Press*, March 18, 2000.
[25] See Office of the Inspector General, Department of Defense, "Military Environment with Respect to the Homosexual Conduct Policy," Report No. D-2000-101, March 16, 2000 (www.dodig.osd.mil). Rcaction drawn from *The New York Times*, March 25, 2000, p. A1; *The Washington Post*, March 25, 2000, p. A1.
[26] See *The New York Times*, Feb. 2, 2000, p. A15.
[27] Reported in *The New York Times*, Feb. 14, 2000, p. A1.
[28] *The Washington Post*, March 26, 2000, p. C3.
[29] The Associated Press, Feb. 10, 2000.
[30] Quoted in *The New York Times*, March 19, 2000, p. A24.
[31] Christina L. Lyons, "Adoption Controversies," *The CQ Researcher*, Sept. 10, 1999, p. 782.
[32] Background drawn from *The Washington Post*, March 29, 2000, p. B1, and the *Washington Blade* (www.washingtonblade.com).

FOR MORE INFORMATION

American Family Association, P.O. Box 3933, Tupelo, Miss. 38803; (662) 844-7370; www.afa.net. Founded by the Rev. Donald Wildmon in 1977, it opposes same-sex marriage and "the movement to normalize homosexual behavior."

Family Research Council, 801 G St., N.W., Washington, D.C. 20001; (202) 393-2100; www.frc.org. The council opposes legal recognition of same-sex relationships, legislation to prohibit discrimination on the basis of sexual orientation and military service by homosexuals.

Gay, Lesbian and Straight Education Network, 121 W. 27th St., Suite 804, New York, N.Y. 10001; (212) 727-0135; www.glsen.org. The organization promotes non-discrimination policies and helps support high school-based "gay-straight alliance" clubs.

Human Rights Campaign, 919 18th St., N.W., Suite 800, Washington, D.C. 20006; (202) 628-4160; www.hrc.org. The organization is a political campaign and lobbying organization working for lesbian and gay equal rights.

Independent Gay Forum, www.indegayforum.org. The forum comprises a group of generally conservative-leaning gay writers, academics, attorneys and activists described as in favor of equality for homosexuals but "dissatisfied" with the current discussion of gay-related issues.

Lambda Legal Defense and Education Fund, Inc., 120 Wall St., Suite 1500, New York, NY 10005-3904; (212) 809-8585; www.lambdalegal.org. The legal center handles a wide array of gay-rights litigation, including employment discrimination, parenting issues, HIV- and AIDS-related discrimination, military and immigration.

National Center for Lesbian Rights, 870 Market St., Suite 570, San Francisco, Calif. 94102; (415) 392-6257; www.nclrights.org. The legal center handles various lesbian-rights issues, with special emphasis on child custody and same-sex adoption issues.

National Gay and Lesbian Task Force, 1700 Kalorama Rd., N.W., Washington, D.C. 20009; (202) 332-6483; www.ngltf.org. The task force, founded in 1973, works for civil rights for gay, lesbian, bisexual and transgendered people.

Servicemembers Legal Defense Network, P.O. Box 65301, Washington, D.C. 20035-5301; (202) 328-3244; www.sldn.org. The organization assists U.S. servicemembers affected by the military's policies on homosexuality.

Bibliography

Selected Sources Used

Books

Adam, Barry D., *The Rise of a Gay and Lesbian Movement* (rev. ed.), Twayne Publishers, 1995.
Adam, a professor of sociology at the University of Windsor, Ontario, relates the rise of gay and lesbian movements in the United States and around the world. The book includes chapter notes, a list of works cited and a three-page bibliography.

Button, James W., Barbara A. Rienzo and Kenneth D. Wald, *Private Lives, Public Conflicts: Battles over Gay Rights in American Communities*, CQ Press, 1997.
Three University of Florida professors examine local conflicts over gay-rights laws and the impact of those struggles on local schools.

Clendinen, Dudley, and Adam Nagourney, *Out for Good: The Struggle to Build a Gay Rights Movement in America*, Simon & Schuster, 1999.
The authors sympathetically trace the rise of the gay-rights movement from the Stonewall Inn riots in 1969 through the late 1980s. The book includes a three-page bibliography. Clendinen is an editorial writer and Nagourney a political reporter for *The New York Times*.

D'Emilio, John, *Sexual Politics, Sexual Communities: The Making of a Homosexual Minority in the United States, 1940-1970* (2d ed.), University of Chicago Press, 1998.
D'Emilio, a professor of gender and women's studies at the University of Illinois in Chicago, traces the early history of the gay-rights movement from the 1940s to the formation and increasing assertiveness of gay-rights groups in the 1950s and '60s. The book was originally published in 1983; the 1998 edition includes a new preface and afterword.

Eskridge, William N. Jr., *Gaylaw: Challenging the Apartheid of the Closet*, Harvard University Press, 1999.
Eskridge, a law professor at Yale, traces the history of anti-gay legislation and enforcement in the United States and examines the advance of gay rights along with the continuation of anti-gay inequities in the law. The book includes several appendices and detailed notes.

—, *The Case for Same-Sex Marriage: From Sexual Liberty to Civilized Commitment*, Free Press, 1996.
Eskridge expanded his unsuccessful representation of a Washington, D.C., gay couple's effort to legally marry into a comprehensive argument for permitting same-sex marriage based on history, law and morality. The book includes detailed source notes, an appendix of court cases, and a 19-page bibliography.

Magnuson, *Are Gay Rights Right?: Making Sense of the Controversy*, Multnomah Press, 1990.
The Minneapolis trial lawyer mounts a sharp attack on what he calls the homosexual-rights movement on grounds of religion, morality, law, and public health.

Marcus, Eric, *Making History: The Struggle for Gay and Lesbian Equal Rights, 1945-1990, An Oral History*, HarperCollins, 1992.
Author Marcus presents first-person accounts by some 50 people who figured in the history of the gay-rights movement since World War II.

Rubenstein, William B., *Cases and Materials on Sexual Orientation and the Law* (2d ed.), West Publishing, 1997.
This law school casebook includes court decisions, statutory provisions and other materials on the full range of gay-rights issues. Rubenstein is an acting professor at UCLA School of Law. The first edition of the casebook was published as *Lesbians, Gay Men and the Law*.

Shilts, Randy, *Conduct Unbecoming: Gays and Lesbians in the U.S. Military*, St. Martin's Press, 1993.
Shilts, a *San Francisco Chronicle* reporter until his death from AIDS in 1994, recounts the largely unacknowledged history of homosexuals in the U.S. military in order to mount a strongly argued attack on the then-existing ban on gay or lesbian servicemembers. The current "don't ask, don't tell" policy is not covered. The book includes detailed source notes and a four-page bibliography.

Articles

Leland, John, "Shades of Gay," *Newsweek*, March 20, 2000.
The cover story in this package of articles on gay-related issues depicts increased tolerance for homosexuals in schools, churches, offices, family life, and politics and government. The story notes a new Newsweek poll that for the first time found that less than a majority of those surveyed — 46 percent — believe homosexuality is a sin.

Reports and Studies

Yang, Alan, "From Wrongs to Rights, 1973-1999: Public Opinion on Gay and Lesbian Americans Moves Toward Equality," National Gay and Lesbian Task Force, 1999.
The report, based on opinion polls over the past decade or longer, finds increasing support for gay rights on a range of issues although most Americans continue to oppose same-sex marriage and believe homosexual relations wrong. Yang is a Columbia University researcher.

Index

Index

Index

Index

Index